AMERICAN AESTHETICS

SUNY series in American Philosophy and Cultural Thought
———————
Randall E. Auxier and John R. Shook, editors

AMERICAN AESTHETICS
THEORY AND PRACTICE

Edited by

WALTER B. GULICK AND GARY SLATER

On the cover:
Artworks by Corey Drieth, American, (1969–), used by permission:
(top left) *Confluence* (gouache/ink/charcoal on wood), 9" × 9" × 1" (2007)
(top right) *Praise* (gouache/colored pencil on wood), 9" × 11" × 1" (2014)

(bottom) *The Light Inside* (1999) by James Turrell, American (1943–)
Medium: neon and ambient light, 13" × 246" × 1416"
Courtesy of the Museum of Fine Arts, Houston
Funded by Isabel B. and Wallace S. Wilson, 2000. Copyright James Turrell.

Published by State University of New York Press, Albany

© 2020 State University of New York

All rights reserved

No part of this book may be used or reproduced in any manner whatsoever without written permission. No part of this book may be stored in a retrieval system or transmitted in any form or by any means including electronic, electrostatic, magnetic tape, mechanical, photocopying, recording, or otherwise without the prior permission in writing of the publisher.

For information, contact State University of New York Press, Albany, NY
www.sunypress.edu

Library of Congress Cataloging-in-Publication Data

Names: Gulick, Walter B., 1938– editor. | Slater, Gary, 1983– editor.
Title: American aesthetics : theory and practice / Walter B. Gulick and Gary Slater, eds.
Description: Albany: State University of New York Press, 2020. | Series: SUNY series in American philosophy and cultural thought | Includes bibliographical references and index.
Identifiers: LCCN 2019049095 (print) | LCCN 2019049096 (ebook) | ISBN 9781438478579 (hardcover : alk. paper) | ISBN 9781438478586 (pbk. : alk. paper) | ISBN 9781438478593 (ebook)
Subjects: LCSH: Aesthetics, American.
Classification: LCC BH221.U5 A48 2020 (print) | LCC BH221.U5 (ebook) | DDC 111/.850973—dc23
LC record available at https://lccn.loc.gov/2019049095
LC ebook record available at https://lccn.loc.gov/2019049096

10 9 8 7 6 5 4 3 2 1

Contents

List of Illustrations   ix

Preface   xi

Acknowledgments   xiii

I. Introduction

1. Toward an American Aesthetics   3
   Walter B. Gulick

II. Philosophical Contributions to American Aesthetics from the Past

2. The Primacy of Aesthetic Judgments: Emerson's Deontological-Transcendentalist Account of Tragedy   39
   Jacob L. Goodson

3. Peirce and Edwards on the Argument from Beauty   59
   Michael L. Raposa

4. A Semeiotic Account of Paintings as Pure Icons that Communicate Beautiful Feelings   75
   David Rohr

5	The Pragmatist Aesthetics of William James *Richard Shusterman*	93
6	Between Nature and Art: Some Analytical Exemplifications of Dewey's Aesthetics *Robert E. Innis*	111

III. American Aesthetics: Contemporary Theoretical Contributions

7	Axiological Landscape Theory: Uniting Aesthetics, Ethics, and Inquiry *Wesley J. Wildman*	139
8	Experience and Signs: Toward a Pragmatist Literary Criticism *Nicholas Gaskill*	157
9	Music, Time, and the Egress of Possibility *Randall E. Auxier*	177
10	Harmony, Existence, and the Aesthetic *Robert Cummings Neville*	211
11	Historical-Aesthetic Complementarity: An American Philosophical Contribution to the Study of Religion *Gary Slater*	235

IV. Applying American Aesthetic Theory to Practice

12	An Exemplary Critic in the Tradition of American Aesthetics: Harold Rosenberg *Leanne Gilbertson and Walter B. Gulick*	257
13	Experiential Immersions in Beauty: A Confluence of James Turrell's Light Spaces and Whitehead's Aesthetics *Vaughan Durkee McTernan*	273

Contents   vii

14 Dialogue: From Rich Experience to Minimalist Expression   283
    Corey Drieth and Walter B. Gulick

15 The Fabric of Thirdness: A Concert Pianist's Peircean
    Interpretation of Performance   297
    Arthur Stewart

16 Inspiring Singers toward Emotional Communication through
    Aesthetic Discovery   311
    Steven Hart

17 Budd Boetticher's Transcendental Westerns, or, Schrader,
    Bazin, Sartre, and Neville Walk into a Saloon   321
    James McLachlan

V. Aesthetic Aspects of a Flourishing Life

18 Resolving the Tension of Everyday Aesthetics in a
    Deweyan Way   339
    Thomas Leddy

19 The Struggle for Centering Things in an Age of Consumerism   359
    David Strong

20 The Dynamics of Selving and the Aesthetics of Ecstatic
    Naturalism   379
    Robert S. Corrington

List of Contributors   397

Index   401

Illustrations

Figure 6.1 Yi Bingshou, *Landscapes*, dated 1814. Metropolitan Museum, New York   118

Figure 6.2 Jan van Eyck, *The Arnolfini Portrait*, 1434. National Gallery, London   119

Figure 6.3 Leonardo da Vinci, *Mona Lisa*, 1503–06. Louvre, Paris   120

Figure 6.4 Auguste Renoir, *Young Girl Bathing*, 1892. Metropolitan Museum, New York   128

Figure 6.5 Paul Cezanne, *The Card Players*, First Version, 1890–92. Metropolitan Museum, New York   130

Preface

This volume attempts the impossible—to chart in adequate fashion a pattern in aesthetic thought and practice that is distinctively American and is relevant not only to all the arts but also to many aspects of daily living. However, it is not necessary to tie down all details of American Aesthetics in this or any other single volume, for the essays in this volume join an ongoing conversation that received its distinctive character in the writings of American pragmatism and process thought. The name American Aesthetics is new, but its practices have a history.

We recognize that there is a danger in naming an ongoing practice that is more a tendency of approach than a movement with self-identified members adhering to clearly defined boundaries. Our basic objective is to point out the often ignored importance of aesthetic judgment in structuring and assessing thought and perception. We believe the classic American philosophers accomplished this in admirable fashion. These thinkers envisioned aesthetic sensibility as a dynamic process open to anyone seeking quality in experience. So care should be taken not to reify American Aesthetics in some way, but rather see its characteristic sensitivities and judgments as facilitators of excellence in experience.

The two of us have much to be thankful for as we have assembled this collection of essays. We will communicate our gratitude separately.

I, Walter Gulick, have experienced warm support for this project going back to the time Gary Slater and I organized the conference on aesthetics for the Institute for American Religious and Philosophical Thought in Manitou Springs, Colorado, in 2016. Many of this volume's contributions derive from that meeting. All who have essays herein have seasoned their philosophical acumen with unfailing cooperation and collegiality. Gary Slater is especially deserving of acclamation in this regard.

He has served as a reliable sounding board, perceptive critic, and dedicated worker throughout our joint activities. Thanks, Gary!

Secondly, I appreciate the support still provided me by Montana State University Billings. For forty-five years MSUB has been my home institution, and I continue to have an office with IT support even as a semiretired emeritus professor.

Thirdly, two women are especially deserving of deep gratitude. I sometimes feel as if I never adequately expressed my appreciation for the love my mother showered on me. This belated public acknowledgment has some relation to my editing this book, for my mother, Helen Gulick, was an art major. I'm sure the art books lying about our house had at least a subterranean influence on my interest in aesthetics. And where would I be without Barbara, loving companion for almost fifty-five years of married life? She expressed her artistic excellence playing the organ and passed on the love of music by teaching keyboard instruments privately. To her I dedicate my work on this book with deep gratitude.

Reflecting on the factors that have made this book possible, I, Gary Slater, am compelled to single out three specific sources of inspiration and support. The first—here as in so much else—has been my family, particularly my wife, Anne. The *American Aesthetics* project developed across an arc that encompassed many professional and personal changes, including the birth of our twin toddlers, James and Rosie. Were it not for the love and partnership that Anne has provided (with a lot of help from her parents), I am certain that I would have possessed neither the stamina nor the sanity to persist.

The second object of thanks is the Institute for American Religious and Philosophical Thought, which is a wonderful community of friends and interlocutors. It gratifies me to think that visitors to these pages might experience the spirit of rich intellectual exchange that has characterized the group since long before I became a member in 2012.

Third, and above all, Walter Gulick deserves enormous thanks for his leadership on this project. The fact that this book exists is a testament to Walter's vision, patience, and tenacity. When he and I began our collaboration on the project in the summer of 2015, I would not have imagined that this book would be the outcome. Yet Walter not only imagined it; he has made it happen. That this book should be the result reflects not simply Walter's efforts during our collaboration, but also his many years of reflection on aesthetics and the American tradition preceding it.

We wish you pleasurable reading.

Acknowledgments

An earlier version of chapter 5 was published as follows:

> Shusterman, Richard. "The Pragmatist Aesthetics of William James." *British Journal of Aesthetics* 51, no. 4 (October 2011): 349–60. © British Society of Aesthetics 2011. Reprinted with permission of Oxford University Press.

An earlier version of chapter 8 was published as follows:

> Gaskill, Nicholas M. "Experience and Signs: Towards a Pragmatist Literary Criticism." *New Literary History* 39, no. 1 (2008): 165–73, 176–83. © 2008 New Literary History, The University of Virginia. Reprinted with permission of Johns Hopkins University Press.

I

Introduction

Walter Gulick's introductory essay sets the stage for seeing how the following essays share in the encompassing tradition that is American Aesthetics. He roots this tradition in the aesthetic thought of the classic American philosophers, primarily Peirce, James, Whitehead, and Dewey, and in a later generation, Langer. American Aesthetics situates aesthetic judgment in two interconnected levels of experience: in precognitive normative feelings of rightness, and in reflective judgments tied to standards of excellence in perception. Aesthetic sensitivity is attuned to ideals of organization and structure with respect to thinking, creating, performing, and evaluating. More narrowly, those indwelling the spirit of American Aesthetics appreciate that aesthetic criticism legitimately considers all factors contributing to the creation and practice of the arts, including historical and cultural background and artist's experience and intentions.

1

Toward an American Aesthetics

WALTER B. GULICK

The discipline of "aesthetics," which once referred to the study of beauty in the arts, has become increasingly blurred in the past two centuries. No longer are representational adequacy and beauty self-evident standards of high aesthetic worth. In fact, creative priority, novelty, and cultural or political critique seem to have largely dethroned beauty in the pantheon of artistic value. Where novelty reigns, unpredictability and challenges to traditional categories of understanding are present. Hence, it may be questioned whether it is possible to make legitimate claims about shared aesthetic patterns in today's diverse and plastic artistic milieu. Generalization is suspect. Yet it is my intent in this essay to make such a claim.[1]

I will argue that there is an identifiable pattern in aesthetic thought and practice that can be labeled "American," and that such labeling distinguishes significant features in the entangled jungle of artistic expression. Within this pattern, aesthetics is understood broadly to elucidate not only the reception, but also the creation and production of art. Moreover, aesthetic factors are recognized not only in the arts, but also in perception, cognition, imagination, and indeed as flavoring experience in general. What I will term American Aesthetics incorporates this broad understanding of aesthetics. American Aesthetics is a living tradition that has greater interpretive power than found in more restricted versions of aesthetics. I argue that the tradition first came to explicit articulation in the writings of the classic American philosophers, especially John Dewey. I will characterize the tradition in terms of three increasingly comprehensive notions of aesthetic judgment, each grounded in feeling. Later in the essay, I will contrast the richness of American Aesthetics with the understanding of aesthetics as found in the analytic tradition, New Criticism, and postmodernism.

For well over a century there have been many attempts by artists to describe and produce art works that are self-consciously American or are deeply immersed in characteristic American issues. Think of the attention to aspects of American life displayed in the works of such diverse artists as John Singleton Copley, Thomas Cole, Herman Melville, Walt Whitman, Mark Twain, Scott Joplin, George Bellows, Charles Ives, Willa Cather, Alfred Stieglitz, Frank Lloyd Wright, William Faulkner, Georgia O'Keeffe, Walker Evans, Aaron Copland, Robert Frost, Jacob Lawrence, John Steinbeck, Thomas Hart Benton, Duke Ellington, Robert Frank, John Ford, Martha Graham, Tennessee Williams, James Baldwin, Pete Seeger, Maya Angelou, Woody Allen, Andy Warhol, Bob Dylan, Cindy Sherman, and countless, countless others. But to what extent have these works of art, distinctively American in theme, been inspired by aesthetic theories that are distinctively American?

Aesthetics—A Definition

To begin answering the foregoing question, it is necessary to specify how I, in reflection upon American philosophy, understand "aesthetics." Broadly speaking, aesthetics is a normative discipline that identifies and assesses patterns, qualities, and relations arising in feeling that shape judgments in all the processes of perceiving, thinking, and making (see the articles by Wildman, Neville, and Shusterman).[2] Beauty, harmony, eloquence, coherence, completion, symmetry—or their negatives, such as ugliness, discord, fragmentation, etc.—such terms are representative of the many aesthetic words describing felt aspects of what we experience. To oversimplify a bit, I understand these aesthetic sensitivities to function at two interconnected levels of reality. At a lower level, they function tacitly in bringing sensation and conception to focal identity. Many of these abilities to discriminate, vaguely accessible as feelings, appear to be innate and shared with other animals. At a higher level of consciousness, many of these feelings have become crystalized into concepts and words, terms we may use in creating and evaluating art.

In its historical origins, aesthetics attended to qualities of excellence in what is perceived. Not all our senses have been accorded equal aesthetic standing in the traditional language of aesthetics. Taste, touch, and smell have, until recent decades, generally been excluded from discourse about aesthetics. Certain kinds of felt satisfactions associated with vision and hearing have been preeminent along with some creative uses of language (for instance, poetry [Gaskill]). Traditionally, aesthetic satisfaction has to do with the pleasurable appreciation of works of art (or scenic beauty) in which appreciation is an end in itself. Aesthetic satisfaction is thus seen as different from satisfactions derived from the achievement of purposes (although an artist or performer may experience both types of satisfaction simultaneously when completing a beautiful work).

As culture has evolved and become more complex, the notion of aesthetics has expanded. Some objects and works of art—perhaps especially music—are primarily evocative. They move the heart and elicit aesthetic experience. A concert hall, vista point, theater, art museum—such venues may be the loci of enthralling experiences of aesthetic pleasure that soar to the heights of peak experiences, to use Maslow's phrase. We humans also actively apply aesthetic sensibility to create works of art and refined experience in general. Aesthetic sensitivity is now understood, especially from the perspective I am labeling American Aesthetics, as applicable to intellectual and active pursuits in daily life in addition to creation, production, and assessment of the traditional arts. Aesthetic judgments can be expressive-of as well as appreciative-of. Communal and cultural flesh are now seen to surround the traditional core of aesthetics restricted to perception and the arts. This volume's essays have been selected to examine telling aspects of that fleshy diversity. A holistic sampling of how aesthetic sensitivity is expressed in America requires that, in addition to ongoing theoretical reflection, attention needs to be given to how that theory is taken up in practice (Stewart, Hart). Theory without practice is impotent; practice without theory is arbitrary.

I develop this essay by emphasizing felt aesthetic sensitivity as a normative force guiding judging and creating. While feeling and judging are among the most subjective aspects of aesthetics, they apply aesthetic sensitivity to physical and mental *objects* of various sorts. However, any quasi-Cartesian emphasis on subjectivity in contrast to objectivity is both simplistic and problematic. Subject and object are fused in aesthetic experience,[3] although they may be distinguished in analysis. Moreover, a rich notion of context is needed to provide the frameworks and meanings that give sense to aesthetic judgments and practices. The lessons of past experiences, biological urgings and processes, natural and built environments, social and cultural influences, personal habits and goals—such are among the many indwelt contextual influences that are molded by aesthetic sensitivities into the felt rightness of particular aesthetic judgments.[4] Attention to context is a crucial aspect of American Aesthetics.

A person's aesthetic feelings and judgments not only derive from the embodied lessons of past experiences, they also exhibit intentionality. They are about something. Aesthetic attention may be devoted primarily to hues, aromas, timbres, and other perceived properties of objects one engages in the world, or to more comprehensive patterns or relationships one experiences.[5] A beautiful rainbow; the three-dimensional form of a sculpture; the attractive arrangement of a website; the pattern of a fugue; a well-crafted architectural rendering; a graceful leap for a rebound in basketball; the unfolding plot of a drama—such are examples of the structures and events *in the world* that may elicit aesthetic responses and judgments.

Authentic engagement with any of the arts may sometimes involve one shifting from mundane everyday consciousness into what sometimes has been called the "realm of the imagination."[6] Imagination in all its gracious mystery must be considered in any comprehensive treatment of aesthetics. Imagination is intimately involved in the creation of art, but it can assist with its appreciation as well. I understand imagination to arise from the incessant and unbidden production of ideas and images in the stream of consciousness. As Susanne Langer notes, a spontaneous feature of human mentality is that it constantly produces symbols and accompanying conceptions.[7] Even when we sleep, the inner fountain of symbols is not turned off. We are immersed in the imagery and thoughts comprising dreams. Artistic imagining can direct nascent images and ideas into novel pathways that produce aesthetic delight or solve aesthetic problems. Imagination is a creative force that becomes art when disciplined by aesthetic judgments, especially those sensitive to socially apt aesthetic categories.

At least three different motivational goals lead to distinct ways of imaginatively engaging a work of art. Most broadly, a person may examine a work to see how it relates to some personal interest external to the object. For example, a historian may want to examine a seventeenth-century Dutch genre painting carefully to see if it artfully illuminates some aspect of life during Holland's Golden Age. That interest guides how the painting is perceived and judged. Secondly, a person may attend to a work of art in terms of favored aesthetic categories in order to experience aesthetic pleasure. Thirdly, aesthetic assessment of a work of art may focus strictly on appreciating *an object or event* and its meaning more fully for its own sake. In the literature influenced by Kant, an approach focusing on the object in and for itself has been called "disinterested." Any pleasure derived would be almost an accidental byproduct of the attention rendered.

The above distinctions provide a basis for evaluating whether the so-called aesthetic attitude toward a work of art has a place in American Aesthetics. The aesthetic attitude relates to an artwork like the third approach I just delineated. In an influential article, George Dickie argues that whatever a person's motivation for viewing an artwork closely, perception is perception, and nothing distinguishes the aesthetic attitude from any other perceptual act of closely examining an art object. That is, his dismissal of the aesthetic attitude is also a rejection of Kantian disinterested attention. There is only attention or inattention. Consequently, he thinks reference to the aesthetic attitude is extraneous and should be eliminated.[8] Well, the actual act of perceiving may not vary from case to case, but what we seek in perceiving includes an intentional, purposive element that does vary. Close perception governed by the aesthetic attitude focuses on the qualities of the art object disconnected from (disinterested in) issues external to the object, such as whether what the object depicts exists or what its practical value might be. If the aesthetic attitude is narrowly defined as a concentration on a person's felt experience of an object's aesthetic qualities (especially such formal qualities as harmony, proportion, unity, and the like), then its purpose is distinguishable from other types of purposeful attention and the term worth retaining. To be sure, our reasons for viewing art closely seem usually to be complex. Judging a painting for its market value, assessing profundity in music, interpreting the political thrust of some performance art, or evaluating eloquence in writing, gracefulness in ballet, the sublime feeling of a cathedral—these diverse judgments include aesthetic elements to different degrees. So it is useful to apply the aesthetic attitude to ascertain the strictly artistic elements at play among impure judgments.

The American Background

Until the past several decades, relatively little attention has been devoted to the possibility of a distinctly American tradition in aesthetics. Self-reliance and problem solving have seemed more American than aesthetic reflection and enjoyment. The high value Americans tend to place on individual freedom can be traced historically to experiences of escape from tyranny in Europe. The perceived opportunity to settle a "wilderness" has fostered an emphasis on the importance of personal initiative and Emersonian self-reliance. The memory of oppressive European social and political hierarchies sustains the ideal of egalitarianism, informality, and the democratic participation of all. The business and trade-generated rise of the middle class has tended to honor competition and practicality more highly than cooperation and display.

But in addition to such essentially middle-class values, upper-class aesthetic sensitivities of a different sort tended to dominate art criticism prior to the twentieth century. In the late nineteenth century, the several movements often jointly termed "aestheticism" were largely borrowed from Europe. Aestheticism's notion of "art for art's sake" emphasized beauty as the highest criterion of aesthetic worth. In practice, however, aestheticism's championing of elitist fine art was supported by wealthy patrons often for reasons of pecuniary value and status. This fine art tradition ignored the service art might provide ordinary persons within democracy. The growth and consolidation of native thought about aesthetics can thus be seen as at least partially an antiestablishment critique of the marriage between the aesthetic perspective and the flaunting of wealth in the Gilded Age. The classic American philosophers, rejecting the reduction of the arts to issues of effete pleasure, decoration, and status seeking, investigated ways the arts could better contribute to broad social and cultural health. American Aesthetics was born.

The works of the many artists mentioned earlier express different reactions to American historical experience. The nineteenth-century reliance on inherited European aesthetic criteria (especially Kantian aesthetics) gradually declined in the twentieth century. Studies of particularistic cultural contexts became more common, as did concern about establishing distinctive American art. Creative work in aesthetic theory was carried out by the classic American philosophers. However, after the devastation of World War II, when America became recognized as the world leader in many of the arts, the urgency of interpreting the new art was mainly carried out in the idiom of either of the two leading philosophical traditions of the time, analytic or continental philosophy. It seems that the resulting aesthetic interpretation was not generally seen as constituting an American tradition, but was, rather, interpreted as just being another expression of Western culture. Distinctive American art, yes; thoughtful work in art history and criticism by Americans, yes; distinctively American aesthetic theory, not so clear.

Classic American Philosophers

It is my contention that conceptions produced by the so-called classic American philosophers provide systematic insights supporting an explicit tradition of American aesthetics. Charles Sanders Peirce, William James, Josiah Royce, George Santayana, Alfred North Whitehead, and John Dewey are generally seen as the classic American philosophers.

It is not the case that these thinkers produce a unified body of aesthetic theory. Their philosophical approaches are varied, even as American culture is varied, and the extent to which they consider aesthetic themes ranges widely. However, Peirce, James, Whitehead, and Dewey are classic American philosophers whose thought about aesthetics largely coheres and reverberates with distinctive American themes. To engage in some useful oversimplification, I see these four thinkers as collectively taking a naturalistic stance that balances empirical evidence with axiological insight, stresses the importance of an aesthetic dimension in experience (especially at its felt, formative stage), is alert to artistic expression as a dynamic affair, and attends to the pragmatic significance of the arts. These four American thinkers and the pragmatic and process traditions they inspire are primary philosophical influences on the following essays.

To this list of American philosophers Susanne Langer should be added. Whitehead is a primary influence on Langer (as is Cassirer), but unlike Whitehead or the other three classic philosophers, she focuses systematically upon the different kinds of aesthetic judgments evoked by different artistic disciplines and specific works of art. Her emphasis on expression, feeling, form, and symbol is consistent with themes in classic American philosophy.

By claiming that the four classic American philosophers provide the most profound and original thought about aesthetics in an American vein, I do not mean to suggest that there were no worthy precursors prior to the late nineteenth century. Jonathan Edwards, Walt Whitman, and especially Ralph Waldo Emerson are examples of writers who successfully married American themes with aesthetic reflection. In his essay "Art," Emerson stresses the importance of producing useful objects that are beautiful so there is no split between the fine and useful arts. He sees the potential among American artisans and artists to rival the work of the great Italians insofar as Americans do not become stuck in previous modes of aesthetic understanding. Emerson secured a lasting place in the world of letters (Goodson); his thought was responded to by Peirce, James, and Dewey among the classic American philosophers. His transcendental view of nature's instructive majesty comes to expression in the paintings of the Hudson River School, although the landscapes of Cole and Church seem better interpreted as American versions of Eurocentric Romanticism rather than as indebted to Emerson. While it is not clear that his aesthetic ideas in "Art" ever had much influence among visual artists, his work as a whole is aesthetically significant.

Besides Emerson and Whitman, America produced strong literary voices in such persons as Henry David Thoreau, Herman Melville, Emily Dickinson, Edgar Allan Poe, and Mark Twain. The content of their writings is deeply embedded in American experience, but the degree to which this work was inspired by native aesthetic reflection is debatable. America produced such skilled landscape artists as Thomas Cole, Frederick Church, Albert Bierstadt, and Thomas Moran, but these figures can be seen as following in a tradition set by seventeenth-century Dutch artists, as well as Nicolas Poussin and Claude Lorrain, and expressed in the nineteenth century by such figures as John Constable, Caspar David Friedrich, J. C. Dahl, and the Barbizon painters. More to the point, America produced no influential aestheticians comparable to England's Samuel Taylor Coleridge, William Morris, John Ruskin, and Walter Pater. The aestheticism that came to prominence in the United States during the last quarter of the nineteenth century was most directly inspired by the aesthetic theory of such nonnative thinkers.

Dewey's *Art as Experience* (1934) is arguably the first groundbreaking comprehensive work on aesthetics by an American. It is surely the most influential single work shaping American Aesthetics. His holistic approach to aesthetics sees it as emerging from bodily based engagement with the world in which perception is conjoined with emotionally charged feeling, intellectual discrimination, and pragmatic concern about meaning and impact. As a fundamental dimension of *experience*, Deweyan aesthetics is not restricted just to the fine arts but is also applicable to pop culture, technological developments, and indeed to daily life (Leddy). Dewey's promotion of democracy and progressive thought, partly a remnant of his early Hegelian leanings, must have a significant place in any tradition of American aesthetics.

None of the three classic American philosophers besides Dewey provides a full, explicit rendering of aesthetics in its various useful permutations. Moreover, the changing understanding of the arts requires ongoing adjustment of the aesthetic theory of Dewey and the other classic

American philosophers. In order to show the continuing relevance of the classic American philosophers, it is important to see how they fit into the worldwide historical flow of aesthetic thought and artistic ingenuity. For an American tradition in aesthetics is far from a completely novel philosophical achievement. Immanuel Kant's *Critique of Judgment* (1790) has had the greatest impact of any Western theory of aesthetics. While I am not claiming Kant's aesthetics directly influenced American Aesthetics in any significant way, I will use it for several purposes:

1. It can serve as a reference point for illuminating how American Aesthetics forms a distinctive tradition in contrast to the traditional dominance of Kantian aesthetics.

2. Kant's thought in his above referenced third *Critique* has less noticed elements that are consistent with and can contribute to American Aesthetics.

4. Kant's claims, modified as appropriate to contemporary experience, helpfully serve as a framework for articulating three progressively inclusive uses of aesthetic judgment.

The Kantian Framework and First Domain of Aesthetic Judgment

Kant's aesthetic theory productively contains elements of Enlightenment attention to reason and a foretaste of Romantic emphasis on imagination and feeling. In his first *Critique*, Kant calls his exposition of the spatio-temporal framework within which empirical knowledge is possible the "Transcendental Aesthetic," alluding to the Greek term *aesthesis*, a reference to sensory perception. He only develops his analysis of the quality inherent in perceiving in his third *Critique*, the *Critique of Judgment*. American Aesthetics follows Kant in paying less attention to the traditional emphasis on the perceived aesthetic object of aesthetic judgment and more attention to that judgment itself and its aesthetic qualities. The judgment that some perceived object is beautiful is based on a feeling that arises prior to the experience being classified and structured through concepts.[9] For beauty as Kant discusses it does not arise from reflection upon pleasure stimulated by perception. That merely gives rise to subjective experience he calls "pleasant" (*CJ* 39, ¶ 3). Recognition of beauty precedes any experience of pleasure (see *CJ* ¶ 9). Beauty results from a primordial harmony between the imagination (in its free play of representation) and the understanding, a harmony Kant thinks is objectively present in all people's perception of an object judged beautiful even though it is subjectively experienced (*CJ* 52, ¶ 9). He claims that beauty is inherent in some sensed objects, and all should agree it is beautiful because the same process of forming a percept is found in all humans. Any pleasure we experience is its own end. We are disinterested in whether the beautiful object exists or not, or whether it is useful (*CJ* 38, ¶ 2). Thus, for Kant the judgment of beauty is based on a self-justified, self-rewarding experience.

Aesthetic theories in the nineteenth century usually followed Kant (and sometimes Schopenhauer) in focusing upon beauty, although generally not understanding beauty in the rarified pure way Kant did. Neither does American Aesthetics believe Kant's grasping for objective purity is sustainable. One problem with Kantian beauty is that he never incorporates the vast range of aesthetic feelings mentioned earlier into his aesthetic analysis, not even when he concocts impure versions of beauty, such as dependent versus adherent beauty. James is especially adept at recognizing the rich varieties of aesthetic judgment needing recognition. Still, the impetus Kant gave to understanding the significance of beauty—or occasionally sublimity, our reaction to something that elicits wonder or awe—is worthy of respect. Tethering aesthetic theory to disinterested judgments of beauty or sublimity represents the first and most common understanding of aesthetics. This first understanding of aesthetics, which I argued earlier applies to the so-called aesthetic attitude, is acceptable, even if of limited use, in American Aesthetics.

The Second Domain of Aesthetic Judgment

As just suggested, American Aesthetics rejects limiting aesthetics to beauty and sublimity alone as aesthetic ideals. An extended usage of aesthetic judgment is important to flesh out if aesthetic theory is to be comprehensive enough to be helpful in interpreting the changing functions and types of art that have emerged since Kant's time. Such cultural expressions as cinema, performance art, political art, and even cuisine, ritual, or landscaping evoke aesthetic responses that should be considered in an inclusive theory. Moreover, artistic creation often produces expressions that are significant but not beautiful. Tragedy in drama, conceptual art, atonal music, war photography—such are among the many artistic expressions to which beauty as commonly understood is not relevant.

Aesthetic responses to all the arts are quite complex, not merely disinterested and formal as in Kant's understanding of beauty. The typical creative artist is very much interested in the content she produces and its success in attracting attention. And the artist is sensitive to past creative experiences, intends outcomes that may shift during the creative process, is influenced by what is or is not going on in the art world, relies upon certain personal skills, and so on. Context again. Does Kant simply dismiss all these factors that contribute to the creative process as not being aesthetic? No, but he diverts from the language of "aesthetic" and the experience of beauty. Rather, he relies upon the concept of "genius." He claims that "genius is a talent for producing that for which no definite rule can be given; it is not a mere aptitude for what can be learned by rule. Hence originality must be its first property" (*CJ* 150, ¶ 46). Genius for Kant is thus creative talent, not just brilliance of mind. The sources of the genius's artistic productivity being mysterious, it might seem that Kant's understanding of creativity tails off into a black box.

This is not the case. Genius is the creative result of what Kant calls spirit, "the name given to the animating principle of the soul" (*CJ* 157, 160, ¶ 49). Spirit produces aesthetical ideas. "And by aesthetical ideas I understand that representation of the imagination which occasions much thought, without however any definite thought, i.e. any *concept*, being capable of being adequate to it; it consequently cannot be completely compassed and made intelligible by language" (*CJ* 157,¶ 49). Aesthetical ideas, then, would seem to be creative images or perhaps even intimations that inspire one toward developing adequate expression of the originating feeling or vague concept. Prosaic language of complete description cannot adequately capture the meaning of an aesthetical idea, but a poem might approximate it. So might dance, a sonata, a sculpture, or a painting, depending on the nature of the aesthetical idea and how it is framed.

Kant's notion of spirit relates in a subterranean and thus generally unacknowledged way to American aesthetic theory. Dewey named his now lost PhD dissertation at Johns Hopkins "The Psychology of Kant." In a letter to W. T. Harris about the dissertation, Dewey writes that Kant "had the conception of Reason or Spirit as the centre and organic unity of the entire sphere of man's experience, and that in so far as he is true to this conception that he is the true founder of modern philosophic method."[10] To be sure, the young Dewey devoted himself more to the

Hegelian expression of spirit than he relied on Kant. Nevertheless, Kant's recognition of the signal importance of aesthetic meaning that exceeds language provides an influential alternative in modern philosophy (and for American Aesthetics) to narrow forms of empiricism centered on mechanistic explanation and the search for certainty.

How does Kant understand the process by which aesthetical ideas and their artistic expression come into being? He suggests that a certain sensitive relation between one's imagination and understanding (the same faculties involved in sensing beauty) generates the work of art. It presumably follows threads of proportion, resemblance, harmony, aptness, association, and the like in its creative thrust, although Kant says little about such leadings other than that the process is bound by no rule. Neither reason nor imagination knows from whence it comes. But the lack of a rule need not imply the lack of standards of judgment. Kant ties the productivity of spirit to the creation of beautiful works of art. However, there is no reason this spirit-driven process should be excluded from broader applications of aesthetic judgment. The felt standards of such aesthetic notions as proportion, resemblance, harmony, aptness, association, and similar qualities of relationship may influence any judgment. These standards are tacitly relied upon in shaping creative work and guiding evaluation. So by extending Kant's notion of spirit slightly we arrive at the second domain of aesthetic judgment, one that interprets art in many normative ways beyond beauty alone.

In his later references to Kant's aesthetics, Dewey seems to forget his earlier appreciation of Kantian spirit and instead pejoratively restricts his treatment of Kantian aesthetics to disinterested judgments of art. He claims Kantian aesthetic judgment is not reflective (wrong) and operates in a mode of isolated contemplation. Dewey states that "the psychological road was opened leading to the ivory tower of 'Beauty' remote from all desire, action, and stir of emotion."[11] These comments by Dewey reflect the common rejection in American Aesthetics of Kant's notion of beauty as the unquestioned standard of aesthetic judgment. Thus Dewey says that Kant's theory of aesthetics

> not only passes over, as if it were irrelevant, the doing and making involved in the production of a work of art (and the corresponding active elements in the appreciative response), but it involves an extremely one-sided idea of the nature of perception. It takes as its cue to the understanding of per-

ception what belongs only to the act of recognition, merely broadening the latter to include the pleasure that attends it when recognition is prolonged and extensive.[12]

While he ignores Kant's discussion of artistic creativity, Dewey sets forth a robust theory that develops potential left unrealized in Kant's account of artistic creation. Thought, emotion, sense, purpose, impulsion—all bound in a passionate pressing forward—are involved in the making of art for Dewey (Innis). Such ideation resonates with the traditional value structure that emerged in American history and became resident in its culture. Thus, aesthetics has for Dewey an extended reach that includes, for example, "subject-matter that is enjoyed in the case of architectural structures, the drama, and the novel, with all their attendant reverberations."[13] Moreover, the felt reach of aesthetic understanding may appropriately involve knowing how the biography of the creator is relevant to the creator's artistic style and intentions. The background experience, sociological status, and psychological state of the creator; historical and cultural conditions in America at the time of creation; artist's intention—all such contextual factors are fair game in aesthetic analysis. Therefore, the traditional American commitment to democracy, endorsement of hard work and the "common man," and suspicion of elitist evaluation of "fine art" frequently underlie aesthetic assessment in the American tradition. "Underlie" is a key term here. For these typical American values, while not abstract and formal like the "pure" aesthetic categories, contribute to the rich evaluation of art characteristic of American Aesthetics.

The Third Domain of Aesthetic Judgment

The making of art can be seen, in Dewey's instrumentalist perspective, as not so different from the taming of a frontier, the founding of a new business, or the solving of a crossword puzzle. Indeed, aesthetic factors are embedded in such exploits. There is no reason Kantian spirit and genius could not be extended beyond the arts to a third domain, one in which aesthetic sensitivity is recognized as being involved in all acts of thinking, making, and doing. In the second half of the third *Critique*, Kant gingerly opens the door to such extension by referring to the satisfactions arising in purposive behavior. Satisfactions arise in intellectual as well as sensible experience. He sees such satisfactions to be generated by, for instance, the *beauty* of numbers and geometrical figures. However, he is reluctant to speak of "intellectual beauty," as then the term *beauty* would "lose all determinate significance" (CJ 212, ¶ 62).[14]

Dewey is not reluctant to speak of aesthetic elements in intellectual endeavor. He states that "*an* experience of thinking has its own esthetic quality. It differs from those experiences that are acknowledged to be esthetic, but only in its materials. . . . Nevertheless, the experience itself has a satisfying emotional quality because it possesses internal integration and fulfillment reached through ordered and organized movement."[15] His version of *an experience* is like a greatly enlarged version of intuition in its unifying function. Dewey in effect claims that each instance of what he calls having *an* experience has a unique aesthetic structure marked by completion and consummation.

> An experience has a unity that gives it its name, *that* meal, that storm, that rupture of friendship. The existence of this unity is constituted by a single *quality* that pervades the entire experience in spite of the variation of its constitutive parts. This unity is neither emotional, practical, nor intellectual, for these terms name distinctions that reflection can make within it. In discourse *about* an experience, we must make use of these adjectives of interpretation. In going over an experience in mind *after* its occurrence, we may find that one property rather than another was sufficiently dominant so that it characterizes the experience as a whole.[16]

Dewey has been criticized by Susanne Langer and others for focusing aesthetic assessment on subjective experience rather than on the object or event that generates the aesthetic experience. In reaction against an overemphasis on psychological interpretations of the aesthetics of art, Langer says that "we might do better to look upon the art object as something in its own right, with properties independent of our prepared reactions—properties which command our reactions, and make art the autonomous and essential factor that it is in every human culture."[17] With respect to the evaluation of art, Langer's criticism seems legitimate for what an art critic might write. Indeed, because art criticism makes essential use of aesthetic categories, it is appropriate to regard it as a species of the holistic genus American Aesthetics. However, perhaps it is best to recognize two related points. Yes, certain objects, created or natural, have the power to elicit glorious aesthetic experiences. But also, a person with an aesthetically sensitive predisposition can recognize in objects aesthetic features to which others are blind. Neither object alone nor person alone can generate aesthetic experience; both are needed.

While Dewey's notion of *an* experience provides a promising basis for the expanded third domain of aesthetic judgment, his illustrations are routinely devoted to works of art. We must turn to others among the classic American philosophers for a dynamic, comprehensive notion of aesthetic sensitivity as relevant to many of the processes of living, not just to art. Thus, Peirce sees aesthetics as the most basic of the normative sciences, fueling even ethical judgments (Rohr). Whitehead writes, contra Kant's disinterested approach, "The concept of completely passive contemplation in abstraction from action and purpose is a fallacious extreme. It omits the final regulative factor in the aesthetic complex."[18] William James contrasts his pleasant, relaxed stay at Chautauqua with an alternative he experiences as more aesthetically compelling.

> [W]hat our human emotions seem to require is the sight of the struggle going on. The moment the fruits are being merely eaten, things become ignoble. Sweat and effort, human nature strained to its uttermost and on the rack, yet getting through alive, and then turning its back on its success to pursue another more rare and arduous still—this is the sort of thing the presence of which inspires us, and the reality of which it seems to be the function of all the higher forms of literature and fine art to bring home to us and suggest.[19]

The Felt Aspect of Aesthetic Judgment

The view that feeling is an essential element in connecting person with environment (including artworks) is central to the epistemology of several of the classic American philosophers.[20] James writes, "Through feelings we become acquainted with things, but only by our thoughts do we know about them. Feelings are the germ and starting point of cognition, thoughts the developed tree."[21] Whitehead describes feeling as constituting the first phase of perception (McTernan). "The crude aboriginal character of direct perception is inheritance. What is inherited is feeling-tone with evidence of its origin: in other words, vector feeling-tone. In the higher grades of perception vague feeling-tone differentiates itself into various types of sense—those of touch, sight, smell, etc."[22] But perhaps it is Susanne Langer who best articulates the broad provenance of feeling within which aesthetic elements may mold judgments. "[T]he thesis I hope to substantiate here is that the entire psychological field—including human conception, responsible action, rationality, knowledge—is a vast and branching development of feeling."[23] She explains that feelings are appropriately regarded as actions rather than entities. "[T]he phenomenon usually described as 'a feeling' is really that an organism feels something, i.e., something is felt. What is felt is a process, perhaps a large complex of processes, within the organism."[24] Aesthetic discernment is such a process.

It is important to differentiate several connotations of "feeling" in order to link it properly with aesthetics.

1. Feeling is what is experienced actively or passively in the physical realm of touching and being touched: "The dress feels silky smooth." Feeling can apply within this embodied sense of the word either to the self-initiated process of feeling something or to the experience of an impact on one.

2. Feeling involves a largely tacit process of retrieval. A felt sensation can have an identity, a particularity that cues the explicit memory of a place, an event, or even an appropriate word: "Hearing my friend talk about his youth evoked feelings about the coziness of my childhood bedroom and the thrill of climbing the back yard tree."

3. Feeling is an intimation or adumbration of an impending coherence or discovery. Peirce's notion of abduction as a form of vague rational intuition is an example of this sort of feeling that is more than a guess but less than a well-founded cognitive state. Feeling in this sense has a place in scientific discovery. Thus, based on a felt intuition of increased coherence, Einstein "adopted a vision in which the electro-dynamics of moving bodies were set beautifully free from all the anomalies imposed on them by the traditional framework of absolute time and space."[25]

4. Feeling is a vague process of discrimination that judges between rational or perceptual alternatives according to

norms of appropriateness, proportion, elegance, profundity, compatibility, beauty, fit, and similar essentially aesthetic terms.

The last two enumerated senses of feeling are most clearly associated with what I am terming the third domain of aesthetic judgment. As felt, this third function of aesthetic judgment has sensitivities that occur in moments of reflective attention. Felt judgments are subjective and not in themselves adequately amenable to logical examination issuing in proof or disproof. The reach of this third function of aesthetical judgment is broad and weighty; it is not limited to the arts. It describes a felt sensitivity to the resources judgment may rely upon in rendering a verdict. Indeed, it gives some intelligibility to the uprising springs of rationality Kant calls "mother wit"[26] and despairs of understanding. That is, the aesthetic norms just suggested in the fourth notion of feeling supply a sort of felt underground nourishment guiding judgment to apt assessments, inferences, or conclusions (Auxier). Here is where noncognitive feeling and cognitively based logic interact, for it is through felt appropriateness to a topic that logic is legitimately employed.

The content of imagination often appears spontaneously, sometimes in the form Kant called aesthetical Ideas. In massaging these Ideas into explicit form, aesthetic categories such as enumerated in the fourth point about feeling are often relied upon. As an example, the cognitive act typically called "intuition" reaches its conclusions through reliance on aesthetic criteria—typically, such criteria as fittingness, completeness, elegance, or harmony. Indeed, it seems as if intuition, as commonly understood, is at its core an aesthetically guided act of recognizing coherence, that is, a basic way of coming to conclusions that is different from logical deduction. If so, then one way of looking at intuition is to see it as the product of a process of integration during which aesthetic criteria act both as filters eliminating extraneous ideas or perceptions and as guides leading the experience to consummation.

Three domains of aesthetic judgment have now been identified. The first domain is the disinterested approach to art that identifies beauty as the aesthetic ideal. American Aesthetics, while it acknowledges beauty as one among many aesthetic standards, reacts strongly against the apotheosis of beauty as *the* aesthetic standard. The second domain, central to American Aesthetics, recognizes that creative imagination, aesthetic sensibility, contextual savvy, and normative vocabulary conjoin in the creation and judging of art in its evolving diversity. The third domain, grounded in the thought of the classic American philosophers, involves the recognition that felt aesthetic criteria can influence any and all judgments, not just judgment about art. Each succeeding aspect is more inclusive than its predecessor.

Characteristics of American Aesthetics

What characteristics would criticism of art consistent with American Aesthetics display? Here are likely attributes: (1) the historical, social, and cultural factors that shape the interpreter's judgments are acknowledged; (2) the particular contextual features that illuminate the meaning of the artwork are explicated; (3) insofar as possible, the specific abstract aesthetic standards used in assessing excellence are identified; (4) the fallible, personal character of judgments would be acknowledged; and (5) how the aesthetic aspects of the artwork(s) lead to conclusions about meaning and significance of the work would be highlighted. Several additional factors are noteworthy: (6) in some arenas of creation, such as literature or creative reflection, aesthetic feeling appropriately takes on linguistic form; but (7) in the visual arts, dance, and music, for instance, creative expression is mediated nonlinguistically and tends to resist adequate translation into language. Nevertheless, (8) all aesthetic theorizing and explicit evaluation must necessarily be discussed in language, so (9) critics with a poetic capacity to communicate felt meanings successfully are worthy of special acclamation.

Those individuals carrying out work in the tradition of American Aesthetics employ relatively abstract aesthetic judgments as indicated in the three domains. But because context is so important in American Aesthetics, American culture and history and social settings also contribute to aesthetic processing. Creation and criticism based on American Aesthetics tend to support and appreciate art with some of the following aspects or characteristics:

- Art that is democratic and anti-hierarchical in its sympathies—art that the informed common person can appreciate—is valued more than art that is pretentious, promoted as an investment, or seen as a producer of status.

- Popular culture, vernacular art, and the aesthetics of everyday life are included within the democratic holism of American

Aesthetics, although with varying degrees of affirmation and acceptance.

- Appreciation does not generally extend to the bland, twee or effete (Norman Rockwell, Grandma Moses, elevator music, classically American though they are). Americans tend to see themselves as hard working, practical persons not overly given to sentimentality.

- The traditions of different cultures and classes are attended to in American Aesthetics, given its openness and egalitarianism. Postmodern attention to voices that have been excluded from attention, while perhaps especially stimulated by such thinkers as Derrida and Foucault, is consistent with American Aesthetic sympathies.

- Novelty of expression is valued as dynamic and perhaps progressive, future-oriented. This aesthetic value may be connected to the American support for individualism and for entrepreneurs, those who challenge established practices and authorities.

- Social, historical, and cultural contexts are seen as important in understanding art, and the life experiences of the artist are part of those contexts. So artistic background and intention have a role to play in assessing the meaning of art works.

- Art with a social message is embraced, especially that which sympathetically examines poverty or racism, critiques commercial excess, and offers positive alternatives to the status quo.

- Nature tends to be viewed as the great source and restorer of spiritual values in art.

Many of the values expressed in this list derive from America's religious heritage. For from the time of the first European intrusions into native soil, religious thought, with its attendant idealism, has shaped the dominant American ethos.[27] Religions tend to be especially sensitive to how all the senses can be utilized as doorways to the sacred. The use of incense, hands-on ordination, holy wafer ingested, the sound of bells, sacred dance—such is the richness of religious aesthetics (Slater). Beyond such experiential aesthetics, the various European denominations bequeathed fine art aesthetic standards to their American counterparts, but the physical, social, and economic conditions prevalent in America often promulgated alternative expressions of those standards. For instance, the traditional white New England Congregational church continued the iconoclastic tradition of its Reformed forebears in England and the continent, but it valorized light in a way that differs from the dusky Dutch Reformed sanctuaries. Music, painting, and sculpture in America usually bypass explicit Christian depiction as found in the Bach cantata and motet or the Renaissance-inspired Madonna and Child. Joshua Taylor notes that "art has rarely served in America as an illustration of religious thought, but rather has often striven to create that environment of mind that makes religion possible. . . . Eventually art itself became both symbol and proof of a persistent human spirituality."[28] Dramatic renderings of nature were seen to proclaim the glories of God's creation.

The important American theologian Jonathan Edwards is one who extolled the beauty of God's beneficent creation; he saw such beauty as physical evidence of divine presence (Raposa). Ralph Waldo Emerson's transcendentalism detached religion from denominationalism. He privileged the individual's direct experience of the divine in nature. Different versions of refined spirituality play significant roles in the thought of Peirce, James, Whitehead, and Dewey. Aesthetic and moral sensitivities, as two species of the ideal, have often been intertwined within American religious contexts. Aesthetic judgment is a primal form of valuing, and religion often functions as a storehouse and champion of those values. American Aesthetics, as a comprehensive approach to aesthetics including attention to social and cultural context, provides some correction to the relative lack of attention given to religion and theology in philosophical aesthetics. Several of the essays in this volume address the intersection of aesthetics and religion.

American Aesthetics is a living tradition that includes content that goes beyond the felt formal purity of much traditional aesthetic theory. Two contemporary philosophers who are exemplars of American Aesthetics are Arnold Berleant and Richard Shusterman. Berleant writes, "It was important for Dewey to set himself apart from the common understanding of experience as a subjective, atomistic, even exotic occurrence and to reclaim its biological and social content and continuity; experience is a natural activity of the human organism in the ordinary activities of living."[29] Shusterman's *Pragmatist Aesthetics* is notable for how it extends aesthetic attention to the body as "the active spirit of human experience."[30] Rap music and the ethics of everyday life are seen as validly subject to aesthetic judgment. Alva Noë's *Strange Tools: Art and Human Nature* is a recent work indebted to Dewey's thought. In suggesting that art is a kind of philosophical practice, Noë also brings something of the third aspect of aesthetics into play.[31] John Kaag thoughtfully relies upon the American philosophical tradition, especially Peirce, in exploring the role of the imagination, with its aesthetic overtones, in different aspects of human flourishing.[32] But perhaps nobody takes the aesthetic dimension of Dewey's philosophy more seriously than Mark Johnson. Aesthetic experiences, he states, must not be sidelined as one mere subjective state of mind among many others. Rather, for Dewey, they are "part of our ability to grasp the meaning and significance of *any and every* developed experience. [Dewey] understood aesthetics, therefore, in a broad sense, as involving form and structure, qualities that define a situation, our felt sense of the meaning of things, our rhythmic engagement with our surroundings, and our emotional transactions with other people and our world."[33]

The contributions of the five contemporary American authors just cited fit philosophically into the broad stream of American Aesthetics. In addition, many *art historians* or *art critics* presuppose and employ the typical emphases of American Aesthetics.[34] Does this mean that the notion of an American Aesthetics is so inclusive, overlapping with historical and critical work, that it serves no distinctive function?

No. The value of American Aesthetics making it attractive to art historians and critics is its inclusiveness and normative force. The authoritative quality of American Aesthetics can best be appreciated by contrasting it with two narrower aesthetic traditions.

New Criticism as Overly Constrained

First, the addition of "American" to the philosophical term "aesthetics" already suggests that we are not dealing with some pure term of reason à la Kant, but rather with a broad notion in which philosophical, psychological, historical, and cultural factors all can have a place. To drive home this point, it is useful to contrast American Aesthetics with the New Criticism movement that came to dominate literary criticism in the middle decades of the twentieth century. T. S. Eliot and I. A. Richards in England along with John Crowe Ransom and Allen Tate in the United

States were influential forerunners of this movement in the 1920s and 1930s. Eliot believed that the ordered world of bygone times had decayed through the advent of scientific instrumentalism, secularistic displacement of religious values, and the rise of lowest common denominator cultural expression. The contrast between Eliot's conservative vision and Dewey's progressivist embrace of modernism is immediately evident.

However, the most far-reaching difference between American Aesthetics and New Criticism is found in the way New Critics came to isolate works of literature—particularly poetry—from their historical, social, and cultural contexts. The advent of New Criticism can be understood as a legitimate reaction against reductionist approaches to literature that psychoanalyzed authors, imposed Marxian categories on literature, or otherwise compromised the integrity of the artwork in some restricted way. Vincent Leitch helpfully summarizes key ideas offered by influential New Critic Cleanth Brooks concerning New Criticism:

> First, New Criticism separates *literary* criticism from the study of sources, social backgrounds, history of ideas, politics, and social effects, seeking both to purify poetic criticism from such "extrinsic" concerns and to focus attention squarely on the "literary object" itself. Second, New Criticism explores the structure of a work, not the minds of authors or the reactions of readers. Third, New Criticism champions an "organic" theory of literature rather than a dualistic conception of form and matter; it focuses on the words of the text in relation to the full context of the work: each word contributes to a unique context and derives its precise meaning from its place in the poetic context. Fourth, New Criticism practices close reading of individual works.[35]

There is merit in New Criticism's focus on the art object as long as it is not thought that this is all aesthetic analysis can or should do. Art criticism that reduces the meaning of art works simply to artistic intention, cultural context, ideological commitments, authorial psychological state, or any other narrow concern is an even more truncated form of criticism than attention to the artwork alone. Fortunately, the Southern sensibility of many of the New Critics lent cultural depth to their critical assessment of literature. But in the more general employment of New Criticism that developed, exclusive attention to the work itself became yet another form of reductionism. Even when carried out by Americans, New Critics' narrow version of aesthetic theory stands in opposition to what I am calling American Aesthetics. The holistic concern of American Aesthetics safeguards a much richer understanding of art and its significance.

So, does the attention American Aesthetics devotes to social, cultural, and historical aspects of American life mean that its relevance is restricted to American art? No, in the sense that *if* its emphases on democratic egalitarianism, applicability to a broad spectrum of thought and practice, sensitivity to historical, social, and cultural context and the like influence aesthetic reflection in other cultures and countries, then it could be said that the values and approach of American Aesthetics apply in those settings. The reference to specific aspects of American culture could be seen as illustrations of a deeper, more broadly applicable aesthetic movement.

High-Art Analysis

A second narrow approach to aesthetics is one that was dominant in American evaluation of the arts, particularly the visual arts, for at least a half-century. The aesthetic critique of many American critics (those not influenced by the classic American philosophers) largely parallels the approach of New Criticism in attending narrowly to the paintings and musical compositions themselves or in relation to their disciplinary antecedents, but not in relation to their larger cultural contexts. Such influential American thinkers about aesthetics as Clement Greenberg, Monroe Beardsley, George Dickie, Peter Kivy, Nelson Goodman, and Arthur Danto (whose thought took on postmodern concerns) have tended to be at least loosely connected to the Anglo-American analytic tradition in philosophy. This tradition tends to focus on defining art and its limits, examining the formal properties of art objects, and reflecting on the progressive achievements of individual artists and movements. When context is considered—as it is by Danto in describing how the art world of museums, art magazines, etc. legitimates what can be considered art—the context is still generally about artistic expressions and developments rather than about the broader social context within which the art has significance. That is, in philosophy, the breadth of concerns of pragmatism and process philosophy in contrast to the narrower analytic concern with rational clarity and rigorous argumentation carries over in aesthetics to the contrast between American Aesthetics and analytic aesthetics. American Aesthetics is *synthetic,* exploring the whole emotion-laden meaning of art; while it may include analysis, dissolving art into its pieces, *holistic* treatment is its aim.[36]

The writings of Harold Rosenberg and Meyer Shapiro[37] express the cultural richness of American Aesthetics, while Clement Greenberg's more sharply focused works can be taken as typical representatives of analytical criticism (Gilbertson and Gulick). In his early (1939) essay, "Avant-Garde and Kitsch," Greenberg offers an analysis of the decline of taste in contemporary society. His critique has overtones of Eliot's critique. And just as Eliot's claims about cultural decadence evolved into New Criticism's focus on poetry in and for itself, so Greenberg's notion of cultural decline evolved into an appreciation of the high art of abstraction. He traced how American abstract expressionism evolved just after World War II from earlier (largely French) forms of modernism into preoccupation with the act and physical nature of painting itself. He had almost no concern with artist intention. Representation, narrative, and social context were also seen as largely extraneous to artistic worth.[38] The following quotation from Greenberg about Barnett Newman's work illustrates his picto-centric interest:

> The limiting edges of Newman's larger canvases, we now discover, act just like the lines inside them: to divide but not to separate or enclose or bound; to delimit, but not limit. The paintings do not merge with surrounding space; they preserve—when they succeed—their integrity and separate unity. But neither do they sit there in space like isolated objects; in short, they are hardly easel pictures—and because they are hardly that, they have escaped the "object" (and luxury-object) associations that attach themselves increasingly to the easel picture.[39]

In sum, Greenberg extolled modernist art with its opposition to popular culture. He valued an "emphasis on high art and self-sufficiency, the preoccupation with medium and purity, the desire to maintain a rigid distinction between art and popular culture."[40]

Is it justified to claim that the classic American philosophers provide a stronger claim to have developed a distinctively American approach to aesthetics than the analytic aestheticians such as Greenberg or philosophers in the analytic tradition like George Dickie and Monroe Beardsley or its continuity in postanalytic philosophy? First, although analytical philosophy has been the dominant style of doing philosophy in America since before World War II, it has European roots in the Vienna Circle, logical positivism, and ordinary language philosophy. It did not originate in American soil as did classic American philosophy. Second, the pragmatism and democratic anti-elitism of the classic American philosophers are deeply reflective of key American cultural traits that are missing among the analytic critics of recent years. To be sure, post–World War II American movements in the visual arts such as abstract expressionism, op art, and minimalism explore and express the very nature of art—its elements and structures—rather than interpret American experience. These forms of artistic expression lend themselves well to the sort of analysis carried out in analytic philosophy. However, even when American culture has been engaged, as in pop art or photorealism, analytic aesthetic has tended to restrict its analysis to surface and formal features rather than delve into deeper contextual meanings. Third, analysis as such is shared among all cultures and is thus not as uniquely a marker of American sensibility as is the thought of the classic American philosophers. In sum, American Aesthetics and aesthetic analysis carried out in analytic philosophy can be seen as in many respects a complementary and useful interpretation of artistic and cultural significance, but the analytic approach tends to be more fine-grained while the concerns of American Aesthetics are more comprehensive and more deeply embedded in American culture.

Finally, one must ask, What is the purpose of aesthetic evaluation? Is it to provide more than clarification of aesthetic terminology and determination of what qualifies as art, more than assessment of artistic elements in perception? If so, then the holistic approach of American Aesthetics, modeled on Deweyan appreciation of the many factors contributing to experiential excellence, is a prime candidate to satisfy this urge for "more." Analytic aesthetics has extended aesthetic inquiry well beyond the traditional emphasis on beauty. But it is still largely formal in its approach to its subject matter. What does American Aesthetics add to the typical analytic approach that I believe makes it a superior basis for understanding and appreciating art? It recognizes that context, purpose, and meaning matter in aesthetics. Perceptual qualities have become increasingly irrelevant in assessing such contemporary forms of art as installations, conceptual art, hip-hop music, or performance art. The scope of artistic creation has expanded greatly since aesthetics was formulated by Baumgarten in the eighteenth century. Artistic intention, tied to the purpose and meaning of a work, can be difficult to ascertain, yet it is often vital to acute interpretation and assessment. Intention and purpose can be nearly impossible to comprehend without some knowledge of what standards or issues are viewed as important within the artistic realm at the time of the work's creation, understanding the artist's interests and previous work, sensitivity to key cultural issues that the work may interpret or represent, and other such issues. Background information has always been important for understanding and evaluating literature, especially poetry. Once it was necessary to understand the classical background to which much poetry alluded to; now the poetic disclosure of meaningful aspects of everyday life often requires sensitive background experience on the part of a reader or listener. While such aesthetic sensibilities as fit, appropriateness, and coherence apply to the creation and organization of a work of art, felt aesthetic judgments of the worth of the work such as being profound, well-made, or provocative require a comparative assessment, viewing the work in relation to relevant cultural background information. The particular meaning of an artwork is tied to the particularity of its *situated* genesis. A comprehensive understanding and assessment of particular works (and the art world as a whole) requires the holistic approach of American Aesthetics argued for in this essay and evident in the essays in this volume.

Postmodernism

Modernist culture gave way to postmodern culture and its many artistic manifestations, including postcolonial critique, feminism, deconstruction, pop art, conceptual art, Fluxus, happenings (and performance art in general), photorealism, queer studies, and neo-expressionism. One way of understanding the diffuse nature of postmodernism with respect to the arts is to see it as a reaction to Greenberg's high-art exclusivity in which painting and sculpture became the only true guides to avant-garde progress. Postmodernists of all stripes tend to replace traditional aesthetic analysis with attention to particularistic studies of the arts and other subject matter in their historical, social, and cultural settings. Steven Best and Douglas Kellner write that "postmodern theory provides a critique of representation and the modern belief that theory mirrors reality, taking instead 'perspectivist' and 'relativist' positions that theories at best provide partial perspectives on their objects, and that all cognitive representations of the world are historically and linguistically mediated."[41] In its openness to diversity, particularity, tradition, and the importance of context, postmodernism is consistent with major themes of American Aesthetics. Does this overlap of interest mean that there is no reason to distinguish the concerns of American Aesthetics from those of postmodernism?

Again, no! The title of the book edited by Hal Foster indicates the reason: *The Anti-Aesthetic: Essays on Postmodern Culture*. Jean-François Lyotard's well-known definition of postmodernism, "incredulity toward metanarratives,"[42] would be seen by many postmodernists as applying to American Aesthetics. The very term *aesthetics* has been regarded as anathema in the postmodern tradition. That is, the search for general patterns underlying creative thought and action, traditionally a central interest in philosophy and a core issue for aesthetics, has largely been occluded within postmodern thought in recent decades. Aesthetics has often been interpreted as striving for a grand theory of the arts, a totalizing project infected by illusions of grandeur.[43] American Aesthetics does not harbor any such illusions.

Postmodern thought continues to be influential today, but its strictures are also being reexamined. Why should reflection about large patterns of cultural influence, human intention, and quality in art be excluded from serious evaluation of the arts?[44] Indeed, the fact that the world of art has become international in the age of the internet and global travel seems to make it more incumbent than ever to have recourse to aesthetic categories to aid in interpreting different traditions of artistic expression and meaning.

Conclusion

The traditional cultural ideals in America of democratic egalitarianism, appreciation of diversity and pluralism, optimism, and generosity of spirit—ideals too often missing, unfortunately, in recent political rhetoric—are manifest in American Aesthetics. These ideal qualities, embedded in classic American philosophy, provide a fruitful framework within which to appreciate efflorescence of artistic talent wherever it may blossom. American Aesthetics is commodious. Within its embrace, all three usages of aesthetic judgment discussed earlier are affirmed. Dewey's emphasis on aesthetic experience continues to be a useful reference point for American Aesthetics, but it must not displace attention from what the experience is about, how art is produced, or what contextual factors influence that experience and its objects (Drieth and Gulick). The visual arts have, of course, long gravitated away from primary attention to beauty and the formal aesthetics of Bell, Fry, and Greenberg. Recently, graphic attention to political and cultural problems has come to the fore. Installations and performance art of various types have tended to overshadow painting as the primary mode of visual expression. In contemporary installations, the embodied perceiver sometimes participates in the work of art. Detached observation of dance seems not as important as it once was, but attention to the importance of the body in all the arts is arguably greater than ever. Film now occupies a central place in contemporary reflection about artistic expression (McLachlan). Yet what especially calls for increased aesthetic attention is the popular visual culture that first surfaced through photography, became public in magazines and books, took on a new role in television, and now is virtually ubiquitous in computer culture through websites, YouTube, and the various social media sites. The tradition of American Aesthetics, with its holistic interest in both the fine arts tradition and popular culture, is ideally positioned to offer informed commentary on the whole panoply of contemporary culture (Strong).

The claim made here for an American tradition in aesthetics is largely descriptive, but I have normative intentions as well. For I believe the thick, holistic approach of American Aesthetics provides an encompassing framework for aesthetic discussion that is much needed today. American Aesthetics and analytic aesthetics are infused with somewhat different sets of values. That does not mean the analytical alternative should be dismissed. It is a complementary approach to aesthetics that has usefully illuminated artistic innovations and meanings for many decades. The two approaches to aesthetics can be and often are productively combined. Hybridization is the norm. Neither should American Aesthetics be seen as some sort of triumphalist patriotic celebration. Rather, in its broad sense it is intended to encourage holistic sensitivity to the felt factors that enhance living by animating creative imagining, doing, and appreciating (Corrington). Insofar as it is devoted strictly to the arts, it is attentive to historical, political, and economic influences shaping American cultural developments. It searches for the integrity and significance of creative work in whatever form it arises. Art matters. Theory matters. Practice matters. American Aesthetics provides resources for evaluating those kinds of mattering and appreciating how and why they occur.

Notes

1. The literature on aesthetics, art criticism, art history, and postmodernism is almost overwhelmingly vast, and my essay has been influenced by more of this literature over the years than I can remember, much less list accurately. However, I am happy to acknowledge help offered me by Phil Mullins, Tom Nurmi, Brian Dillon, and Gary Slater in thinking through some of the claims made in this paper. An anonymous publisher's reader offered much appreciated editorial suggestions.

2. Wesley Wildman's article in this volume places aesthetic sensitivity among the value-laden kinds of responsiveness of organisms to their physical and social environments. Robert Neville describes how harmony is a primal trait of existence. Shusterman shows how James illuminates the aesthetic factors shaping experience. In the text I will indicate in parentheses those authors whose articles in this volume bear upon the points at hand.

3. This is a view that John Dewey emphasizes: "For the uniquely distinguishing feature of esthetic experience is exactly the fact that no such distinction of self and object exists in it, since it is esthetic in the degree in which organism and environment cooperate to institute an experience in which the two are so fully integrated that each disappears." *Art as Experience* (New York: Capricorn Books, 1958 [1934]), 249.

4. Arnold Berleant develops a rich, holistic notion of the many factors involved in aesthetic appreciation in his early work *The Aesthetic Field: A Phenomenology of Aesthetic Experience* (Springfield, IL: C. C. Thomas, 1970). In Berleant's *Art and Engagement* (Philadelphia: Temple University Press, 1991), he describes the aesthetic field as an integration of four aspects: "the creative, the objective, the appreciative, and the performative, replacing [Kant's notion of] disinterestedness with engagement and contemplation with participation" (4). While this list of four aspects would seem not to include the historical, social and cultural context that I take to be crucial to the approach of American Aesthetics, the body of his work, devoted to environmental aesthetics and social context, affirms these issues. "To recognize the social context in the creation, appreciation, and use of the arts is to strengthen their importance and their powers, not weaken them" (*Art and Engagement*, 209).

5. D. W. Prall's classic work, *Aesthetic Judgment* (New York: Thomas Y. Crowell, 1967 [1929]) continues to serve as an excellent exposition of the various material elements to which aesthetic judgment may refer.

6. John Anderson is among those who make use of this phase. See his *The Realm of Art* (University Park: Pennsylvania State University Press, 1967), 19.

7. "The symbol-making function is one of man's primary activities, like eating, looking, or moving about. It is the fundamental process of his mind, and

goes on all the time." Susanne Langer, *Philosophy in a New Key* (Cambridge: Harvard University Press, 1957), 41.

8. See Dickie's 1964 article "The Myth of the Aesthetic Attitude," in *The Philosophy of the Visual Arts*, ed. Philip Alperson (New York: Oxford University Press, 1992), 30–39.

9. Immanuel Kant, *Critique of Judgment*, trans J. H. Bernard (New York Hafner, 1966 [1790]), 48, ¶ 7 & 8. Henceforth citations from this work will be referenced in the text as CJ.

10. Dewey to Harris, January 17, 1884. Dewey mentions the title of his dissertation in a letter of May 28, 1888, to T. R. Ball. Both letters are quoted in George Dykhuizen, *The Life and Mind of John Dewey*, ed. Jo Ann Boydston (Carbondale: Southern Illinois University Press, 1973), 37.

11. John Dewey, *Art as Experience*, 253.

12. Ibid.

13. Ibid., 254.

14. In this paragraph, Kant notes that the natural world has aspects that are purposeful for human use in ways that induce aesthetic pleasure. Kant's aesthetic theory is not limited to beauty.

15. *Art as Experience*, 38

16. Ibid., 37.

17. Susanne Langer, *Feeling and Form* (New York: Charles Scribner's Sons, 1953), 34. Langer in her critique of Dewey's emphasis on personal experience further states, "Bell's assertion that every theory of art must begin with the contemplation of 'the aesthetic emotion,' and that, indeed, nothing else is really the business of aesthetics, seems to me entirely wrong. To dwell on one's state of mind in the presence of a work does not further one's understanding of the work and its value. The question of what gives one the emotion is exactly the question of what makes the object artistic; and that, to my mind, is where philosophical art theory begins" (*Feeling and Form*, 39).

18. Alfred North Whitehead, *Adventures of Ideas* (New York: Mentor, 1955 [1933]), 264. While Whitehead was born in England and did not emigrate to the United States until after his career was well underway, it is appropriate to include him among the classic American philosophers because of his influence in the States while teaching at Harvard, and because his greatest influence by far has been in America.

19. William James, "What Makes a Life Significant?" in *Essays on Faith and Morals* selected by Ralph Barton Perry (Cleveland and New York: Meridian Books, 1962), 290.

20. Jonathan Edwards early on spoke of the importance of the affections in shaping belief and thought. Henry James's novels are rife with exemplifications of Victorian sentiment that may have influenced his brother William in his emphasis on feeling.

21. William James, *Principles of Psychology*, vol. I (Dover, 1950 [1890]), 222.

22. Alfred North Whitehead, *Process and Reality: An Essay in Cosmology* (New York: Harper Torchbooks, 1957 [1929]), 182. Whitehead states his philosophical objective thusly: "The philosophy of organism aspires to construct a critique of pure feeling, in the philosophical position in which Kant put his *Critique of Pure Reason*" (*Process and Reality*, 172–73).

23. Susanne Langer, *Mind: An Essay on Human Feeling*, vol. I (Baltimore: Johns Hopkins University Press, 1967), 23.

24. Ibid., 21.

25. Michael Polanyi, *Personal Knowledge: Towards a Post-Critical Philosophy* (New York: Harper Torchbooks, 1964 [1958]), 144.

26. Kant, *Critique of Pure Reason*, 177 (A 133, B 172). Farther along, Kant also writes, "This schematism of our understanding, in its application to appearances and their mere form, is an art concealed in the depths of the human soul, whose real modes of activity nature is hardly likely ever to allow us to discover, and to have open to our gaze" (183 [A 141, B 180]).

27. Speaking of religious influence throughout the history of American culture, Debra Koppman states a broadly held view that the "often unspoken assumptions about religious beliefs and the meaning of symbols profoundly inform the development of theory, criticism, and interpretation of art." "Thou Art: The Continuity of Religious Ideology in Modern and Postmodern Theory and Practice," in *Reclaiming the Spiritual in Art: Contemporary Cross-Cultural Perspectives*, ed. Dawn Perlmutter and Debra Koppman (Albany: State University of New York Press, 1999), 145.

28. Joshua C. Taylor, "The Religious Impulse in American Art," in *Art, Creativity, and the Sacred*, ed. Diane Apostolos-Cappadona (New York: Crossroad, 1984), 104.

29. Arnold Berleant, *Aesthetics Beyond the Arts: New and Recent Essays* (London and New York: Routledge, 2016 [Ashgate, 2012]), 161.

30. Richard Shusterman, *Pragmatist Aesthetics: Living Beauty, Rethinking Art*, 2nd ed. (Lanham, MD: Rowman and Littlefield, 2000), 274. See also Schusterman's entry, "Pragmatism," in *The Routledge Companion to Aesthetics*, 3rd ed., ed. Berys Gaut and Dominic McIver Lopes (London and New York: Routledge, 2013), where on 97–101 he lists seven major themes of pragmatist aesthetics.

31. Alva Noë, *Strange Tools: Art and Human Nature* (New York: Hill and Wang, 2015).

32. John Kaag, *Thinking through the Imagination: Aesthetics in Human Cognition* (New York: Fordham University Press, 2014).

33. Mark Johnson, "Dewey's Big Idea for Aesthetics," in *Rethinking Aesthetics: The Role of the Body in Design*, ed. Ritu Bhatt (New York: Routledge, 2013), 38. Johnson's *The Meaning of the Body: Aesthetics of Human Understanding* (Chicago: University of Chicago Press, 2008) is a fuller development of the crucial role aesthetics ought to play when discussing meaning in life.

34. Several works in literary criticism and music criticism may be listed to illustrate that the sort of concerns expressed in this essay evoke wider, although perhaps still minority, attention. *A Return to Aesthetics: Autonomy, Indifference, and Postmodernism*, by Jonathan Loesberg (Stanford: Stanford University Press, 2005) and *American Literature's Aesthetic Dimension*, ed. Cindy Weinstein and Christopher Looby (New York: Columbia University Press, 2012) argue for the use of aesthetic criteria to understand postmodernism, despite its rejection of aesthetics, and to avoid reductionist allegiance to either formal analysis of literature or political and cultural historicism. Rita Felski in *The Limits of Criticism* (Chicago: University of Chicago Press, 2015) suggests that critical analysis of literature has been handicapped by the prevalence of a hermeneutics of suspicion that ignores the many other rich modes of appreciating literature. Theodore Gracyk's *Listening to Popular Music: Or, How I Learned to Stop Worrying and Love Led Zeppelin* (Ann Arbor: University of Michigan Press, 2007) may be taken as an example from the vast literature on popular culture of those works that pay attention to aesthetic issues. These books and essays, however, do not stake out a theory of American Aesthetics.

35. Vincent B. Leitch, *American Literary Criticism from the Thirties to the Eighties* (New York: Columbia University Press, 1988), 26.

36. See Alejandro García-Rivera, *A Wounded Innocence: Sketches for a Theology of Art* (Collegeville, MN: The Liturgical Press, 2003), ix. Garcia-Rivera makes a strong plea for regarding the "symbols, imagery, and music" of all the arts, especially in their folk art form, as basic to the cultural and religious identity of people throughout all the Americas—see especially chapter 5. Hence, it is reasonable to see the comprehensive approach of American Aesthetics as applying, at least in theory, to Latin America as well as the United States.

37. For Rosenberg, see the article on his approach to aesthetics in this collection. The title of art historian Meyer Schapiro's important article, "On the Social Basis of Art" (in *Art in Theory, 1900–2000*, ed. Charles Harrison and Paul Wood [Oxford: Blackwell, 2003]), describes well the contextual basis of his aesthetic interests.

38. Suzi Gablik describes Greenberg's limited aesthetic perspective in memorable language: "Only the 'dictates of the medium'—pure paint and the flatness of the picture plane—were held to be worthwhile concerns for painting. The very idea of content was taken to be a hindrance and a nuisance, and looking for meaning was a form of philistinism." *Has Modernism Failed?* (New York: Thames and Hudson, 1984), 23.

39. Clement Greenberg, *Art and Culture: Critical Essays* (Boston: Beacon Press, 1961), 226–27.

40. Richard Hertz, *Theories of Contemporary Art* (Englewood Cliffs, NJ: Prentice-Hall, 1985), v.

41. Steven Best and Douglas Kellner, *Postmodern Theory: Critical Investigations* (New York: Guilford Press, 1998), 4.

42. Jean-François Lyotard, *The Postmodern Condition* (Minneapolis: University of Minnesota Press, 1984), xxiv.

43. F. J. W. Schelling's work *The Philosophy of* Art, based on lectures from 1801 and 1804, is a prime example of seeing art as the indispensable vehicle for reaching romantic totality.

44. Postmodern sensibility has sponsored eclectic use of material from diverse genres, media, and historical epochs with a consequent blurring of previous boundaries. Pam Meecham and Julie Sheldon are among those who have noted a renewed interest in aesthetics as a means of sorting out what is of compelling worth within the new art forms. See their *Making American Art* (London and New York: Routledge, 2009), 186. A work that appears to have been relatively ignored but that is consistent with the approach of this essay is David Kenneth Holt, *The Search for Aesthetic Meaning in the Visual Arts: The Need for the Aesthetic Tradition in Contemporary Art Theory and Education* (Westport, CT: Bergin and Garvey, 2001).

II

Philosophical Contributions to American Aesthetics from the Past

The essays in this section explore how different aesthetic elements in the philosophical writings of key American thinkers continue to offer persons today significant insights in theology, philosophy, and the arts, as well as in everyday living.

Jacob Goodson's central claim is that Emerson suggests a shift of the object of tragedy from one of events, as with Aristotle, to one of temperaments. This shift is an auspicious step in the expanded sense of aesthetics taking root in American Aesthetics. Instead of addressing the question of whether the generally optimistic Emerson appropriately recognizes the tragic element of life, Goodson's essay offers the more precise and fruitful question of whether Emerson's account of tragedy is legitimate with respect to ordinary life. Goodson recovers a neglected aesthetic feature in Emerson by claiming that he democratizes the tragic and thereby makes this category applicable to all human beings.

Michael L. Raposa claims that both Jonathan Edwards and C. S. Peirce understand an aesthetic sensibility to be critical for perceiving God. Each construes nature as the site of divine semiosis, with an accurate reading of the signs embedded in nature possible only for those endowed with the appropriate aesthetic sensibility. The concept of beauty is relied upon by Peirce in his peculiar version of the ontological argument, while Edwards makes use of beauty in his argument from design. Raposa's essay illuminates an identifiable thread of aesthetically relevant philosophical theology arising within American thought.

The premise of David Rohr's article is that pragmatism in general, and Peirce in particular, provide powerful tools for conceptualizing how aesthetic inquiry and creation work. Rohr utilizes Peircean vocabulary to distinguish between emotional, behavioral, and rational interpretation as continuous, distinct, but also intertwined modes of experience. Artistic creation, he claims, manifests "self-reflective semiosis" in which aesthetic intention is enacted, evaluated, and then modified in an unfolding form of aesthetic dialectic. Paintings and other aesthetic products function as signs, as Rohr illustrates with reference to the work of Van Gogh, Gerhard Richter, and Ira Glass.

Richard Shusterman's development of pragmatist aesthetics is an important expression of core concepts in American Aesthetics. His essay reveals that although William James wrote no specific treatise on aesthetics, he had a keen regard for the arts and aesthetic assessment. James's *Principles of Psychology* is shown to be the source of penetrating insights into the role that aesthetic sensitivity and judgment plays in the development of thought and action. For James, aesthetic criteria of selection greatly shape rational and practical decision making. Shusterman convincingly demonstrates that James's aesthetic thought decisively influenced Dewey's aesthetic theory and the pragmatist aesthetics Shusterman himself develops.

Robert Innis celebrates the richness of John Dewey's 1934 masterpiece, *Art as Experience*. Innis shows how Dewey's work, in its profound assimilation and synthesis of elements from Peirce and James, understands art and aesthetic experience as crucial tools for bringing embodied humans into organic, existential bonding with nature. Indeed, aesthetic judgments are seen by Dewey as one of the more powerful ways in which humans adjust to and find significance in the surprises and challenges of living. Innis illustrates his theoretical exposition by exploring how Dewey reflects on the aesthetic significance of Chinese art, Michelangelo's *Moses*, one of Renoir's "Bather" paintings, and other artworks.

2

The Primacy of Aesthetic Judgments

Emerson's Deontological-Transcendentalist Account of Tragedy

JACOB L. GOODSON

Introduction

Most scholars of Ralph Waldo Emerson's philosophy conclude that he makes room for neither the ancient aesthetic category of tragedy nor the Existentialist phrase "the tragic sense of life."[1] Even the most sympathetic reader of Emerson on this issue, Newton Arvin, concludes his essay "The House of Pain"[2] (1959) with these words: "Emerson . . . is bound to disappoint . . . if we look in his work for a steady confrontation of Tragedy as a sustained and unswerving gaze at the face of Evil. They are not there, and we shall lose our labor if we look for them."[3] According to Arvin, Emerson ought to be interpreted within the Augustinian tradition emphasizing the moral impact of sinfulness and should never be interpreted within the Aristotelian tradition that focuses upon the aesthetic category of tragedy.

This claim about Emerson's work strikes me as deeply misguided and wrong: much more than universalizing Augustine beyond Christian theological reasoning,[4] Emerson democratizes Aristotle's aesthetic categories and virtue theory. By the claim "democratizes Aristotle's *aesthetic* categories," I mean that Emerson makes the categories of comedy and tragedy applicable to all citizens of particular polities and social bodies;[5] by the claim "democratizes Aristotle's . . . *virtue* theory," I mean that Emerson makes the virtue of courage available to all human beings—not only to the male elite.[6] These two moves become decisive for understanding Emerson's aesthetics and ethics. Unlike the Existentialist turn in modern philosophy toward internal anxiety as representative of our deepest fears and the cause of our own personal tragedies, Emerson maintains the Aristotelian notion that tragedies involve observable outward objects; whereas Aristotle identifies *events* as the object of tragedy, however, Emerson shifts the object of tragedy to those observable *temperaments*: tragedy "consists in temperament," Emerson writes, "not in events."[7] Also, in the same essay, he displays ease in offering aesthetic judgments such as, "This [temperament] is not beautiful," and calling one possible response to tragedy "tuneful." The question is not (as scholars of Emerson's philosophy continually ask), Does the overly optimistic Emerson account for tragedy?[8] The question, rather, is: Do we accept Emerson's account of tragedy as a legitimate account of the tragic elements of ordinary life?[9]

Emerson makes tragedy less dramatic than Aristotle does but thinks that everyday tragedies within ordinary life require aesthetic judgments.[10] Emerson's notion of tragedy serves as an example for how American philosophers seek to change the definition of aesthetics. Emerson seeks to apply aesthetic judgments beyond art, literature, and music because of his preoccupation with domestic life and ordinary life. Emerson thinks that aesthetics provides the most serious and sobering ways to make judgments on our character in relation to the tragedies that we experience in our everyday lives. The aesthetic dimension of Emerson's understanding of tragedy concerns the type of judgment that we make on the observable temperaments of others and ourselves.[11] We learn this through a close reading of Emerson's early lecture entitled "Tragedy" and his later essay "The Tragic."

Emerson's Tragic Sense

Emerson informs his audience that he intends to "enumerate the tragic elements in our constitution" and evaluate the validity of each of them: two of which he dismisses; one he accepts but only on Kantian deontological terms; and the final one he fully defends.

First, the ancient literary understanding of tragedy: what Emerson labels "the belief in Fate of Destiny."[12] Emerson labels this ancient literary understanding of tragedy "a terrible idea" and laments how much of a hold

Antigone and Oedipus have over us as citizens of the Western world. His lamenting extends beyond Western civilization; he also rejects these types of stories found in Ancient Israel, India, and within Islam. He concludes, "Hence the antique Tragedy which was founded on this faith [in Fate or Destiny] can never be reproduced."[13] This conclusion often serves as a kind of proof-text for saying that Emerson offers no account of tragedy, but in fact he simply says that the ancient literary and moral understanding of tragedy should have no hold for a modern conception of tragedy and within the modern world.

The second enumeration of tragedy concerns being held down or limited "by the laws of the world."[14] We might expect Emerson to defend this one, especially in relation to his defense of the significance of "self-reliance," but we would be wrong to make this prejudicial judgment. He breaks down the phrase, "the laws of the world," into four categories: "Disease, Want, Insecurity, Disunion."[15] He considers disease a troubling part of life but not quite "tragic." We learn later that "madness" seems to be the disease of the mind, and this type of disease ought to be granted as tragic because it impacts our observable temperament. The sickness or unhealthiness of the body, however, does not achieve the status of tragic.

What he calls "want" concerns the imagined need for "external goods." The desire for wealth becomes Emerson's primary target, and both the lack of wealth and being impoverished ought to be understood as "good"— neither is tragic in itself. We tend to view poverty as a tragedy based upon systemic greed, which causes oppression and suffering. Emerson, however, thinks that the wealthy remain at a disadvantage because they fail to develop the skills necessary to live properly and think for themselves. The word *tragedy* should be used to describe neither poverty nor wealth.[16]

Does insecurity lead to tragedy? Emerson answers this question in the negative by contrasting faith with insecurity. He defends faith as a virtue directed toward God with effects that determine our own sense of security: "My faith is perfect that what is from God shall be more wise, more fair, more gracious, more manifold, more rejoicing than aught the soul had already."[17] The virtue of faith does not provide a response to the tragedies caused by insecurity; rather, Emerson seems to understand insecurity strictly as a vice that opposes faith. Being insecure does not lead to tragedy but, more simply, to further vices. We should recognize Emerson's difference from Aristotle on this point. For Aristotle, on the one hand, a singular vice of "a great man" brings about his fall or his tragic story. In Aristotle's *Poetics*, a tragedy involves the following: (1) the major characters in a tragedy are significant human beings (i.e. they are gods, heroes, and/or kings); (2) the protagonist's life, and the underlying conditions for his life, go from good to bad; (3) the protagonist has a "tragic flaw," which brings about his downfall; (4) the protagonist has connections with several people, which means that his downfall becomes a catastrophic event for himself and for others; (5) the purpose of a tragedy, in relation to the audience, is *catharsis*: to cleanse or purify the soul (why do our souls need cleansing?—because we each carry around "fear" and "pity" within ourselves).[18] For Emerson, on the other hand, a singular vice is merely a singular vice. Sometimes a vice is just a vice.

By "disunion," Emerson means death. From Aristotle onward, philosophers have considered death to be the height of the tragic. Emerson disagrees: death is simply part of life, and philosophers have deceived us by making death *extra*-ordinary rather than part of *the ordinary*. The word *disunion* signals the extra-ordinariness of death found within philosophy: for death gets explained through the lens of the disunion of the soul from the body. Death should not be considered a tragedy but, more simply, a necessary part of ordinary life.

After dismissing death, disease, insecurity, and money as the causes of tragedy, Emerson tells his audience: "The next tragic element in life is the hindrance of private felicity by vice."[19] The contrast Emerson makes here concerns the Aristotelian emphasis on particular evil dispositions versus the Kantian focus on the general tendency to use "persons as things." If we understand vice in the Kantian sense of a general tendency to "use persons as things," then this gets us closer to an understanding of tragedy within our everyday lives. This aspect of Emerson's understanding of tragedy can be labeled deontological, where our relation to family and friends becomes an act of slaveholding. Emerson writes: "We swell the cry of horror at the slaveholder and we treat our laborer or farmer or debtor as a thing; women; children; the poor; and so we do hold slaves." He continues, "In the base hour, we become slaveholders. We use persons as things, and we think of persons as things."[20] For Emerson, relating to other persons as "things"—instead of persons—leads to relational tragedies within our domestic or ordinary lives. At this point in his argument, Emerson's place in the tradition of philosophical reflections on tragedy ought to be described as deontological—which applies mostly to problematic features of our relationships rather than viewing tragedy in terms of the downfall of a single individual.

Emerson labels the fourth type of tragedy—which he defends as "the proper tragic element"—as "Terror." Terror connects with tragedy because it provides a singular word not for definite evils but "indefinite" evils: "an ominous spirit which haunts the afternoon and the night; idleness and solitude, ignorance and [general] vice."[21] He writes this passage a bit differently in "The Tragic": "After we have enumerated famine, fever, inaptitude, mutilation, rack, madness, and loss of friends, we have not yet included the proper tragic element, which is Terror, and which does not respect definite evils but indefinite [evils]; an ominous spirit which haunts the afternoon and the night, idleness and solitude."[22] In both versions, Emerson emphasizes relationality—not an individual downfall—as the focal point for the tragic. He claims "[u]ngrounded fears, suspicions, half knowledge, and mistakes [that] darken the brow and chill the heart of men" are not problems because of how they make individuals *feel* but become problems because of how they encourage individuals to act against others and judge others in inappropriate ways. We should expect neither Terror nor tragedy to go away, but we can set our reactions and temperaments in such a way that we avoid inappropriately judging others and improperly using others. To this end, Emerson highlights four responses to the tragedy of Terror: composure, temperance, "the just application of the intellect to the facts," and sympathy.[23] In short: Emerson argues that particular dispositions are not the cause of the tragic, but particular dispositions help us live into the everyday tragedies that we face in ordinary life.

I imagine that any Aristotelian-leaning reader will assume that these responses are types of moral virtues—how else do we understand composure, temperance, and sympathy?—but Emerson seems deliberate about not calling these responses moral virtues. Instead, he envelopes his description of these four responses with aesthetic language: "Tragedy is in the eye of the observer, and not in the heart of the sufferer";[24] "I think we fly to Beauty as an asylum from the terrors of finite nature";[25] and, "Nature is the beautiful asylum to which we look in all the years of striving and conflict as the assured resource when we shall be driven out of society by ennui or chagrin or persecution or defect of character."[26] I believe Emerson deliberately places the first quotation before explaining the four responses and the latter two quotations immediately after his explanations of the four responses in order to suggest that the tragic elements of everyday life involve aesthetic judgments instead of moral judgments. By doing so, Emerson thinks we ought to offer a different type of judgment on the tragic elements of domestic life: aesthetic judgments. The tragedies that we experience are neither good nor bad; we might say, morally, "Tragedy is what it is." However, we can make aesthetic judgments on the tragic aspects of life—which involves disciplining both our speech and thinking to make the following judgments: (1) the problem with using other people, in ordinary life, strictly as a means to one's own end leads to relational *ugliness*; (2) while all of us live in *conditions* of "Terror," the tragedy is that he or she neither appreciated nor escaped into "the Beauty" of life around them; and most fitting for the twenty-first century, (3) while terrorism can be considered a moral problem, the American reaction to terrorism ought to be considered an aesthetic problem in the sense that we allow the moral problem of terrorism to remake us into ugly human beings who perpetuate horror based upon our fears.

Emerson turns toward the power of the intellect in his final paragraph of the later essay, "The Tragic," and reflects on how the "intellect" serves us best for working through the tragedies encountered within ordinary life. Emerson writes:

> The intellect is a consoler [during everyday tragic experiences], which delights in detaching or putting an interval between a man and his fortune [or misfortune], and so converts the sufferer into a spectator and his pain into poetry. It yields to [the] joys of conversation. . . . Hence also the torments of life become tuneful tragedy, solemn and soft with music, and garnished with rich dark pictures. But higher still than the activities of art, the intellect in its purity and the moral sense in its purity are not distinguished from each other, and both ravish us into a region whereunto these passionate clouds of sorrow cannot rise.[27]

The intellect allows us to respond to tragedy in "tuneful" ways, which prevents us from becoming ugly in our response to the tragic. The intellect consoles us by leading us to a healthy and proper detachment from the tragic, which involves both caring for the self and recognizing others in their personhood. The intellect empowers us to cope with and work through everyday tragic experiences without falling into sorrow. Emerson's turn toward the intellect, I suggest, warrants an account of intellectual virtue for helping us know when to make aesthetic judgments versus moral and religious judgments.[28]

The Primacy of Aesthetic Judgments

I believe that Emerson sees himself as offering both a deontological and Transcendentalist account of tragedy. *Deontological,* because Emerson seeks to shift the claim of the tragic from the sense of an individual downfall to relational tragedies within our domestic or ordinary lives—these relational tragedies occur when we develop the general tendency to use other persons strictly as a means toward our desired ends. *Transcendentalist,* because Emerson's account of tragedy tries to make sense of the role of "Terror" as part of the *conditions* of ordinary life and as a rule for thinking.

Terror and Tragedy in the Twenty-first Century

Although he never connects it with his own "readings" of Emerson's essays, Stanley Cavell understands what it means for Terror to turn ordinary persons into ugly monsters; in the following passage, Cavell reflects upon the concept of horror and gives us the terms necessary for understanding what I mean by making aesthetic judgments on the tragic elements found in ordinary life:

> I do not suppose that what I have, when I am horrified, *is* horror; it may only be "horror." What is the object of horror? At what do we tremble in this way? Fear is of danger; terror is of violence, of the violence I might do or that might be done to me. I can be terrified of thunder, but not horrified by it. And isn't it the case that not the human horrifies me, but the inhuman, the monstrous? Very well. But only what is human can be inhuman. Can only the human be monstrous? If something is monstrous, and we do not believe that there are monsters, then only the human is a candidate for the monstrous.
>
> If only humans feel horror ... then maybe it is a response specifically to being human. To what, specifically, about being human? Horror is the title I am giving to the perception of the precariousness of human identity, to the perception that it may be lost or invaded, that we may be, or may become, something other than we are, or [what] take ourselves [to be].[29]

Toward the end of the semester when teaching the course, "Warfare and Ethics,"[30] I read this passage aloud during my lecture on Talal Asad's *On*

Suicide Bombers.³¹ Asad claims that American citizens tend to justify the horrors caused by American policies and soldiers but then, unreflectively, react out of moral disgust when they learn that Muslims perform suicide bombing missions.³² I read this passage from Cavell and then ask the students, "How do we follow Asad's observations and not become the horror or the monsters that we claim are against 'us'? Does the development of a deeper comprehension of our friends and enemies within different religious traditions, and who view the history of politics differently from us, prevent us from becoming monsters toward them? As Americans, we are on the verge—and perhaps we have already crossed the line—of becoming the horror that we seek to eliminate." I remain uncertain what it means as an American to think of war as part of our ordinary lives, but I think this discussion about horror and monsters illustrates Emerson's point about learning to make aesthetic judgments on ourselves when we live under and within *conditions* of Terror.³³

Cavell, furthermore, writes that classical tragedy requires an extra-ordinary response—either moralistic or religious—because of how we have become accustomed to think of tragedy "as made up of pity and terror" simply in our gaze, "as if what we witness is the subjection of the human being to states of violence, to one's own and to others."³⁴ Examples of this gaze at terror come in the forms of thinking that terror results from "the causes and consequences of human rage, jealousy, ambition, pride, self-arrogance."³⁵ Suppose, however, "that there is a mode of tragedy"—Cavell teases out—"in which what we witness is the subjection of the human being to states of violation a perception that not merely human law but human nature itself can be abrogated."³⁶ This type of tragedy involves the way in which we abject others who are like us but refuse our gaze.³⁷ In Cavell's words: "The outcast [in our ordinary life becomes] a figure of pity and horror; different from ourselves [though] not different."³⁸ For Cavell, this "suggests . . . that if there is a worry it is [neither a classically tragic nor] a skeptical worry, not something beyond the field of everyday life."³⁹ If not "beyond the field of everyday life," then the temptation toward ugliness—or choose your favorite aesthetic judgment about negative human behavior (dreadful, ghastly, hideous, horrible, horrid, repulsive, revolting)—remains constant and unavoidable.⁴⁰

I find this especially true in the twenty-first century where we can escape neither tragedy nor opportunities to display our response to the tragic elements of everyday life. For the classical understanding of tragedy, going about one's business means avoiding the tragic; according to Emerson's

Transcendentalism and for the *conditions* of the twenty-first century, going about one's business means bearing and witnessing everyday tragedies.[41] These everyday tragedies, on their own, do not belong in the category of aesthetics; our responses to these everyday tragedies require an aesthetic judgment because our responses to tragedy require a truthfulness often concealed, covered up, or downplayed in moralistic or religious language.

Significantly, Emerson's *Conduct of Life* builds on insights from his writings on tragedy. In his interpretation of Emerson's *The Conduct of Life*, for instance, Michael Lopez furthers my point. He writes, "Civilization cannot . . . simply be defined as virtue, morality, and 'good energy'; it exists, rather, as the complex end product of what we now call, in the wake of Nietzsche and Freud, the 'sublimation' of destructive or immoral impulses."[42] Lopez continues, "Culture cannot exist without those 'wicked' energies that give it 'muscle'; even our 'representations of the Deity' depend on those forces we associate with hell."[43] Those "forces we associate with hell" reflect the ugly realities that we make for ourselves.

Emerson teaches us that aesthetic judgments reveal much more about us than moralistic or religious judgments tend to do. I have in mind here the ways in which neighbors tend to describe a mass shooter or a serial killer as an overall "good person." In terms of religious judgments, within my own tradition of Lutheranism, we tend to downplay the *impact* of our sinful actions (we acknowledge the significance of sin but tend to emphasize confession and absolution) and focus instead on God's forgiveness. While this focus seems to be the proper theological stance toward sinful actions, it also gives us more reason to connect our judgments about tragedy with aesthetic language if we wish to make a harsher and more sobering judgment on our sinful and wrongful actions.

Tragedy after Emerson?

I conclude by reflecting upon how tragedy gets understood in those philosophers who come after and follow Emerson: Friedrich Nietzsche, William James, Josiah Royce, John Dewey, Reinhold Niebuhr, and Cornel West. By concluding in this way, I am able to show the significance of Emerson's own account of tragedy in relation to these other theories.

Companion or Godfather? This becomes Lawrence Buell's question, in his chapter called "Emerson as a Philosopher?" about Emerson's relationship to Friedrich Nietzsche and William James.[44] Buell argues that

James views Emerson as his "godfather" whereas Nietzsche views Emerson as his "companion": "Nietzsche found in Emerson 'a kind of freedom and spiritual openness that was lacking in his own [German] culture' "[45] whereas James kept Emerson at a distance of admiration in the sense that James absorbs "Emersonian idealism into a more robust pluralism," and "James revives Emerson even as he monumentalizes him."[46] Who is Emerson's true heir when it comes to his account of tragedy: James or Nietzsche? Additionally, according to Cornel West, Reinhold Niebuhr's greatest contribution to American Philosophy involves his robust account of sin and tragedy against the optimism of Emerson's Transcendentalism and the progressive humanism of John Dewey's pragmatism. Are Niebuhr and West the true heirs to Emerson's Transcendentalism?

Nietzsche *after* Emerson? Like Emerson, Nietzsche critiques the moralism of Aristotle and Socrates. Adrian Poole describe Nietzsche's critique of moralism in these terms:

> In *The Birth of Tragedy* . . . Nietzsche sees in ancient Greek drama the collision of fundamentally opposed principles: he calls them Dionysius and Apollo. . . . For Nietzsche, pain is an inevitable corollary of the Life-Force, and as such it is to be welcomed rather than lamented. . . . And it is this violence, pain, and conflict that Nietzsche insists is essential to ancient Greek culture. . . .
>
> Nietzsche tries to be fair to Apollo, but the thrust of his writing is towards celebration of Dionysius, who is at once creator and destroyer, the force behind form, or better, the force that drives *through* all human forms, making and unmaking them, including all human artefacts. Apollo is the name for the contrary principle that gives form to force. Apollo individuates and differentiates. Apollo presides over structures, over limits and contours and shapes; Dionysius presides over the process of generation that makes forms possible, but also perpetually dissolves them. . . . [Nietzsche] makes Aristotle's idea of *katharsis* look puny and pallid by comparison.[47]

Like Emerson, Nietzsche finds that the category of the tragic ought to be limited to aesthetic judgments as well. The difference between Emerson and Nietzsche seems to be that Nietzsche refuses to make negative aesthetic judgments on tragic moments associated with our relationships and, instead, wants to make negative aesthetic judgments exclusively on aspects of culture.[48] Emerson's account of tragedy seems appropriately nestled between Immanuel Kant's *Critique of the Power of Judgment* and Nietzsche's *The Birth of Tragedy*. In terms of scholarship on Emerson's Transcendentalism, one of the problems of downplaying or neglecting Emerson's account of tragedy is that American philosophers have failed to place Emerson in his proper place between Kant's Transcendental Idealism and Nietzsche's reflections on culture.

William James *after* Emerson? Unlike Emerson and Nietzsche, William James does not provide us with a specific textual work on tragedy. Although he does not offer readers a text specifically on tragedy, James tends to write in what Stanley Cavell describes as "the mode of what we may perhaps call . . . tragic [writing]."[49] Both Emerson and James think that courage remains crucial for coping with the tragedies that we experience in our lives: Emerson puts much more emphasis on the role of the intellect in this process of coping whereas James continually downplays an independent role for the intellect in our daily lives and suggests instead that we need moral and physiological responses. In terms used within this essay, James would be categorized as a moralist—even to the extent that he, like Aristotle, tends to think that heroic individuals might overcome the ordinary. Cornel West writes, for instance, "Jamesian rhetoric of moral heroism intends to energize people to become exceptional doers under adverse circumstances, to galvanize zestful fighters against excruciating odds."[50] Emerson, too, defends heroism and moral courage; in my interpretation of Emerson's Transcendentalism, however, intellectual courage serves us better for coping with and working through everyday tragedies that we experience in ordinary life.[51] James remains more moralistic than Emerson on the question of the tragic.

Josiah Royce *after* Emerson? Royce accounts for tragedy, and we have two interpretations of what this account actually achieves. Royce discusses tragedy in (at least) two texts: "The Problem of Job"[52] and *The Problem of Christianity*.[53] The first interpretation comes from Cornel West in his essay "Pragmatism and the Sense of the Tragic,"[54] and we find the second interpretation in William Elkins's response to West's argument in his essay entitled "Suffering Job? Scriptural Reasoning and the Problem of Evil."[55] West claims that the problem with classical pragmatism concerns its neglect of "the sense of the tragic," but Royce tries to correct this problem by providing an account of the tragic in relation to the problem of evil. According to West, however, Royce's account of tragedy lacks explanatory power—especially in relation to the "tragicomic" achievement of Anton Chekhov.[56] Elkins counters West's interpretation by showing what the explanatory power of Royce's sense of the tragic actually looks like. Elkins argues that the point of Royce's sense of the tragic involves knowing (1) how to repair "the conditions that cause evil" and (2) how to repair philosophical misrepresentations of what evil entails.[57] While Absolute Pragmatism—and not Transcendentalism—becomes Royce's way to theorize about (1), returning to the Book of Job in the Hebrew Bible is Royce's way to think through (2). In relation to the terms developed in the present essay, both Elkins and West equate tragedy with evil. It seems to me that the reason for this relates to Royce's overreliance on religious judgments and theological reasoning for his reflections on tragedy. It would be helpful and interesting to outline an Emersonian interpretation of the Book of Job.[58] It stands that Royce exclusively makes religious judgments on tragedy and, thereby, deflects his readers *away from* the tragedies we experience in our everyday lives and *to* the bigger philosophical problem of evil and the religious problems of philosophy.

John Dewey *after* Emerson? It could be argued that Dewey seems to be the true heir to Emerson's Transcendentalism; both thinkers share overly optimistic temperaments, and both thinkers remain committed to spreading democracy in more intense and intentional ways throughout American culture and society. On the question of tragedy, however, I find these two thinkers very far apart from one another—which ought to be a surprising judgment to those readers very familiar with Dewey's *Art as Experience*. Seemingly close to the account developed in the present essay, in Dewey's *Art as Experience* we find a connection between tragedy and horror: "The peculiar power of tragedy to leave us at the end with a sense of reconciliation rather than with horror forms the theme of one of the oldest discussions of literary art."[59] Aha! Now, we see the difference: Dewey thinks that tragedy leads to "reconciliation" instead of "horror." Although Emerson never uses the word *horror* (Cavell does), Emerson does not think that tragedy gets cleaned up so well—which is what the word *reconciliation* suggests. Later in *Art as Experience*, Dewey praises William Shakespeare for "employing the comic in the midst of tragedy" because it helps to "relieve the strain" for Shakespeare's audience.[60] Dewey claims that comic interruption of tragedy "punctuates tragic quality" in ways that bring "to definite perception values that are concealed in ordinary experience because of habituation."[61] Dewey accounts for tragedy only for the purpose of explaining and exploring how to overcome the tragic and how tragedy leads to reconciliation.

Stephen C. Pepper's interpretation of Dewey's understanding of tragedy furthers my point. Pepper writes, "Pragmatism is a theory of conflict, celebrating struggle and vigorous life in which every solution is the beginning of a new problem, in which every social ideal is an hypothesis of action, in which values thrive on conflicts."[62] He continues, "The inference almost comes of itself that vital quality will thrive on tragedy. . . . Yet Dewey gives us the conciliatory . . . theory of tragedy."[63] Tragedy gets treated within pragmatism as a form of conflict, and conflicts ought to be overcome; Dewey wants to appease his readers about tragedy—not encourage them to face the tragedies of everyday life with intellectual courage but, rather, with the certainty that conflicts will be overcome and tragedy will end in reconciliation. Without engaging Emerson's turn toward aesthetic judgments in his account of tragedy, Stephen Pepper further critiques Dewey's theory of tragedy on the grounds that Dewey deprives us "of a pragmatic theory of *ugliness*."[64] Pepper seeks a "pragmatic theory of ugliness" because he is surprised that when Dewey talks about the category of ugliness he does so in more traditional terms "that things are ugly in themselves" and not ugly in relational terms.[65] Within a Transcendentalist account of tragedy, we either respond "tunefully" or with ugliness to tragedy—which requires relational dispositions (what Emerson calls "observable temperaments") between persons. Pepper concludes that Dewey's pragmatism reduces ugliness into a "pseudo-concept." The contrast between Dewey's pragmatism and Emerson's Transcendentalism becomes sharp: for Emerson, ugliness serves as an aesthetic judgment that we make on ourselves and those closest to us as a way to articulate the serious and sobering problems of faulty responses to tragedy. Dewey's pragmatism does not get us anywhere close to making such aesthetic judgments either on ourselves or those closest to us in our ordinary lives.

Niebuhr and West *after* Emerson? Cornel West claims that Reinhold Niebuhr ought to be considered "*the* Emersonian figure in mid-century America,"[66] with the caveat that Niebuhr's intensely pessimistic temperament counters Emerson's overly optimistic temperament.[67] West sides with Niebuhr's descriptions of the "harsh and tragic world" over and against what he considers as Emerson's total neglect of tragedy. West thinks that Niebuhr holds "the most complex view of the 'tragic' in the pragmatist tradition," and West uses Niebuhr's "complex view" of tragedy in developing a key component of what West calls prophetic pragmatism: "Prophetic pragmatism is a form of tragic thought in that it confronts candidly individual and collective experiences of evil in individuals and institutions—with little expectation of ridding the world of *all* evil."[68] Both Niebuhr's and West's accounts tie tragedy to human agency, sinful actions, and vicious intentions. Admitting that he concurs with this claim, West quotes an argument made by Raymond Williams against making aesthetic judgments on tragic actions: "The tragic action, in its deepest sense, is *not* the [aesthetic] confirmation of disorder."[69] Both Niebuhr and West articulate religious judgments as the best way to think about the tragic, and West—more so than Niebuhr—encourages moralistic responses to tragedy as well.[70]

I obviously disagree with what West considers as Emerson's total neglect of tragedy, but I believe that West and I have a more interesting disagreement in terms of the proper response to tragedy: I agree with Emerson that aesthetic judgments offer a more in-depth and sobering response to the everyday tragedies that we experience in ordinary life. I continue to worry that moralism invites self-righteousness, and religious judgments fail to address the actual problems that come with the everyday tragedies that we experience in ordinary life.[71]

Notes

I feel a constant temptation toward what Emerson warns against in terms of making others strictly a means for my own desired ends—namely, instrumentalizing others for the sake of my own thinking and writing. I name this temptation but wish to claim neither that I avoid it nor commit it; the former claim would involve self-righteousness while the latter claim would require more moral certitude than I possess about myself. By naming it, I simply want to set up my profound gratitude for the beauty of having such helpful, insightful, and wonderful colleagues, friends, and students. Morgan Elbot reads every word that I write, and she consistently improves the argumentation and style of my writing. Lindsey Graber, Phil Kuehnert, and David O'Hara read an earlier draft of this essay and provided a healthy mix of affirmation and confusion; I appreciate the affirmation, and I take responsibility for the confusion. Randall Auxier, Robert Corrington, Walter Gulick, Lisa Landoe Hedrick, Michael Raposa, Gary Slater, and Wesley Wildman offered constructive responses to the presentation version of this essay.

1. See Miguel de Unamuno, *The Tragic Sense of Life* (New York: Dover, 1996).

2. Arvin borrows his the title for his essay from this sentence by Emerson: "He has seen but half the Universe who never has been shown the House of Pain." Emerson, "Tragedy," in *The Early Lectures of Ralph Waldo Emerson, 1838–1842: Volume III*, ed. Robert E. Spiller and Wallace E. Williams (Cambridge: The Belknap Press of Harvard University, 1972), 103.

3. Newton Arvin, "The House of Pain," in *Emerson: A Collection of Critical Essays*, ed. Milton Konvitz and Stephen Whicher (Englewood Cliffs, NJ: Prentice-Hall, 1962), 59.

4. I agree with Michael Lopez's judgment on the question of Emerson's relationship with Christian moral reasoning: "It is, in fact, Emerson's theory of power that makes *The Conduct of Life* a fundamentally anti-Christian book. The will to power, the 'spawning productivity' . . . that sets the universe in motion exists, for Emerson, outside the boundaries of any Christian definition of good and evil, moral and immoral. This is Emerson's central philosophical lesson: the always tangled coexistence of positive and negative force. While Christian morality defines good and evil as opposites, Emerson portrays them as simply different points on the same continuum of power. Vice is not the opposite of virtue, but 'the excess or acridity of a virtue.'" Lopez, "*The Conduct of Life*: Emerson's Anatomy of Power," in *The Cambridge Companion to Emerson*, ed. Saundra Morris and Joel Porte (New York: Cambridge University Press, 1999), 258.

5. Very early in his career, Emerson wrote in this direction; see Emerson's "Tragedy" and "Comedy," in *The Early Lectures of Ralph Waldo Emerson, 1838–1842: Volume III*, ch. 7 & 8.

6. For a critique of Emerson's ultimate failure on the standards of feminist philosophy, see Erik Ingvar's *Emerson as Priest of Pan: A Study in the Metaphysics of Sex* (Lawrence: University Press of Kansas, 1982).

7. Emerson, "Tragedy," 110; Emerson, "The Tragic," in *The Complete Writings of Ralph Waldo Emerson* (New York: Wm. H. Wise, 1929), 1371.

8. Stanley Cavell claims it is not "the tragic" that Emerson wishes to avoid or overcome but, rather, a sense of nihilism: "Yet a more-than-tragic emotion of thankfulness is still not the drift, or not the point. The point is the achievement not of affirmation but of what Emerson calls 'the sacred affirmative' . . . the heart of a new creation. This is not an effort to move beyond tragedy but to move beyond nihilism, or beyond the curse of the charge of human depravity and its consequent condemnation of us to despair; a charge which is itself, Emerson in effect declares, the only depravity." Cavell, *Emerson's Transcendental Etude* (Stanford: Stanford University Press, 2003), 16.

9. While I build upon suggestions found in Stephen Whicher's "Emerson's Tragic Sense" (1953), I go much farther in terms of emphasizing the role of tragedy within Emerson's Transcendentalism. Whicher claims that Emerson's "chasm cuts deep . . . between a vision that claims all power now, and an experience that finds none." Whicher concludes that this "chasm *is* the Emersonian tragedy,

a tragedy of incapacity." In this regard, tragedy applies to questions concerning the self: "Emerson's thought of the self was split between a total Yes and a total No, which could not coexist, could not be reconciled, and yet were both true." See Stephen Whicher, "Emerson's Tragic Sense," in *Emerson: A Collection of Critical Essays*, ed. Milton Konvitz and Stephen Whicher, (Englewood Cliffs, NJ: Prentice-Hall, 1962), 39–45.

10. For the argument that Aristotle's categories of comedy and tragedy no longer apply at all, see Stanley Hauerwas's "How to Be Theologically Funny," in *The Work of Theology*, (Grand Rapids: Wm. B. Eerdmans, 2015), ch. 12. I find that Emerson's account of tragedy stands as a midpoint position between Aristotle's moralistic account and Hauerwas's wholesale dismissal of the ancient category of tragedy.

11. Emerson limits the "others" here to family, friends, and anyone else who plays a significant role within one's own domestic or ordinary life (see Emerson, "Domestic Life," in *The Complete Writings of Ralph Waldo Emerson*, 652–61).

12. Emerson continues: "that the Order of nature and events is constrained by a law not adapted to man nor man to that, but which holds on its way to the end, blessing him if his wishes chance to lie in the same course—crushing him if his wishes lie contrary to it—and careless whether it cheers or crushes him" (Emerson, "Tragedy," 105).

13. Ibid., 106.

14. Ibid.

15. Ibid.; see 106–109.

16. Emerson writes: "The brave man will always be rich in the best sense; he will do the dictates of his character and genius, will do substantially the same things whether rich or poor, will make the same impression" (Emerson, "Tragedy," 108).

17. Ibid.

18. For a helpful and interesting critical reflection on Aristotle's *Poetics*, see Angela Curran's "Feminism and the Narrative Structure of Aristotle's *Poetics*," in *Feminist Interpretations of Aristotle*, ed. Cynthia A. Freeland (University Park: The Pennsylvania State University Press, 1998), ch. 11.

19. Emerson, "Tragedy," 109.

20. Ibid.

21. Ibid., 110.

22. Emerson, "The Tragic," 1371.

23. See Emerson, "Tragedy," 112–16.

24. Ibid., 111; Emerson, "The Tragic," 1371.

25. Emerson, "Tragedy," 117.

26. Ibid.

27. Emerson, "The Tragic," 1373.

28. Ann Louise Keating also emphasizes Emerson's turn toward the intellect in her essay on Emerson's account of tragedy, but she (1) does not consider how this requires a consideration of intellectual virtue and (2) remains too close to Arvin's interpretation of Emerson's Transcendentalism. She properly claims that "Emerson believes that Reason enables thinkers to confront the abyss and recognize the Darkness as part of the whole" but wrongly concludes that Emerson's "belief in the abyssal Soul enables him to move from the Tragic to the affirmative, from Understanding's view of the parts to Reason's vision of the whole. As an intellectual act, the affirmative offers far more than either wishful thinking or escape. Indeed, it provides a valid way of perceiving and so changing the world." Ann Louise Keating, "Renaming the Dark: Emerson's Optimism and the Abyss," *American Transcendental Quarterly* 4, no. 4 (Dec. 1990), 305ff.

29. Stanley Cavell, *The Claim of Reason: Wittgenstein, Skepticism, Morality, and Tragedy* (New York: Oxford University Press, 1979), 418–19.

30. RELG 323: Warfare and Ethics, College of William & Mary, 2010–2013.

31. Talal Asad, *On Suicide Bombers* (New York: Columbia University Press, 2007).

32. Asad asks, "What is horror?" Horror "is not a motive" but, rather, "a state of being." "Unlike terror, outrage, or the spontaneous desire for vengeance," Asad claims, "horror has no object." He concludes that horror remains "intransitive." Asad also turns to Stanley Cavell's description of "horror" (see Asad, *On Suicide Bombers*, 68–69).

33. For more reflections on Cavell's account of horror, see Peter Dula's *Cavell, Companionship, and Christian Theology* (New York: Oxford University Press, 2010), ch. 5.

34. Cavell, *The Claim of Reason*, 419.

35. Ibid.

36. Ibid.

37. I use the word *abject* relying on Julia Kristeva's development of this word in her masterful book: *Powers of Horror: An Essay on Abjection*, trans. Leon S. Roudiez (New York: Columbia University Press, 1992).

38. Cavell, *The Claim of Reason*, 419.

39. Ibid., 419–20.

40. For an insightful commentary on Cavell's own account of tragedy, see Graham Ward's "Philosophy as Tragedy or What Words Won't Give," *Modern Theology* 27, no. 3 (July 2011): 478–96. Ward does his best to recover religious judgments and theological reasoning in relation to tragedy.

41. My claim in this sentence resembles what Stanley Hauerwas means by the phrase "bearing reality"; see Hauerwas's "Bearing Reality," in *Approaching the End: Eschatological Reflections on Church, Politics, Life* (Grand Rapids: Wm. B. Eerdmans, 2013), 139–57. Hauerwas relies on the work of Stanley Cavell and

Cora Diamond in his grappling with "the difficulty of reality." Of course, Hauerwas displays more confidence in religious judgments and theological reasoning than Emerson allows.

42. Lopez, "*The Conduct of Life*: Emerson's Anatomy of Power," 259.
43. Ibid.
44. Lawrence Buell, *Emerson* (Cambridge: The Belknap Press of Harvard University, 2004), ch. 5.
45. Ibid., 239.
46. Ibid., 240.
47. Adrian Poole, *Tragedy: A Very Short Introduction* (New York: Oxford University Press, 2005), 63–64.
48. See Friedrich Nietzsche, *The Birth of Tragedy*, trans Ronald Speirs (New York: Cambridge University Press, 1999), 1–116.
49. Cavell, *Emerson's Transcendental Etudes*, 207.
50. West, *The American Evasion of Philosophy* (Madison: The University of Wisconsin Press, 1989), 59.
51. For more on courage as an intellectual virtue, see my *Strength of Mind: Courage, Hope, Freedom, Knowledge* (Eugene, OR: Cascade Press, 2018).
52. Josiah Royce, "The Problem of Job," in *Studies of Good and Evil: A Series of Essays upon Problems of Philosophy, Problems of Life* (New York: D. Appleton, 1906), ch. 1.
53. Royce, *The Problem of Christianity* (New York: MacMillan, 1913).
54. Cornel West, "Pragmatism and the Sense of the Tragic," in *The Cornel West Reader* (New York: Basic Civitas Books, 2000), ch. 10.
55. William Wesley Elkins, "Suffering Job? Scriptural Reasoning and the Problem of Evil," *Journal of Scriptural Reasoning* 4, no. 1 (July 2004).
56. West writes: "Chekhov's tragicomic sensibilities go so far beyond and cut so much deeper than anything in pragmatism that even Royce comes up short" (West, "Pragmatism and the Sense of the Tragic," 174). The relation between Chekhov's "tragicomic sensibilities" and Emerson's nondramatic account of tragedy deserves its own essay.
57. See Elkins, "Suffering Job?," paragraph 7.
58. To my knowledge, Henry Bugbee comes the closest to offering such an interpretation in his "A Way of Reading the Book of Job," http://faculty.salisbury.edu/~jdhatley/Bugbeejoba.htm): accessed Sept. 2, 2015.
59. John Dewey, *Art as Experience* (New York: Perigee Books, 1980), 96.
60. Ibid.
61. Ibid.
62. Pepper, "Some Questions on Dewey's Aesthetics," in *The Philosophy of John Dewey: The Library of Living Philosophers*, ed. Paul Arthur Schilpp (New York: Tudor, 1939), 386.
63. Ibid.

64. Ibid.," 387; emphasis added.
65. Dewey, *Art as Experience*, 204.
66. West, *The American Evasion of Philosophy*, 150.
67. I spell out the relationship of West's prophetic pragmatism to Niebuhr's Christian realism and Emerson's Transcendentalism in "Prophetic Pragmatism or Prophetic Reasoning?" in *Introducing Prophetic Pragmatism*, co-authored with Brad Elliott Stone, (Lanham, MD: Lexington Books, forthcoming).
68. West, *The American Evasion of Philosophy*, 228.
69. Raymond Williams, *Modern Tragedy* (Stanford: Stanford University Press, 1966), 83; emphasis added. West quotes the full passage in *The American Evasion of Philosophy*, 229.
70. Reinhold Niebuhr has numerous reflections on tragedy, but the best place to start with Niebuhr's view of tragedy remains *Beyond Tragedy: A Christian Interpretation of History* (New York: Scribner and Sons, 1937).
71. Randall Auxier provides an extremely helpful summary of my argument: "Goodson argues that Emerson democratizes Aristotelian and other classical ideas about tragedy (including ancient Israel, Egypt, and Islam), moving the emphasis from the 'dramatic' (dominated by moral ideas) to the aesthetic (which calls forth a more self-reflexive and flexible kind of judging). The classical, dramatic, moralizing view, Emerson says, has no place in the modern world. In the tradition of Emerson, Goodson also cites Reinhold Niebuhr and Cornel West as philosophers exemplifying the American attitude toward the tragic. Of particular interest, also, is Goodson's excellent analysis of his application of Emerson's category of 'Terror' within the tragic to contemporary problems with terrorism and the monstrosities it begets in the sleep of reason." Randall Auxier, personal correspondence, June 14, 2016. For readers who wish to test my interpretation of Emerson's account of tragedy, I encourage using my thesis as a framework for making sense of Emerson's "Fate" (Emerson, "Fate," in *The Complete Writings of Ralph Waldo Emerson*, 521–35).

3

Peirce and Edwards on the Argument from Beauty

MICHAEL L. RAPOSA

I

In my 1989 book on Charles Peirce's philosophy of religion, I suggested that his 1908 article "A Neglected Argument for the Reality of God" ought best to be understood as defending an idiosyncratic version of the ontological argument.[1] This suggestion rubbed against the rather widespread consensus among Peirce's interpreters that the article clearly presented some form of the argument from design. But that consensus seemed problematic to me because, in other writings, Peirce not only had admitted to defending some version of the ontological proof (albeit *not* Anselm's), but also had clearly rejected all arguments from design (for reasons in some ways similar to those of David Hume). It was revealing to me, furthermore, that Peirce began the Neglected Argument by identifying God as *Ens necessarium*. Now on Peirce's account, the specific feature of the *idea of God* that makes belief in the reality of such a being virtually irresistible for one who is properly disposed is its great *beauty*. Moreover, to be thus disposed is to be skilled at "musement," a term that Peirce coined, but the concept that it labels was one for which he claimed indebtedness to Friedrich Schiller's aesthetics.

I want to explore Peirce's aesthetics in this paper as background for properly understanding his Neglected Argument. While I do not claim any direct lines of historical influence, I want also to link Peirce's deliberations here to the earlier philosophical theology of Jonathan Edwards. However "heavenly intelligences" might be able to communicate with one another, Edwards insisted that in *this* world the human mind can communicate with other minds only through some process of mediation. Inferring divine intentions based on inference from the design observed in nature is one such process. (And so Edwards, unlike Peirce, did not rule out the possibility of a coherent argument from design.) But Edwards gave clear priority to another way of communicating, involving the perception of nature as embodying the symbols of a divine presence. For one who is properly predisposed to see, the world will appear (in Peirce's words) as God's "great poem." For both Edwards and Peirce, then, nature is to be understood as divine semiosis, and an accurate reading of the signs embedded in the "book of nature" is possible only for one who is endowed with the appropriate sense of beauty. I want to explore here the specific work that the concept of beauty does for each thinker in their respective arguments for the reality of God, while also investigating further how each of them portrays this distinctive aesthetic capacity or sensibility.

II

Within the context of Peirce's account of the normative sciences, logic is dependent upon ethics to the extent that a theory of correct thinking must be rooted in a theory of right behavior in general. Moreover, no such theory of behavior can be properly articulated without some understanding of that which is admirable in itself, apart from any extrinsic reason for its being so. Consequently, the science of ethics, in turn, is dependent upon the normative science of "esthetics,"[2] since it is the task of the latter to determine the nature of that which is truly and intrinsically admirable, what Peirce often referred to as the *summum bonum*. Now by his own admission, Peirce's deliberations in the field of aesthetics were woefully underdeveloped, especially in comparison to his numerous and remarkable achievements in logic. Nevertheless, this admission does not belie the great importance that he attached to aesthetics, its primacy for him among the normative sciences, in addition—given the high priority of these sciences within Peirce's architectonic system—to its crucial role informing Peirce's philosophizing about religious topics.

If Peirce wrote relatively little about aesthetics, his attention was nevertheless drawn to its subject matter very early on in his philosophical career. Along with Whatley's *Elements of Logic* and Kant's first Critique, Schiller's *Aesthetic Letters* is one of the philosophical works to which Peirce devoted serious consideration while still a teenager. Indeed, a brief essay written by Peirce about Schiller as a high school assignment in 1857 has now been published in the first volume of the ongoing chronological edition of Peirce's *Writings*.[3] Half a century later, Peirce was still claiming indebtedness to Schiller, as he formulated his Neglected Argument and then reflected subsequently on the key factors shaping its development. I want to suggest that the influence of Schiller's aesthetics on Peirce's thought was consistently steady during the intervening decades, as he moved from an early articulation of pragmatism to the mature position that he referred to as "pragmaticism."[4] My present interest is primarily focused on the later work. Nevertheless, without denying any development in Peirce's philosophy, I have rather persistently argued that the distinction between "pragmatism" and "pragmaticism" ought best to be conceived as marking a contrast between Peirce's somewhat anomalous philosophical perspective and that of certain other thinkers, rather than as indicating some dramatic transformation of his own thought during the period extending from the late 1860s (when his first significant publications appeared) to the early twentieth century.[5]

After some preliminary considerations, the Neglected Argument begins in earnest with Peirce's prescription for musement, a form of playful engagement with nature that, while Peirce admitted it might eventually "flower" into religious meditation, he most immediately characterized as resembling "esthetic contemplation" (CP 6.458).[6] Several months after the publication of this article, Peirce was queried during his correspondence with Victoria Lady Welby about what he meant by the use of that invented term. Peirce's response was that it was "thoroughly soaked" by Schiller's ideas and that musement was intended to convey nothing beyond what the latter had designated as *Spieltrieb,* the play impulse. If soaked in Schiller's thought, nevertheless, I would argue that the pot in which Peirce's concept of musement was stewed contained a few other ingredients, most notably his own reflections on phenomenology and on the logic of abduction. At the same time, none of these ingredients is neatly separable from the others, but rather, all are artfully blended together in the mix.

How can this playful mode of thought best be characterized? In the first place, it has no predetermined agenda or goals. The muser will allow attention to be drawn by this or that aspect of experience, but without being completely "captured" by any one of them. So it may begin passively enough with a "drinking in" of impressions, but soon develops into a "lively give and take," as in an animated conversation (CP 6.459). It is in a certain sense disinterested ("involves no purpose"), while nevertheless resulting in a "lively exercise" of one's powers. Faithful to Schiller's earlier portrayal of it, this type of play behavior skillfully mediates between the purely passive and the active. The muser is bound by nothing and so is potentially aware of anything that may appear. Schiller characterized such a state of mind as perfect freedom. Buddhists refer to it (or something very much like it) as the achievement of what they call "mindfulness." I have argued elsewhere that success in musement presupposes the cultivation of a certain skill, somewhat analogous to the fine motor skills required for juggling.[7]

I want to underscore this observation, originally Peirce's and later echoed by my own, that it takes a certain degree of training to be able effectively to engage in musement. Only after considerable practice is it likely that the God-hypothesis will regularly and forcefully suggest itself to the muser. Peirce *predicts* that this will be the case but then he also *invites* his readers to take up the practice and to test it for themselves, much as if they were participating in an experiment.[8] He also predicts that once the hypothesis suggests itself to an individual, she will find it to be an irresistible plaything, much like a loose tooth is for the tongue.[9] Eventually, the muser will pass from playfully considering the hypothesis about God's reality to earnestly believing it, not least of all—and here is the crucial point for present purposes—because if its great beauty.

I want to propose that the concept of beauty works at different levels in Peirce's argument, first attracting the muser to the hypothetical idea of God as one lovely enough to be entertained (CP 6.465) and then causing that person to fall in love with the idea, so that she actively embraces it as true and fashions a life to be lived in conformity with it as an ideal (CP 6.467). Now in reviewing the characteristics of the God-hypothesis that contribute to its plausibility, Peirce mentions both its "beauty" and its "august practicality." Oddly enough, on Peirce's account, these two features of the hypothesis may be regarded as amounting to pretty much the same thing. The beauty of the idea of God consists, at least partially, in its providing an ideal for human living, what Josiah Royce would have referred to as a "life plan."[10] Peirce once described esthetic contemplation as consisting in the ability to prescind from "temporary urgencies" in order to discern "what may lie hidden in the icon" (CP 7.555). Yet, the capacity to take a "long-run" view of human conduct rather than focusing narrowly on immediate effects is precisely one of the characteristics that distinguished Peirce's pragmaticism from what he regarded as cruder forms of pragmatism. It is also how Peirce understood the nature of self-control, not as volition exercised in the moment, but as the cultivation of specific habits over extended periods of time. And so it should hardly be surprising to observe that toward the end of his article on the Neglected Argument, Peirce turned to a discussion both of his pragmaticism and of the nature and importance of self-control (CP 6.478–85).

Two years before the publication of that article, in the draft of an essay entitled "Issues of Pragmaticism," Peirce had concluded that "it is by the indefinite replication of self-control upon self-control that the *vir* is begotten, and by action, through thought, he grows an esthetic ideal, not for the behoof of his own poor noddle merely, but as the share which God permits him to have in the work of creation" (CP 5.403, note #3). This rather oddly articulated conclusion is one for which Peirce explicitly reported some indebtedness to Schiller's aesthetic letters. The aesthetic education of human beings, the careful and deliberate cultivation of aesthetic sensibilities, is a phenomenon that Schiller described at great length in those letters. In doing so, he provided the template for what Peirce was later to portray as musement.[11] This 1906 reference to the "share which God permits" humans to have in creation is a clear indication that the ideas soon to be embodied in his Neglected Argument were then already at the point of percolation.

Why characterize such an argument as "ontological" rather than "teleological" however? It is easy enough to understand why readers have often assumed that Peirce was developing his own somewhat peculiar version of the argument from design. The muser is directed to the contemplation of nature—its beauty, variety, harmony, etc.—eventually formulates the hypothesis that a divine intelligence might be its designer and creator, and then proceeds to embrace that hypothesis. Yet the proponents of teleological arguments, from its earliest versions to contemporary intelligent design proposals, typically interject God as a hypothesis to account for what science itself would otherwise seem incapable of explaining. They also regularly employ analogical reasoning. They focus on a specific phenomenon in nature, such as blood clotting for example,[12] that they claim begs for some kind of intelligent intervention as a presupposition in order to be understood. This strategy is nothing like the one that Peirce enacted in the Neglected Argument. He was firmly convinced that the scientific method is the most reliable method available to human inquirers for the purpose of "fixing belief." He conceived of musement as a practice not set apart from scientific inquiry but as constituting the initial stage of what might very well become such an inquiry. In fact, his argument never trades on the inadequacies or limitations of science, nor does it proceed by way of analogy. Like Hume, Peirce was aware that we do not have access to any other worlds with which we might hope to compare the creation of this one. Also, following Hume, Peirce conceded that the attempt to find in the universe "any design embracing it as a whole is futile, and involves a false way of looking at the subject" (CP 6.419).

Rather, as with Anselm so too for Peirce, it is the *idea* of God's reality that proves to be irresistible to anyone who contemplates it in the appropriate manner. To think (hypothetically) that God *might* be real eventuates in the virtually indubitable belief that such a God *must* be real, for both thinkers albeit for very different reasons. So both arguments can be identified as "ontological," although Peirce's version is also clearly "experimental." The Neglected Argument's conclusion, unlike Anselm's, is not the upshot of some form of deductive reasoning. Instead, it is an inductive claim about our abductive proclivities and predispositions. Belief in God, properly conceived, is not shown to be inevitable by logic but rather, by experience. This is the rationale for Peirce's invitation to his readers that they should themselves engage in musement in order to test his results with this practice. The argument supplies the rubric for an experiment. Contemplation of the variety, order, and design displayed in nature provides the *occasion* upon which the hypothetical idea of God is likely to arise and be entertained, not the *evidence* needed to conclude that belief in such a God must be true. The muser's instinctive response to the beauty of the idea constitutes her primary motive both for entertaining and embracing it.

If any "evidence" for the truth of the hypothesis is to be gathered, it will be only in the long run, and will consist not in showing how God trumps some scientific hypothesis as an explanation for the natural world, but rather in how the idea of God serves so perfectly as an inspiration and norm for those lives lived in conformity with it. The experiment that begins with musement is extended in this fashion. On Peirce's account, such lives will also be beautiful, the deliberate development "by action, through thought" of an aesthetic ideal. In his various discussions of the normative sciences, this sort of development, the embodiment of ideals in specific habits of conduct, is how Peirce came to understand the *summum bonum*, as the growth of what he called "concrete reasonableness." Beauty is a quality of experience, thus to be correlated with Peirce's category of "firstness"; but it is most perfectly manifested as living semiosis, by ideas growing and spreading like wildflowers in a meadow, and so more precisely to be categorized, in Peirce's terms, as the "firstness of thirdness."

In fact, it was not Anselm's but the nineteenth-century British philosopher William Johnson Fox's version of the ontological proof that Peirce claimed to find compelling.[13] In a letter written to William James, one again just a few years before his publication of the Neglected Argument, Peirce indicated the form in which he found such an argument to be so persuasive. "The esthetic ideal, the altogether admirable, has *as ideal*," he explained to James, "necessarily a mode of being to be called living." He added that this "ideal is not a finite existent"—Peirce was careful in the Neglected Argument also to distinguish God's reality from any kind of misguided claim about divine existence—and then Peirce concluded that "the human mind and the human heart have a filiation to God" (CP 8.262). "It is impossible," he insisted, "to think that the object of one's love is not living."[14] This impossibility is not a logical one deduced from the definition of God as "that than which nothing greater can be conceived." For the individual who has performed Peirce's experiment carefully and consistently, the impossibility of doubting God's reality is one that will be experienced rather than inferred. Now, Peirce has a lot to say about how this will be true only to the extent that the concept of God remains quite vague. But it would be a distraction, at this juncture, to explore all of the implications for philosophical theology of Peirce's logic of vagueness. Instead, a few general remarks will have to suffice.

In the first place, the God-idea must be regarded as vague because it is *instinctive*; the training in indifference that is characteristic of musement is designed to liberate any such natural or instinctive cognitive predispositions and to give them free play. The Neglected Argument is intended to make explicit, then, a certain vague idea of God that may now exist in the mind only *habitualiter*. Like a therapist working with someone to penetrate those regions of the mind that lie below the threshold of consciousness, Peirce invites his reader to engage in a kind of "free association" with the universe. This cognitive play also requires the sort of disinterestedness that Kant and Schiller portrayed as being characteristic of aesthetic experience. Far from being an attempt to circumvent science for theological purposes, as Peirce explained to Lady Welby in one of his 1908 letters glossing the Neglected Argument, "every true man of science," that is, every scientist who perceives the universe as a concrete embodiment of the reasonableness that governs it, even if he "does not explicitly recognize that he believes in God," nevertheless, on Peirce's reckoning, "has Faith in God."[15] This tendency displayed in Peirce's remarks—i.e., to make what was at first only implicit now somewhat explicit—is also, it seems to me, one of the general characteristics of that family of arguments that we tend to classify as "ontological."

I qualify the adjective *explicit* here with the adverb *somewhat* because Peirce was insistent that one can reduce the vagueness of the idea of God by only the slightest of measures before one renders it problematic and the belief in it dubitable. Even in Anselm's argument, the contention that God must be greater than any conceivable being does not entail that one must be able to conceive of God clearly; that is, the affirmation of divine existence does nothing to reduce the divine mystery. On Peirce's account, use of the word *God* was to be preferred to philosophical substitutes such as "the Absolute" for the very reason that the former is much more vague than the latter. As it arises naturally in musement, the idea of God will necessarily be both vague and anthropomorphic. Regarding the second of these two characteristics, it is a distinctive feature of Peirce's philosophy (which was, after all, a form of objective idealism) that for him "all conceptions are at bottom" anthropomorphic. Moreover, "to say . . . that a conception is one natural to man, which comes to just about the same thing as to say that it is anthropomorphic, is as high a recommendation as one could give to it in the eyes of an Exact Logician" (CP 5.47). The claim that God can best be conceived as being "vaguely like a man" (CP 5.536) also supports Peirce's rationale for the related assertion that this conception supplies for human conduct its highest ideals and purposes.

III

Jonathan Edwards was not preoccupied with the task of formulating any sort of argument for the existence of God. On his account, the true saint will simply discern the presence of God everywhere in nature. She will do so by virtue of a grace-infused sense of beauty that allows her to perceive what others cannot. Moreover, just as Peirce described the skillful muser as "earnestly loving" his "strictly hypothetical God" (CP 6.467) and Josiah Royce understood the embodiment of true loyalty as being displayed in someone who had "somehow fallen in love with the universe,"[16] for Edwards, the "true virtue" of the saint will manifest itself as a "benevolence to being in general."[17] The experience of divine beauty readily inspires loving devotion. This or that finite being, or some collection of beings, may be beautiful in a "secondary" and "inferior" sense, but only being in general—that is to say, only God—should be regarded as perfectly beautiful.

Now, the problem with secondary beauty for Edwards is that it will be the characteristic of an object "when considered only with regard to its connection with, and tendency to, some particular things within a limited, and as it were a private sphere."[18] So too, on Peirce's reasoning, the *summum bonum* as the goal of inquiry in aesthetics will necessarily be general (CP 1.613). Its beauty will not be a function of its relationship to this or that particular thing, nor can it be considered beautiful because it serves this or that particular purpose. Rather, the *summum bonum* would have to be regarded as such under all conceivable circumstances.

The otherwise significant differences between Edwards's Calvinist theology and Peirce's pragmaticism can be safely ignored only in an inquiry operating with the limited goals of the one in which I am presently engaged. But there are certainly some interesting similarities between these two perspectives. Musement for Peirce takes practice, but what is thereby eventually revealed to the skillful practitioner is the presence of a basic human instinct, a natural "filiation to God." Similarly, for Edwards, consistent Christian practice is chief among all the signs of God's grace being operative in the saint, not as its *cause* but as the most reliable *sign* of its presence.[19] True virtue is in some special sense "perfected" in practice but not in any way that fundamentally augments what divine grace has already accomplished within a person through conversion. Divine beauty is manifested in the consistently virtuous conduct of the saint, much as (to use one of Edwards's favorite analogies) light radiates outward from its source in the sun. In any event, I want to attend especially to the semiotic features of this argument. Discernible patterns of behavior are *signs* that have as their object some habit or virtue possessed by the person who behaves in that fashion. Such habits themselves signify whatever ideal they might happen to embody. Moreover, the persons who embody them are drawn to these ideals by their great beauty, and motivated to act accordingly by a certain kind of love.

For Edwards, the Christian might come to know God either through Scripture or the design in nature, or through both. It is possible also to know "God a priori from the necessity of his existence and perfections." Consequently, Edwards's perspective accommodates the possibility of both a teleological and the more traditional ontological argument for God's existence. Nevertheless, the primary and ultimate way of knowing God, at least for the saint, is to "see him . . . in images."[20] This way of knowing is to be distinguished from any mode of inference based on what one observes of God's effects, thus, from any kind of design argument. What is perceived in nature is not, in this case, to be regarded as *evidence* for God's existence, but rather, as a *sign* of God's presence. For the saint, this involves the recognition as a symbol of "anything that being from him has resemblance of him, as the sun's majesty and green fields and pleasant flowers of his grace and mercy," as well as in "the soul of man that is made in the image of God."[21] It is to recognize all of creation, using Peirce's language, as being "perfused with signs" (CP 5.449), also, to read these signs as being religiously meaningful. (To conceive of nature in this fashion and to engage in the disciplined practice of such reading is what I refer to as "theosemiotic.")[22]

Edwards was enough of a pragmatist *and* a fallibilist to realize that one could certainly be mistaken about how one perceives both the world and oneself. The saint sees the world truly because of an acquired sense of beauty, a fundamental transformation of her character, for which divine grace alone is responsible. Yet being in possession of such a sense is not something that one can know about intuitively or through a simple act of introspection. Its presence is something about which one can conclude based only on the evidence supplied by certain reliable signs, chief among these being a certain consistency in one's religious practices. While it may appear to be a conceptual challenge to link Edwards's talk about "seeing" God "in images" to that family of arguments that I have been calling "ontological," his theology is clearly (and by his own clear and explicit admission) designed for the elucidation and defense of an "experimental religion." "By their fruits you will know them" is a pearl of biblical wisdom that supplied both Edwards's theology and Peirce's pragmaticism with their guiding rationale.

Edwards's theology is also essentially semiotic in character. The human knowledge of God is always necessarily mediated to persons and so always also a matter of interpretation. Even the saint's experience of the divine beauty in nature represents a semiotic event, the meaning of which must be illuminated and the authenticity of which must be tested in actual practice. The more consistently it is thus tested, the more reliable will be the knowledge that it yields. Almost anyone can persist in practice for the short run. But Edwards was fond of distinguishing counterfeit spirituality from what he regarded as true saintliness by using metaphors, for example, by contrasting the ephemeral flash of a comet with the steady brightness of a star shining in the night sky. In any event, all of the actions that constitute consistent Christian practice are to be regarded and analyzed in decisively semiotic terms. "There is a language in actions," Edwards observed, "and in some cases, much more clear and convincing than in words."[23] As with the "book of nature," so too does human behavior constitute a text for our reading, its religious meaning never revealed in a single episode (such as suddenly speaking in tongues or reciting a passage from scripture that springs to mind), but only gradually over time.

IV

Several decades after Peirce's publication of the Neglected Argument, recorded in one of the terse entries from her manuscripts later published posthumously, Simone Weil presented to readers her own version of "an experimental ontological proof." "It is only by directing my thoughts towards something better than myself," she suggested, "that I am drawn upwards by this something. If I am really raised up, this something is real. No imaginary perfection can draw me upwards even by the fraction of an inch."[24] Weil understood with great depth of insight (and much like William James also did, I might suggest)[25] the profound importance of *how* and to *what* we choose to direct our *attention*. For Peirce, Edwards, and Weil, love begins with an act of attention and bears fruit in disciplined conduct, a certain pattern of practices. It is important not to neglect among the latter, however, the practice of paying attention itself. The capacity to experience great beauty may be ingrained—a gracious affection for Edwards or a natural instinct as on Peirce's account. But God's gift (for Edwards) can be "perfected" in practice by the cooperative saint, even as the muser (for Peirce) can expose and develop a natural inclination that may otherwise remain unconscious and obscure.

Saint Anselm framed his ontological argument as a form of prayerful meditation, as did Duns Scotus when he developed his later modal version of it. Yet the logic of their arguments was at its core deductive. Now, the role that deduction plays in explicating any hypothesis, that is, in identifying what would necessarily be entailed were that hypothesis shown to be true, is an important aspect, at least I would contend, even of the playfully meditative form of thought that Peirce described as musement. Nevertheless, the logic of musement is essentially abductive. It is the logic of sign-interpretation, and all interpretation necessarily does lean on the deductive explication of hypothetical ideas (in order to evaluate their explanatory power), as well as some preliminary inductive testing of their merits. To wander too far down the road of explication and testing however, as Peirce warned, would be to risk converting play "into scientific study" (CP 6.459). From Peirce's point of view, I think the risk involved here is that of making a category mistake. Scientific study in itself is a noble enterprise and Peirce's 1908 article presents what is actually a series of "nested" arguments, with the "Humble Argument" consisting in musement comprising only its innermost core. But that core differs—in its purposive purposelessness, its fresh awakening to beauty wherever it appears, its free and vigorous exercise of human thought, feeling, and imagination—from all of the later philosophical commentaries on such an exercise, including the one in which I am presently engaged.

Nevertheless, there is a natural progression from Peirce's religious musings early in the Neglected Argument to his discussion later in that same article of the logic of pragmaticism and the nature of scientific inquiry. The purported instinctiveness of the God-hypothesis does not mark it as a special case, but rather links it to every other instance of hypothesis formation. Peirce speculated that human beings have evolved in such a way that the human mind has become attuned to the universe in which it lives and moves and has its being. In his view, among the most important instincts that humans have developed are those that enhance our capacity for human reasoning, most especially, hypothetical reasoning. This is how Peirce eventually came to understand "simplicity" as a valuable criterion for the selection of hypotheses. Rather than focusing on logical simplicity, Peirce now suggested that one ought to prefer "the simpler Hypothesis in the sense of the more facile and natural, the one that instinct suggests" (CP 6.477).

It is well known that Peirce was a great admirer of the medieval scholastics, especially Duns Scotus, and that he believed that the progress of science rested on certain necessary assumptions about the reality of universals, as he put it, about a "reasonableness energizing in the universe." Yet Peirce's pragmatic use of deduction was quite different from the way it was employed by medieval thinkers, as already evidenced by the contrast observed between his version of the ontological argument and Anselm's. (Edwards also creatively adapted the medieval tradition for his own theological purposes.)[26] Rather than believing that inquiry could generate conclusions that must be regarded as necessarily true, Peirce was a committed fallibilist; he understood the role of deduction as being essentially explicative. Contra Anselm or Scotus, we cannot deduce that God exists, but we *can* deductively explicate the God-hypothesis in order to clarify what other sorts of things would have to be the case *if* that hypothesis were true. Testing whether or not they are in fact the case is the business of induction; like all of the other classical pragmatists, Peirce was a thoroughgoing experimentalist.

Moreover, much like these other pragmatists (most especially James and Dewey, but for this discussion it is also important to include Edwards's "experimental religion" in the mix), Peirce had a nuanced and capacious understanding of what it means to "conduct an experiment." For all of them, the scientific method was too important for its practice to be restricted to the laboratories of specialists in the physical sciences. All of human life was a laboratory on their account, the making of inferences a ubiquitous and ongoing aspect of human experience. Peirce conceived the constant testing of hypothetical ideas in practice as crucial to the spread of concrete reasonableness in the world. Here the hypothesis about God does represent a special case in point, its validity to be tested only by a vast community of inquirers, over an extended period of time (even across generations), living their lives in conformity to that hypothesis as an ideal. There are two complementary concepts of "experience" informing Peirce's pragmaticism, as any idea deserving to be authorized by reason must enter consciousness through the "gate of perception," but then make its exit at the "gate of purposive action" (CP 5.212).

Peirce thus believed his argument for the reality of God to be connected to a "theory of the nature of thinking" (CP 6.491), a theory for which his portrayal of musement can only serve as introduction. Yet as all thought is rooted in this kind of cognitive play, it is an introduction to which Peirce invited his reader consistently to return, not permanently, but in recurring "half hours" (CP 6.459). This returning is itself a kind of practice, its "fruits" a renewal and deepening of human aesthetic and spiritual sensibilities. Each return or "replay" is also a rereading (*relegere*) of that "great poem" inscribed in the book of nature, an activity that both directs and disciplines attention in a way that is characteristic of many forms of religious ritual and meditation.

Paying attention to the beauty in nature, catching a "glimpse" of some "fragment" of its design, the vague discernment of its purposes—these are all features of what we would typically regard as the task of "natural theology." That Edwards was explicitly engaged in such a task and that Peirce approached it in some of his later philosophical meditations are conclusions supported by the evidence presented in this essay. What is not warranted is the conclusion that, in doing so, they were also engaged in "arguing from design" (although Edwards himself did not demur from such forms of argument). Their perspectives represent a different approach to what might be called natural theology, as I have suggested, a distinctively semiotic approach.

Now, to perceive "intelligent design" only in those rare instances where the appeal to natural causes for explanation seems unsatisfactory or incomplete is to invest one's faith in a "God of the gaps." Such a God is threatened with extinction as soon as natural explanations are discovered or repaired. For a person of deepened sensibilities, the rising and setting of the sun, the power of a winter storm and the gentleness of a summer breeze, the smile of an infant, an act of human creativity or of love, even the generation of new species through a natural process of evolution—all of these are radiant with beauty, potentially of religious significance. Indeed, the predisposition to find God only in the exceptional risks spiritual blindness, the failure to recognize the divine in all of those mysterious yet tangible and everyday occurrences that signify its presence.[27]

Notes

1. Michael L. Raposa, *Peirce's Philosophy of Religion* (Bloomington: Indiana University Press, 1989), 130–31.

2. This is the spelling of the word that Peirce himself preferred, but one that I will use only in quoting him.

3. Charles S. Peirce, "The Sense of Beauty never furthered the Performance of a single Act of Duty," in the *Writings of Charles S. Peirce: A Chronological Edition, Volume I,* ed. Peirce Edition Project (Bloomington: Indiana University Press, 1982), 10–12.

4. This influence has been carefully explored in a useful article by Jeffrey Barnouw; see " 'Aesthetic' for Schiller and Peirce: A Neglected Origin of Pragmatism," *Journal of the History of Ideas* 49, no. 4 (Oct./Dec., 1988): 607–32.

5. Most recently in Michael L. Raposa, "Pragmaticism among the Pragmatists: A Brief History and Future Prospects," *Cognitio: Review of Philosophy* 16, no. 2 (2015): 321–34.

6. These references in my text are to Charles S. Peirce, *The Collected Papers of Charles Sanders Peirce,* ed. Charles Hartshorne, Paul Weiss (Volumes 1–6) and

Arthur Burks (Volumes 7–8) (Cambridge: Harvard University Press, 1935, 1958). "CP 6.458" should be read as "volume 6, paragraph 458."

7. For Schiller on freedom, consult Friedrich Schiller, *On the Aesthetic Education of Man: In a Series of Letters,* ed. Elizabeth M. Wilkinson and L. A. Willoughby (Oxford: Clarendon Press, 1967), especially the discussion embodied in the twentieth letter. For a clear and accessible account of Buddhist teachings about mindfulness, consider Thich Nhat Hanh's *The Miracle of Mindfulness,* trans. Mobi Ho (Boston: Beacon Press, 1975). I first compared musement to juggling in "Phenomenology as Phaneroscopy: Theology in a New Key," *American Journal of Theology and Philosophy* 27 (Jan. 2006): 84–98.

8. Peirce's invitation, along with some extended advice for the prospective muser, appears in CP 6.458–61. I characterized musement as a kind of experiment for which the Neglected Argument supplies the rubrics in *Peirce's Philosophy of Religion,* 134.

9. The oddness of this example is perhaps mitigated by consideration of the root meaning of the word *play,* not as a subjective human attitude or activity, but as embodied in the to-and-from movement of something not completely fastened or tied down. See Hans-Georg Gadamer's reflections on "Play as the Clue to Ontological Explanation," in *Truth and Method* (New York: Continuum, 1975), 91–119.

10. Josiah Royce, *The Philosophy of Loyalty* (Nashville: Vanderbilt University Press, 1995), 78–81.

11. I suggest some of the ways in which Schiller's analysis of the *Spieltrieb* may have shaped Peirce's thinking about musement in *Peirce's Philosophy of Religion,* 128–29.

12. The example is taken from Michael Behe's defense of intelligent design in *Darwin's Black Box: The Biochemical Challenge to Evolution* (New York: The Free Press, 1996).

13. William Johnson Fox, *On the Religious Ideas* (London, 1849).

14. This last remark is taken from a variant of the same letter sent to James, to be found in Peirce's unpublished manuscripts, also quoted and cited in *Peirce's Philosophy of Religion,* 130–31.

15. Charles S. Peirce, *Semiotic and Significs: The Correspondence between Charles S. Peirce and Victoria Lady Welby,* ed. Charles S. Hardwick (Bloomington: Indiana University Press, 1977), 75.

16. Josiah Royce, *The Problem of Christianity* (Washington, DC: The Catholic University of America Press, 2001), 270.

17. Jonathan Edwards, *The Nature of True Virtue* (Ann Arbor: The University of Michigan Press, 1960), 3.

18. Ibid., 2.

19. On the idea that practice constitutes an important sign, consult Jonathan Edwards's *Religious Affections, The Works of Jonathan Edwards,* Vol. 2, ed. John

E. Smith (New Haven: Yale University Press, 1959); and also, my commentary in "Jonathan Edwards' Twelfth Sign," *International Philosophical Quarterly* XXXIII (June 1993): 153–62.

20. Jonathan Edwards, *The "Miscellanies,"* ed. Ava Chamberlain. In volume 18 of *The Works of Jonathan Edwards* (New Haven: Yale University Press, 2000), No. 777, 428ff. Consider also Perry Miller's discussion of these remarks in his Introduction to Edwards's *Images or Shadows of Divine Things* (New Haven: Yale University Press, 1948), 32–33.

21. Edwards, *Images or Shadows of Divine Things*, 33.

22. Having originally used this term as the title for the final chapter of *Peirce's Philosophy of Religion* and discussed its meaning in numerous publications since then, it now supplies the title for my book-in-progress, on *Theosemiotic: Religion, Reading and the Gift of Meaning* (under contract with Fordham University Press).

23. Jonathan Edwards, *The Distinguishing Marks of a Work of the Spirit of God*, ed. C. Goen (New Haven: Yale University Press, 1972), 238.

24. Simone Weil, *Gravity and Grace* (London: Routledge and Kegan Paul, 1952), 90.

25. For a brief consideration of the importance of the concept of attention in William James's philosophy, consult the final chapter my book on *Meditation and the Martial Arts* (Charlottesville: University of Virginia Press, 2003).

26. See Sung Hyun Lee's important account of Edwards's indebtedness to and adaptation of the medieval scholastic tradition in *The Philosophical Theology of Jonathan Edwards* (Princeton: Princeton University Press, 1988).

27. This last paragraph is adapted from my short essay intended as a critique of intelligent design arguments, previously published as "Finding the Divine in the Everyday," *Lehigh Alumni Bulletin* 92 (Winter 2006), 21–22.

4

A Semeiotic Account of Paintings as Pure Icons that Communicate Beautiful Feelings

David Rohr

In a commonsense, intuitive way, an artwork—whether a painting, symphony, poem, or sculpture—functions as a sign for those who "interpret" that artwork. The goal of this essay is to replace this vague intuition with a technical account grounded in C. S. Peirce's *semeiotic*—his theory about signs, reference, interpretation, communication, etc.—of how and why paintings are signs. Section 1 explains the basics of Peirce's semeiotic and classifies paintings as pure icons and their primary interpretants as emotional interpretants. This means that a painting's primary meaning consists in the visual feelings experienced by the painting's interpreters. Relying on insights from John Dewey's *Art as Experience*, Vincent van Gogh's letters to his brother Theo, and the film *Gerhard Richter Painting*, section 2 analyzes the process of painting as a cycle of action, feeling, and aesthetic judgment that continues until the painter judges that the painting is aesthetically excellent or beautiful.[1] This account helps to explain *how* paintings become capable of communicating the specific feelings they do. Section 3 concerns the role of great paintings in the wider, communal process of aesthetic inquiry. Interpreting beautiful paintings results directly in the cultivation of beautiful feelings and, over time, slowly refines the community's aesthetic ideals, while broadening and deepening its aesthetic appreciation.

Paintings as Pure Icons Interpretable Via Emotional Interpretants

This section introduces Peirce's conception of semeiosis and his most important classifications of signs and interpretants, employing the latter to classify paintings as pure icons and their primary interpretants as emotional interpretants.

The central concept of Peirce's semeiotic is *semeiosis* or sign-based interpretation. Semeiosis involves an irreducibly triadic relation between three relata: (1) a representing *sign*, (2) a represented *object*, and (3) an *interpretant* that interprets the object via the sign. The sign represents the object to the interpretant and the interpretant interprets the object via the sign. The following everyday examples, with sign [S], interpretant [I], and object [O] labeled, help to render this abstract definition more tangible:

1. Noticing a road sign with a wavy arrow [S], Beth brakes in preparation [I] for the curvy road ahead [O].

2. After noticing several piles of bear poop [S], Ben, fearing a bear [O] is close, quickly descends [I] the hill he hiked up.

3. Based on a prescription [S] written by Matt's doctor, Matt's pharmacist collects [I] the medicines [O] needed to treat Matt's illness.

If the sign is approximately true, then the interpretant usually fits with or is adapted to the reality of the object, given the interpreter's interests and purposes. Braking allows Beth to navigate the curvy road safely; Ben descending the hill decreases his chances of encountering a bear; and Matt's pharmacist, knowing nothing about Matt's illness, gathers exactly those medicines Matt needs. In light of the interpretant's adaptedness to the object, Peirce described semeiosis as a communication of "form" from the object, through the sign, and into the interpretant:

> [A] Sign may be defined as a Medium for the communication of a Form. . . . As a *medium*, the Sign is essentially in a triadic relation, to its Object which determines it, and to its Interpretant which it determines. . . . That which is communicated from the Object through the Sign to the Interpretant is a Form. . . .

[I]n respect to the Form communicated, the Sign produces upon the Interpretant an effect similar to that which the Object itself would under favorable circumstances.[2]

Thus, an apt synonym for semeiosis is in*form*ation, a process that forms, shapes, or organizes the interpretant to fit with the object based upon a sign's representation of that object.

Peirce proposed several important divisions of signs and interpretants, but only two are important here. Peirce's most fundamental classification of signs divides them according to how they represent their objects. *Icons* represent their objects because the icon's inherent qualities are like the object's qualities. *Indices* represent their objects through direct physical relations—whether causal relations or simple spatiotemporal proximity—with those objects. *Symbols* represent their objects because an instinct or convention determines that interpreters will interpret the symbol as standing for that object.

Peirce did not divide icons into genuine and degenerate cases, as he did with indices and symbols, but he did distinguish between icons in general and "pure icons." In his words,

> the character that fits [the icon] to become a sign of the sort that it is, is simply inherent in it as a quality of it. For example, a geometrical figure drawn on paper may be an *icon* of a triangle or other geometrical form. . . . A pure icon . . . serves as a sign solely and simply by exhibiting the quality it serves to signify. The relation to its object is a degenerate relation. It asserts nothing. . . . An *icon* can only be a fragment of a completer sign. . . . It will be observed that the icon is very perfect in respect to signification, bringing its interpreter face to face with the very character signified. For this reason, it is the mathematical sign *par excellence*. But in denotation it is wanting. It gives no assurance that any such object as it represents really exists. (*P*, 306–307)

Because a pure icon "asserts nothing" and is "wanting" "in denotation," it "can only be a fragment of a completer sign." The terse definition of an icon offered above somewhat misleadingly suggests that an icon stands for an object, when, in fact, an icon by itself cannot denote any object other than itself. Icons only function as likenesses of objects other than themselves when they are combined with other signs, whether icons, indices, or symbols. Typically, icons function in combination with other icons: to recognize her sister's face as similar, one must already know what Jamie's face looks like; fingerprints from a crime scene are only informative when matched with fingerprints in a police database; etc. Although icons depend on other signs to select their objects, their distinctive significance remains precisely that of a pure icon—a capacity, grounded in the icon's inherent qualities, to represent anything with similar qualities. Considered apart from other signs, every icon is a pure icon.

If every icon is a pure icon, why draw the distinction? The most important reason is that some pure icons are interpreted as such. Peirce gives the example of "a triangle or other geometrical form" and describes the pure icon as "the mathematical sign *par excellence*" because it "bring[s] its interpreter face to face with the very character signified." Obviously, most geometrical diagrams also involve indices and symbols—the letters labeling the diagram's points and lines are degenerate indices, and those partly iconic points and lines are also partly symbolic because, for example, due to established conventions, we interpret them as extensionless in spatial dimensions in which the drawn points and lines are necessarily extended. With that said, a geometrical diagram of a triangle that is unaccompanied by any symbolic label or attached index referring the diagram to a particular object is a pure icon that is capable of representing any triangle with points, lines, and angles similarly related. Insofar as a pure icon has an object, that object is a mere possibility—the possibility of something exhibiting the same or similar qualities. Looked at another way, a pure icon is its own object: its significance is grounded in its inherent qualities and it only represents other things insofar as they possess the same or similar qualities. In Peirce's words, "A pure icon does not draw any distinction between itself and its object. It represents whatever it may represent. . . . It is an affair of suchness only" (*P*, 163). The paradoxical identity of the pure icon with its object is helpfully explained by T. L. Short: "Music is a limiting case of sign, as is the pure icon in general. A pure icon does not signify anything that it does not contain. The feeling as contained in the sounds is the sign, in itself is the object, in the experience of the listener is the interpretant; the distinctions among these three are relational, not substantive."[3] "The red color embodied can serve to focus attention on that color in itself, independently of its occurring anywhere. The color in itself is the object; as embodied, it is the sign."[4]

In order to understand how the same quality of feeling can define a pure icon, its object, and its interpretant, consider a scarlet color sample at a paint store. The scarlet sample is the sign. As a pure icon, its significance consists in its ability to stand for anything the same or similar in color (for example, paint purchased using such a sample). In that sense, the only object the scarlet sample can represent is the same scarlet color that grounds its purely iconic significance. Likewise, the interpretant of the color sample is the same scarlet color, now felt by an interpreter who is viewing the sample.

The preceding example anticipates my classification of paintings. If a mere patch of scarlet color is a pure icon, so is the complex composition of colors exhibited by a painting. While some paintings represent specific objects through titles or realistic depictions of otherwise recognizable objects, an untitled abstract painting is a pure icon that, in Short's words, "does not signify anything that it does not contain." Rather than representing something else, such a painting's only object is the mere possibility of something defined by the qualities the painting exhibits. Many paintings possess additional significance via involved icons, indices, and symbols, but every painting clearly possesses the same purely iconic significance as an untitled abstract—in Short's words, "The icon with additions is, in itself, an icon without additions."[5] Like music and other pure icons, a painting's qualities are simultaneously the ground of its significance, the object it represents, and, as discussed below, its primary interpretant.

Recall that an interpretant is the upshot of a process of semeiosis: via the sign's representation of the object, the interpretant is informed about the object. Peirce thought interpretants consisted of three kinds of things, namely, feelings, efforts, and thoughts:

> Corresponding to [the object] there is something which the sign in its significant function essentially determines in its interpreter. I term it the "interpretant" of the sign. In all cases, it includes feelings, for there must, at least, be a sense of comprehending the meaning of the sign. If it includes more than mere feeling, it must evoke some kind of effort. It may include something besides, which, for the present, may be vaguely called "thought." I term these three kinds of interpretant the "emotional," the "energetic," and the "logical" interpretants. (P, 409)

Logical interpretants are signs that interpret other signs. Thus, a definition interprets the word defined, an argument's conclusion interprets its premises, and a book review interprets the reviewed book. *Energetic interpretants* are efforts, whether external actions or mental efforts, that interpret signs. Examples include using a grocery list to purchase groceries, decelerating after seeing a speed limit sign, and arriving at the same place and time as other participants in a meeting scheduled by email. *Emotional interpretants* are feelings that interpret signs. Examples of emotional interpretants include the joy we feel upon hearing good news, fear caused by nearby gunfire, and the complex sequence of feelings we experience while reading a novel.

Peirce's emotional/energetic/logical division of interpretants is rich in philosophical implications, two of which are especially important here. First, because Peirce's doctrine of interpretants *is* his account of meaning,[6] this division implies that a sign's meaning is expressible as or translatable into, not only other signs, but also practical actions and mere qualities of feeling. Peirce's pragmaticism is the doctrine that habits of action are the "ultimate" or essential interpretants of our intellectual concepts (see *P*, 398–433). More pertinent to this essay is Peirce's striking thesis that "Qualities of feeling may be meanings of signs."[7] Peirce's favorite examples of emotional interpretants were musical: "[T]he interpretant may be a feeling. Thus, an air for a guitar, if considered as meant to convey the genuine or feigned musical emotions of its composer, can only fulfill this function by exciting responsive feelings in the listener" (*P*, 430). According to Peirce, music is a sign whose essential function is to convey feelings from the music's composer to the music's listeners. Likewise, this essay contends that paintings are pure icons whose primary meaning is only expressible through emotional interpretants, namely, the visual feelings interpreters experience while viewing the painting.[8]

The second philosophical implication of Peirce's division of interpretants is the anthropological correlate to the first: presumably, signs have three kinds of meaning because human beings interpret signs through three streams of interpretation consisting of feelings, efforts, and symbolic thoughts. According to Peirce, "Nomenclature involves classification; and classification is true or false, and the generals to which it refers are either reals in the one case, or figments in the other" (*P*, 354). If Peirce is right that human beings interpret signs through three kinds of interpretant, then the physical and/or physiological bases for these interpretive capacities ought to be empirically discernible. My best guess is that our capacity for emotional interpretation is grounded in our sensory nervous system (perceptual qualia being basic emotional interpretants), energetic interpretation is grounded in our motor nervous system, and logical interpretation is grounded in human languages and other symbol systems that evolve continuously across millennia while the language-interpreting brains that evolution depends upon develop from a single cell into a mind-numbingly complex network of one hundred billion neurons only to become fungi food after death. If the kinds of interpretant Peirce identified are indeed grounded in these three information systems, this would provide an important physiological and physical support for the naturalness of Peirce's classification of interpretants.

Like all hypotheses, Peirce's emotional/energetic/logical division of interpretants must ultimately be judged by its fruitfulness.[9] One example of that fruitfulness is especially pertinent here: if human beings interpret reality through feeling, effort, and symbolic thought, perhaps this explains why our normative, self-critical inquiries divide naturally into aesthetics, ethics, and logic, respectively. Only potentially controllable things merit criticism (*P*, 240–41), and it is essential to the idea of an interpretation both that it is partially subject to the interpreter's control and that it can be performed either well or poorly—i.e., adaptively or maladaptively relative to the interpreter's interests. Thus, if our species interprets nature through three interpretive modalities, it is unsurprising that our normative, self-critical inquiries cluster around three branches, with aesthetics criticizing feeling, ethics criticizing effort and action, and logic criticizing symbolic thought. Presumably, the ultimate goal of these normative inquiries is to cultivate excellence in each interpretive capacity. We must think with symbols, so we ought to develop true rather than false thoughts and theories. We must act in a world with others, so we ought to cultivate good rather than evil actions and habits. We must feel through our senses, so we ought to seek beautiful rather than ugly feelings. The fact that a plausible account of the *raison d'être* of these normative inquiries is implicit in Peirce's division of interpretants is one of many instances of that division's theoretical fruitfulness.

Developing the preceding account of normative inquiries is beyond the scope of this essay. However, because it resurfaces in section 3, a brief defense of this conception of aesthetics is necessary. Defining aesthetics as the normative criticism of *feelings* or emotional interpretants might seem strange. As John Dewey observed, our object-oriented tendency is to imagine that aesthetics is about external artworks:

> [T]he existence of the works of art upon which formation of an esthetic theory depends has become an obstruction to theory about them. For one reason, these works are products that exist

> externally and physically. In common conception, the work of
> art is often identified with the building, book, painting, or statue
> in its existence apart from human experience. Since the actual
> work of art is what the product does with and in experience,
> the result is not favorable to understanding.[10]

Rather than being about beautiful external objects such as artworks, Dewey consistently conceives aesthetics as about beautiful *experience*, whether the experience is of an artwork, craft, or natural scene. He says, for example, "By common consent, the Parthenon is a great work of art. Yet it has esthetic standing only as the work becomes an experience for a human being" (*D*, 2); "To be truly artistic, a work must also be esthetic—that is, framed for enjoyed receptive perception" (*D*, 49). On Dewey's account, an artwork only fulfills its function when it is experienced by an interpreter. Obviously, the matter of an artwork is also essential, whether it is oil on canvas, the bronze of a sculpture, or the instruments played by an orchestra. But if they were never experienced, sculptures would be mere lumps of bronze and symphonies nothing but complex fluctuations in air density. To put the point negatively, it would be absurd to pass aesthetic judgment on a painting one has never viewed or a novel one has never read. An artwork makes its appeal to us through one or more of our senses, and, short of interpreting it through the relevant sense(s), we cannot judge the aesthetic value of that artwork.

After introducing Peirce's conception of semeiosis, his icon/index/symbol classification of signs, and his energetic/emotional/logical classification of interpretants, this section employed the latter to classify paintings as pure icons whose primary interpretants are emotional interpretants, namely, the visual feelings interpreters have while viewing the painting. This initial classificatory effort raises two questions that the next sections attempt to answer: How are paintings capable of communicating the feelings they do? If aesthetics is a normative inquiry that criticizes feelings, what norms ground this inquiry?

The Process of Painting and the Endowment of Paintings with Beautiful Feelings

This section addresses the first question above. Via appeals to van Gogh's letters, *Gerhard Richter Painting*, and John Dewey's *Art as Experience*, I analyze the process of painting as a cycle of self-criticism wherein the painter acts upon the painting, experiences that action's consequences in visual feeling, judges the aesthetic value of the resultant feeling, and continues acting upon the painting until the resulting feeling is judged to be aesthetically excellent. A similar process of self-criticism occurs during the extended process of artistic training. We shall begin with the latter.

Although a writer rather than a painter, Ira Glass's comments about artistic training seem to me to transcend genre:

> Nobody tells this to people who are beginners. I wish someone told me. All of us who do creative work, we get into it because we have good taste. But there is this gap. For the first couple years you make stuff, it's just not that good. It's trying to be good, it has potential, but it's not. And your taste is why your work disappoints you. . . . We know our work doesn't have this special thing that we want it to have. . . . It's only by going through a volume of work that you will close that gap, and your work will be as good as your ambitions.[11]

Glass suggests, as does Dewey, that the indispensable characteristic of an artist is keen aesthetic taste (*DI*, 51). Without such aesthetic taste, the artist could not detect the flaws in their immature works, and, therefore, could not improve. As Glass suggests, mastering the techniques required to create artworks that satisfy the artist's aesthetic taste requires lots of practice. The artist tries and tries and tries, struggling to create something that they regard as genuinely beautiful.

Concurring with Glass, Vincent van Gogh said the following about learning to draw: "What is drawing? How does one learn it? It is working through an invisible iron wall that seems to stand between what one *feels* and what one *can do*."[12] Van Gogh's letters to his brother Theo document a great artist breaking through this iron wall, allowing the depth of what he felt to flow through masterly technique onto his canvases. Consider the following six quotations, arranged in chronological order from 1882, two years after van Gogh began drawing, to 1888 when he arrived in Arles and began, in Meyer Schapiro's words, "a new art—his first new art."[13]

"I have made a drawing of a boy from the Orphanage who is blacking shoes. It may be this is done by a hand that does not quite obey my will, but still the type of the boy is there. And though my hand may be unruly, that hand will learn to do what my head wishes" (*VG*, 97).

"I do not regret a single moment that I did not go on at first with water-colour and oil painting. I am sure I shall make up for that if only

I work hard so that my hand does not falter in drawing and in the perspective" (*VG*, 143).

"Last night something happened to me. I had been at work on those three pollard oaks at the bottom of the garden at home for three days; the difficulty was the tufts of Havana leaves; how to model them and give them form, colour, tone. I had toiled on them for the fourth time. In the evening I took the work to an acquaintance of mine in Eindhoven who has rather a stylish drawing-room, where we put it on the wall. Well, never before was I so convinced that I shall make things that do well" (*VG*, 308).

"I have been [in Arles] only a few months, but tell me this: Could I in Paris have done the drawing of [these] boats *in an hour*? And without the [perspective] frame? I do it now without measuring, just letting my pen go" (*VG*, 356).

"Ideas for my work come to me in swarms, so that although solitary I have no time to think or to feel; I go on like a steam-engine at painting. I think there will hardly ever be a standstill again" (*VG*, 383).

"I wrote early this morning; then I went away to go on with a picture of a garden in sunshine. Then I brought it back and went out again with a blank canvas, and that also is finished. And now I write again. . . . What a country! I cannot paint it as lovely, but it absorbs me so much that I let myself go, never thinking of a single rule; I have no doubts, no hesitation in attacking things. I am beginning to feel that I am quite a different creature from the one I was when I came here" (*VG*, 387–88).

Vincent's letters document a profound transformation in his artistic ability. Despite great effort and careful attention to rules, he initially lacked the technical skills needed to create artworks that satisfied his acute aesthetic sensibilities. But by the time he reached Arles, Vincent painted effortlessly, thoughtlessly, and extremely rapidly, churning out canvas after canvas that he found aesthetically satisfactory and that art critics today consider masterpieces.

The method of Vincent's transformation can be characterized as a process of self-criticism *directed at* his behavioral, painterly technique and *prosecuted by* his keen aesthetic taste. Summarized in broad strokes, the process involves: (1) acting to create a drawing or painting; (2) observing the finished drawing or painting; and (3) judging its aesthetic value, usually concluding that the composition is unbalanced, the perspective off, or the modeling too flat. Negative aesthetic judgments concerning immature artworks provide the basis for improving the artist's technique, ultimately allowing her to create more aesthetically satisfying artworks in the future. Vincent's descriptions of his maturation are revealing. Early on he says that his "*hand* . . . does not quite obey my will" and that he needs to "work hard so that my *hand* does not falter in drawing and in the perspective." Years later he has a breakthrough moment and becomes "convinced that I shall make things that do well," but this occurs only after *viewing* his painting of pollard oaks displayed on his friend's wall. In the final quotation, we find Vincent drawing and painting "without the [perspective] frame . . . without measuring," "never thinking of a single rule," with "no doubts, no hesitation in attacking things."

Based on van Gogh's letters, learning to draw and paint requires making many immature drawings and paintings, passing critical aesthetic judgments upon these immature works, and struggling to improve future drawings and paintings in light of negative aesthetic judgments of prior work. According to Gerhard Richter and John Dewey, a similar cycle of self-criticism occurs during the creation of a single painting. The film *Gerhard Richter Painting* (2012) is aptly named, as it consists of extended scenes of Richter painting abstracts by scraping long plastic squeegees across the surface of his paintings, dragging and smearing the paint as he goes. The impact of each squeegee stoke is massive, altering the surface of the painting so drastically that Richter effectively unveils a whole new painting. After each drastic transformation, Richter steps back and contemplates the new painting. He often takes days or weeks to decide what to do next. Eventually, he usually decides to apply more paint or make another revelatory squeegee stroke. As portrayed in the film, Richter's painting process consists of him acting upon his paintings with either brush or squeegee, standing back to pass aesthetic judgment upon the action, squeegeeing again, contemplating some more, etc., until he is aesthetically satisfied. He describes this process as follows:

> INTERVIEWER: So the question is: You paint without a plan but you know exactly when it's right. So what's the correlation between planlessness and making the judgment: "Now it's a painting?"

> RICHTER: Each step forward is more difficult and I feel less and less free until I conclude there's nothing left to do. When, according to my standard, nothing is wrong anymore, then I stop. Then it's good.

> INTERVIEWER: And what is right and wrong? The wrong consciousness, material, or process?

> RICHTER: It just doesn't look good. Then it's wrong. . . . We're all completely equal here. The producer and consumer, artist and observer, both must have one quality: to be able to see if it's good or not. To make that judgment.[14]

According to Richter's description, he cycles between action and experience, altering each painting repeatedly until, according to his aesthetic "standard," "there's nothing left to do" because "nothing is wrong anymore," and he judges the painting to be "good" or beautiful.

John Dewey describes the process of artistic creation in similar terms: "A painter must consciously undergo the effect of his every brush stroke or he will not be aware of what he is doing and where his work is going" (*D*, 47).

> As we manipulate, we touch and feel; as we look, we see; as we listen, we hear. The hand moves with etching needle or with brush. The eye attends and reports the consequences of what is done. . . . Until the artist is satisfied in perception with what he is doing, he continues shaping and reshaping. The making comes to an end when its result is experienced as good—and that experience comes not by mere intellectual and outside judgment but in direct perception. (*D*, 51)

Dewey posits a similar cycle of action, emotional interpretation, and aesthetic judgment as that proposed above. The artist "continues shaping and reshaping" and "the eye . . . reports the consequences of what is done" until the "result is experienced as good." Like Richter and van Gogh, Dewey affirms that the artist's aesthetic judgment concerning the beauty of the artwork is the final arbiter determining when the work is finished.

Based on the reflections of Glass, van Gogh, Richter, and Dewey, the process of painting appears to involve a cycle of action, emotional interpretation, and aesthetic judgment. The painter acts upon the painting, feels the result of this action through vision, passes aesthetic judgment on that visual feeling, and acts in order to modify and improve the painting until emotional interpretation of the painting satisfies the artist's aesthetic taste. Implicit in this account is an answer to the first question raised above: How do paintings become capable of communicating the feelings that they do? The obviously true, but superficial answer is that the painting's qualities, and, therefore, the feelings it conveys to others, are determined by the painter's actions. However, the purpose of those actions is to create a beautiful painting, the emotional results of the painter's actions are continually criticized according to the painter's aesthetic ideals, and the cycle only concludes when the artist judges that her visual experience of the painting is aesthetically excellent. Thus, the painting's capacity to communicate feelings to other interpreters is determined first and foremost by the artist's experience of the painting and her judgment that that experience is beautiful. Because paintings made by great painters were experienced and judged to be beautiful by those painters, they are usually capable of communicating genuinely beautiful feelings to their interpreters. Via a beautiful painting, we *experience with* the painter, feeling the beauty of the world through the eyes of one who has dedicated their life to the creation and appreciation of beauty. Just as the writings of a philosopher keep that philosopher's thought alive long after their death, an artwork preserves the artist's experience beyond the grave. Via great art, great souls such as Beethoven, Rodin, and van Gogh stay with us, teaching us to feel the beauty of the world with greater keenness and depth.

Beautiful Paintings and the Norms that Ground Aesthetic Inquiry

On the basis of Peirce's semeiotic classifications, section 1 posited that paintings are pure icons whose primary meanings are interpretable only through emotional interpretants, specifically, the visual feelings experienced by interpreters who view the painting. Section 2 hypothesized that the visual feelings that finished paintings communicate are feelings the painter experienced and judged to be beautiful. Of course, such judgments are not always shared by the wider community of aesthetic interpretation. Often enough, however, there is wide agreement that particular paintings are genuinely beautiful. The function of beautiful paintings, on the preceding account, is to communicate beautiful visual feelings from the painter to the painting's interpreter. If beautiful paintings reliably communicate beautiful visual feelings, then the feelings they communicate can function as norms or exemplars upon which to ground future aesthetic judgments. Appealing once more to Dewey and van Gogh, this section examines the role that finished paintings, especially the masterpieces of great painters, play in the wider communal process of aesthetic inquiry. The interpretation of beautiful paintings advances aesthetic inquiry by directly causing interpreters to experience beautiful feelings and by slowly refining the aesthetic ideals of the wider community of aesthetic inquiry.

Dewey discusses the role of normative artworks in artistic training, saying, "When the old has not been incorporated, the outcome is merely eccentricity. But great original artists take a tradition into themselves. They have not shunned but digested it" (*D*, 165). He observes that "whether they are set up on their own account or are derived from masterpieces, standards, prescriptions, and rules are general while objects of art are individual. The former have no locus in time. . . . In order to get concreteness, they have to be referred for exemplification to the work of the 'masters'" (*D*, 313). The process by which the old is incorporated and painters "take a tradition into themselves" occurs, first and foremost, through the emotional interpretation of artworks in that tradition. Only through such emotional interpretation can the interpreted paintings function as aesthetic norms capable of guiding the interpreting painter's subsequent works. If aesthetics is rightly conceived as a critical inquiry whose ultimate purpose is to cultivate excellent emotional interpretants—i.e., beautiful rather than ugly *feelings*—then it makes sense that the norms governing that inquiry would themselves be *feelings*, namely, the beautiful feelings one has while interpreting great art. Just as logic criticizes arguments on the basis of exemplary or valid arguments; and ethics criticizes actions on the basis of exemplary or virtuous behaviors, habits, and persons; aesthetics appeals to exemplary or beautiful feelings, whether caused by viewing a beautiful natural scene, a beautiful craft with a nonaesthetic function like a quilt or shield, or a beautiful artwork created for purely aesthetic purposes, like a painting, sculpture, or symphony.

The normative role played by great artworks is illustrated by van Gogh's letters, which are filled with praise for the masters and masterworks Vincent sought to emulate. Here are four examples: "I am fairly carried away by Rubens's way of drawing the lines in a face with dashes of pure red, or of modeling the fingers in the hand by the same kind of dashes. I know he is not so intimate as Hals and Rembrandt, but they are so alive, those heads! Rubens . . . succeeds in expressing . . . a mood of cheerfulness, of serenity, of sorrow by the combination of colours" (*VG*, 314). "In order to make notes from nature . . . a strongly developed feeling for outline is absolutely necessary. . . . Beside me is hanging a landscape study by Roelofs, but I cannot tell you how expressive that simple outline is, everything is in it" (*VG*, 144). "The root of all figure painting depends enormously on the modelling directly with the brush. With Gericault and

Delacroix the figures have backs even when one sees them from the front; there is atmosphere around the figures—standing out from the paint. It is to find this that I am working" (*VG*, 320). "To paint in one rush—as much as possible in one rush! What struck me most on seeing the old Dutch pictures again was that most of them had been painted quickly; that Frans Hals, Rembrandt, Ruysdael dashed off a thing from the first stroke, and did not retouch it very much" (*VG*, 303).

In these passages, all written before his maturation in Paris and Arles, van Gogh recognizes in the works of prior masters various aesthetic excellences—Ruben's use of unnatural coloration, Roelof's expressive outlines, Gericault's and Delacroix's modeling of figures, and the rapid, energetic brushwork of Hals, Rembrandt, and Ruysdael—that his own paintings lacked. The paintings of these great artists provided a higher aesthetic standard against which van Gogh could compare and criticize his immature paintings. Eventually, this norm-based criticism resulted in van Gogh's mature paintings embodying the same aesthetic virtues he admired in these masters' works: unnatural coloration that increases vibrancy and modulates emotional tone; bold, expressive outlines that capture the energy of his subjects; robust modeling of faces, hands, books, branches, fruits, and flowers; and rapid, energetic brushwork, which imbues his final works with such anguished intensity. Concerning his originality, van Gogh's paintings speak for themselves. His letters reveal that this originality was matched by reverence for and careful study of works by great artists such as Millet, Rembrandt, Delacroix, and Hokusai.

Like van Gogh, most artists are profoundly influenced by artworks made by other artists. This influence is often detectable in an artist's oeuvre, as the influence of Japanese woodblock prints is upon van Gogh's work. Despite giving issue to such concrete, observable effects, artistic influence occurs primarily through feelings, namely, the emotional interpretants the influenced artist has while studying another artist's work. In general, one cannot be aesthetically influenced by an artwork that one has not emotionally interpreted.

The fact that merely observing great works of art can influence the observer's aesthetic standards and ideals has important implications for understanding the normativity of aesthetics. One objection to construing aesthetics as a normative inquiry is that "it is idle to criticize as good or bad that which cannot be controlled" (*P*, 188) and feelings are not subject to our control, at least not in the same way actions and thoughts are. The emotional interpretants that interpret a painting are only a specific kind of perceptual feeling, and, as Peirce argued at length, perception is beyond our capacity to control and, therefore, beyond rational criticism (P, 291–92, 226–30, 240–41). I cannot choose to see green grass as red or to taste a sour lemon as salty. Therefore, criticizing perceptual feelings, whether of artworks or anything else, would seem to be idle.

Although our emotional interpretations are beyond our control in the preceding sense, we can nevertheless act for the purpose of undergoing certain experiences. For the sake of beautiful experiences, we hike up mountains, sit beside flowing waters, savor fine foods and wines, decorate our homes' interiors and plant flowers outside them, transform tools like shields and blankets into beautiful crafts, and create artworks such as paintings, sculptures, and symphonies that serve no function other than generating beautiful experiences. All painters aim to create paintings that communicate beautiful feelings to interpreters. But whether the feeling that is actually communicated through a painting is really beautiful is a separate question, which concerns the judgments of the wider community of aesthetic inquiry. Whatever else we want to say about this wider process of aesthetic judgment involving both art critics and the public, the obvious fact is that certain artworks are more frequently interpreted, more carefully preserved, and more highly valued by the wider society. Through the repeated experiential interpretation of such classic artworks, not only are beautiful feelings directly cultivated, but the aesthetic ideals of the wider community of aesthetic inquiry are also slowly refined, while their aesthetic appreciations are broadened and deepened. Via interpretation of beautiful art, human beings can bring their capacity for emotional interpretation under normative, critical control and guidance, allowing us to pursue excellence, not only in our actions and thoughts, but also in our feelings.

Notes

I am deeply grateful to this volume's editors for their invaluable feedback on earlier drafts of this essay.

1. Throughout this essay, I use "beauty" and its cognates to mean simply "aesthetic excellence." Many aesthetic values are important in contemporary visual arts. Rather than asserting the predominance of beauty over such values, my vague use of this term is meant to be inclusive of these more specific aesthetic values. "Beauty" must not be confused with prettiness or pleasantness. Even degrading

and repulsive paintings such as those of Francis Bacon can be beautiful in this vague sense.

2. Charles Sanders Peirce, *The Essential Peirce: Selected Philosophical Writings*, vol. 2 (1893–1913), ed. The Peirce Edition Project (Bloomington: Indiana University Press, 1998), 544n22. Hereafter citations to this work are indicated in the text as (P___).

3. T. L. Short, *Peirce's Theory of Signs* (Cambridge: Cambridge University Press, 2007), 205.

4. Ibid., 217.

5. Ibid., 218.

6. Ibid., 263: "In general, it seems best to declare that Peirce gave the term 'meaning' no special place in his semeiotic and that his theory of the interpretant, in its various divisions, is his technical counterpart to the tangled uses 'meaning' has in ordinary language."

7. Charles Sanders Peirce, *Papers*, 1849–1914, Manuscript Collection in the Houghton Library, Harvard University: MS 318.

8. Clearly, paintings can also be interpreted through words such as an art critic's review. However, all such symbolically mediated judgments of the painting qua artwork can only be secondary meanings, interpretations that would be utterly unfounded if not based upon prior emotional interpretation of the painting.

9. Peirce illustrated this point using scripture: "Not that the highest recommendation of a science necessarily lies in the utility of its practical applications, but . . . the surest sign of health and vigour in anything that lives and grows . . . lies in its fertility. It is the moral of the fig-tree, which expresses . . . the very essence of the method of science: *the hypothesis which brings forth predictions that ripen into verifications is preserved*, while the hypothesis that is barren of such good fruit is hewn down and cast into the fire. It is the breeder's selection" (*Papers* MS 624.51–52; see Mt. 7:19, 21:18–22).

10. John Dewey, *Art as Experience* (New York: Penguin, 1934), 1. Further citations from this source are indicated in the text as (D___).

11. Neal Martin, "Encouraging Advice for Beginning Writers from Ira Glass," *Neal Martin: Dark Fiction Writer: Fantasy, Horror, Thrillers*, http://www.npmartin.com/2015/08/13/encouraging-advice-for-beginning-writers-from-ira-glass/; published Aug. 13, 2015, accessed June 10, 2016.

12. Van Gogh, *Dear Theo: The Autobiography of Vincent van Gogh*, ed. Irving Stone (New York: Plume, 1937), 164. Hereafter this work is cited in the text as (VG___).

13. Meyer Schapiro, *Vincent Van Gogh* (New York: Harry N. Abrams, 2003), 10.

14. *Gerhard Richter Painting*, film directed by Corinna Belz (Berlin, Zero One Film, 2012).

5

The Pragmatist Aesthetics of William James

Richard Shusterman

[In section I, Shusterman notes that the young William James, although frustrated in his desire to become a painter, retained his passionate concern for the arts and their importance even as he began his career teaching physiology at Harvard in 1872. He fruitfully employed aesthetic ideas and artistic examples in his 1890 masterpiece *Principles of Psychology*.]

II

A good way to introduce James's aesthetics is by noting why he never wrote a treatise in this field. He believed that the general formulae, abstract principles, and verbal criteria that philosophical aesthetics offers simply cannot do justice to the nameless qualities that make aesthetic experience so powerful and that make works of art so different in value and in spirit even if these works can be described in similar terms.

> The difference between the first- and second-best things in art absolutely seems to escape verbal definition—it is a matter of a hair, a shade, an inward quiver of some kind—yet what miles away in point of preciousness! Absolutely the same verbal formula applies to the supreme success and the thing that just

misses it, and yet verbal formulas are all your aesthetics will give.

If discursive formulae fail to capture what is aesthetically essential, the ineffable "je ne scais quaw [sic]" of quality, James concludes that "no good will ever come to Art as such from the analytic study of Aesthetics, harm rather, if the abstractions could in any way be made the basis of practice." Convinced pragmatically that "imitation in the concrete is better for results than any amount of gabble in the abstract," he not only eschewed the project of formulating a systematic aesthetic theory but also mocked the pretensions of philosophers who did.[1]

German philosophers, renowned for their conceptual systematizations, were singled out for special ridicule. "Why does the *Aesthetik* of every German philosopher appear to the artist like the abomination of desolation?" he asks rhetorically, while suggesting that the problem is the lifelessly abstract conceptualizations of its "system of categories" and "the gray monotony" of its "universal" essences.[2] If this seems like a swipe at Hegel's conceptualism in contrast to the particularism of Kant's aesthetic, James shows equal antipathy to the latter, invoking it to complain of academic philosophy's dull obfuscations and stultifying jargon. "Think of the German literature of aesthetics, with the preposterousness of such an unaesthetic personage as Immanuel Kant enthroned in its center!"[3]

Kant's emphasis on the particularity of aesthetic judgement (that defies conceptual definition and generalization) and its essential ground in feelings of pleasure or displeasure should indeed appeal strongly to James, who also insists on the ineffable particularity and affective dimension of aesthetic value. Kant's treatment of aesthetics in terms of the complex, co-operative workings of human perception as grounded in our diverse mental and affective powers (of imagination, understanding, reflective judgment, and feeling) should also find sympathy in James, who likewise viewed aesthetics as primarily a perceptual matter based in human psychology.[4] Could James's apparent antipathy to Kant's aesthetics then be due to the sharp Kantian opposition of the aesthetic to the practical, while a pragmatist aesthetic would want to have them more closely connected and reconciled? This seems likely, but a proper understanding of James's thinking on such matters requires a closer look at the key pragmatist themes expressed in his diverse remarks on aesthetics, especially in his *Principles of Psychology*, but also elsewhere.

III

We should begin, however, by showing how James pragmatically uses examples from aesthetics and art to formulate and defend his theories in other philosophical fields. One of James's central arguments in epistemology, ontology, and philosophy of mind is that the world we perceive or experience is not a fixed, independent, immutable given but rather a product of human selection in which the selective process involves different levels and can be likened to artistic creation, especially because the criteria for selection are in large part aesthetic. At the lowest level, says James, "our very senses themselves [are] but organs of selection" (*PP*, 273) that create "a world" by receiving only certain ranges of stimuli and shaping them into sensory sensations. Attention then further shapes our experienced world by selecting which sensations it will notice. But what, then, governs attention's selection? James follows Helmholtz in maintaining "that we notice only those sensations which are signs to us of *things*"; and things James in turn defines as "special groups of sensible qualities, which happen practically or aesthetically to interest us, to which we therefore give substantive names, and which we exalt to this exclusive status of independence and dignity" (*PP*, 274). In other words, if attention selects a group of sensations worth noting from the larger group of sensations that our sense organs have selected, then our mind makes a further selection. "It chooses certain of the sensations to represent the thing most truly, and considers the rest as its appearances, modified by the conditions of the moment" (*PP*, 274).

Thus, James maintains, "the mind is at every stage a theatre of possibilities," creating "mental products" by selecting, shaping, and combining "data chosen" from the lower levels (PP, 277). "The mind, in short, works on the data it receives very much as a sculptor works on his block of stone . . . and the sculptor is alone to thank for having extricated this one" from the many other sculptural possibilities in that block of stone. "Just so the world of each of us," James continues, "howsoever different our several views of it may be, all lay embedded in the primordial chaos of sensations," from "the mere matter" available to all. If this "black and jointless" manifold of space and "swarming atoms" is what "science calls the only real world," James counters that "the world we feel and live in" is instead "that which our ancestors and we, by slowly cumulative strokes of choice, have extricated out of this, like sculptors, by simply rejecting certain portions of the given stuff. . . . How different," James concludes, "must be the [experienced] worlds . . . of ant, cuttle-fish, or crab!" (*PP*, 277).

Aesthetic examples from other arts are likewise deployed when James argues for the essential contextuality of sensory perception. "In the senses," James explains, "an impression feels very differently according to what has preceded it; as one color succeeding another is modified by the contrast, silence sounds delicious after noise, and a note, when the scale is sung up, sounds unlike itself when the scale is sung down." In the same way, just as "the presence of certain lines in a figure changes the apparent form of the other lines, and as in music the whole aesthetic effect comes from the manner in which one set of sounds alters our feeling of another," so all our perceptions depend on the contexts in which they are situated (*PP*, 228).

Moreover, when James argues that the perception of felt time—its sense of haste, slowness, or rhythm of intervals—"is a qualitative, not a quantitative judgment," he highlights the point by describing it as "an aesthetic judgment, in fact" (*PP*, 583). In advocating his famous theory of emotion, James looks to the arts for evidence of "widespread bodily effects by a sort of immediate physical influence, antecedent to the arousal of an . . . emotional idea," and claims,

> In listening to poetry, drama, or heroic narrative, we are often surprised at the cutaneous shiver which like a sudden wave flows over us, and at the heart-swelling and the lachrymal effusion that unexpectedly catch us at intervals. In listening to music, the same is even more strikingly true.[5]

IV

I now turn from James's use of aesthetic examples to his articulation of four key themes in pragmatist aesthetics, themes that resurface with Dewey in more explicit form and sustained argument.[6]
1. The first theme could be called somatic naturalism. Art and aesthetic experience are not otherworldly emanations from a divine ethereal Muse but rather embodied expressions of natural energies engaged in our living interaction with our natural and cultural contexts, but also mediated and refined through these contexts. That art and aesthetic experience are often self-consciously cultivated through the most sophisticated and intellectual cultural forms does not belie their roots in more basic somatic feelings,

forms, and pleasures based on our evolutionary heritage. Our highest artistic expressions and most sublime aesthetic experiences, no matter how culturally mediated, are ultimately grounded (like our culture itself) on underlying aesthetic dispositions that have evolved in conjunction with the biological and experiential development of our bodies and our brains (which, of course, are part of our bodies). Thus an ant, crab, or cuttlefish cannot have the aesthetic experience and aesthetic tastes that we do since their somatic makeup and basic instincts are very different to ours.

For James, aesthetic judgment is most fundamentally about perceptual feelings that give pleasure or displeasure, and all perceptual feelings are essentially somatic. Not only do they require bodily organs for sensing and bodily actions for attention, our perceptions also come "invariably" with "some awareness" of "our own bodily position, attitude, condition" (*PP*, 234–35). Our embodied perceptual feelings of pleasure are thus linked to somatic instincts and appetites that are shaped by our evolutionary and personal history. James's somatic pragmatism, then, does not reject the appetitive from the aesthetic domain. There is continuity between more basic, appetitive pleasures and more abstract and refined forms. The sensuous pleasures of taste in food thus have an aesthetic character in essentially the same way as the formal harmonies of music. As James puts it, "Aesthetic principles are at bottom such axioms as that a note sounds good with its third and fifth, or that potatoes need salt" (*PP*, 1264).

Insisting that emotions are essentially bodily, James notes that much of art's aesthetic appeal is due to the pleasing emotions it engenders through its wide-ranging excitement of "the bodily sounding board" that the perception of beauty can produce: "A glow, a pang in the breast, a shudder, a fulness of the breathing, a flutter of the heart, a shiver down the back, a moistening of the eyes . . . and a thousand unnamable symptoms besides, may be felt the moment the beauty *excites* us" and fills us with pleasure (*PP*, 1084). James calls these "secondary pleasures" (*PP*, 1083) because he recognizes a more subtle primary aesthetic emotion that does not rely on the reverberations of other body parts but only on the pleasure received through the specific teleceptors and the brain that grasp the artwork's design: "[T]he pleasure given us by certain lines and masses, and combinations of colors and sounds, is an absolutely sensational experience, an optical or auricular feeling that is primary, and not due to the repercussion backwards of other sensations elsewhere consecutively aroused" (*PP*, 1082).Yet even an optical or auricular feeling is a bodily feeling, involving the body's active attention. Moreover, James insists that in most cases, "this simple primary and immediate pleasure in certain pure sensations and harmonious combinations of them" is considerably enriched by "added secondary pleasures; and in the practical enjoyment of works of art by the masses of mankind these secondary pleasures play a great part" (*PP*, 1083).

James is far from disdaining this enjoyment, which he links to Romantic taste, in contrast to classic taste that tends to see these secondary pleasures as gratuitous, distracting ornaments. His democratic pragmatist spirit is likewise far from disdaining the aesthetic needs of the masses, and he further insists that even very refined aesthetes include such secondary somatic enjoyment in their aesthetic appreciation, though they may be unaware of it.[7] A philosopher of pluralistic continuities rather than exclusive, rigid dualisms, James affirms not only a continuum of taste between the extreme poles of Romanticism and Classicism in which individuals can express their own aesthetic preferences, but also a continuum of aesthetic forms from the most simple to the most refined. This idea of a continuum, where the more primitive forms are not condemned or relegated to nonaesthetic status, expresses the pluralistic democratic theme of pragmatist aesthetics and its affirmation of popular art.

Before turning to this theme, I should note two further points about James's somatic naturalism. First, it includes a strong appreciation of the human body as muscular and dynamic. James would not "be satisfied with a more delicate and intellectual type of beauty" that has no place for "well-developed muscles" and physical fitness. He "cannot believe that muscular vigor will ever be a superfluity" in our evolutionary future because somatic fitness provides one's "indwelling soul" with experiential aesthetic "satisfaction" of "sanity, serenity, and cheerfulness." Thus, "quite apart from every consideration of its mechanical utility," it is "an element of spiritual hygiene of supreme significance."[8] Second, James's aesthetic of evolutionary somatic naturalism is not a crude instrumentalism according to which our aesthetic drives, tastes, and artworks are direct, explicit adaptations in the struggle for survival. They are instead the complexly indirect results of other somatic adaptations that may have had survival value. Our basic aesthetic reactions, says James, are in this sense "accidental" in origin though apparently "permanent in us now."

> In fact, in an organism as complex as the nervous system there *must* be many such reactions, incidental to others evolved for utility's sake, but which would never themselves have been

evolved independently, for any utility they might possess. Sea-sickness, the love of music, of the various intoxicants, nay, the entire aesthetic life of man, we shall have to trace to this accidental origin. (*PP*, 1097)[9]

2. Affirming that our aesthetic pleasures and artistic drives are grounded in instincts of our somatic evolutionary heritage but also shaped by our sociocultural environment and personal experience, James recognizes a plurality of legitimate aesthetic satisfactions and artistic forms in which the more refined rest on the more primitive. Beyond the aesthetic harmony of salt with potatoes, he notes the instinctive aesthetic satisfactions of mimicry, which "gives to both bystanders and mimic a peculiar kind of aesthetic pleasure" that underlies the appeal of dramatic art, whose appeal James also traces to the empowering pleasure of "stretching one's personality" beyond its conventional limits (*PP*, 1027–28). James regards play as a basic impulse and a legitimate aesthetic form that is both grounded in "the excitement yielded by certain [other] primitive instincts" and provides the basis for higher forms of play, including those that we regard as highest and ultimately accord the status of fine art. James underlines the very broad and diverse "sort of human play into which higher aesthetic feelings enter," referring "to that love of festivities, ceremonies, ordeals, etc., which seems to be universal in our species" (*PP*, 1044–45).

"The lowest savages have their dances, more or less formally conducted. The various religions have their solemn rites and exercises, and civic and military power symbolize their grandeur by processions and celebrations of divers sorts. We have our operas and parties and masquerades" (*PP*, 1045). James notes that "[a]n element common to all these ceremonial games, as they may be called, is the excitement of concerted action as one of an organized crowd. The same acts, performed with a crowd, seem to mean vastly more than when performed alone." We feel "a distinct stimulation at feeling our share in . . . collective life" (*PP*, 1045).

Thus, James, like Dewey, insists on the important social dimension of aesthetic experience and art's communicative power, grounding it in basic social instincts that form "a primitive element of our nature." James, moreover, cautions how the power of this collective aesthetic feeling has its stubbornly problematic expressions. "The formation of armies and the undertaking of military expeditions would be among its fruits" (*PP*, 1045); and he elsewhere explicitly argues that one of the prime reasons for resistance to the end of war is essentially aesthetic . . . [an] unwillingness to envisage a future in which army-life, with its many elements of charm shall be forever impossible, and in which the destinies of peoples shall nevermore be decided quickly, thrillingly, and tragically by force, but only gradually and insipidly by "evolution."[10]

2b. The democratic pluralism of James's aesthetics is combined with a distinct meliorism. First, James urges a meliorism of perception, the need to liberate ourselves from "a certain blindness" we have concerning the tastes and feelings of "people different from ourselves." To make this point, James invokes "a personal example" of his own blindness to the rustic charm and homey meaning of some settlement clearings in the North Carolina woods that initially struck him as "hideous, a sort of ulcer, without a single element of artificial grace to make up for the loss of Nature's beauty" in the previously pristine forests, until he looked at it through the perspective of his local guide who appreciatively had such a dwelling for his home. More broadly, James notes, "we grow stone-blind and insensible to life's more elementary and general goods and joys," including the simple somaesthetic satisfactions of "seeing, smelling, tasting, sleeping, and daring and doing with one's body," and we need to emancipate ourselves from such blindness by heightened perception of the diverse possibilities of vital joy and meaning that surround us.[11] Still more broadly, we need to develop a greater sensitivity to the aesthetic joys and moral ideals of other people different from us and whom we snobbishly regard as beneath us because of our entrenched "ancestral blindness" or inherited "ancestral intolerances." We need a "widening of vision" to "wean us away from that spurious literary romanticism on which our wretched culture . . . is fed." For beauty, nobility, and divinity lie "all about us, and culture is too hidebound to even suspect the fact."[12]

This leads to a second dimension of James's aesthetic meliorism. If our aesthetic pleasures and artistic forms are in large part evolutionary products of the world we inhabit and the experiences we have had, they are not, however, narrowly limited by that world and its established order of things. Although our perceptions and actions are guided by entrenched habits, although our tastes and pleasures are also shaped by habitual experiences (and resultant expectations) in our material and social worlds, what we seek to create and enjoy aesthetically through imagination and art are instead *better* worlds of experience. As James puts it,

> Although the elements [in works of art] are matters of experience, the peculiar forms of relation into which they are woven are incongruent with the order of passively received experience. The world of aesthetics and ethics is an ideal world, a Utopia, a world which the outer relations persist in contradicting, but which we as stubbornly persist in striving to make actual. (*PP*, 1235)

James admits, of course, "that habitual arrangements may also become agreeable" by the power of familiarity. "But," he adds, "this agreeableness of the merely habitual is felt to be a mere ape and counterfeit" of the superior harmonies and stimulations that aesthetic and ethical imagination can give us, and that we idealists can then try to actualize in the real world (*PP*, 1235). As Emerson potently put it, "There is higher work for Art than the arts. . . . Nothing less than the creation of man and nature is its end."[13]

3. A key theme of pragmatist aesthetics is the continuity and combination of the aesthetic with the practical, a theme expressed in the integration of art and life, the recognition that bodily appetites and desires can also be aesthetic, and the appreciation of the functionality of art and aesthetic experience. If Kant defined the aesthetic by its opposition to the practical, the appetitive, and the merely agreeable in sensation, he also defined it by opposition to cognitive, conceptual judgments of truth. Kant's tripartite division of the aesthetic from the practical and from conceptual truth is reflected (and symbolically reinforced) through his three famous critical masterpieces: *The Critique of Pure Reason*, *The Critique of Practical Reason*, and finally *The Critique of Judgment*, which treats the aesthetic. Thereafter, the aesthetic has often been contrasted not only with the practical but also with the rational (and thus sometimes even portrayed as "reason's absolute other").[14] In 1884, James initially deployed a similar tripartite distinction, at least for rhetorical purposes, to urge the study of emotions as a necessary complement to the study of "cognitive and volitional performances" through the "sensorial and motor centers" of the brain. For in contrast to "the perceptive and volitional parts of the mind," James complains, "the *aesthetic* sphere of the mind, its longings, its pleasures, and pains, and its emotions, have been . . . ignored."[15] But distinctions do not necessarily imply oppositions, and a key theme in the *Principles of Psychology* is the close co-ordination and overlap of the aesthetic with the rational and practical.

James argues that our knowledge and rational thinking rely most heavily on aesthetic and practical considerations. We have already noted his view that aesthetic selective shaping explains the transformation of sensations into perceptions and then of perceptions into things. But he goes farther in affirming that aesthetic and practical factors are what determine for us the *real* properties of things. For instance, from among "*all the visual magnitudes of each known object we have selected one as the* REAL *one to think of and degraded all the others to serve as its signs*. This 'real' magnitude," claims James, "is determined by aesthetic and practical interests. It is that which we get when the object is at the distance most propitious for exact visual discrimination of its details" (*PP*, 817). In the same way, "*when two sensorial sense-impressions, believed to come from the same object, differ, then* THE ONE MOST INTERESTING, *practically or aesthetically,* IS JUDGED TO BE THE TRUE ONE" (*PP*, 818; italics and capitals in all the James quotes are in the original).[16] Thus, for example, "The real color of a thing is that one color-sensation which it gives us when most favorably lighted for vision." The case is similar, he continues, for "its real size, its real shape, etc.—these are but optical sensations selected out of thousands of others, because they have aesthetic characteristics which appeal to our convenience or delight" (*PP*, 934).

Although James typically gives equal mention to aesthetic and practical factors in determining what we take as the true properties of things and thus the objects of our knowledge, this last example implies the priority of the aesthetic because the practical—what will "appeal to our convenience"—is explained in terms of "aesthetic characteristics." The point is that certain aesthetic qualities (e.g., clearness or vividness) are what render those sensory properties practical or convenient (and hence worth selecting) for our use in treating those things of which they are perceptual properties.

Beyond the cognitive question of the true properties of things, James also explains the whole practice of conceptual classifications as emerging from aesthetic gratification.

> It is, for some unknown reason, a great aesthetic delight for the mind to break the order of experience, and class its materials in serial orders, proceeding from step to step of difference, and to contemplate untiringly the crossings and inosculations of the series among themselves. The first steps in most sciences are purely classificatory. (*PP*, 1242)

Moreover, James argues, beyond this initial stage of classification, aesthetic factors continue to function in our choice of scientific theories. "*That theory will be most generally believed which, besides offering us objects able to account satisfactorily for our sensible experience, also offers those which are most interesting, those which appeal most urgently to our aesthetic, emotional, and active needs*" (*PP*, 940).

Thus, James continues, "The two great aesthetic principles, of richness and of ease, dominate our intellectual as well as our sensuous life" (*PP*, 943).What we want are theories that are "rich, simple, and harmonious," which sounds like the classic definition of beauty as unity in variety. "The richness," James argues, "is got by including all the facts of sense in the scheme; the simplicity, by deducing them out of the smallest possible number of . . . primordial entities." Simplicity provides the aesthetic sense of ease because it tends to make things clearer and more "definite," while complexity strains our limited powers of attention and memory (*PP*, 943–44). But we can once again see the aesthetic as underlying (or pervading) also practical considerations about choice of theory, since James describes the simplicity criterion in terms of the "law of least effort," which (like simplicity) constitutes a powerfully practical consideration.

Far broader than most ordinary theories are the general philosophies through which we view the world. James here insists on the fundamental primacy of aesthetics for choice of theory, explaining (in his book *A Pluralistic Universe*) the different philosophical worldviews as expressing different "tastes in language" or in personality. Agreeing with Hegel that philosophy's aim is to render the world less strange and "make us more at home in it," James realized that different men feel at home in different ways with different visions of life, declaring that "it would be pitiful if [such] small aesthetic discords were to keep honest men asunder."[17] Philosophy moreover arises, says James, from an essentially aesthetic drive of "scientific curiosity" or "metaphysical wonder" with which "the practical . . . has probably nothing to do. . . . The philosophic brain responds to an inconsistency or a gap in its knowledge, just as the musical brain responds to a discord in what it hears." The urge and satisfactions of philosophical thinking are in this sense like "many other aesthetic manifestations, sensitive and motor" (*PP*, 1046).

If aesthetic factors thus underlie much of our rational thinking, even underpinning key practical interests on which our cognitive life also relies, then Jamesian pragmatism would have to reject a strict Kantian compartmentalization of the aesthetic as opposed to the practical. James, moreover, sometimes explains our positions on practical issues of ethics in terms of aesthetic factors. If war is one example, then cleanliness and chastity provide others. Finally, given the Jamesian view that all voluntary actions are implicitly guided by kinaesthetic ideas based on felt movement, then all practical actions, for him, would involve (at least implicit) aesthetic feelings of whether these actions are smoothly or effectively performed or instead frustrated. Smooth performance not only gives pleasure but also tends to improve the efficacy of the action, whose overall practical value thus also includes those helpful, pleasurable feelings. Here, aesthetic and practical interests so closely blend or overlap that they certainly cannot be separated in actual experience, even if we can intellectually try to distinguish them thereafter.

For James, then, aesthetic experience is not confined to a pure, disembodied, compartmentalized, formal appreciation of fine art or natural beauty. It finds expression in a broad spectrum of life experiences that not only display prominent aesthetic interests (of richness, vividness, harmony, unity, and pleasures of perception and feeling) but that also can contain strong practical and cognitive interests. The very same experience, for James, could be cognitive, practical, and aesthetic; and we variously label it one or the other according to which aspect seems most dominant or pertinent, according to our current perspectives, purposes, and contexts.

4. That the aesthetic is continuous with the practical and cognitive and that all these different factors or interests can be integrated in the unity of experience points to the final key theme of pragmatist aesthetics I will consider here: the centrality of aesthetic experience and its unifying power of nameless quality. This theme lies at the heart of Dewey's aesthetics, which first put pragmatist aesthetics on the philosophical map, and which I believe is deeply indebted to James. In defining art as experience, Dewey sought to remind us that art's ultimate value lies not in a collection of physical objects that we identify as artworks, but instead in the absorbingly vital aesthetic experiences that engage and reward us through the creation and appreciation of those objects and other elements of our experience. Dewey followed James in placing experience at the core of his entire philosophical project, since this rich notion can unify many of the divisive dualisms that thwart our thinking and our lives.

Dewey identified the core of aesthetic experience in a unifying, nameless quality that resists conceptual description or explicit foregrounded reference because it instead forms the necessary unifying background for the foregrounding of what can be explicitly noticed, distinguished, and named in experience. This unifying quality is what integrates the vastly different elements that combine to form one coherent experience in our consciousness. Dewey thus argued that this qualitative core of aesthetic experience must be present and necessary to all coherent experience, for it is what brings the diverse experiential elements together in a coherent form. In advocating the pervasive importance of aesthetic experience and its unifying power and richness, Dewey essentially borrowed from James's arguments for the unity of consciousness. I close this paper by showing how, thus demonstrating another way that Jamesian psychology provides a crucial source for pragmatist aesthetics.

In his famous chapter "The Stream of Thought," James argues that a person's stream of thought has no abrupt "breaks in quality." Rather, "Within each personal consciousness, thought is sensibly continuous." This is why James describes consciousness as a "river" or a "stream" rather than a "chain" or "train" that instead imply linkage of discrete "bits" rather than a full merging that flows (*PP*, 231, 233). James emphasizes this full merging by choosing to define "continuous" as "that which is without breach, crack, or division" (*PP*, 231), and Dewey echoes this (in his most famous chapter of *Art as Experience*, "Having an Experience") by defining aesthetic experience as a smoothly continuous flow "without seam and without unfilled blanks," a "continuous merging" with "no holes, mechanical junctions, and dead centers." (*AE*, 43)

In "The Stream of Thought," James distinguishes between "flights" and "perchings" in the flow of consciousness in order to show that what might seem to be sharp breaks in this stream are not really violations of its continuity but rather the product of a conceptual "confusion" and "a superficial introspective view" (*PP*, 233,234,236).The confusion is mistaking the subjective thought in consciousness for the discrete object of that thought in the world. "A silence may be broken by a thunder-clap," James explains, but this shock forms precisely part of our continuous stream of conscious experience as a transitional "state that passes straight over from the silence to the sound." It "is no more a break in the *thought* than a joint in a bamboo is a break in the wood" (*PP*, 233–34).We overlook the continuity because we typically focus on the "perchings" (the salient, distinctive resting places) in the stream of consciousness, while not noticing the many things that connect them in our consciousness, including the contextual transitions and relations between them that form the background of our experience. Our consciousness of the thunder thus "is not thunder *pure*, but thunder-breaking-upon-silence-and-contrasting-with-it," and is "quite different from what it would be were the thunder a continuation of a previous thunder." Our "*feeling* of the thunder is also a feeling of the silence as just gone" (*PP*, 234), and thus is continuous with that silence though also quite different. We normally overlook this fundamental continuity because we fixate on the two perchings (the silence and thunder) rather than the transitive feelings (or flights) that link them.

Yet, for James, every feeling or content of consciousness is far more complex than the substantive image or perching by which we name it. Rather, it also includes a whole contextual penumbra of "transitive states," "*feelings of tendency*," "feelings of relation," or "other unnamed states or qualities" (*PP*, 239–40) that though nameless and unnoticed constitute a vague halo of context that helps constitute the meaning and quality of what we experience. "Every definite image in the mind," writes James,

> is steeped and dyed in the free water that flows round it. With it goes the sense of its relations, near and remote, the dying echo of whence it came to us, the dawning sense of whither it is to lead. The significance, the value, of the image is all in this halo or penumbra that surrounds and escorts it. (*PP*, 246)

This "halo of felt relations," James continues, forms a "*psychic overtone*" or "*fringe*" whose felt quality essentially guides our consciousness, selecting and organizing the elements and focus of our thought so as to render them coherently unified in terms of their felt "sense of affinity" to that quality. "Any thought the quality of whose fringe lets us feel ourselves 'all right' [may be considered] . . . a relevant and appropriate portion of our train of ideas" (*PP*, 247, 249, 250).

Dewey explicitly cites this Jamesian theory when explaining the integrated unity of the different phases of aesthetic experience as a continuity of successive "flights and perching" (*AE*, 62). He likewise borrows the Jamesian distinction between the discrete physical things we experience and the actual contents of consciousness in our experiential stream that instead are vague, continuous, and essentially shaped by an indefinite "qualitative background," "an indefinite total setting," "an enveloping, undefined whole" (*AE*, 197, 199) whose felt unity determines the direction of our conscious experience and the focal elements, parts, or objects into which we carve up that experience, even though the experience itself is a continuous, unified, flow. Thus, even if aesthetic experience stands out as "*an* experience" because of its distinctive quality, Dewey likens it to "a river" versus a pond because of its directional flow (*AE*, 43).

James argues that we fail to notice the transitive elements of qualitative background since they "have no names" (*PP*, 243). Our words name only the particular substantive objects, elements, or perchings in our stream of consciousness, but not the complex, indefinite background into which these elements or perchings merge, nor the nameless qualities or feelings of tendency through which the specified elements are united and guided into a directional flow. In the same way, Dewey insists that in aesthetic experience "no verbal symbols can do justice to [its] fullness and richness of thought,"[18] and "there is no name" to specify its immediate quality (*AE*, 197). Its unifying quality cannot be described nor even be specifically pointed out, Dewey argues; for if it could be specifically named and specified, it would then lose its flowing structuring immediacy and would instead turn into a foregrounded object of reflection. In James's more colorful language, "As a snow flake crystal caught in a warm hand is no longer a crystal but a drop," so trying to "arrest" the immediate transitive qualities of flow would amount to really annihilating them (*PP*, 237).

If James's theory of the unity of consciousness provides the formative model for Dewey's notion of aesthetic experience, was James himself aware of the aesthetic import of his psychological views? He surely was when discussing the vague qualitative penumbra of nameless feelings of tendency that guide our aesthetic experience. "What," James asks, "is that shadowy scheme of the 'form' of an opera, play, or book, which remains in our mind and on which we pass judgment when the actual thing is done?" His answer is "the halo of felt relations" that constitutes the "*psychic* overtone . . . or *fringe*" of our experience of that aesthetic object (*PP*, 246–47, 249). This shadowy, nameless but immediately felt quality organizes the elements of consciousness, determines the direction of its experiential flow, and underlies the specific properties we later articulate in our verbal descriptions of the work and our judgments of it. Dewey's theory of the immediate quality of aesthetic experience fulfills the same unifying, organizing, and directing function, and he indeed extends it beyond the field of art into a transcendental argument that such immediately felt quality is necessary for all coherent thought, an argument clearly inspired by James's phenomenological account of the unity of consciousness.

Although Dewey's argument can be challenged,[19] the debt of his pragmatist aesthetics to James cannot. Their evolutionary pragmatist approach of continuity is important not only for insisting on the pervasiveness of the aesthetic dimension in experience, and thus reconciling the aesthetic with the somatic and appetitive as well as with the practical and rational, but it also helps integrate art with life by connecting (and respecting) both high and popular culture. Their pragmatist direction is, moreover, crucial for reconnecting aesthetics to philosophy of mind, redirecting it to questions of perception and practical performance that were central to Alexander Baumgarten's founding project of aesthetics as a science of sensory perception.

Notes

1. William James, *The Correspondence of William James*, vol. 8 (Charlottesville: University of Virginia Press, 2000), 475–76.

2. William James, "The Sentiment of Rationality," in *Collected Essays and Reviews* (London: Longmans, 1920), 122–23.

3. William James, *A Pluralistic Universe*, in *William James: Writings 1902–1910*, ed. Bruce Kuklick (New York: Viking, 1987), 638.

4. I confess to having all too readily followed James (and Dewey) in being hypercritical of Kant, though my own pragmatist aesthetics shares with him (much more than with Hegel) an emphasis on pleasure, perception, and the experiential particularity of aesthetic reactions that cannot be reduced to the conceptual. See Richard Shusterman, *Pragmatist Aesthetics: Living Beauty, Rethinking Art* (Oxford: Blackwell, 1992). I owe this point to Hyijin Lee.

5. William James, "What Is an Emotion?" *Mind* 9 (1884): 188–205, quotation 196. This passage is repeated with only very minimal stylistic variations in *PP*, 1072.

6. I individuate and discuss these four key themes in "Dewey's *Art as Experience*."

7. James notes that "[t]he more *classic* one's taste is, however, the less relatively important are the secondary pleasures felt to be in comparison with those of the primary sensation as it comes in" (*PP*, 1083–84).

8. William James, "The Gospel of Relaxation," in *Talks to Teachers on Psychology and to Students on Some of Life's Ideals* (New York: Dover, 1962), 102–103. James's somaesthetic taste was equally devoted to clothing, and he once suggests that their aesthetic qualities count more for us than the body's. "We so appropriate our clothes and identify ourselves with them that there are few of us who, if asked to choose between having a beautiful body clad in raiment perpetually shabby and unclean, and having an ugly and blemished form always spotlessly attired, would not hesitate a moment before making a decisive reply" (*PP*, 280).

9. One might challenge James here by arguing that aesthetic pleasures themselves have some survival value because they make life worth living. Moreover, the communicative pleasures of art that James insists upon can also be seen as promoting survival by raising group consciousness, solidarity, and communicative skills.

10. William James, "The Moral Equivalent of War," in *The Writings of William James*, ed. John McDermott (Chicago: University of Chicago Press, 1977), 666.

11. William James, "On a Certain Blindness in Human Beings," in *Talks to Teachers*, 114–15, 126–27. This criticism of blindness is linked to the democratic thrust of James's aesthetic. "We are trained to seek the choice, the rare, the exquisite exclusive, and to overlook the common. We are stuffed with abstract conceptions, and glib with verbalities and verbosities; and in the culture of these higher functions the peculiar sources of joy connected with our simpler functions often dry up" (ibid., 126).

12. William James, "What Makes a Life Significant?" in *Talks to Teachers*, 135, 131.

13. Ralph Waldo Emerson, "Art," in *The Essential Writings of Ralph Waldo Emerson*, ed. Brooks Atkinson (New York: The Modern Library, 2000), 280. Emerson also prefigured all the central themes of pragmatist aesthetics that Dewey later formulated systematically without acknowledging their Emersonian source. See Richard Shusterman, "Emerson's Pragmatist Aesthetics," *Revue Internationale de Philosophie* 207 (1999): 87–99.

14. See Jürgen Habermas, *The Philosophical Discourses of Modernity* (Cambridge: MIT Press, 1987), 94; and Richard Shusterman, *Practicing Philosophy: Pragmatism and the Philosophical Life* (New York: Routledge, 1997), ch. 4.

15. James, "What Is an Emotion?" 188.

16. More generally with respect to sensations, James claims "the more practically important ones, the more permanent ones, and the more aesthetically apprehensible ones are selected from the mass, to be believed in most of all" (*PP*, 934).

17. *A Pluralistic Universe*, 634–35. Cf. "A philosophy is the expression of a man's intimate character, and all definitions of the universe are but the deliberately adopted reactions of human characters upon it" (ibid., 639). Different characters have different aesthetic tastes or needs, so that James can recognize how some philosophers would see "formal or aesthetic superiorities of monism to dualism" (ibid., 643), while others will instead follow the dualistic "philosophical faith, bred like most faiths from an aesthetic demand" (*PP*, 138).

18. See John Dewey, "Qualitative Thought," in *John Dewey: The Later Works*, vol. 5 (Carbondale: Southern Illinois University Press, 1984), 250.This paper was published in 1930 when Dewey was preparing for his 1931 William James lecture series on aesthetics, having received the lecture invitation in 1929.

19. See Richard Shusterman, *Practicing Philosophy* (London: Routledge, 1997), 163–66.

6

Between Nature and Art

Some Analytical Exemplifications of Dewey's Aesthetics

ROBERT E. INNIS

Nature as Matrix and Medium

John Dewey's writings on art and the aesthetic are of extraordinary interest and importance for uncovering what he called in *Art as Experience* "the immense variety of interactions between the live creature and his world" (*AE*, 317).[1] The originating matrix of these interactions is nature as a network of forces, energies, and situations, what he called in *Experience and Nature* the "moving unbalanced balance of things" within which we live and which engages us on all levels: physical, vital, psychological, semiotic.[2] Life, on Dewey's account, is a constant interplay of endogenic impulses toward the immediate environment and nature as a whole and of exogenic processes of being affected or impacted by it. For Dewey, the basic condition of our relation to nature is the "felt relationship between doing and undergoing as the organism and environment interact" (*AE*, 217), an interplay elicited by features of the environment pressing upon us and the immanent demands of organisms. These environmental features are marked by distinctive determining qualities and forms of resistance to us, challenging us and at the same time enabling us, giving rise to various modes of accommodation and adaptation, with the aim of establishing equilibrium between the organism and multileveled nature as a whole.

Such an equilibrium in a universe permeated by the creative processes of the emergence of novelties is never fully stable on any level. Our lives are marked by constant efforts to keep our balance and to utilize and transform the very resources of the environment to deal with it instrumentally and practically and to perceive it in its harmonies and luring qualities that we dwell in for their own sakes. In the cumulating heightened vitality that arises in our encounters with nature, Dewey writes, "there abides the deep-seated memory of an underlying harmony, the sense of which haunts life like the sense of being founded on a rock" (*AE*, 23). The lack, however, of such a memory is a mark of a life trajectory without such an ontological ground. Rather than being present in memory, such an underlying harmony then becomes the object of longing. Its absence can be due to multiple factors, from the "bustle and ado of modern life" (*AE*, 216) to the desolate existential landscapes of poverty, starvation, and disease in the great struggle of life on both individual and social planes. Dewey approvingly cites Santayana to the effect that "every living experience owes its richness to . . . 'hushed reverberations'" (*AE*, 23).[3] These reverberations are grounded in the universal structure of the ideal of a rhythmic swing and sway of the organism's engagement with its environments if it is able, without deviation, to follow courses of development in unison with them. But clearly, life can also be often haunted by the absence of such reverberations and rendered experientially impoverished. Our existence can be mired in deadening situations of disorder and negative energies.

Dewey writes, looking at the "normal" structures of experiencing, that "in a world made after the pattern of ours, moments of fulfillment punctuate experience with rhythmically enjoyed intervals" (*AE*, 23). These intervals are what make up the inner harmony of what Dewey called consummatory experiences in which experience is brought by various means to a "fulfillment that reaches to the depths of our being—one that is an adjustment of our whole being with the conditions of existence" (*AE*, 23). Such adjustments, coming to terms with the environment, are not permanent states. The achievement of equilibrium is only one phase in a continuous process and "is at the same time the initiation of a new relation to the environment, one that brings with it potency of new adjustments to be made through struggle" (*AE*, 23). Art and the development of the inner and outer conditions of aesthetic experiences are essential forms of realizing and employing the very powers and qualities of nature to institute new adjustments.

Dewey's fundamental picture of the organism-environment/nature relationship is one not just of oscillation between activity and passivity toward "the given" but a constant circuit or spiral of engagements that is participatory and reconstructive. In his fundamental 1896 paper criticizing the "reflex arc" account of experiencing, Dewey had pointed out that the organism never responds merely *to* the environment but rather *into* it.[4] The organism is not a passive mirror but an agent that constitutes the meaning of the environment by its actions and its perceptual acts. The organism is self-moving, wandering in the field of nature, appropriating its powers for both its practical and vital uses and for its expressive uses when, as in the case of art, experience "goes out into symbolization." Going out into symbolization, however, involves both the grasp *of*, and being grasped *by*, the richness of experience itself as *emblematic* of domains of meaning beyond the merely physical or instrumental or the analytically conceptual.[5] This "going out into symbolization" generates *presentational forms*, configurations of significance that elude capture in discursive language.

It is precisely art's role and power to use the very materials of nature to create artifacts with which we resonate at all levels of our existence. But, for Dewey, the *aesthetic* is by no means to be confined to the vast collections of artifacts that make up what we now, in one way or the other, call works of art. It extends to experience as a whole inasmuch as we do not pass over it to something else, using it as mere instruments or pointers, but, to allude to a core idea of Michael Polanyi's, inasmuch as we "dwell in" it and experience it for its own sake as a domain of harmonious wholes. There is an aesthetic dimension to, and perception of, nature just as there is a specifically artistic transformation and exploitation of its natural powers and materials that enables us to construct a second nature that differentiates out into the varied forms of art in which we express the infinitely variable aspects of the world and give flesh to meanings of our existence in all their breadth and depth.

Dewey exemplifies the aesthetic dimension of nature itself as an object of consummatory experiences not so much by his own descriptions as by adducing some passages from W. H. Hudson, R. W. Emerson, George Eliot, as well as snatches of poetry, including the nature-loving Romantics. Fusing the descriptive and the normative, Dewey writes that "nature is the mother and habitat of man, even if sometimes a stepmother and an unfriendly home" (*AE*, 34). The mothering or nourishing side of nature is clearly outlined in passages cited from W. H. Hudson. Hudson writes, "I feel when I am out of sight of living, growing grass, and out of the sound of birds' voices and all rural sounds, that I am not properly alive" (cited AE, 35).[6] Being "properly alive" means attending to what Dewey called the "sensuous surface of the world," exemplified in Hudson's account of his childhood as being "just a little wild animal running around on its hind legs, amazingly interested in the world in which it found itself" (cited AE, 131). As if doing an inventory of the senses, Hudson writes that he "rejoiced in colours, scents, in taste and touch: the blue of the sky, the verdure of earth, the sparkle of light on water, the taste of milk, of fruit, of honey, the smell of dry or moist soil, of wind and rain, of herbs and flowers; the mere feel of a blade of grass made me happy; and there were certain sounds and perfumes, and above all certain colours in flowers, and in the plumage and eggs of birds, such as the purple polished shell of the tinamou's egg, which intoxicated me with delight" (cited in AE, 130).

Dewey insightfully notes that what Hudson enumerates is not isolated sense qualities. The experiences he catalogues are of *objects*. "The sight, smell, and touch immediately appealed to are means through which the boy's entire being reveled in acute perception of the qualities of the world in which he lived—qualities of things experienced not of sensation" (AE, 131). It is the object that has significance, not the sense organ alone. "The connection of qualities with objects is intrinsic in all experience having significance" (AE, 131). This connection occurs through the body, which is bound to the natural world and which is quickened by the qualities that lure us through it toward deeper and more nuanced perceptions of the environment with their resonances and reverberations. In this respect, Dewey writes:

> It is not just the visual apparatus but the whole organism that interacts with the environment in all but routine action. The eye, ear, or whatever, is only the channel *through* which the total response takes place. A color as seen is always qualified by implicit reactions of many organs, those of the sympathetic system as well as touch. It is a funnel for the total energy put forth, not its well-spring. Colors are sumptuous and rich just because a total organic response is deeply implicated in them. (AE, 127)

Art's purpose is to engender such a total organic response, even if it such a response has many gradations and tones.

Hudson's love of sensory detail and particularity, of experiential uniqueness, is, as he importantly admits, rooted in his childhood and the freedom he had to safely wander in nature. It was first and foremost nature's diversity and rich blooming that attracted him and filled him with joy and was carried over to his later life. Dewey contrasts Hudson's account with a cognate passage from a mature Emerson to which Dewey thinks it is spiritually linked. Emerson writes: "Crossing a bare common, in snow puddles, at twilight, under a clouded sky, without having in my thought any occurrence of special good fortune, I have enjoyed a perfect exhilaration. I am glad to the brink of fear" (*AE*, 35).[7] This passage exemplifies a metaphysical mood, a global all-encompassing *tone* elicited by a situation and a place and not individual objects. Emerson's exhilaration and gladness on the brink of fear arose with no thematic or operative effort on his part. Such experiences happen to us, come to us, and are not something that we do or are explicitly searching for, although after they occur we realize their life-enhancing character as revealing and satisfying a deep longing. They interrupt us, both setting us in motion and at the same halting us and holding us in their embrace, much as Rollo May in his *My Quest for Beauty* describes in his existentially deep essay on "Poppies in Greece," which saved his life and kept him alive when he was on the cusp of despair.[8]

Dewey also cites (*AE*, 23–24) a passage from George Eliot's *The Mill on the Floss* that exemplifies the aesthetic aspect of our deep existential bond with ordinary nature, if we only attend to or have access to it:

> These familiar flowers, these well-remembered bird-notes, this sky with its fitful brightness, these furrowed and grassy fields, each with a sort of personality given to it by the capricious hedge, such things as these are the mother tongue of our imagination, the language that is laden with all the subtle inextricable associations the fleeting hours of our childhood left behind them. Our delight in the sunshine on the deep-bladed grass to to-day might be no more than the faint perception of wearied souls, if it were not for the sunshine and grass of far-off years, which still live in us and transform our perception into love.[9]

The "still living in us" of past perceptions, their sedimentation into habits of attending and feeling, Dewey calls "fundedness." These habits literally "fund" our existence, a kind of existential capital upon which we rely to realize our lives.

Like a drumbeat, in *Art as Experience* Dewey returns time and again to the omnipresence of nature as the ground of our lives. It is the ultimate surrounding frame and system of constraints in which human life takes place. It also, in its potential expressive powers, enters into all art forms as their medium or substance transformed into form. "Matter becoming medium" is a core thesis or organizing principle of Dewey's aesthetics. The grinding of pigments; the shaping and carving of stone; the organization of sound whether produced by the human body or reed, drum, or string; the harnessing of bodily movement; the marking and construction of surfaces, including the surfaces of the human body; the development of chisel, pen, and brush; the building of dwellings to shelter us and our gods; and so forth; all belong to nature *in* art. They are the tools for the bodying forth of nature. They make up the "substance" of art in general and in the particular modes in which it appears. The theme of nature as matrix and medium runs through *Art as Experience* as central thread or motif and, of course, one of the main chapters of *Experience and Nature* is devoted to art. So, it is important to realize that Dewey's aesthetics is fundamentally naturalistic in the literal sense.[10] It is concerned with meaning-infused and meaningfully-structured matter. Such matter is the ultimate support of all art and in the case of nature the ultimate object of perception. The transformation of nature into a materially and semiotically sheltering foundation of our lives give us a specifically human "place" in nature.

In what follows, I intend, keeping close to Dewey's examples, to examine and extend more explicitly, albeit in schematic and allusive fashion, the fertility and analytical relevance of central categories of Dewey's approach to art and the aesthetic dimension. In such a way it will be possible to make concrete the foundations of Dewey's account of the ultimate experiential contours and implications of the transformative interactions between us and nature that take place in art and aesthetic perception.

The Scroll and the Smile: Experience Has No Edges

In a remarkable passage, a continuation of a Jamesian insight, Dewey argued that the open field of experience is an encompassing, moving, ever-receding horizon. This is a central insight of his pragmatist account of the organism-environment relationship. He writes:

Things, objects, are only focal points of a here and now in a whole that stretches out indefinitely. This is the qualitative "background" which is defined and made definitely conscious in particular objects and specified properties and qualities. . . .

For although there is a bounding horizon, it moves as we move. We are never wholly free from the sense of something that lies beyond. . . . We might expand the field from the narrower to the wider. But however broad the field, it is still felt as not the whole; the margins shade into that indefinite expanse beyond which imagination calls the universe. This sense of the including whole implicit in ordinary experiences is rendered intense within the frame of a painting or poem. (*AE*, 197–98)

This phenomenologically accurate observation can be illustrated in three examples, two taken from Dewey and a remarkable parallel passage from another work written with no connection to Dewey but linked to one of the examples.

First of all, there are numerous references to Chinese painting in *Art as Experience*, although the bulk of Dewey's allusions, interpretations, and judgments are, with rare exceptions, to the art of the Western world. The references and juxtapositions are of great theoretical and analytical import in showing the essential openness of Dewey's aesthetics. Dewey had pointed out that in his opinion "craftsmanship alone is not art" and that the "thorough relativity of technique to form in art" has been often ignored. What example does he give? He claims that the special form of Gothic sculpture was not due to lack of dexterity any more than is the special kind of perspective found in Chinese painting (*AE*, 147). Dewey had remarked that "works of art express space as opportunity for movement and action," including, I would say, spiritual action. And, in light of the primacy of the category of quality in Dewey's aesthetics, such a space is, as Dewey says, "a matter of proportions qualitatively felt" (*AE*, 213), which is not dependent on the actual physical dimensions of a painting or even a poem.

Spaciousness, Dewey rightly remarks, is a characteristic feature of Chinese painting and especially the tradition of landscape painting, with its metaphysical import. Such paintings do not need frames because they are not centralized. Rather, "they move outwards, while panoramic scroll paintings present a world in which ordinary boundaries are transformed into invitations to proceed" (*AE*, 213). They have an auratic margin of

Figure 6.1. Yi Bingshou, *Landscapes*, dated 1814. Metropolitan Museum, New York.

an ever-receding "beyond." An invitation to proceed *involves* us, elicits *participation*. We do not just respond *to* such a painting, we respond *into* it and into the self-generating nature coming to appearance in it, within which we ourselves are. As Dewey put it, "[N]ature in this meaning is not 'outside.' It is in us and we are in and of it" (*AE*, 336). Nature is the complex of generative processes into which and within which we enter into forms of relationships and participation that transcend our starting points, taking us out of ourselves and "putting us into play." Works on Chinese painting emphasize this dynamic openness that is bound to a profound stillness of contemplation and absence of agitation that is manifested in Chinese painting, which holds in delicate balance both a displacement of the human and at the same time an image of the human ability and need to recognize displacement. What appears to be the strangeness of Chinese painting is really something that is proper to what all art demands of us:

Figure 6.2. Jan van Eyck, *The Arnolfini Portrait*, 1434. National Gallery, London.

that "we install ourselves in modes of apprehending nature that at first are strange to us" (*AE*, 337) but can lead to an "insensible melting" in which barrier and limiting prejudices are dissolved by our entering into a new "spirit" or qualitative matrix embodied in an art work.

Such a leading, both existentially in terms of being affected and attuned in different ways and in terms of seeing analytical connections, allows Dewey to note a remarkable parallel and intersection. Western painting, governed for a period of its existence by progressive attempts to "picture the world" through exact representation of its empirical properties, attempted to be a realization of the "objective eye." This involved the evolution not just of monocular perspective but of very different uses of pigments and brush work. Dewey nevertheless illuminatingly contended that by these different means Western painting, even in spite of its "highly centralized" form, was able to "create the sense of the extensive whole that encloses a scene that is carefully defined" (*AE*, 213), that is, objects with clearly defined edges. Dewey gives as an example Van Eyck's famous "Jean Arnolfini and Wife," which is able to "convey within a defined compass the explicit sense of the outdoors beyond the walls" (*AE*, 213). This is a remarkable insight, issuing a challenge to us to scrape away the veneer of

Figure 6.3. Leonardo da Vinci, *Mona Lisa*, 1503–06. Louvre, Paris.

perceptual habits and to attend to the backgrounds of appearances and not just their foregrounds, even if we are also made aware of the gulf in metaphysical premises and worldviews out of which Chinese landscape painting and such a work as Van Eyck's arose and were determined.

I would like, going further, to adduce a third, quite unexpected example, of the importance of the background, not analyzed or even mentioned by Dewey but whose presence in our culture has been so domesticated that we have a very difficult time attending to or *being with* what is before us: the *Mona Lisa*, exemplar par excellence of what François Cheng called "an enigmatic smile that seems to want to say something."[11] This is true enough and universally recognized. Cheng, however, remarks on the "look" as a total quality, encompassing the eyes and the smile, a remark reminiscent of the centrality of the category of quality that Dewey creatively developed, in multiple formats, from Peirce.[12] The look is indeed more than the eyes. "The beauty of the look comes from a light that wells up from the depths of Being. It can also come from an external light that illuminates it" (47). Following St. Augustine's reflections in his "Sermon on Providence," Cheng writes about beauty that it "results from the encounter between the interior of a being and the splendor of the cosmos. . . . This encounter in some way annihilates the separation of the internal and external" (47), precisely the core of Dewey's idea that the encounter between humans and the environing world involves participation and mutual penetration. Nature is as much in us as we are in nature, the beauty of which forms a "landscape." Verlaine, Cheng remarks, wrote that "[y]our soul is a chosen landscape," which the Chinese aesthetic tradition called a "feeling-landscape," marked by forms of attunement. Such a landscape also exemplifies Dewey's fundamental notion of *fundedness*: it is made up of "memories and dreams, fears and desires, experienced and anticipated scenarios" (47), which constitute the very quality of our lives, the ramified felt matrix of our existence.

But Cheng goes farther, and indeed, by citing another analysis of the *Mona Lisa*, confirms the importance of Dewey's great insight into the edgelessness of our moving fields of experience and of the decentering that Dewey ascribes to Chinese painting. But the lesson of the analysis of *Mona Lisa* is nevertheless surprising and shows the analytic value of Dewey's core insight. The question Cheng poses is whether there is, as he puts it, a "key to unlock the mystery" (47) of the Mona Lisa's look. The answer to this question is startling and unexpected, to say the least. He asks whether in fact the key is to be found in "that misty landscape behind her, both distant and near" (47). He cites a long passage from *Le Sel et le Vent* by France Quéré, which I reproduce here as a text consonant with Dewey's phenomenological orientation with its focusing on funded reverberations, resonances, organic responses, memories.

> In forms of rocks and lakes burst the strange soundings of an interior world. . . . At the height of the [Mona Lisa's] shoulders, an ochre landscape of hilly terrain begins, which the efflorescence of the rock runs through. To the left, the path opens onto the gray waters of a lake, striated by the shadows of the overhanging rocks. These are thrust faults, manes, fierce necks, deformed muzzles that rise above the waters in a burst of petrified anger. A prehistoric violence blocks the view. . . . To the right, beside the young woman's turned-up mouth, the path follows the course of the muddy river, threading its way up from level to level, among the fallen rocks, finally reaching the shore of a second lake, higher than the first. . . . This is another world, immaterial, immensely contemplative, toward which the smile and the movement of the eyes subtly direct us. A dim glow makes the high altitude lake just barely iridescent. But the maledictions of the shadows and obstructions are vanquished. Other rocks rise, but they no longer shade or enclose anything. Their shadow traces a ring, suggests transparency, leaves the mirror of the waters intact. . . . Between the two purified shores opens a gap where the gold of the water and the light merge, and extend together toward infinity. Is this a god who welcomes the traveler? Is it the joy of an enlightened intelligence at the height of its meditation? . . . Is it childhood rediscovered, made more beautiful by the distances of memory? . . . A human dream begins there, at the height of the eyes and the pure forehead. Its dawns are even more beautiful than the hills of Florence in the sun's first rays.[13]

Cheng comments that, looked at this way, the *Mona Lisa* "no longer appears to us as the simple portrait of a socially prominent woman, but as the miraculous manifestation of that potential beauty the universe promises from the very first" (49). The beauty of her face is not that of a single isolated face but the realization of a transfiguration arising from "the encounter of interior light and another light forever offered but so often obscured. *Transfiguration* is understood here as that which is transformed from within, and also as that which shows through in the space of life between the finite and the infinite, between the visible and the invisible" (49). The "space of life" that Cheng refers to has no firm or defined edges. Within life there are, as Dewey noted, pragmatic edges, but in the concrete world in which we live out our lives they are labile borders and not abstractions belonging to another "ideal" world. Life is lived both "on" and "at" the edge. We also see in the Quéré text the detailed engagement with the landscape, an oscillation between identifying and being grasped by the "tone" or "determining quality" of a landscape that becomes a mirror of the soul. We can see here in a different way the matrix of nature as determinate of an art work, although it is clear that the global notion of a landscape is not able to fully encompass on its own the distinctiveness of Dewey's aesthetics and approach to the analysis of art works.

Indeed, it is clear with respect to painting that Dewey had a special, but by no means exclusive, affection for the great impressionists and postimpressionist painters. Three art works from the Barnes Foundation, Renoir's *The Bathers*, Cézanne's *Still Life with Peaches*, and Matisse's *Joie de Vivre*, are represented in the eight illustrations that were included in the original and critical addition of *Art as Experience*. Renoir and Cézanne play central roles in exemplifying the point and fertility of Dewey's analytical framework. They are, for him, prime paradigms of painting and of major philosophical importance. It is worthwhile and very enlightening to see where they appear and what role they pay in the development of Dewey's argument.

Paradigms of Painting:
On Representation, Expression, and Abstraction

First of all, as to Cézanne, references are strewn throughout *Art as Experience*, in different contexts of the general discussion of art and aesthetic experience, which is linked with allusions, interpretations, and criticisms of various artists and art works. Writing about the role of color and color qualities, Dewey writes that line generally, but not absolutely, has a stable constancy of *some* sort but that this is not the case with color. Change of light and other conditions introduce variances. The motivation for this remark is the misplaced attempt to discover pure or simple qualities independent of relational contexts. Experiential qualities, even studied scientifically, Dewey holds, "cannot shut out the resonances and transfers of value" due to their attachment to objects. Moreover, the attempt to separate design and color is misplaced. In this context, Dewey has recourse to a passage from Cézanne: "Design and color are not distinct. In the degree in which color is really *painted*, design exists. The more colors harmonize with one another, the more defined is design. When color is at its richest, form is most complete. The secret of design, of everything marked by pattern, is contrast and relation of tones" (*AE*, 127). For Dewey, the philosophical lesson is that opposing "quality as immediate and sensuous to relation as purely mediate and intellectual is false in general theory, psychological and philosophical" and, in the case of art, "absurd" (*AE*, 127). Relations go all the way down.

The interplay between doing and undergoing that makes up the spiral or circuit of experiencing that defines the ultimate contours of the organism-environment relation also undercuts any attempt to separate the "esthetic and artistic" as passive and active respectively. Mere perfection in execution can end up as pure technique, Dewey claims, resulting in a product with a mechanical feeling. Indeed, for him "there are great artists who are not in the first ranks as technicians (witness Cézanne), just as there are great performers on the piano who are not great esthetically, and as Sargent is not a great painter" (*AE*, 54). Right after this critical observation, Dewey contends that technical perfection is not the same as true artistic craftsmanship. What he says surely is influenced by the practice of Cézanne. For Dewey, craftsmanship to be artistic entails that the craftsman must hold in view in the process of production those who will perceive and enjoy the product, including the artist who must know when the work is finished and fulfills the felt schema out of which the artwork emerges and which it realizes, what Langer called the artist's "idea." The artistic success of this process is determined by its being "loving"; the craftsman "must care deeply for the subject matter upon which skill is exercised" so that it is "framed for enjoyed receptive perception" (*AE*, 54). When Dewey refers to the "constant observation" necessary for the artist as producer of the art work we cannot help but think of Cézanne's obsession with Mont Sainte-Victoire, as a manifestation of telluric forces, an inexhaustible source of inspiration and lure for his painting, which exemplifies the synthesis of "outgoing and incoming energy" in perception and production.

Indeed, later on in the chapter on "The Expressive Object," returning to the topic of whether "drawing" is essential to painting, Dewey establishes the pivotal nature of the distinction between recognizing and perceiving aesthetically. We do not go to painting to recognize objects because the artist has employed, with high skill, drawing as a "means of exact outline and definite shading," reproducing reality as it is. Drawing, for Dewey, is

> drawing *out*; it is extraction of what the subject matter has to say in particular to the painter in his integrated experience. Because the painting is a unity of interrelated parts, every designation of a particular figure has, moreover, to be drawn *into* a relation of mutual enforcement with all other plastic means—color, light, the spatial planes and the placing of other parts. This integration may, and in fact does, involve what is, from the standpoint of the shape of the real thing, a physical distortion. (*AE*, 98)

But this very distortion does not contravene what Dewey thinks is the ultimate goal of art: to capture every shade of expressiveness of the world. The goal, that is, is not to copy the world but, to allude to a notion from Susanne Langer, to *present* the *forms of the world*, the forms in which the world appears as configurations and fields of significance. Representing the significances of the world is not re-producing the world but producing *expressive objects* that both draw out, shape, and inform the *how* of appearing.

It is at this point in Dewey's discussion that the discussion about expressiveness and meaning turns to the central notion of "abstraction" and abstract art and its repudiation of representation as the highest goal of art. Cézanne, for Dewey, is a prime exemplar for showing the falseness of the opposition between representation and expressiveness and their connection with the putative goal of any so-called naturalism, in painting in particular and of art in general. Representation, Dewey thinks, is no more objective than expression. The absence of representation in a painting, as in the case of abstract art, does not make it "merely expressive" in the sense of a mirror of an individual subjectivity without any perceptual logic to it. Nor are the distortions present in Cézanne and El Greco or the blatant flatnesses of Matisse's painting, such as the *Red Studio* or the *Joie de vivre*, merely expressive with no links to the world.

Dewey's conception of the nature of abstraction, especially in painting, has critical importance. If linear outlines are restricted to merely reproducing with accuracy particular shapes, they have limited expressiveness.

They are either just "realistic" copies or they are the capturing of types, of generalized kinds of things that allow us to recognize them. *Aesthetically* drawn lines, Dewey notes, have increasing expressiveness in that they can embody "the meaning of volume, of room and position; solidity and movement" such that "they enter into the force of all other parts of the picture, and they serve to relate all parts together so that the value of the whole is energetically expressed" (*AE*, 99). But, Dewey claims, showing the influence of Albert Barnes, that the history of painting has progressed "from giving a pleasing indication of a particular object to become a relationship of planes and harmonious merging of colors" (*AE*, 99), as in the work of his beloved Cézanne, Renoir, and many others who receive positive mention throughout *Art as Experience*.

As to abstract art proper in the strict sense, which was just emerging, Dewey has recourse to citing a fertile passage from Barnes's *The Art in Painting*. In this passage we can see how overcoming the tension or opposition between representation and expressiveness with regard to painting also illustrates a core feature of Dewey's whole aesthetic theory and can be extended to the art as a whole, *mutatis mutandis*. Here is the passage:

> Reference to the real world does not disappear from art as forms cease to be those of actually existing things, any more than objectivity disappears from science when it ceases to talk in terms of earth, fire, air and water, and substitutes for these things the less easily recognizable "hydrogen," "oxygen," "nitrogen," and "carbon." . . . When we cannot find in a picture representation of any particular object, what it represents may be the qualities which *all* particular objects share, such as color, extensity, solidity, movement, rhythm, etc. All particular things have these qualities; hence what serves, so to speak, as a paradigm of the visible essence of all things may hold in solution the emotions which individualized things provoke in a more highly specialized way.[14]

Dewey continues by drawing out the philosophical lesson of Barnes's exemplary formulation:

> Art does not, in short, cease to be expressive because it renders in visible form relations of things, without any more indication of the particulars that have the relations than is necessary to

compose a whole. Every work of art "abstracts" in some degree from the particular traits of objects expressed. . . . There is no *a priori* rule to decide how far abstraction may be carried. . . . Abstraction is usually associated with distinctively intellectual undertakings. Actually it is found in every work of art . . . for the sake of expressiveness of the object. (*AE*, 100–101)

The movement toward the impersonal and the abstract that marked the various forms of art when Dewey was composing his *Art as Experience* did not mean a movement away from a true naturalism which aimed at capturing in forms what Schelling called the "potencies" in things. There is, on Dewey's account, no rigid opposition between the abstract and the concrete, between the drive toward simplification and toward the proliferation of internal specifications, between direction and allusive indirection, between the overarching controlling *tone* of death and darkness in the presented subject matter and the light and air of another. Taken to extremes, we have imbalance, impenetrability, or the unbearably obvious and trivial, mere illustration or a merely scientific exercise. The key is arriving at an equilibrium of form and matter, a unity that is the point of all art. It is the defining feature of art to be informed by and express what Dewey calls "adequate sympathy" with, as I indicated at the beginning, "the immense variety of interactions between the live creature and his world" (*AE*, 317).

These interactions involve selection, whose directive source is interest, "an unconscious but organic bias toward certain aspects and values of the complex and variegated universe in which we live" (*AE*, 100). The artist works both with and within "the infinite concreteness of nature" and follows the logic of his selective interest while adding "to his selective bent an efflorescence or 'abounding' in the sense or direction in which he is drawn" (*AE*, 101). At the same time there has to be maintained some intrinsic reference, at some level of specificity, to the environment's qualities and structures, which make up some objective frame of reference that cannot be ignored, but which is transfigured in art in multiple ways.

A comment on the nudes of Renoir illustrates this theoretical or analytical point. They give delight, Dewey says, but are not in the least pornographic, as can be clearly seen from the reproduction of Renoir's *The Bathers* in *Art as Experience*. While his nudes do not repudiate the "voluptuous qualities of flesh" but actually heighten our awareness of

Figure 6.4. Auguste Renoir, *Young Girl Bathing*, 1892. Metropolitan Museum, New York.

them, nevertheless Renoir abstracted *from* the conditions of their physical existence. There is also a positive form of abstraction operative that, through the medium of color, transfers bare bodies, naked bodies, into a new dimension or realm. According to Dewey the ordinary associations of naked bodies disappear:

> The esthetic expels the physical, and the heightening of qualities common to flesh with flowers ejects the erotic. The conception that objects have fixed and unalterable values is precisely the prejudice from which art emancipates us. The intrinsic qualities of things come out with startling vigor and freshness just because conventional associations are removed. (*AE*, 101)

Dewey remarks that paradigmatically in the case of Renoir there is manifested a love of the substance of common life. Renoir exploited the power of "every plastic means—color, light, line, and planes, in themselves and in their interrelations—to convey a sense of abounding joy in intercourse with common things. . . . What is expressed is the experience Renoir himself had of the joy of perceiving the world" (*AE*, 134). This is precisely the goal that motivated Dewey both in his aesthetics and in his general philosophical project: to create an environment that satisfied our needs for stability and harmony in our everydayness which is not alien to the aesthetic dimension.

Dewey emphasizes Renoir's great ability to take hold of the phases of objects that especially interest him and, within the limits of the art work under production, to grasp and embody "the total esthetic quality of an experience" (*AE*, 135), which has a property that Dewey called "livingness," a quality of moving from within and that can absorb us, as in Renoir's paintings of children reading or sewing. Renoir in Dewey's estimation shows us the richness of everydayness if it is properly attended to, provided, of course, that its frames, both natural and constructed, embody forms of what we could call "aesthetic rationality." Nature is the omnipresent originating and shaping frame or matrix of our lives. Artworks, as Dewey has clearly shown, arise within this originating frame by the creative transformation and transfiguration of nature itself upon which they bear in multiple ways. They shape nature and our perception of nature, both human and nonhuman, by capturing in a unique way every aspect of an infinite play of forms as they manifest themselves in our experience, shaping us and locating us in places and times.

Shaping Nature: Qualities of Space-Time in Art and Life

In line with his metaphysical vision, Dewey sees nature as a processive system of space-time. In the chapter on "The Common Substance of the Arts," Dewey remarks that "space and time—or rather space-time—are found in the matter of every art product" (*AE*, 210). In painting, for example, space relates and is a factor in the constitution of form. But, Dewey notes, it is also felt directly or experienced as a quality and Dewey ascribes to James a key role in establishing that sounds had more than a temporal quality; they were also spatially voluminous, as musicians know. While science aims to reduce the qualities of space and time to relations captured in equations, it is the prime function of art to "make them abound in their own sense as significant values of the very substance of all things" (*AE*, 210–11). While the power drive of science is toward formal relations in a space-time field grasped mathematically, such relations in experience are "infinitely diversified and cannot be described, while in works of art they are *expressed*" (*AE*, 211). Art, on Dewey's account, involves selection, not universalization. Its object is the uniquely significant, not the irrelevant, and its result is compression and intensification of experience, pushing us across thresholds of habit and custom.

It is traditionally thought that the plastic arts—painting, drawing, sculpture, architecture—engage the spatial aspects of change, while the literary arts and music focus on the temporal aspects of experience. However, the difference, Dewey says, is one of focus or emphasis. They share a common substance: the space-time matrix of our lives. Dewey adduces a striking example of this: a close correspondence between the opening bars of Beethoven's fifth symphony and the "serial order of weights, of ponderous volumes, in Cézanne's 'Card Players'" (*AE*, 212). Each has a "voluminous quality," conferring on each of them power, strength, and solidity—"like a massive, well-constructed bridge of stone," expressing the enduring and the structurally resistant (*AE*, 212). These are *felt* qualities that are embodied both spatially in a picture and temporally in a set of complex sounds.

Figure 6.5. Paul Cezanne, *The Card Players*, First Version, 1890–92. Metropolitan.

Space and time, as qualitative space-time, is "infinitely diversified in qualities" (*AE*, 212). Dewey is in full agreement with Peirce and James that existence itself is qualitatively defined, what Peirce called its "firstness" and James foregrounded in his famous notion of the different feelings of "and," "but," "then," "until," and so forth. This infinite diversification of space and time can be reduced, he claims, to three general themes: Room, Extent, Position—Spaciousness, Spatiality, Spacing—and the temporal correlates: Transition, Endurance, and Date. These dimensions are distinguishable in thought but have no separate existence (*AE*, 212).

Dewey distinguishes three interlocked aspects of this space-time matrix, all of which manifest both aesthetic and everyday consequences. They unfold what was latent in the beginning section of this essay dealing with nature as matrix.

1. Space is, first of all, as he puts it, *Raum*, roominess, not just in the physical sense but in the existential sense of a "breathing space" that allows us to live with a sense of potentiality and to live and move in multiple dimensions. Likewise, there is a space of time that makes possible the accomplishment of anything significant. Inasmuch as *omnis determinatio est negatio*, that is, value arises out of limitation, infinite room, whether of time or space, leads to dispersion: "[L]imitations must bear a definite ratio to power; they involve cooperative choice; they cannot be imposed" (*AE*, 213). Dewey goes on to say that "works of art express space as opportunity for movement and action" whose proportions are "qualitatively felt" and notes that a lyric poem can have it while a "would-be" epic does not and indeed, as many of us have experienced, a miniature painting can immensely supersede a canvas covered by acres of paint. This is clearly seen in the exceptional sense of spaciousness already noted in Chinese paintings and also, Dewey perspicuously notes, in an individual portrait of Titian in which "infinite space, not just the canvas, is behind the figure" (*AE*, 213).

2. Space and time in experience, Dewey writes, are also "occupancy, filling. . . . Spatiality is mass and volume, as temporality is endurance, not just abstract duration" (*AE*, 213). In our experience there is the shrinking and expanding of colors and sounds just as there is the rise and fall of both colors and sounds. But neither is free-floating and isolated. Colors especially belong to objects in a "world possessed of extent and volume" and sounds both return and proceed, displaying intervals and progression that belong to them and not just isolated tones. They have identity and continuation, but that does not mean, Dewey says, that they are associated with natural objects, although clearly they can be: brooks murmur, leaves

whisper and rustle, wave ripple, surf and thunder roar, wind moans and whispers. Nevertheless, empty time, he states, does not exist, nor is there such an "entity" as time. "What exists are things acting and changing, and a constant quality of their behavior is temporal" (*AE*, 214). This is a matrix of art works and not just of nature. Volume is an experiential quality independent of the physical characteristic of mere size and bulk, which can be objectively measured. Small landscapes, Dewey insightfully says, can open onto unlimited space or embody qualities of fragility and frailness without being aesthetically weak. Solidity and massiveness, or their reverse, can mark a wide range of artworks of different genres.

3. Spacing, the third property, involves place or position, "distribution of intervals through spacing" (*AE*, 214) and contributes to realizing the individualization of parts. Rightness of placing is integral to the immediate qualitative value of a position, its "just-right-ness" that is directly felt. This is also a mark of the "fittingness" or "aura" that is grasped in the encounter with a work that "works." What Dewey called the power of the concrete is manifested both in energy of position as well as of motion. Intervals and spacings can be favorable, or unfavorable, to the manifestation of energy, while others frustrate and block. This is especially so, Dewey remarks, in the case of the "bustle and ado of modern life" that renders "nicety of placing the most difficult for artists to achieve" (*AE*, 216). But I think this remark bears more upon life outside the projects of art and is a manifestation of Dewey's hesitation about the distortions of modern life, a topic I have explored elsewhere.[15]

Dewey summarizes his position in the following way, having recourse once again to the central and indispensable idea of "quality."

> I have said that the three qualities of space and time reciprocally affect and qualify one another in experience. Space is inane save as occupied with active volumes. Pauses are holes when they do not accentuate masses and define figures as individuals. Extension sprawls and finally benumbs if it does not interact with place so as to assume intelligible distribution. Mass is nothing fixed. It contracts and expands, asserts itself and yields, according to its relations to other spatial and enduring things. While we may view these traits from the standpoint of form, of rhythm, balance and organization, the relations which thought grasps as ideas are present as *qualities* in perception and they inhere in the very substance of art. (*AE*, 217)

A Final Word Connecting Us to the Beginning

The basic condition of our lives, Dewey writes, is the felt relationship "between doing and undergoing as the organism and environment interact" (*AE*, 217). The poised readiness to meet the impacts of the environment and to endure and persist is matched by active response, not just *to* it but *into* it. From our position in the world of space and time we go out into the environment seeking opportunities for further action: instrumental, intellectual, aesthetic. The ultimate significance of art, on Dewey's account, is that it avails itself of every component of nature to create out of its transformations harmonious wholes that embody the felt qualities and senses of things and "to the construction of which the self has surrendered itself in devotion" (*AE*, 190).

Notes

1. *Art as Experience*, in *The Later Works of John Dewey*, vol. 10, ed. Jo Ann Boydston, intro. Abraham Kaplan (Carbondale: Southern Illinois University Press, 1987; original publication 1934), cited hereafter as *AE*. This essay takes up and rotates in a different way themes in Dewey's aesthetics that I have treated in a number of other essays. See especially the following: "The 'Quality' of Philosophy: On the Aesthetic Matrix of Dewey's Pragmatism," in *The Continuing Relevance of John Dewey: Reflections on Aesthetics, Morality, Science, and Society*, ed. Larry A. Hickman, Matthew Caleb Flamm, Krzysztof Skowroński, and Jennifer A. Rea (Amsterdam: Rodopi, 2011), 43–60; "Dimensions of an Aesthetic Encounter," in *Semiotic Rotations: Modes of Meaning in Cultural Worlds*, ed. SunHee Kim Gertz, Jaan Valsiner, and Jean-Paul Breaux (Charlotte, NC: Information Age Publishing), 113–34; "Energies of Objects: Between Dewey and Langer," in *Das Entgegenkommende Denken*, ed. Franz Engel and Sabine Marienberg (Berlin: Springer Verlag, 2016), 21–38; "Dewey's Peircean Aesthetics," forthcoming in *Cuadernos de sistemática Peirceana*; "Aesthetic Naturalism and the Ways of Art: Linking John Dewey and Samuel Alexander," forthcoming in *Rivista della storia di filosofia*; and "Peirce and Dewey Think About Art," forthcoming in *Semiotica*.

2. *Experience and Nature*, in *The Later Works of John Dewey*, vol. 1, ed. Jo Ann Boydston, intro. Sidney Hook (Carbondale: Southern Illinois University Press, 1981; original publication 1925), 341.

3. George Santayana, *Reason in Common Sense*, vol. 1 of *The Life of Reason* (New York: Charles Scribner's Sons, 1905–06), 65.

4. "The Reflex Arc Concept in Psychology," first published in *Psychological Review* III (July 1896), 357–70. Reprinted in *The Essential Dewey*, vol. 2, ed.

Larry A. Hickman and Thomas M. Alexander (Bloomington: Indiana University Press, 1998), 3–10.

5. This is Susanne Langer's great theme, continuing Ernst Cassirer's work, developed in her *Philosophy in a New Key, Feeling and Form*, and her great trilogy *Mind: An Essay on Human Feeling*. I have traced the trajectories of her thought and its linkages with the pragmatist tradition in my *Susanne Langer in Focus: The Symbolic Mind* (Bloomington: Indiana University Press, 2009).

6. These passages are from W. H. Hudson, *Far Away and Long Ago: A History of My Early Life* (New York: E. P. Dutton, 1918), 3, 331, 231, 232.

7. This passage is taken from Ralph Waldo Emerson, "Nature," in *The Complete Works of Ralph Waldo Emerson*, 1, 9.

8. Rollo May, *My Quest for Beauty* (Dallas: Saybrook, 1985), ch. 1.

9. George Eliot, *The Mill on the Floss* (New York: Athenaeum Club, 1900), 44.

10. See my "Aesthetic Naturalism and the Ways of Art: Linking John Dewey and Samuel Alexander" cited in endnote 1.

11. François Cheng, *The Way of Beauty: Five Meditations for Spiritual Transformation*, trans. Jody Gladding. (Rochester VT: Inner Traditions, 2006), 44. Citations in text.

12. See my "The 'Quality' of Philosophy," "Dewey's Peircean Aesthetics," and "Peirce and Dewey Speak About Art," cited in footnote 1.

13. *Le Sel et le Vent* (Paris: Bayard, 1995), 150–52; cited in Cheng, 47–48.

14. Albert C. Barnes, *The Art in Painting*, 3rd ed., revised and enlarged (New York: Harcourt, Brace and World), 36 and 35 of 3rd edition; cited in *AE* from 2nd edition, 99. For a differently oriented naturalistic account of abstraction in abstract art see Eric Kandel, *Reductionism in Art and Brain Science* (New York: Columbia University Press, 2016). Abstraction goes all the "way down" as well as all the "way up."

15. See my *Pragmatism and the Forms of Sense: Language, Perception, Technics* (University Park: Pennsylvania State University Press, 2002), ch. 5 on "Pragmatist Aesthetics as Critique of Technology."

III

American Aesthetics

Contemporary Theoretical Contributions

The field of American Aesthetics continues to attract thought-provoking explorations by contemporary philosophers and theologians developing the pragmatist and process traditions initiated by the classic American philosophers. This section features both broad-ranging expositions of the comprehensive field of value and more narrowly defined theoretical treatments of how the tradition of American Aesthetics illuminates the work of specific artists and artistic domains.

Wesley J. Wildman expands the notion in evolutionary biology of fitness landscapes to include a temporal dimension of intentional journeying in relation to a landscape of value bearing possibilities. In Wildman's axiological landscape theory, active choice is determinative and in its irrevocability sets the stage for new choices. The open option of organismic choice undermines any largely deterministic theory of value development and distribution. Things show up as objective affordances (availabilities) merged with subjective valuation. In his exposition of landscape axiological theory, Wildman makes use of Whitehead's organic metaphysics, big bang theory, Beethoven as the creator of musical beauty, and Islamic extremism. The resulting theory is pluralistic and context dependent; it employs a framework-relative approach to truth, but in its generality it cannot replace sensitive aesthetic particularism.

Nicholas Gaskill begins his account of pragmatist literary criticism by following Peirce in placing aesthetics at the level of Firstness—as inherent in immediately felt qualities having the power to produce rich artistic experience in a world of becoming. While it is clear how the visual arts and music may be rooted in nonreflective Firstness, how can literature, unfolding in the mediation of language (Thirdness), be seen as aesthetic like those other arts? Gaskill refers to Dewey's use of James's notion that relations, often coded as conjunctions in language, are real and integrate sensation and language. Therefore, aesthetically informed literature does not simply represent a preexisting world but constitutes experience. Pragmatist imagination precedes logical reasoning so that in literary experience, reader, text, and context enter into a dynamic constellation full of novelty and rich with possibilities for reconstructing life.

Does possibility play an important role in human experience? Randall E. Auxier claims that by eliminating inappropriate possibilities of notes and moves, the core meanings resident in the performance of music and dance can shine forth. The very egress of possibilities reveals human limitations. Auxier accepts in general Heidegger's emphasis on being toward death, the ultimate limit, as productive of human meaning, but he creatively deepens Heidegger's thought through his analysis of aesthetic inspiration. Edgar Allan Poe's stories create imagery illustrating how the increasing closure of possibilities in time can potentially heighten appreciation of life. The gaps between possibilities and actuality, feeling and symbols, Langer's presentational and discursive symbols—these openings, as when Miles Davis holds off for a moment before playing the right note, provide for the savored moments of heightened personal response to possibilities.

Drawing upon themes developed throughout his career, including axiology, determinacy, harmony, and ontology, Robert Cummings Neville argues that everything determinate is a harmony of essential and conditional features. Neville follows Jonathan Edwards in postulating that to exist is to be beautiful, although good inner harmony may not be experienced as good in its relationships. From Whitehead, Neville borrows the notions of narrowness, width, triviality, and vagueness to describe how the form of a harmony is related to its components. These terms are used in support of his claim that value arises from density of being, and elegance is the aesthetic trait of things fitting together with complexity and simplicity. Finally, Neville turns to how his general theory relates to the arts in an American context, and he offers seventeen points of interpretation illustrating the application of his theory.

Gary Slater delves into the way aesthetics can be meshed with historical investigations to uncover deeper cross-cultural and transhistorical understandings of religious phenomena than have previously been accomplished. Aesthetic judgments, he claims, apprehend the rich sights, sounds, and smells that are basic to the creation of religious meanings;

the aesthetic is where we really live. Slater turns to Robert Corrington's ecstatic naturalism to explore the ways the arts can expand the imagination and confound cultural boundaries. Slater finds that Dewey views history as a holistic system of social and cultural relations that enhances aesthetic insight and promotes empathy for that which is different. Peirce's categories provide a way of integrating the thought of Corrington and Dewey and help illuminate how religious traditions of all times and places can be fruitfully compared.

7

Axiological Landscape Theory

Uniting Aesthetics, Ethics, and Inquiry

WESLEY J. WILDMAN

Introduction

The purpose of this essay is to articulate a comprehensive hypothesis about the nature of value, in as much detail as space permits. I do not present an argument for this hypothesis or make detailed comparisons with alternative hypotheses. Rather, my aim is to introduce this hypothesis into the ongoing scholarly conversation about axiology.

Most discussions of value in human life are partitioned into practical, domain-specific spaces. Some people study aesthetics, which is value in the realm of beauty; some investigate ethics, which is value in the realm of goodness; some examine inquiry, which is value in the realm of truth. There are specialized subdiscourses as well. Within aesthetics, for example, we have the aesthetics of film, the aesthetics of garden landscapes, and the aesthetics of art. Each subdiscourse generates a distinctive body of literature, existing alongside many other, similarly specific subdiscourses. If scholars put diverse fields of study together, it's still usually within a domain-specific partition, as when aesthetics is treated as a philosophical specialization even though much of the literature in aesthetics is generated within many distinct subdiscourses. But there are highly abstract literatures in aesthetics, ethics, and inquiry as well.

What's the point of a highly abstract treatment of, say, aesthetics that aims to make sense of value in the realm of beauty? I think the aim is to say what we mean by beauty as such. It's a pleasingly antinominalist impulse but there's a price paid for indulging it—abstractions about aesthetics are often difficult to relate to concrete instances of things we are prepared to call beautiful. This in turn raises sharp questions about whether all those abstractions are worth the trouble when we could be expending the same energy in more concrete analyses of instances of beauty, or indeed in the creation of beautiful things. Yet we speak as if there really is affinity among beautiful things, so the curious and theoretically minded aesthetician is naturally drawn to ask the fundamental question: What is beauty? The same goes for a general theory of goodness and a general theory of truth: it's natural for some kinds of minds to want to think about what is goodness as such, what is truth as such, and how to create the good and the true; and there is a price paid by abstract distancing from the many concrete instances of goodness and truth.

What, then, ought we say about axiology, in the specific sense of the study of value as such with the highest degree of abstraction? One usage of axiology confines it to a hallway within the mansion of value theory—the hallway in which we worry about what processes, objects, people, and qualities are good, and ponder the many modes of the good. Just as everyone passes through the mansion hallway on the way to their rooms, so axiology is relevant to everyone pursuing ethical inquiries. Thus, axiology is both central in the sense of being a common concern and marginal in the sense of being off to one side of the range of interests among most experts.

I prefer to use axiology in a more general sense, encompassing all three of the transcendentals of beauty, goodness, and truth (in this I follow such thinkers as Edwards 2010, Frondizi 1971, and Neville 1995). To pursue the mansion image a little farther, axiology in my sense is the main staircase from which the beauty-as-such hallway, the goodness-as-such hallway, and the truth-as-such hallway radiate outward. It is doubly abstract, then, but it is also relevant to absolutely everything happening in the mansion of value. In short, axiology is the theory of value as such, with every kind of value in the interpretative picture. It's a kind of speculative metaphysics, inevitably, and will strike some as pointless because of that. But the questions raised within axiology understood in this general way are fair questions, deserving of careful consideration and detailed analysis.

These questions include the following.

1. Can the axiological character of reality be simultaneously objectively encountered by interpreters, in some respects, and subjectively construed by interpreters, in other respects?
2. Can the axiological character of reality be simultaneously a matter of both individual conscious experience and socially ordered construction?
3. Are some values incommensurable, untranslatable, or uncommunicable?
4. What are the connections between the axiological character of reality and fundamental physics and mathematics?
5. How does evolutionary biology illumine changes in the way the axiological character of reality is interpreted?
6. How do biological organisms engage the axiological features of reality, in both social and neurological terms?
7. What is the phylogenetic history of human axiological sensitivity?
8. Does understanding axiology in the most general terms have any practical application to the human challenge of creating the beautiful, the good, and the true?

The axiological theory I venture in this chapter answers these and other related questions.

Philosophically, I consider myself a pragmatist with a methodological commitment to fallibilism, which in practice means I seek correction capable of improving promising hypotheses, or overthrowing deficient ones. Thus, I am hopeful that this theory of value can be improved through conversation with others who have given themselves over to wondering about the deep axiological puzzles of reality.

Summary of the Hypothesis: Basic Answers to Basic Questions

The way of thinking about value as such that I am proposing here is called "axiological landscape theory." It is offered with greater attention to the role of value in cosmic evolution and incorporates the insights of biological and cultural evolution more comprehensively than existing approaches, including, as we shall see, the notion of a fitness landscape. Axiological landscape theory employs the concept of a landscape of axiological possibilities, complete with structures and dynamics. Natural processes from cosmic development to the axiological sensitivity of living organisms navigate this landscape, realizing some possibilities and foreclosing others, like choosing to hike down one valley rather than another. This process of realization and foreclosure defines determinate histories of value in everything from the mathematizable regularities of nature to organism-environment interactions, including human appraisal and construction of value. In social species, when neurological complexity permits (as it does for human beings), the exploration of the landscape of axiological possibilities is corporate and ways of perceiving value can be profoundly influenced by social inhibition or enhancement.

In axiological landscape theory, aesthetics, ethics, and inquiry are collaborative ventures of determining value histories. The theory merges the social construction of value, individual creativity in axiological appraisal, and the givenness of axiological potentials in environmental affordances. Thus, telegraphing answers to the eight questions above, I assert that:

1. The axiological character of reality is simultaneously objectively given as valuational possibilities afforded, and subjectively construed as valuational possibilities sensed and realized;

2. The axiological character of reality is simultaneously individual, as an adventure in axiological awareness, and social, as a corporate process of construing value potentials and determining value histories;

3. Uncommunicable value may exist but we can't speak about it, while incommensurable values are a practical problem to be resolved through creative translation using the tools of specialized discourse communities;

4. Fundamental physics and mathematics express the determinate value histories arrived at in reflexive cosmic exploration of the axiological landscape, particularly in the early phases of the universe;

5. Evolutionary biology underlines the exploratory character of the axiological landscape and natural selection illustrates what it means to realize some value possibilities while foreclosing others;

6. Evolutionary theory also explains what it means for a species (such as our own) to awaken to intense axiological sensitivity;

7. Evolutionary theory sheds bright light on how biological organisms develop the neurological capacity for such axiological sensitivity and the social capacity for the exploration and construction of value; and

8. The abstractions of axiological landscape theory can be highly relevant to practical questions of value creation and appraisal.

Background: Fitness Landscapes, Axiological Pluralism, Determinate Histories, Appraisal Dimensions

Summary in place, let's fill in some background. Axiological landscape theory makes good use of the analogy of a landscape. This application of the analogy is related to the concept of fitness landscapes employed since the 1930s in evolutionary biology, thanks especially to American geneticist Sewall Wright (1889–1988). Fitness landscapes are also known as adaptive landscapes since they depict the relative fitness of organisms (on the vertical axis) plotted against genomic variation (on the horizontal axis). Over time, subpopulations within a species can move about within a fitness landscape, depending on changes in genes and resultant behavioral capacities. Fitness landscapes can be enhanced in 3-D by adding an axis for a second dimension of genetic variation, or for time so that changes in the fitness landscape itself can be visualized. Greater complexity than that complicates convenient visual portrayal.

Inclusive fitness is the characteristic of an organism that tends to be optimized through natural selection. While there are many sources of evolutionary change, including genetic drift and non-random mating patterns, natural selection probabilistically confers reproductive success more on some organisms than others. All of this happens within an environment that is, in a variety of senses, competitive. Maybe caloric resources are scarce, predators are plentiful, or there are strong preferences about sexual partners—in all cases, we have competition. What inclusive fitness means in detail varies depending on the nature of the environment and the kinds of competition prevalent within it. There are a lot of chances in life, so surviving and reproducing is a stochastic business. But the evolutionary process is essentially a non-random fitness-optimizing algorithm that plays a huge role in determining the distribution of genomic variations in every species.

The biological realm is extravagant, if not profligate. Ever since people began relatively comprehensive study of animals and plants in the time of Aristotle, the diversity of biological organisms has repeatedly astonished us. From ants to antelopes, from bacteria to brains, and from clams to coyotes—and that's just animals—there seems to be no end to the exploratory eagerness of the biological world. Charles Darwin's Tree of Life, as well as more accurate and detailed descendants of that diagram, express the initially astounding claim that all this diversity is historically and biologically related. After we grasp the idea of natural selection, though, this claim quickly loses its astounding quality and instead seems obvious. Well, it was always obvious, in a way: obvious enough for Aristotle himself to have thought of it and rejected it as implausible—which it was, given what he knew at the time. Right on the heels of the dawning obviousness of the historic genetic relatedness of all earth creatures there is a deeper astonishment that life is so fecund, so creative, so sensitive to context, so good at solving fitness challenges, so pervaded with predation and fear, and so much a matter of creaturely embodiment.

It's here that an enhancement to fitness landscapes becomes useful: we can move from a two-dimensional to a three-dimensional landscape by introducing a dimension of time that records both movements of organisms within fitness landscape and changes in the fitness landscape itself. This brings historical sensitivity to the landscape idea, making the hills and valleys resemble branches in the Tree of Life itself, always moving outward, away from the trunk, and never turning back the clock. The profligacy of life has somehow combined with moments of historic determination to produce some organisms where others might have existed instead.

There are countless examples of determinate evolutionary histories, but let's focus on one. The preservation of skeletal structure across millions of species makes some body plans common and other thinkable body plans entirely absent in our ecology. We detect awareness of the strangeness of this kind of historic particularity in the fantastic depictions of alternate bodily structures in the literature and art of myth and fantasy—think of the Hydra from Hesiod's *Theogony* or Fred Hoyle's Black Cloud. Somehow, somewhere, somewhen, there was a key, unplanned collaboration of random variation and natural selection that yielded the historic line of body plans that dominates our planet. We assume that many alternatives were possible, based on invertebrates such as octopuses if nothing else, and thus that a historic determination made all the difference.

This suggests that the evolutionary process is akin to walking through a landscape (or climbing up through the Tree of Life). Sometimes the process branches and continues along two different valleys, each with distinctive competitive pressures and matched optimization of inclusive fitness. Sometimes entire valleys of organisms are wiped out by a comprehensive change in conditions for which those organisms are ill-prepared. Presumably, entire valleys of biological possibilities are never realized at all. Within any given valley, organisms compete in the corresponding biological niche. Those with higher inclusive fitness reproduce successfully and often, perhaps because they display superior problem-solving skills, are better providers and protectors, or possess robustness in the face of ecological changes. The list of fitness-conferring characteristics depends on organism capabilities and the ecological niche they inhabit.

The historical quality of the evolutionary process is deeply impressive. There is directional path dependence in the process that translates in the landscape analogy to a journey in which we explore some possibilities and not others, in a specific order. The landscape analogy invites us to think of this journey as a movement through a host of possibilities, some of which are realized and others foreclosed due to this directional path dependence. Unlike a journey in a geographical landscape, once you are in one valley of this type of landscape, you cannot go back and choose another valley. Past events limit present possibilities just as present events constrain future possibilities. And at every step along the way, the possibilities are at least as rich as the profligacy of life itself.

We need a second enhancement to the concept of fitness landscapes to make sense of axiological realities as we experience and create them. So far we have three dimensions: we started with organism characteristics on the horizontal axis and inclusive fitness on the vertical, and then added a historical dimension. But inclusive fitness is not the only relevant dimension of appraisal. Complex cognition and sensory capacities, along with the interaction of biology and culture, produce new possibilities that are not easily comprehended within the framework of inclusive fitness, as when we protect and nurture babies who would certainly have died in the pain-filled history of our species' past; or as when we prize human rights to such an extent that we reorganize social and economic realities to give formerly marginalized people a chance at a healthy and safe life.

This might potentially be understood in terms of inclusive fitness by noting that radically changed environments can change the conditions for fitness. For example, in the history of our species there has never been a greater probability that people on the autism spectrum will reproduce and be very good at providing for offspring. The social landscape has changed and the meaning of inclusive fitness has changed with the mutating niche. High school manifestations of phylogenetically virtually timeless fitness criteria (think of the strong and popular jock who gets the pretty girls) quickly vanish when it comes to producing and providing for offspring in a high-tech world.

But reducing everything to a single appraisal system—namely, inclusive fitness in mutating niches—really doesn't work. Think of the suicide bomber who self-destructs while swept away by a religious-political vision of the way things could and should be. Or the saintly person who loves strangers unconditionally when there is no associated fitness gain. Or obsessed artists such as Van Gogh who subordinate everything in life to creating artistic portrayals of the sublime. Who knows what appraisal systems might be possible in the axiological landscape, but already our species has manifested quite a few, enabling us to detect affordances that, while always virtually present as possibilities, once lay beyond the reach of our perceptual abilities.

This multiplying of dimensions of appraisal from the evolutionary given inclusive fitness to the evolutionarily emergent alternatives greatly complicates the axiological landscape in precisely the way needed to make sense of axiology, ethics, and inquiry. But one final enhancement is still needed.

Fitness landscapes were originally used to talk about the frequency and spread of genetic variations (alleles) that conferred inclusive fitness in a wider population of organisms, on the assumption that the landscape itself was static. We have already seen that the landscape can change, modifying evolutionary niches slowly or quickly depending on the change. But even the inclusive fitness appraisal system operates on all aspects of an organism that are exposed to selection through behavior or biological reactivity—and that's a lot of aspects. Thus, we need multiple dimensions to express the various ways that organisms differ from one another, some as variations in individual tendencies, some as variations in the focus of social intensification.

A person obsessed with the sublime probably has a brain that is particularly sensitive to intense configurations of value, and this makes a sharp contrast with those who are tone deaf to such features of the axiological landscape. Those who are susceptible to fanaticism can be identified and cultivated by groups that have a use for them, while those stabler and broader in judgment find fanaticism repulsive and are useless for the same groups. Those who tend to enter easily into dissociative states are more likely both to appreciate the strange and to benefit from the fitness benefits of unleashing placebo healing mechanisms, while those who lack this tendency tend to sense reality as a flattened-out environment for practical manipulation. All these individual characteristics, and a host of others—from reflexive tendencies to cultivated skills, and from features that drive group formation to features enhanced by group participation—are simultaneously active in the axiological landscape.

Key Concepts: Value, Possibility, Virtuality, Potential, Landscape, Affordance, Engagement, Determination, Realization, Foreclosure

This multidimensional conception of an axiological landscape significantly broadens the original idea of a fitness landscape, first by infusing it with temporality and historicity, rendering it sensitive to both chance events and deliberate decisions; second by generalizing the landscape to express value possibilities of all kinds, rather than solely values related to inclusive fitness in evolutionary niches; and third by introducing intense sensitivity to individual differences, potentially amplified and muted by sociality. This is a conception of value as such that promises a high degree of generality as well as rich applicability to the wildly diverse contexts in which we talk about values. Here's how it works.

Value possibilities define the axiological landscape. Value possibilities are objective as possibilities but virtual in their objectivity because they may or may not be concretely realized anywhere at a given time. The form of their virtual objectivity is environmental affordance, by which values might or might not be realized, depending on the flow of events and the behavior of organisms. Affordances are structured possibilities, perceived and engaged differently depending on the qualities of events and organisms. Affordances are something like complex, curling, multidimensional manifolds. Organism engagement of those affordances in the first instance is akin to a simplifying slice through the manifold, reducing the dimensions to the tractable minimum needed to formulate action plans and engage the world so manifested. We analyze the abstracting, simplifying slicing of engagement in terms of an organism's perceptual and cognitive capacities, which are always particular to phylogentic history, individual propensities, and patterns of social learning; and in terms of the kinds of valuational appraisal in play within any given situation. This is why we routinely encounter different valuational perspectives in the presence of the same affordance, which in turn is the experiential basis for the philosophical stance of valuational pluralism.

Environmental presentation or manifestation of affordances is the potent fuel of the axiological landscape. Those potentialities are made available and then engaged or not. Every engagement and every nonengagement involves both realizing and foreclosing possibilities. In this way, organism engagement of an environment takes on path-dependent directionality, which is in effect an accumulating history of determinations. Just as our own bodies bear in their muscular-skeletal depths a history that realized some possibilities and foreclosed others, so all our adventures in values are marked by a barely traceable but extremely important axiological lineage.

Psychologists treat affordances more concretely, as the way a bit of the world shows up as graspable, comprehensible, or navigable to a particular species. For human beings, most things we call "doors" show up as openable, in part because we have the physiological capacity to grasp door handles and the imagination to picture what's on the other side. But they don't show up that way to snakes, for which the door handle is not tractable cognitively or physiologically; or to ants, for which most doors are probably like floating walls, barely relevant to their travel activities. The way things show up as graspable, comprehensible, or navigable is the very foundation of valuation. The way things show up is objective affordance merged with subjective valuation. Affordance theory in psychology did us the very great favor of pointing to valuation at the very root of the biological world.

Some semiotic theories go further, atomizing macroscopic processes of valuation such as navigating doors into a flux of accreting sign events in which one thing shows up for another thing as something in particular, as valuable in a particular way. The most aggressive semiotic theories build "one thing showing up for another thing as valuable in a particular way" into the prevailing understanding of causation, thereby implanting valuation into the very roots of physical nature. This is the foundation of all di-polar metaphysical schemes: value isn't added to the physical, it doesn't emerge from the physical, and it is not opposed to the physical; nor is the physical a masked expression of more fundamental valuational processes in the manner of absolute idealism; rather, physicality and valuation are co-primal in the causal nexus of reality. The theory of affordances invites precisely this kind of generalization. Thus, affordance theory and semiotic theory are good partners for axiological landscape theory.

Axiological landscape theory enjoys many resonant connections with other thinkers, from Aristotle to Whitehead, from Peirce to Buchler, and from Neville to Corrington. I'll focus for a moment just on Whitehead's approach in *Process and Reality* (1929). Whitehead's primordial nature of God is approximately the axiological landscape in its virtuality. The initial aim is the presentation of axiological affordances. Prehension in actual occasions is the abstracting, simplifying slicing that occurs in an organism's apprehension of affordances. Concrescence is the realizing of some possibilities and the foreclosure of others as apprehension of value possibilities transitions with historical implacability into action plans and creaturely determinations. Most importantly, perhaps, axiological landscape theory is evocative of the most reflexive interpretations of Whitehead's philosophy of organism. These are the interpretations in which God's presentation of the initial aim is wholly automatic, a reflexive process that does not admit even of traces of intentionality or purpose. Hartshorne sensed the impersonal automaticity of Whitehead's account of God and took decisive steps to render God intelligible as a personally ordered society of actual occasions. This, felt Hartshorne, was the only way to make of a process deity something that could be properly religiously relevant.

How do axiological landscape theory and Whitehead's philosophy of organism differ? Most importantly, axiological landscape theory makes far more explicit the historical lineage of value determinations, the individual differences in value apprehension, the role of sociality in structuring valuational apprehension, and the host of appraisal systems that are relevant in the philosophy of organism. This additional conceptual machinery is what allows axiological landscape theory to move so freely and in detail over so many valuational domains of life, connecting aesthetics, ethics, and inquiry.

Also, axiological landscape theory has nothing to say about the consequent nature of God, which is the most speculative and least empirically compelling aspect of Whitehead's philosophical vision in *Process and Reality*. This effectively eliminates a vital reason for using God language at all, and of course axiological landscape theory does not require God concepts. If there were an ultimate transcendental condition for the possibility of the axiological landscape, an ontological ground for the suchness of reality, a Whence for all that is, then that might be worthy of the name God. But such a God would be no personal being, nor any being at all. Rather, the axiological landscape in its multidimensional plurality and ambiguity and historicity would be the finest symbolic presentation of its character, akin to the way the Logos is the first reflexive presentation of Plotinus's One.

Finally, axiological landscape theory does not require Whitehead's reformulation of causation. Causation is a deep philosophical problem and dominant theories now and for a long while have great difficulty registering the co-primordiality of valuation and physicality in the root of reality. Consider the so-called hard problem of consciousness to see how difficult the challenge is. Whitehead's theory of causation (prehension, concrescence, sociality) has the very great virtue of directly addressing that deep philosophical problem. Axiological landscape theory requires such a solution as well but it is free to take or leave Whitehead's specific version of it and embrace an alternative, say, Corrington's (and arguably Peirce's) semiotic flux that runs all the way down and all the way up the levels of complexity in nature. Neutrality about the specific reformulation of causation is arguably an important virtue in an axiological theory at the current time. But the greatest theoretical virtue of axiological landscape theory is the extra detail in the mechanisms that make axiological analyses so interestingly fruitful. And with that we pass from speculative metaphysical exposition to practical application.

Applications of Axiological Landscape Theory

To illustrate axiological landscape theory in action, I'll quickly work through a series of illustrations in diverse domains of value designed to illustrate different aspects of the theory and to demonstrate its cross-domain generality.

Consider big-bang cosmology. In the early phases of our universe's development, the same thing happens everywhere and we have homogeneity. This homogeneous process of expansion involves symmetries prevailing and then breaking, transitions expressed in the exquisite mathematics of group theory, which is the analytical language of symmetry. Surely this is a case of let those who have ears to hear, listen for the mathematical music, because appreciating the abstract mathematics of symmetry and symmetry-breaking transitions is not for everyone.

Cosmic expansion is a stochastic process governed by statistical regularities so strictly that variations get averaged out and the process is thoroughly deterministic. There's historical directionality, however, as space-time expansion lowers density and temperature, thereby permitting forces to be distinguished and elementary structures to form. The inflationary phase of big-bang cosmology freezes statistically explicable inhomogeneities in density, creating the beginnings of what will become the cobweb of galaxial structures that we now detect in the cosmos. It is these frozen inhomogeneities that cause the universe to become transparent to light at different rates, giving rise to the patterned cosmic microwave background radiation that has told us so much about the early universe. Here we have the manifestation of value possibilities that are necessarily construed so narrowly and simply by the available objects and processes that we see an inevitable realization of possibilities—akin to a one-way hike down a long non-branching valley within the axiological landscape. This is an essentially deterministic journey, lasting more than ten billion years in which nothing surprising happens, no choices arise, and the raging sea of probabilities in which particle interactions occur is governed with rigid law-like statistical regularity.

Before the beginning, in standard inflationary big-bang cosmology, there appears to be a spawning of universes in a quantum vacuum, a process known as bubble nucleation, with only certain types of proto-universes capable of lasting long enough for anything interesting to happen within them. Here again, though, we have a statistical process so homogeneous that variations average out and deterministic regularity is the rule.

Inside universes that last long enough for interesting forms to arise, as in our universe, the complexification of form we see in living organisms permits the apprehension of formerly undetectable and therefore unrealized value possibilities. For instance, some bacteria can detect a chemical gradient and, to their reproductive benefit, move along that gradient using machinery refined through natural selection. The development of the chemical machinery of photosynthesis was a game changer for the entire ecology of our planet. And all this happens above seething tectonic plates and within a thinned-out solar disc that occasionally delivers asteroid collisions so violent that all complex life is wiped out. We haven't had one of those for a while, fortunately. This marks the entry of historical sensitivity into organism appreciation of the axiological landscape of possibilities. The historical path dependence here is not the homogeneous, statistical averaging kind by which the early universe yields galaxial structures. Rather, this is extremely particular historical path dependence, places and times of emergent complexity that leave a permanent mark on an ecosystem, new forms that spread out and supplant older forms because of a competitive advantage in a process that can never be wound back.

The chance formation of light-sensitive cells conferred on organisms possessing such cells a capacity to detect a new realm of value possibilities, with attendant inclusive fitness advantages. This formed the basis for an evolutionary pathway to visual perception, with attendant fitness advantages. Visual perception is adaptive because it confers pronounced survival advantages on organisms that possess it, which is why visual perception has evolved several times independently—an instance of so-called convergent evolution. As with many adaptations, however, visual perception has side effects. So much of cultural expression depends on vision, for example, just as fine cuisine is a wonderful side effect of the sense of taste. Sensory modalities unleash appraisal systems we weren't expecting but which subsequently dramatically affect behavior.

As an example, consider Ludwig van Beethoven (1770–1827). As he lost his hearing he became increasingly desperate and frustrated but he also produced famously sublime music that still stands as the phase change between the Classical and Romantic periods in the history of Western music. Hearing developed in the first instance for its survival benefits but its existence sponsors a novel system of value appraisal related to the aesthetics of sound. The species variations in this capacity are pronounced, as there are many sounds we cannot detect that other species can. But human cognition makes of the human aural capacity a playground for aesthetic experimentation.

Beethoven's third symphony, the "Eroica" of 1804, activates many aspects of axiological landscape theory. It marked a career transition for him as he confronted the established classical tradition with dissonance, syncopation, wild key changes, and violent variations in dynamics and texture. Axiological landscape theory explicitly registers the way established tradition sets aesthetic expectations through socialization, abstracting and simplifying environmental affordances so that people hear as beautiful what conforms to their training. But the right kind of mind, under the right kind of unique pressures, can slice the affordance manifold in a different way, realizing new possibilities foreclosed by others, and foreclosing yet other possibilities. And so it was that Beethoven heard possibilities of syncopation, dissonance, and dramatic emotion where some others could not hear the beauty in it. This was the precisely the kind of historical determination that took the bulk of Western music down a new valley in the axiological landscape, stabilizing new aesthetic sensibilities that call upon new geniuses to evoke the novel in the presentation of the familiar. We need to learn some music history even to appreciate what was so striking about the third symphony at the time it was composed, which is a clear indication of how much aesthetic sensibilities have changed, even among those with a fondness for classical music.

We've now talked about mathematics, cosmology, evolutionary biology, a wide variety of biologically based axiological appraisal systems, and the aesthetics of musical beauty. Let's switch gears to morality. To guide us here, consider Omar Mateen, the probably self-radicalized Islamic extremist, and definitely self-proclaimed ISIS sympathizer, who on June 12, 2016, shot and killed forty-nine people and injured many others in an Orlando club before being shot and killed in a gun battle with police. Some have claimed that Mateen exhibited a pattern of hatred toward gay and lesbian people, and of violent behavior, thereby explaining it as a tragedy of mental instability. People have also put it down to the allegedly violent and intolerant nature of Islam, an assertion typically made without a lot of nuanced historical awareness. In my own axiological analysis of this terrible moment in this country wrestling with religious extremist violence, I want to steer clear of easy reductive explanations and instead honor the research performed by courageous psychologists and anthropologists showing that religious extremists perpetrating violence have the same range of personality, education, and mental health as the regular population. In my view, a necessary step for grasping the axiological nature of this event is to acknowledge frankly that Mateen saw what he did as good—everything was good, from his hatred toward homosexuals to his systematic dehumanizing of victims, from the moral vision that inspired him to his righteous anger at the killing of ISIS fighters, and from his casing possible targets to the actual killings. With that acknowledgment in place, we can go on to understand how goodness could ever be so apprehended and realized.

Axiological landscape theory is particularly well suited to comprehending the alien good because of its sensitivity to context, to individual difference, to the social construction of the good, and to historical lineages of moral determinations that structure moral apprehension. The resulting moral pluralism frustrates some moral philosophers, who correctly judge that it exchanges the sharp edge of prophetic critique and moral orientation for the infinite nausea of perpetually legitimate moral contrasts. That's essentially correct, in my view. Axiological landscape permits but does not dictate a prophetic moral stance for or against what Mateen did; in fact, it affords and grounds both possibilities—what he did, and what the police did to stop him. Whatever prophetic moral stances we adopt, therefore, they cannot be derived from or dictated by axiological landscape theory; they can only be explained by and accommodated within that theory. Naturally, traditional personal theists will not welcome this separation of the axiological grounding of moral possibilities from the concrete apprehension of moral norms suited to governing behavior. A lot of nontheists might not be comfortable with this separation, either.

Axiological landscape theory invites us deeply into the intricacies of the moral ambiguities of life, teaching us how to narrate Mateen's story until we, too, might learn to see the good as he does, even though this experience of axiological empathy underwrites our resolve to resist his vision of the good with every fiber of our being. Axiological landscape theory also helps us see dynamic patterns in structured axiological possibilities, as when repeated lying causes most people to stop trusting me, while being reliable and empathic causes most people to have confidence in me. These dynamic structures don't determine the moral good but they do meaningfully constrain what can be said about the moral good. Thus, axiological landscape theory presumes or implies moral pluralism, moral objectivity, and moral rationality, in respects that sit somewhat awkwardly with many traditional moral theories. This awkwardness of fit is just right, I think.

The public has been exposed to several television series in recent years that drive home moral pluralism, from the realization of moral ambiguity to perspectivalism of moral appraisal. One example is *Game of Thrones*, which the writers self-consciously depict as being centrally about conflicting visions of the good. Another example is *Dexter*, the story of a serial killer with a profoundly unfamiliar moral code. I am fascinated by the impact such television programs may have on moral ways of seeing in the people who watch them. Whatever we say about that, I think such dramatic manifestations of moral pluralism are essentially correct about the moral character of life, which is compactly and richly described in axiological landscape theory. Of course, Schopenhauer and Nietzsche already taught us this, long ago.

As a final example, let's consider an instance of inquiry. To keep things connected, we'll focus on research into religious-extremist violence. There is a seething, squirming vipers pit's worth of conflicting viewpoints about this topic, which means that a host of explanatory hypotheses are inserted into public discussion without enough time or energy to evaluate even a few of them. What does axiological landscape theory say about the nature of religious-extremist violence? Is there a truth to be uncovered in this line of inquiry? Or is axiological landscape theory as pluralistic in regard to truth as it is in regard to morality and aesthetics?

Axiological landscape theory encourages a framework-relative approach to truth. Axiological affordances are complexly multidimensional, and we abstract and simplify this complexity in our engagement of those affordances, as we have seen. Thus, while the meaning of truth is word-world correspondence, neither word nor world is ever comprehensively at our disposal for analysis and inquiry, so correspondence can be assessed in a host of respects—obvious or subtle depending on perspective. This kind of perspectivalism is very far from epistemic relativism. The objectivism of axiological landscape theory permits without determining judgments of better and worse characterizations of a phenomenon such as violent religious extremism. The full truth may be as inexpressible as the affordances engaged in these phenomena are. But framework-relative assertions can be accurate, particularly when they are made with full awareness of the limitations of interest and perspective involved. In short, axiological landscape theory implies moral pluralism, not moral relativism.

Doesn't this correspond to our experience precisely? For example, I can see truth in some sense, from some angle, in most of the perspectives on violent religious extremism I encounter: the liberal haters and the conservative haters, the freedom haters and the authoritarianism haters, the secularism haters and the religion haters. These apparently contradictory truths do not actually conflict when framework dependence is taken into account. This is actual word-world correspondence in action. Axiological landscape theory helps us analyze and track the influence of the conceptual frameworks within which truth claims are made and come to seem internally incorrigible.[8] This relativizes any given truth claim while protecting the objectivity of truth as a kaleidoscopically complex reality sustaining plural moral evaluations.

Conclusion

Axiological landscape theory offers a way to see the entire range and variety of axiological phenomena in a consistent account of value as such. The comprehensiveness and consistency is welcome to the philosophical inquirer but the abstraction associated with any account of anything as such, and value as such above all, must be embraced. In practice this means tolerating its limitations and moving beyond them when possible.

For this reason, general theories of value such as axiological landscape theory can never replace exquisite sensitivity to concrete situations in which values are apprehended and engaged. But then neither can intricate appreciation of axiological details supplant general theories of value.

Notes

1. See Aristotle, *Physics*, Book II, Part 8, in *The Basic Works of Aristotle* (New York: Random House, 1941).

2. See Hesiod, "Theogony," in *Hesiod*, 2 vols., trans. Glenn Most (Cambridge: Loeb Classical Library, 2006–07); Fred Hoyle, *The Black Cloud* (London: William Heinemann, 1957).

3. For works not mentioned elsewhere, see Charles Sanders Peirce, *Values in a Universe of Chance: Selected Writings of Charles S. Peirce*, ed. P. P. Wiener (Mineola, NY: Dover, 1958); Justus Buchler, *Metaphysics of Natural Complexes* (New York: Columbia University Press, 1966); and Robert Cummings Neville, *Normative Cultures, Axiology of Thinking*, Vol. 3 (Albany: State University of New York Press, 1995).

4. Alfred North Whitehead, *Process and Reality: An Essay in Cosmology* [1929], corrected edition, ed. David R. Griffin and Donald W. Sherbourne (New York: Free Press, 1978).

5. Charles Hartshorne, *The Divine Relativity, A Social Conception of God* (New Haven: Yale University Press, 1948).

6. Robert S. Corrington, *A Semiotic Theory of Theology and Philosophy* (Cambridge, UK; New York: Cambridge University Press, 2000).

7. See Friedrich W. Nietzsche, *Beyond Good and Evil: Prelude to a Philosophy of the Future* (Harmondsworth; Baltimore: Penguin, 1973); Arthur Schopenhauer, *The World as Will and Representation* (Mineola, NY: Dover, 1969).

8. See Stephan Körner, *Categorical Frameworks* (Oxford: Blackwell, 1970).

8

Experience and Signs

Toward a Pragmatist Literary Criticism

NICHOLAS GASKILL

Could there be a pragmatist literary criticism? Richard Rorty doesn't seem to think so.[1] The thinkers lumped under "classical pragmatism" made only passing references to literature, and only William James's magpie delight in gathering quotations from Stevenson, Whitman, Tolstoy, and others even approaches an analysis of texts. Why then turn to pragmatism for a method of reading and interpretation? For calisthenics: "Pragmatism unstiffens all our theories, limbers them up and sets each one at work."[2] This essay seeks to put theories of meaning and representation in literary criticism on the stretching bar by reorienting them toward pragmatist conception of process, action, and experience. In particular, it asks "What does a text *do*?" rather than "What does a text *mean*?" and then traces the difference that this difference makes.

Understanding literary meaning in terms of the effects literary texts produce requires the aesthetics of John Dewey and the semiotics of Charles Sanders Peirce. Their related projects emphasize transactive, unfolding experience and suggest that art—through its relation to quality or Firstness—constitutes the means by which immediate experience and its novel possibilities enter into intelligent life. Thus, pragmatist conceptions of art contribute to Deweyan projects of reconstruction: the continual processes of adjusting the elements of an evolving situation toward the creation and realization of meaningful experiences.[3] Where Dewey's *Art as Experience* provides the explicit corrective to aesthetic theories based on the subject or on representation, Peirce's doctrine of signs insists on the distinctness of literary language even as it accounts for its effects in extraliterary procedures. In literary experience or the sign-production event, reader, text, and context enter into a dynamic constellation within which virtual reconstructions of relations are created and pushed forth into future experience. Peirce's artistic signs, Dewey's qualitative binding, George Herbert Mead's "enlarged" personalities, and James's correctives to our "certain blindness" all circulate within the orbit of this conception of literary aesthetics and its connection to life. A pragmatist literary criticism explores these transactive relations and absorbs the effects texts produce in order to generate new concepts, modes of thinking, and ideas that bring the possibilities and affects of literary experience within the reconstructive process of intelligence.

Aesthetics, Quality, Possibility

Peirce and Dewey—consummate men of science as they were—both turned to aesthetics late in their careers to investigate that which precedes, surrounds, and regulates logical inquiry. Yet neither concerned himself with formal criteria or with dealing authoritative judgments upon canonical works, and neither accepted the enshrinement of art apart from the everyday. Rather, they considered the aesthetic as a phase or formation of experience and discussed the arts as points at which the "universe of experience" entered into the "universe of discourse." Dewey's aesthetic theory, based on his transactive notion of experience, offers pragmatist strategies for reconstructing our accounts of art. Peirce's semiotic, based on his transactive triadic sign, sets these strategies within the realm of sign-production and interpretation. Combined, these discourses constitute a starting point for a pragmatist literary criticism, one that attends to the effects produced within an aesthetic experience permeated by Deweyan quality and Peircean possibility.

Above all else, Dewey's aesthetic theory disposes of false distinctions between art and everyday life. Even his title speaks this message: *Art as Experience*. The idea stirs him to rare lyrical images, as in his appropriation of the Romantic trope of the mountain top. "Mountain peaks do not float unsupported," Dewey explains; "they do not even just rest upon the earth. They *are* the earth in one of its manifest operations." Likewise, the "refined" qualities of aesthetic experience do not hover in an ethereal realm beyond what we commonly call experience; instead, they are experience in one of its forms.[4] Specifically, the aesthetic denotes "the clarified and intensified development of traits that belong to every normally complete experience;" its characteristics are shared by all experience, though in less palpable or less realized manners (*LW*, 10:53). Dewey thus directs attention away from art objects and toward the experiences art makes available by redefining the "the actual work of art" as "what the product does with and in experience" (*LW*, 10:3). He gives art the Peircean pragmatist workout; he asks, "what effects, that might conceivably have practical bearings,"[5] artworks have and locates the meaning of our conception of art in these effects.

Dewey's claims about aesthetic experience and works of art rely on his philosophy of transactional experience. The Darwinian model of life as the unfolding of, and adaptation to, chance variations provided Dewey with an image of experience as the mutually constitutive interaction of an agent and an environment. Such a model sees individual subjects and objects not as primary elements but as the results of a reflective process that returns to and divides up an experience. Thus, Dewey substituted "transaction" for "interaction," as the latter still smacked of substance-based thinking. Pragmatism is all process. It recognizes change and variation as rules rather than exceptions, and it counts a creative capacity for novel adaptation among the characteristic features of experience. Experience grows, and as it does so it holds a relation to its own unfolding, its own capacity to become something other than it is. Call this the relation to the possible.[6] Discrete elements of a situation exist as virtual possibilities that might be actualized, though within experience they are indistinguishable. Experience is not subjective, though it does have possible subjects in it. Dewey needs this account of "pure" experience for his philosophy of effective human action; his empiricism, like James's, must be radical.[7] For our efforts to make a difference, the world must be in process and the future must not be settled. A transactional notion of experience thus prepares the way for a concrete program of action. For his theory of art, this means that aesthetic experiences create new, unprecedented modes of experience and manners of living in relation to the qualities, contexts, and readers involved.[8]

Peirce's semiotic shares with Dewey's experience-based aesthetic this emphasis on process and transactive situations. He defines a sign as that which stands in a triadic relation *to* an "object" and *for* an "interpretant," and he refers to the material element within this relation—what we might call the "signifier"—as the "representamen." A Peircean "sign," then, denotes the dynamic interaction between representamen, interpretant, and object within a particular use or context, called the "ground."[9] It refers to the *action* of signs, the sign-event, which always includes sign-production since an interpretant in one sign enters into new contexts as a representamen. The nature of signs is to move, to grow, to produce more signs; Peirce's universe is a sign-producing machine. But the world is not a linguistic text, and there is plenty "outside" of words. Of Peirce's ten classes of signs, only three apply to language. Another version of the definition helps to explain: a sign is "anything which is so determined by something else, called its Object, and so determines an effect upon a person, which effect I call its interpretant, that the latter is thereby mediately determined by the former."[10] Signs create and register *effects*, ranging from those produced by a red room to those produced by an imagist poem. Peirce makes clear that phenomenal effects should not be conceived of as simply subjective: "just as a rainbow is at once a manifestation both of the sun and of the rain," so are signs effects of all their various elements (5:283). He abandons the logic of representation and correspondence, a logic that has no place in a world of becoming. His semiotics deals with the constituents of signs in their dynamic processes, just as Dewey's aesthetics begins with the transactive aesthetic experience in its unfolding.

Dewey and Peirce provide a way of looking at art as a distinct phase of experience—or category of sign-production—that is nonetheless continuous with, and dynamically related to, other modes of life. They emphasize that meaning resides in process and in the dynamic relations of elements in a situation and thus call us to abandon aesthetic inquiries based on, or directed toward, autonomous "texts" or "readers" or "language" and instead engage the relations and modes of experience literature makes available.[11] But before looking at the effects literary experience produces in nonliterary realms, we must elaborate the characteristics of experience that pragmatism marks as the source of art: what Peirce calls Firstness and Dewey calls quality.

Peirce thinks in threes. Throughout his career he developed three basic categories that received several different inflections depending on the type of inquiry to which they were applied. In brief, Firstness is the category of quality, Secondness of actual existents, and Thirdness of laws or mediating relations. As phenomenological—or, in Peirce's preferred term, phaneroscopical—Firstness refers to "certain qualities of feeling, such as the color of magenta, the odor of attar, the sound of a railway whistle," as separate from their actual instantiation in objects (1:304). As such, a First is a "mere may-be" that might become embodied, a virtual possibility that does not inhere in a subject (1:303–304). It is "an immediate, uninterpreted, qualitative aspect of a phenomenon" that cannot appear in experience as such but must be "prescinded"—or abstracted—from objects (Seconds).[12] Peirce sees Firstness as flowing throughout and around experience, undergirding consciousness and yet unable to appear in thought. "[T]he Immediate (and therefore in itself unsusceptible of mediation—the Unanalyzable, the Inexplicable, the Unintellectual) runs in a continuous stream through our lives," he explains; "it is the sum total of consciousness," but it only enters thought by being submitted to a Third (5:289). Firsts function as the virtual elements in experience that may be actualized within actual events or objects, and literary language strikes a distinctive balance between the immediacy of Firstness and the intelligibility of Thirdness. Aesthetics is the "science of possibility."[13]

John Dewey developed Peirce's notion of Firstness under the name of "quality" in "Qualitative Thought," a 1930 essay that builds on Dewey's first serious thoughts about art in *Experience and Nature* (1925) and generates key concepts for *Art as Experience* (1934). Dewey begins the article as a critique of subject-predicate logic that follows from his commitment to transactive experience. He claims that attributes such as "red" or "sweet" are qualities that pervade a situation rather than attributes that belong to an object, and he explains that when thought returns to an experience and differentiates its elements—for example, into "sweet" and "that thing"—it transforms quality into an object within a different sort of experience. It moves from a First to a Third. Dewey likens the realm of quality to "the big, buzzing, blooming confusion of which James wrote" and specifies this expression as referring to "not only the state of a baby's experience but the first stage and background of all thinking on any subject." Firstness flows through our lives; it precedes and surrounds consciousness. Yet quality as such is not "merely buzzing and blooming"; "[i]t buzzes to some effect; it blooms toward some fruitage."[14] It binds the elements of an experience and moves them toward some goal. Dewey goes so far as to argue that all felt association—which informs logical association—depends on qualitative binding. "The only way that form or pattern can operate as an immediate link," he maintains, "is by the mode of a directly experienced *quality,* something present and prior to and independent of all reflective analysis, something of the same nature which controls artistic construction" (*LW,* 5:259). Earlier, Dewey specifies this "logic of artistic construction" as "the logic of what I have called qualitative thinking," and he explains that the "material of the fine arts consists in qualities" (*LW*, 5:251; *LW*, 10:45). Art trucks in quality, and because situations in their qualitative unity shape the direction and nature of thought, aesthetics precedes logic. Peirce thought likewise, and even situated his version of creative intuition—abduction—at the initial stage of scientific inquiry.[15]

Pragmatist aesthetics supplements and nourishes logical inquiry by investigating the world of qualitative Firstness that antecedes and influences discourse. In this view, art "gives us symbols that make us aware of more of our experience in the world of signs," which, as Peirce makes plain, is broader than the signs of language use or even of conscious thought.[16] Dewey and Peirce never worry that literary analysis might expose our conscious lives as hopelessly trapped in linguistic signs. Rather, they assert that a "universe of experience . . . surrounds and regulates the universe of discourse" and that even though it "never appears as such within the latter," it affects it at its frontier: art.[17]

Literature, Sensation, Relations

To claim for the visual arts and for music a relation to Firstness and ineffable quality is one thing. To affirm as much for literature seems quite another. Dewey insists that "[i]t cannot be asserted too strongly that what is not immediate is not esthetic." But how can language, which is complete mediation—thoroughly Third—fit the bill? For Dewey, the trick lies in disposing of the idea that "only certain *special* things—those attached to eye, ear, etc.—can be qualitatively and immediately experienced" and in accepting James's contention that relations are real and vividly experienced (*LW*, 10:123). He argues that James's recognition of the deep and intimate experiences we have of conjunctions helped philosophy to see that even mediating or "abstract" elements in experience can be vividly "had."[18] Dewey finds proof for James's radical revision of empiricism in "[e]very work of art that ever existed," and he claims that one of literature's lessons for philosophy is the intricate way in which intellect and sensation are bound in experience (*LW*, 10:125). This curious mix of sensation and language allows pragmatism to set forth an account of literature based on the new modes of living—constellations of relations and patterns of relating—created within aesthetic experience.

Poets have long recognized the corporeal effects of literary language. Emily Dickinson reported, "If I read a book and it makes my whole body so cold no fire can ever warm me, I know that is poetry. If I feel physically as if the top of my head were taken off, I know that is poetry."[19] Dewey acknowledges such signs as indications of poetry, but he refuses to go so far as to agree with A. E. Housman's contention—compatible with Dickinson's criteria—that poetry is "more physical than intellectual."[20] Rather, he sees literature as the successful fusion of the intellectual and sensual; it "absorbs the intellectual into immediate qualities that are experienced through the senses that belong to the vital body." We experience poetry both immediately and intelligently, and "words serve their poetic purpose in the degree in which they summon and evoke into active operation the vital responses that are present whenever we experience qualities" (*LW*, 10:220). Literature hits our whole person because its interpretant "has the mode of being of Firstness."[21] It has the form of a Third (symbolic, linguistic) with the force of a First.[22] Thus, literary signs do not refer to or represent an experience; they "constitute one" (*LW*, 10:91).[23]

This relation to qualitative Firstness not only enables literature's effects on the vital body but also constitutes its relation to possibility. A First is a mere may-be unconnected to actual events or existents and "can only accede to the 'object' level through a *chance* activation of its possibility in the imagination."[24] Literature's fictive elements solicit and demand the imagination's participation in ways that engage qualities not actually existing in the world and instantiates them within and through the aesthetic experience. As such, literary language is neither true nor false; it is creative and the configurations that it offers are novel, undetermined, and forceful because of this relation to Firstness as quality and possibility. The pragmatist imagination thus resembles Bergsonian intuition: an unreflective response to the virtual elements of an evolving situation rather than a fanciful adventure into unearthly realms.[25] It involves locating and arranging undetermined elements of an event toward the end of reconstructing relations in a consummatory experience—vital moments of enjoyed meanings that then direct and influence future projects. Like the related concepts of abduction, intuition, and qualitative thought, pragmatist imagination precedes logical reasoning and exists merely as "had" rather than as well reasoned or understood. It may remain ineffable and be "unexpressed in definite ideas which form reasons and justifications" and "yet [be] profoundly right" (*LW*, 5:249).[26] While all of our experiences have an imaginative element to them, encounters with literary texts foreground the life-functions of arranging and selecting aspects of a situation such that Dewey insists on their ability to offer new modes of experience. Throughout *Art as Experience*, he claims that art creates and constitutes "unprecedented object[s]" of "new experience," and what might appear as a tired argument for a mystical quality of literature should be understood within the pragmatist emphasis on reconstructive action in a world thick with habits (*LW*, 10:95).[27] In other words, Dewey recognizes that some situations comprise elements more malleable than others, and he holds that the fictive qualities of literature make for especially plastic and open-ended experiences. The linguistic medium has everything to do with this capacity. Dewey describes the material of the language arts as "charged with meanings . . . absorbed through immemorial time" and thereby endowed with "an intellectual force superior to that of any other art" (*LW*, 10:244). He celebrates the ability of words to "preserve and report the values of all the varied experiences of the past, and to follow . . . every changing shade of feeling and idea," and he argues that literature's "combinations and permutations" of its medium have the "power to create a new experience, often times . . . more poignantly felt than that which comes from things themselves" (*LW*, 10:245). Because literary signs combine the intensity of Firstness with the meanings of Thirdness, they lend to art the ability to control and to create experiences full of sensation infused with the "funded meanings" of past experience. Dewey follows the pragmatist precedent of recognizing the force of "the animal life below the human scale" but also looking for ways to direct such experiences toward meaningful—that is, intelligently apprehended and enjoyed—reconstructions that contribute to the social process (*LW*, 10:24).[28] Literary language carries the fullness of sense but in a medium more resonant with the ways in which we carry out our intelligent lives.

Literature accomplishes this clarification and reconfiguration of the processes of living by experimenting both with the relations in experience and with our modes of relating.[29] As mentioned earlier, pragmatism insists that relations are real and constitutive. Changing the relations in which a thing stands to other things creates something new. Of course, there are limits to how radical these reconstructions can be—Dewey knows that the world pushes back—but the Darwinian emphasis on mutually adaptive organisms participating in an evolving environment leads pragmatism to emphasize the relational character of processual identity. As experience develops, new relations emerge and with them new meanings and possibilities. Mead's favorite illustration is organic: with the appearance of a certain kind of gastrointestinal organ-system, grass becomes "food," and a new meaning and relation enters the world.[30] Dewey prefers to emphasize cultural developments: "Some existent material was perceived in the light of relations and possibilities not hitherto realized when the steam engine was invented. But when the imagined possibilities were embodied in a new assemblage of natural materials, the steam engine took its place in nature as an object that has the same physical effects as those belonging to any other physical object" (*LW*, 10:277). Within aesthetic experiences of literature, new configurations of relations between immediately felt ideas, the reader, and her context emerge and take "[their] place in nature." These bindings occur through the creation and direction of a quality made to pervade the situation in which these elements come together. As mentioned above, Dewey argues that associations only come about through such qualitative binding; they begin not with logical reasoning but with an intuition of "a directly experienced *quality,* something present and prior to and independent of all reflective analysis" (*LW*, 5:259). In aesthetic constructions, we often recognize this binding quality as emotion, "the moving and cementing force" that "selects what is congruous and dyes what is selected with its color, thereby giving qualitative unity to materials externally disparate and dissimilar" (*LW*, 10:49).[31] Every use of metaphor involves an intuition of a pervading quality that transverses two ideas, objects, or experiences and "assimilates" them to one another (*LW*, 5:261). Such language fosters new aggregates of the elements of pure experience and adds them to the world; each reading of a poem, Dewey insists, "creates something new, something previously not existing in experience" (*LW*, 10:113).

This qualitative embedding of elements within an aesthetic experience "intensifies and clarifies" the selection and reconfiguration that characterize everyday mechanisms of attention. Thus, literature offers new styles of life by creating new possibilities for feeling and perceiving, new manners of attending to the world. In an experience of literary signs, a reader's transaction with these affects and percepts modifies the relations she recognizes and pursues; the qualitative constellations made palpable in the aesthetic experience change the reader's *modes of relating* to both self and environment. These modes are multiple and involve our ways of feeling, thinking, and associating in the world.

Peirce understood the qualitative links in aesthetic experience to associate sensations and affects, and his characterization of the literary sign emphasizes art's capacity to modify both our affective investments and our manners of thinking. Because the interpretant within a literary sign-event has the character of a First, the experience of such signs contributes to the cultivation of what Peirce calls "habits of feeling" (1:574). Qualitative glue joins the reader with new objects or affects in the world and causes her to *feel* connections previously dumb or insensible. We need only look as far as advertising to recognize the ways in which qualities of aesthetic constructions continue to create non-preexisting connections to the end of establishing habits. And these tactics remind us that ways of feeling can issue in behavior and action. The same goes for ways of thinking: Peirce's formula for establishing the meaning of a thought process is "simply to determine what habits it produces" (5:400). Because thinking for Peirce consists in creating relations between sensations, ideas, states of feeling, and so forth, it receives a jolt when art shifts our experience of the world's relations. The intense and qualitatively controlled experiences afforded by literary signs thus have the power to shift our perspective—to "move" us—enough to modify the belief systems that affect our undertakings and investments. It is not that this only happens in art. It is that within aesthetic experiences, which have often—but not always—been linked to "art objects," the normal processes of attention and selection are focused to the end of producing a more concentrated or marked instance of the emergent properties of one situation guiding the reconstruction of another.[32] Sign-events always press forward; they spill into other contexts, setting the terms and influencing the relations. Literary signs, Peirce explains, provide opportunities to adjust our associations of feeling and our ways of thinking about ourselves and our responsibilities; they participate in the construction of habits that issue in action. . . .

Criticism, Theory, Philosophy

When works of art are successful, Dewey asserts, their creators "are entitled . . . to the gratitude that we give to inventors of microscopes and microphones; in the end, they open new objects to be observed and enjoyed." Artists offer new ways of perceiving and feeling the world, and critics, we might add, are those who have learned how to deploy the "modes of perception" and the styles of experience these instruments make available.[33] They offer instruction manuals, user's guides that demonstrate how a text's creations might be implemented in the world. These guides are pragmatist when they begin with the aesthetic experience and articulate "what a work of art is *as an experience*" rather than how an art product matches up to a predetermined criterion (*LW*, 10:313; emphasis added). They investigate the *effects* of a literary work, often by conjoining it to other texts, contexts, and events and considering what is produced. With the help of theory, pragmatist criticism uses the possibilities and qualities of literature to stimulate thought and to focus inquiry.

Pragmatism insists on the continuity of literature and life; therefore, it promotes an engaged criticism that both articulates the modes of experience rendered in works of art and follows the extratextual effects they produce. These goals require an immanent means of evaluation and demand techniques that can apprehend the connective movements of an aesthetic experience in its growth. Dewey argues that successful critics follow the development of aesthetic quality and then wed this understanding with propositional statements that lead readers to more vivid experiences of literary texts. Their interpretations and analyses of formal techniques connect with the initial text and "effect a heightening and deepening of a qualitative apprehension" (*LW*, 5:251). Critics help readers to think qualitatively and to take on the modes of feeling and perceiving that artists create, and we count those critics best who make possible more productive or desirable experiences of literary works. Yet a particular text contains the potential to activate any number of modes of experience; there is no one "life" behind a literary work. Thus, critics do not seek to establish the meaning of a text but rather to produce meanings—with meaning understood pragmatically as effects. Note the balancing act: pragmatist criticism recognizes the importance of context and the dynamic, power-laden, and situational interactions within which meaning is produced at the same time that it addresses the "objective" elements of a text to anchor claims and direct readers.[34] There are some relations and reconstitutions a poem simply will not sustain; texts, like other things in the world, push back.

This attention to the formal elements of a text must be understood as an emphasis on what particular styles, genres, techniques, and syntaxes do within an aesthetic experience rather than as a taxonomy of properties belonging to texts-in-themselves. Dewey terms this latter formalism "legalistic" or "judicial criticism" as it tends to impose a preexisting set of criteria that deems a work good or bad. These academic modes affect a posture of critical distance that Dewey claims is neither possible nor desirable when discussing works of art. Pseudoscientific stances in criticism subject texts to extraneous rules or totalizing ideas that occlude the experiences texts make available and stunt any productive possibilities of literature. (In this regard, recent ideological modes are as guilty as the conservative "great works" tradition of Dewey's time.) Dewey therefore names "the source of failure of even the best of judicial criticism" as "its inability to cope with the emergence of new modes of life—of experiences that demand new modes of expression" (*LW*, I0:307). Pragmatism invites critics to connect with literary texts, to explore the styles of life immanent to them, and to extend the effects they might have. Far from leaving a poem on the dissection table, it puts literature to work in the world and follows the transformations of the affective and intellectual currents it produces.[35]

Within this critical program, literary analysis examines the nuances of language not to make a claim about the failure of signification or to emphasize poetic slips in meaning but rather to consider what particular uses of language set in motion.[36] We have already seen how Peirce's semiotics—in emphasizing the process of sign-events in which an interpretant of one sign becomes the representamen of another—makes sense of how literary texts produce new signs that circulate in nonliterary events. Critics working from this model would both follow and advance the mobility of signs by attending to the contextual connections surrounding works and by setting them in new constellations. Of course, the conjugation of literary and nonliterary texts is quite familiar; the pragmatist addition is to think of these combinations as creating new effects and possibilities in their own right. Furthermore, pragmatism's twin emphases on real relations that constitute identity and on modes of relating that comprise thinking and consciousness endow the configurations that emerge from critical productions with ontological weight. Peirce's description of the meaning of thought can thus be applied to the meaning of criticism: "[N]o present actual thought (which is a mere feeling) has any meaning, any intellectual value; for this lies not in what is actually thought, but in what this thought may be connected with in representation by subsequent thoughts" (5:289). Criticism explores the value of the "mere feelings" rendered in literature by investigating the ways in which the signs they produce might form relations with other signs.

The transformative constellations produced by criticism involve the extraction of affects and percepts from literary works to be employed in the philosophic construction of concepts.[37] Critics take the qualitative Firstness characteristic of aesthetic productions and then create logical tools of thought worthy of these sensory and affective complexes. James performs such an operation in "On a Certain Blindness in Humans" when he looks to Walt Whitman to articulate a particular manner of existing in the modern world. He locates in Whitman's writings a way of enjoying felt relations contrary to practical or economic standards of value: "[C]onsidered either practically or academically," Whitman is "a worthless unproductive being."[38] Yet in his ability to "be rapt with satisfied attention . . . to the mere spectacle of the world's presence" he constitutes "one way, and the most fundamental way, of confessing one's sense of its unfathomable significance and importance."[39] Once James has pulled from Whitman this rapturous, panoramic mode of seeing the world and feeling the crowd, he considers what it might do for ethical philosophy.[40] In particular, he suggests that the Whitmanian ability to bring life "down to the non-thinking level, the level of pure sensorial perception" helps us to respect "the significance of alien lives" and to adjust our social behavior accordingly (W, 857, 841). Throughout the essay, James turns to literature—Stevenson, Wordsworth, and Tolstoy in addition to Whitman—to address the problem of "the blindness with which we all are afflicted in regard to the feelings of creatures and people different from ourselves" and to find a mode of experience suited to ethical living in the modern world (W, 841).

James's contention, gleaned from Whitman, that thought can be aided by the "non-thinking" demonstrates the conception of philosophy at the heart of a pragmatist literary theory. In short, philosophy needs art. Just as thinking requires the buzzing, blooming world of quality and the active subject requires the transactive experience of nonidentity, so too do the ventures of philosophy need the "unique control" of art (LW, 1 0:301). Literary theory is simply philosophy that allows itself to be so controlled. Its project is to think and to think clearly, but it remains open to the nonphilosophical intuitions about the nature of experience made most manifest in our encounters with art. By drawing from literature, theory seeks to "enrich and clarify current impoverished notions of rationality, by restoring to it its affective and imaginative components."[41] Because it views literature not as a separate realm but as an intensification of the characteristics of everyday life that make visible the workings of all experience, pragmatist literary theory applies its lessons from literature to the reconstructive projects applicable to our contemporary cultural and political scene. It builds on an aesthetic grounded in experience and thus, by its engagements with the modes of experience rendered in literary works, equips itself "to indicate the factors and forces that favor the normal development of common human activities into matters of artistic value" (*LW*, 10:17). In this way, pragmatist theory continues Dewey's project of reconstructing the unrealized or dumb activities of life into intelligent, community projects. Through theory, pragmatism proclaims, we learn to make our lives and our communities works of art.[42]

In this light, Dewey and Peirce are at their most pragmatist when they turn to art.[43] Their respective aesthetics work to "unstiffen" their theories of logic and science, and to bring out the qualities of experience that might be redirected and reshaped toward productive social ends. Pragmatism does not allow artworks to languish in an ethereal realm or an ivory tower. It "sets each one at work," treating it as a quality or style of experiencing the world that might feed back into philosophy and keep it in vital connection with present social problems.[44] Pragmatist critics would work for these ends, investigating the manner by which literature's effects might be directed to cultivate efficacious habits in individuals and communities. They would begin with the thoughts of James, Peirce, Dewey, and Mead but draw equally from any traditions that proved efficacious for setting in motion the possibilities of a text. Their method would help mark criticism's unique contribution to the community project without falling into overly grandiose claims and, in so doing, it might stake out the difference that literature makes.

Notes

1. In an interview published as "Worlds or Words Apart? The Consequences of Pragmatism for Literary Studies," Edward Ragg asks Rorty if he thinks that "pragmatism . . . has certain things to recommend to people studying literature." The latter, with characteristic nonchalance, replies: "No, I guess I don't." Richard Rorty, *Take Care of Freedom and Truth Will Take Care of Itself: Interviews with Richard Rorty*, ed. Eduardo Mendieta (Stanford: Stanford University Press, 2005), 125.

2. William James, *Writings, 1902-1910* (New York: Library of America, 1987), 510.

3. "Reconstruction" runs throughout Dewey's wide body of work, and in each case it refers to the human capacity to reshape the emerging world so as to bring the dumb, inarticulate aspects of experience under intelligent control. Within the reconstructive process, an individual acts "as the agent who is responsible through initiative, inventiveness and intelligently directed labor for recreating the world, transforming it into an instrument and possession of intelligence." John

Dewey, *Reconstruction in Philosophy* (1920), in *The Middle Works, 1899–1924*, ed. Jo Ann Boydston (Carbondale: Southern Illinois University Press, 1976), 12:108.

4. Dewey, *Art as Experience* (1934), in *The Later Works, 1925–1953*, ed. Jo Ann Boydston (Carbondale: Southern Illinois University Press, 1981), 10:9. Subsequently cited as *LW*, 10.

5. Charles Sanders Peirce, *Collected Papers*, vols. 1–6, ed. Charles Hartshorne and Paul Weiss, vols. 7–8, ed. Arthur Burks (Cambridge: Harvard University Press, 1931–35, 1958), 5:402. Parenthetical citations for Peirce's *Collected Papers* will follow the conventional method of volume number followed by page number.

6. In *Parables for the Virtual: Movement, Affect, Sensation* (Durham: Duke University Press, 2002), Brian Massumi names this relation of a thing or experience to its own becoming-other in the process of growth "the virtual." He also attends more rigorously to the philosophic distinction between the possible and the potential. According to his definitions, I am speaking of the "potential," "the immanence of a thing to its still indeterminate variation, under way" (9). However, I will continue to use "possibility" in order to keep the terms those of the pragmatists.

7. These sentences attempt to make sense of an apparent split in pragmatist thinking. On the one hand, the classical pragmatists are concerned with effective human action in the world, and this project requires a responsible subject pursuing coherent projects. On the other, they are deeply interested in a vision of a subjective experience from which subjects emerge. Witness the "unpersonalized feeling" of Peirce's Firstness (6:33), the "pure experience" of James's radical empiricism, and the "I" or the "biologic individual" in George Herbert Mead. Rather than try to dismiss the half that seems more mystical (as Rorty asks us to do in "Dewey between Hegel and Darwin"), I argue that the belief in the impersonal quality of experience allows the pragmatists to introduce a radical novelty into their philosophy of action and to make sense of our ethical connections to the lives of others. Rorty, *Philosophical Papers*, vol. 3, *Truth and Progress* (Cambridge: Cambridge University Press, 1998), 290–306.

8. For a thorough and illuminating account of Dewey's aesthetic in light of his other writing, see Thomas M. Alexander, *John Dewey's Theory of Art, Experience, and Nature: Horizons of Feeling* (Albany: State University of New York Press, 1987) and his "The Art of Life: Dewey's Aesthetics," in *Reading Dewey: Interpretations for a Postmodern Generation*, ed. Larry Hickman (Bloomington: Indiana University Press, 1998), 1–22.

9. Too many others have devoted their time to translating Peirce's esoteric vocabulary into more familiar terms—for example, those of Ludwig Wittgenstein and Roman Jakobson—for this study to dwell on such connections. Suffice it to say that Peirce's triadic sign acts differently from Saussure's dyadic one. For helpful "translation" work, see Gérard Deledalle's *Charles S. Peirce's Philosophy of Signs: Essays in Comparative Semiotics* (Bloomington: Indiana University Press, 2000).

Also see parts 7 and 8 of *Peirce's Doctrine of Signs: Theory, Applications, and Connections*, ed. Vincent Colapietro and Thomas Oshewsky (New York: Mouton de Gruyter, 1996) and Thomas Winner's "Peirce and Literary Studies with Special Emphasis on the Theories of the Prague Linguistic Circle," in *Peirce and Value Theory: On Peircean Ethics and Aesthetics*, ed. Herman Parret (Philadelphia: John Benjamins, 1994), 277–300.

10. Charles S. Peirce, *The Essential Peirce: Selected Philosophical Writings*, vol. 2 (1893–1913), ed. the Peirce Edition Project (Bloomington: Indiana University Press, 1991), 478.

11. John K. Sheriff helpfully frames the implications these ideas have for literary criticism: "Peirce's demonstration of the interdependence of imagination and reality, private choices and public signs . . . subjectivity and objectivity—as equals—shows that many of the problems that have plagued literary studies are artificial problems deriving from misguided efforts to define readers, texts, or language as autonomous and to define correct understanding or interpretation as completed objective fact." John K. Sheriff, *The Fate of Meaning: Charles Peirce, Structuralism, and Literature* (Princeton: Princeton University Press, 1989), 138–39.

12. Carl R. Hausman, "Charles Peirce's Categories, Phenomenological and Ontological," in *Categories: Historical and Systematic Essays*, ed. Michael Gorman and Jonathan J. Sanford, Studies in Philosophy and the History of Philosophy, vol. 41 (Washington, DC: The Catholic University of America Press, 2004), 101.

13. Pere Salabert, "Aesthetic Experience in Charles S. Peirce: The Threshold," in *Peirce and Value Theory*, ed. Parret, 196.

14. Dewey, "Qualitative Thought" (1930) in *Later Works, 1925–1953*, 5:254. Subsequent citations will appear parenthetically as *LW*, 5.

15. When Peirce distinguishes the three normative sciences of aesthetics, ethics, and logic, he explains that "Ethics . . . must appeal to Esthetics for aid in determining the *summum bonum*" and that Logic "must appeal to ethics for its principles" (1:191). Elsewhere, he claims that "[e]sthetics . . . appears to be possibly the first indispensable propedeutic to logic" (2:199). For commentaries on the place of aesthetics in Peirce's thought, see sections 2 and 3 of the aforementioned collection by Parret.

16. Sheriff, *The Fate of Meaning*, 90.

17. Dewey, *Logic: A Theory of Inquiry* (1938), in *Later Works, 1925–1953*, 12:74.

18. James sets forth this founding principle of radical empiricism in "Does 'Consciousness' Exist?" and elaborates on conjunctive relations in "A World of Pure Experience" (*Writings, 1902–1910*). His insight resonates with Peirce's scholastic realism and his adamant contention that laws and relations (Thirds) are every bit as real as objects or qualities.

19. Emily Dickinson, *Letters*, ed. Thomas Johnson (Cambridge, MA: Belknap Press, 1958), 2:474.

20. A. E. Housman, *The Name and Nature of Poetry* (New York: Macmillan, 1933), 45.

21. Sheriff, *The Fate of Meaning*, 76.

22. Not surprisingly, Peirce had a name and a class for this type of sign: a Symbolic Rheme, class-8 (2:261). For a discussion of art in terms of this class of signs, see Sheriff, ch. 5.

23. Elsewhere, Dewey brings out the distinction between scientific and literary language by comparing the way that they deal with emotion. "In reality," he explains, "poet and novelist have an immense advantage over even an expert psychologist in dealing with an emotion. For the former build up a concrete situation and permit *it* to evoke emotional response," and the latter merely provide "a description" (*LW*, 10:73).

24. Salabert, "Aesthetic Experience," 198.

25. When explaining "intuition" in "Qualitative Thought," Dewey flatly states, "Bergson's contention that intuition precedes conception and goes deeper is correct" (*LW*, 5:249).

26. For other pragmatist accounts of imagination and its relation to literary studies, see Gilles Gunn's "The Pragmatics of the Aesthetic" and Winifried Fluck's discussions of the "fictive" in "Pragmatism and Aesthetic Experience," both in "Pragmatism and Literary Studies," ed. Winifried Fluck, special issue, *REAL: The Yearbook of Research in English and American Literature* 15 (1999): 3–19, 227–42.

27. Dewey claims that when an artist extracts an element of experience and reconstellates it within a work of art, it "becomes a qualitative part of a new qualitative design" by virtue of "its new relationships" (*LW*, 10:102). Likewise, he states that "[t]hrough art, meanings of objects that are otherwise dumb, inchoate, restricted, and resisted are clarified and concentrated, and not by thought working laboriously upon them, nor by escape into a world of mere sense, but by creation of a new experience" (*LW*, 10:138).

28. This emphasis can be traced from Dewey's pedagogical writings on "play" through his turn to aesthetics in the 1920s and 1930s.

29. "The limits of . . . esthetic potential," Dewey explains, "can be determined only experimentally and by what artists make out of it in practice" (*LW*, 10:292).

30. George Herbert Mead, *Mind, Self, and Society from the Standpoint of a Social Behaviorist* (Chicago: University of Illinois Press, 1934), 215.

31. Because these emotions are "attached to events and objects in their movement" (*LW*, 10:48), they function like Brian Massumi's "affects:" the "life-glue of matter" that binds elements in a situation in their movements of growing-together (Massumi, *Parables for the Virtual*, 227).

32. *Art as Experience* makes plain the way in which aesthetic experience is not limited to art objects. For a version of pragmatist aesthetics that focuses on this democratization of aesthetic experience, see Richard Shusterman, *Pragmatist Aesthetics: Living Beauty, Rethinking Art*, 2nd ed. (Lanham, MD: Rowman

and Littlefield, 2000). For a more recent account of the continuity between the aesthetic and the everyday, see Hans Ulrich Gumbrecht, "Aesthetic Experience in Everyday Worlds: Reclaiming an Unredeemed Utopian Motif," *New Literary History* 32, no. 2 (2006): 299–318.

33. Dewey, *Experience and Nature* (1925), in *The Later Works, 1925–1953*, 1:293.

34. Peirce's doctrine of signs expresses this idea by insisting that the relations between the elements of the triadic sign are controlled by a "ground."

35. I have in mind Walter Benjamin's claim, in "Surrealism: The Last Snapshot of the European Intelligentsia," that "intellectual currents can generate a sufficient head of water for the critic to install his power station on them." Walter Benjamin, *Reflections: Essays, Aphorisms, Autobiographical Writings*, trans. Edmund Jephcott, ed. Peter Demetz (New York: Harcourt, Brace, Jovanovich, 1978), 177. Pragmatist criticism directs its attention to the nature of the current, the mechanisms of transference, and the operations and objects the energy powers.

36. It is on this point that my version of pragmatist literary criticism diverges most sharply from Richard Poirier's. In *Poetry and Pragmatism* (Cambridge: Harvard University Press, 1992), Poirier construes pragmatism as a way of using language, one that maintains a skepticism of its tools. "If pragmatism works," he claims, "then it works the way poetry does—by effecting a change in language, a change carried out entirely *within* language, and for the benefit of those destined to inherit the language." His emphasis on "the actual inadequacy of language to the task of representing reality" and his claim that pragmatism "shies away" from "historical crises" puts his readings at odds with my own attention to a "universe of experience" that surrounds the "universe of discourse" and to the extratextual effects rendered by styles of writing (132, 133). In brief, Poirier's is a pragmatism of the linguistic turn based on Emerson and James; mine is one of transactive experience and semiotic production rooted in Dewey and Peirce.

37. The language here, though true to the pragmatists, is that of Gilles Deleuze. Indeed, Deleuze has done more for articulating a pragmatics of literary criticism than any of the American "neopragmatists." In particular, see Gilles Deleuze, *Essays Critical and Clinical*, trans. Daniel W. Smith and Michael A. Greco (Minneapolis: University of Minnesota Press, 1997) and "On the Superiority of Anglo-American Literature," in *Dialogues*, trans. Hugh Tomlinson and Barbara Habberjam (London: Athlone Press, 1987) for his idea of a "literary clinic" and for his thoughts on pragmatism. *What Is Philosophy?* (New York: Columbia University Press, 1994), coauthored with Felix Guattari, addresses the relation between the production of affects and percepts in art and their reconstellation in philosophy into concepts.

38. William James, *Writings, 1878–1899* (New York: Library of America, 1992), 851 (hereafter cited as *W*).

39. Alan Trachtenberg offers a perceptive reading of the "processual" mode of perception that Whitman develops and that James appropriates, in "Whitman's Lesson of the City," collected in *Lincoln's Smile and Other Enigmas* (New York: Hill and Wang, 2007), 125–39.

40. Victorino Tejera, "The Primacy of the Aesthetic in Peirce and Classical American Philosophy," in *Peirce and Value Theory*, ed. Parett, 95.

41. Theory and criticism are not essentially separate, though their functions might be differentiated. In the above account, theory should be understood as directing and enabling the extracting tools of criticism, just as criticism grounds theory and acts as its necessary interface with literature. It is not within the scope of this essay to detail the ways in which a pragmatist approach would address important topics in contemporary theory and criticism. Suffice it to say that the philosophy of pragmatism has key concepts to contribute to theoretical disputes about identity, ideology, and culture and that a pragmatist literary criticism would draw from novels, poems, plays, and so forth to refine these concepts and to test their limits.

42. For other critics who counter the argument—favored by many neo-pragmatists—that pragmatism goes astray when it turns to aesthetics, see Ross Posnock, *The Trial of Curiosity: Henry James, William James, and the Challenge of Modernity* (New York: Oxford University Press, 1991); Jonathon Levin, *The Poetics of Transition: Emerson, Pragmatism, and American Literary Modernism* (Durham: Duke University Press, 1999); and Joan Richardson, *A Natural History of Pragmatism: The Fact of Feeling from Jonathan Edwards to Gertrude Stein* (Cambridge: Cambridge University Press, 2007). Each of these studies makes important contributions to the formulation of a pragmatist aesthetics useful to literary criticism and theory.

43. In his most famous statement of this idea, Dewey argues that "[p]hilosophy recovers itself when it ceases to be a device for dealing with the problems of philosophers and becomes a method, cultivated by philosophers, for dealing with the problem of men." "The Need for Recovery in Philosophy" (1917), in *The Middle Works, 1899–1924*, 10:46.

9

Music, Time, and the Egress of Possibility

RANDALL E. AUXIER

The thesis advanced by this essay is that aesthetics, as an exercise in applied ontology, provides an indispensable clue to the structure of possibility. In immediate aesthetic experience, most clearly illustrated in music and dance, we can recover, in example and in theory, the traces of our immediate experience of possibility. These descriptions belonging to aesthetics have profound implications for our scientific understanding of the natural world, as well as for our social philosophies of law, economics, religion, and all other social forms. If I am correct in what I assert and defend in the following, the clues to the structure of possibility we discover in our most intense aesthetic experiences also provide the ground of what we mean by "person," which is not only irreducibly social, but dependent upon the creation of a certain kind of "place" which lies virtually above the spaces created in the variable overlapping of temporal modalities in the flux.

It will not be possible to explore this overlap of temporal modalities here, but I have treated it elsewhere.[1] The full investigation of what "person" is in light of the clue we find in the immediate experience of possibility will also await another study, and will remain here a provocative suggestion. Nevertheless, some work has been done along these lines.[2]

This inquiry is divided into three major parts. First, I will examine some features of the relationship of possibility exhibited in time and music. We will follow some insights taken from Edgar Allan Poe into a new understanding of, for lack of a better phrase, the "shadow cast by possibility upon actuality." In the second part, I will describe the relation between possibility as a continuum and temporal unfolding and its reductions into space and place. The aim is to show how an "egress of possibility," which has been illustrated in Part I, gives way to a symbolization that encompasses and expands our ideas about finitude, especially as related to death and ultimacy.

This second part also offers a naturalization of Whitehead's eternal objects—his view has always been naturalistic, indeed radically empirical, but it is often misinterpreted. Still, I go beyond Whitehead's explicit words and offer some slight terminological modifications and additions that will help, I think, in avoiding those misinterpretations in the future. I will draw upon Langer's aesthetics to describe a theory of the symbol.

Finally, in the third part I will examine the *advent of person* in the *place* established in a "hiatus," in rest that maintains creative tension, and in the *immediate experience* of egress, and of the ingress that is left behind as a residuum of egress. Taking a point of departure from Ralph Ellison's observations about jazz, I will examine some of the "acts" of Miles Davis to suggest that, in keeping with Bergson's views, *personality* is *built up* in the *withholding* of the act, and indeed, *consists* in what can be accomplished "between the beats."

Throughout this study I will be drawing on the neglected philosophical ideas of Edgar Allan Poe. Poe as a philosophical thinker was far ahead of his historical epoch, but what interests me most among the many ideas he explored are his views about time and its relation to death. He was interested not just in physical death but in ultimate limitation, and I will show that his account is more comprehensive and insightful than philosophers usually realize, and that his view contributes significantly to the aesthetic aspect of a temporal ontology.

Part I: Possibility in Time and Music, and Being toward Death

Edgar Allan Poe often began his short stories with philosophical discourses foreshadowing the deepest layers of the problem to be posed by the story itself. In his story "The Island of the Fay" (1841), he begins thus:

> "*La musique*," says [Jean-François] Marmontel, in those "Contes Moraux" which in all our translations, we have insisted upon calling "Moral Tales," as if in mockery of their spirit—"*la*

Music, Time, and the Egress of Possibility 179

> *musique est le seul des talents qui jouissent de lui-même; tous les autres veulent des témoins."* ["Music is the only talent which gives pleasure of itself; all the others require witnesses."] He here confounds the pleasure derivable from sweet sounds with the capacity for creating them. No more than any other *talent*, is that for music susceptible of complete enjoyment, where there is no second party to appreciate its exercise. And it is only in common with other talents that it produces *effects* which may be fully enjoyed in solitude.[3]

Poe corrects the writer by reminding him that persons are social to the core, and talents are either plural or impotent: there is no enjoyable effect that comes of a single talent, taken alone. In this case, the music must find its listener, and the *creation* of music and its *performance* are not the same talent. The talent for listening with understanding and discernment is a third, which we call "having a good ear." Not all composers or performers have this talent, although it is true that most successful musicians have at least a dose of all three. I will foreshadow what I have to say later by using Whitehead's more technical language for making this same point on a cosmological scale, and it is this: possibilities *ingress* in ordered groups. In other writings I (and my co-author) have substituted the word *collections* for *groups,* to avoid confusion with group theory in mathematics.[4] The *order* in the case of the talents required for the creation and enjoyment of music (and they are more than the three to five I have mentioned) is an organic fusion of possibilities that concretely invest the body of any musician, and invest it with a sufficient intensity, depth, history, and potency to burst forth upon release *as* music. These possibilities are potencies, what Whitehead calls "real potentiality."[5]

The same may be said of the power to speak a language or fix an automobile. Possibilities of this sort are actively immanent in what we are and we take these powers with us wherever we go, a movable feast of possible action, the overwhelming bulk of which is not being enacted in any given moment. Let us say, for example, that you have the ability to write excellent stories. But you aren't writing one now. Still, it's possible. Such possibilities are "positively prehended," in Whitehead's terms, as *part* of the actual world. They are "in" the prehending actual entity as genuine capacities with a concrete history. Disuse removes them gradually from *relevance* to present action, but the history remains a part of the actual world of all the successors to any actual entity.

These possibilities do perish into the past, but slowly. Still, there is something in music that tempts us to favor it as a welcome guest into our individual bodies, to carry a certain groove into our steps or an alluring melody as an aural image playing at the edge of expression—an "ear worm," as musicians call it. But the creation of such music involves an expulsion of something from within the body as surely as listening involves an invitation—or invasion—from beyond. I will explore this process in connection with a discussion of Miles Davis's music later.

Poe might as well have said that Martmontel was focusing too narrowly on what is *actual* in music and neglecting its relation to *possibility*—which is crucial to its creation and to casting light upon its enjoyment as the *guest* of the body. There are certainly uninvited guests (E. S. Brightman called them the "non-rational given"),[6] but we must first consider those which insinuate themselves in our bodies by invitation. It is a vitalizing experience.

In Poe's view (and in my own), this issue of life, and of the *space* life creates, and within which that creation is possible, is perhaps the most mysterious of all.[7] He says:

> [S]ince we see clearly that the endowment of matter with vitality is a principle—indeed, as far as our judgments extend, the leading principle in the operations of Deity,—it is scarcely logical to imagine it confined to the regions of the minute, where we daily trace it, and not extending to those of the august. As we find cycle within cycle without end,—yet all revolving around one far-distant centre which is the God-head, may we not analogically suppose in the same manner, life within life, the less within the greater, and all within the Spirit Divine? In short, we are madly erring, through self-esteem, in believing man, in either his temporal or future destinies, to be of more moment in the universe than that vast "clod of the valley" which he tills and contemns, and to which he denies a soul for no more profound reason than that he does not behold it in operation.[8]

Poe was without question a panexperientialist, and an ontological optimist. However, this inquiry, henceforth, is not going to be an uplifting adventure. This is a study in tragic loss, ultimate loss. It is about being toward death, and is a reworking of that topic. I intend to include everything Heidegger said, because all of it is astute and finds confirmation in experience, but also to broaden and resituate the relation of life and death *to possibility*, which, in spite of our habits of interpretation regarding him, is a topic Heidegger grasps only vaguely, I think, and he does not work out a full theory of possibility, as he perhaps would have if had he been able to finish his projected plan for *Being and Time*. He left us with many valuable insights, but not a systematic account of possibility.[9] Whitehead's account of the negative prehension of possibility, its "elimination" as he calls it, is needed in order to grasp the full range of implications for this idea of being toward death, but Whitehead left his idea less than fully articulated in a different way. Still, his suggestions lead to a broader and more concrete grasp of the possible, both as experienced and as eliminated from experience.

Unfortunately, Heidegger also distanced himself, and understandably so, from the "natural standpoint" in order to avoid scientism and the way what he called "the technical interpretation of thinking," sent to us from Plato and Aristotle through Western history,[10] tends to leave us unconscious of the soul of nature, as Poe puts it. Heidegger also wanted to avoid what Whitehead called "misplaced concreteness" and "vacuous abstraction," all of which characterize the dogmatic science of his day (and of our own— indeed, it seems to me that our science is far worse on this score). But Heidegger gave up too easily on the prospect of reconstructing empirical philosophy so that it does not fall into these errors. As he himself said, in citing Hölderlin, where grows the danger, there also is the saving power.[11]

My view about how to do this is different. I don't think a "free relation with technology" is proving to be a workable approach. And science will not be relinquishing its hold over our process of fashioning for ourselves the objects of knowledge that fulfill desire of the technological sort at any point in the foreseeable future. We will have more technological desire and greater mediation in the future. One must therefore reinvigorate scientific thinking with a sense of its relatedness to, dependence upon, and embeddedness within nonscientific values.

The best way to accomplish this task is to teach science the fundamental character of possibility, to insist that good science deal with possibility intelligently rather than ignorantly, and to formalize for science a set of formal principles that must be considered wherever a knowledge claim is to be couched in a scientific hypothesis. Heidegger needed, in short, to grasp radical empiricism, to study Whitehead's *The Concept of Nature* and *Science in the Modern World*, in order to encounter someone who shared all of his criticisms of scientific thinking but who realized that reclaiming nature for responsible philosophy would require more than Heidegger's poetics and romantic yearnings for the absent gods.

Whitehead was surely no less enamored of poetry, but he was also a practitioner of science who saw both its foibles and its possibilities. Similarly, Heidegger might have studied the well-informed critique of science to be found in Cassirer's *Substance and Function*, as well as his works on relativity theory and quantum theory, and most importantly, the third volume of the *Philosophy of Symbolic Forms*.[12] There is far more to science than the technical interpretation of thinking and we cannot set it aside philosophically by returning to the thing, the ringing of the fourfold, and thinking that dwells.

One advantage of keeping scientific inquiry within one's sights, in philosophical thinking, as something more than a pathology of thinking is that it keeps one from either romanticizing nature overmuch or holding the process of knowledge-creation as unimportant to the pursuit of philosophical meaning. Music is a fair example of how measure and proportion find a home in our precognitive experiential processes. These processes yield, upon reflection, all sorts of dynamic formalizations that serve as genuine reasons why some vibratings of the world-process *do* settle within our bodies while others do not. There is such a thing, in actuality, as aesthetic value, and it can be formalized in many ways without destroying the experience and its value to us.

By "settling within the body," I mean the dynamic joining of one "history," one "physical route," with another in a sufficiently intense way as to contribute to the "life" of the dominant route. Such settling is always an accretion of value, *but it is not always invited*. These are not always elective affinities, and musical experience is nonesuch—I take this to be Poe's point in correcting Montmartel. As I said, music is sometimes an invader, as we shall see, but sometimes it is merely more like an annoying street evangelist with a religious tract, or a vacuum cleaner salesman at the front door, or even a lost traveler asking directions. Music is often a ringing at the ears, the side doors of the body, but it is sometimes a rumbling beneath one's seat. But as such a visitor, it enters not as a primitive or meaningless noise. It is already a fully formed *symbol* by the time it knocks. Otherwise it is not music. That second route that settles and joins itself to our physical history has its own order. It is a symbol of something the world accommodates as possible and as actual.

Music, Time, and the Egress of Possibility

Susanne Langer says that "a genuine symbol can most readily originate where some object, sound, or act is provided which has no practical meaning, yet tends to elicit an emotional response, and thus hold one's undivided attention."[13] She actually does not mean "undivided attention" literally. It is an idiom. In fact, it is the music that has interrupted the continuum whereby our experience is carried along with the general flux, and in the moment the music appears, we almost cannot help relinquishing the more generalized temporal process for the more condensed and intensified symbol that offers itself as a substitute. She continues:

> Certain objects and gestures appear to have this phenomenological, dissociated character for some apes, as well as for man; sounds have it for man alone. They annoy or please him even when they are not signs of anything further; they have an inherently interesting character.[14]

I do not accept her claim that sounds operate this way only in the case of humans, but I do think they operate on humans in a way that is nearly impossible for humans to ignore, especially at the onset, and that they carry a saturation of symbolic (albeit precognitive) meaning for us that is evident to us alone.

The formation of such symbols plays a part in expelling the "accursed share" (to use Bataille's phrase), that excess of energy that builds up within the bodies of organisms with centralized nervous systems and which *must be* wasted because it cannot find sufficiently dense *place* for the magnitude and the intensity of action that would be required to maintain its full intensive value; such energy must therefore expel itself into the abyss of the *space* from which it originated, overrunning its *place*.[15] The portion that can be conserved for a time is the symbol. When we cast out the unneeded (and eventually unwanted) energy from within, most of the energy is wasted, dissipated by means of the act, but those portions we expel as symbols (granting that it is only a tiny fraction of the energies we must lose) can condense into nuggets of endurance. They can be propagated in accordance with the various fields of energy from which they are formed and to which they contribute.

Sound waves, for example, are heavy, and difficult to propagate, and have a high entropy, so they dissipate quickly. But encoded as information, with a lower entropy, whether mechanically or digitally, they can be revived, almost resurrected, and rereleased with much of their form intact. The meaning of the whole buildup thus abjected can join with otherwise alien physical routes and, as settling there, can be moved from one space to another, and can contribute to the transformation of spaces into places, into virtualized regions of meaning. The physical energy expended by Miles Davis while playing the trumpet during his many performances is mostly lost, dissipating in the cracks and crannies of Birdland and thousands of other spaces. But the *music* holds. Some of it holds in the bodies of those who were present, some by the reduction and heavy mediation of recording, but the music still *means* in either case.

The advent of a musical experience creates a buildup of the kind that compels abjection, which is why we begin to sway and stomp and even prance about as it takes hold (or sing along, tap a foot, or talk about it later). Our response is both an expulsion of what is building up within our bodies and a seeking of equilibrium with the *im*balance introduced by the "visitor," the new symbol seeking to settle. This expulsion is unproblematic when the symbol is *contrasted* with what was given up in order to have it (the silence, or whatever else is incompatible with the visit of the symbol). But the dance is not incompatible. Rather, the dance stands over against the music and conveys *its own* meaning, as a separate symbol, and hence division (between what is abjected and what is conserved) is met with counterdivision (some of what was conserved is re-added to the conserved whole by way of response, while still more is lost).

Yet, all is not in balance; a further tension emerges between what is possible and what is actual *within* our activities—to breathe out a particular melody is to leave all other tones unsung; to enact one train of rhythm in dance is to leave all other possibilities for the organizing of the flow of that durational epoch forever unenacted. The same is true of the act by which one thought becomes determinate to the exclusion of its incompatible near competitors. One movement (whether it is a logical procession of inclusions and entailments or a melody), or more to the point, a *continuum* of movement, is expected to exclude, or defer, or condense an infinity of others that are *not* explicitly enacted (although part of the richness of the act will derive from their having been *suggested*), while carrying their reality, their meaning and unmeaning, along its own path. There is just *a* melody or *a* groove or an intensive logical movement to the thinking, a "just this and none other" which employs temporal passage, transition, as a vehicle for packing the meanings of all the movements *not* enacted into the single movement enacted, or *expirated* (and please do note this word) in the case of a sung melody or a trumpet played. It is easier to see the abjection in singing and wind instruments than in dancing or playing stringed and percussive instruments. But the abjection, the elimination of the unenacted in favor of the act, is there in all cases, and it *is* an abjection. Still, it is easier to see the form when something expires, and the suggestion of death in this term is no mere play of language.

We might not want to treat the excluded or occluded or merely alluded-to possibilities as dead, or dying, at this point in the account. After all, possibilities, qua possible, are immortal—or, as Whitehead puts it, "eternal." They are indifferent to actuality and still exist in the mode of the possible even when no potency remains in them and they have become "might-have-beens." But "negatively prehended eternal objects" (in Whitehead's terms) are not only intelligible, their proximity to actuality conditions and, at one end of the structure of meaning, even *begets* meaning. These are not wind eggs, as Socrates fretted over in the *Theaetetus*, but highly organized modes of delimitation conditioning allowances and affordances.[16]

What you *might be doing* but are not, at this moment, is every bit as crucial to the structure and continuum of meaning as what you *are* doing, and in many situations, the *undone* overruns the positive act in its determinative role in the generation of meaning. Sometimes, for example, what we *don't* say is what we really mean, and all competent interpreters know it, and the meaning is intensified precisely because the thought is *un*said. But, qua actual, these broader constellations of possibility will never *ingress* as "collections" of possibilities. Rather, they *egress* in deference to whatever ingresses.[17] *It is a kind of death.*

Here we arrive at the point to be rethought and reconstructed. The egress of possibility is broader than death, is a part of every real moment and event, and most importantly, it contributes to all meaning and to all experience an ongoing ultimacy. There is no way to reclaim an unenacted constellation of possibilities, and while we make such constellations determinate in thinking, we will never succeed in making them definite contributors to the physical cosmos. It is a kind of intelligibility (call it "mind" if you insist) that exhibits for us our limits irrevocably in all that we do.

In considering this contrast between definite and merely determinate possibilities, under the heading of life and death, and the borderland between (with which he was so fascinated),[18] Poe puts it like this in "Island of the Fay":

> The . . . eastern end of the isle was whelmed in the blackest shade. A sombre, yet beautiful and peaceful gloom here pervaded all things. The trees were dark in color, and mournful in form and attitude, wreathing themselves into sad, solemn, and spectral shapes that conveyed ideas of mortal sorrow and untimely death. The grass wore the deep tint of the cypress, and the heads of its blades hung droopingly, and hither and thither among it were many small unsightly hillocks, low and narrow, and not very long, that had the aspect of graves, but were not; . . . I fancied that each shadow, as the sun descended lower and lower, separated itself sullenly from the trunk that gave it birth, and thus became absorbed by the stream; while other shadows issued momently from the trees, taking the place of their predecessors thus entombed.

One could hardly conjure a better visual image of actualities that almost are not, that hover between existing and never having existed. This is the barely actual, but determinately possible in prose. Poe continues:

> This idea, having once seized upon my fancy, greatly excited it, and I lost myself forthwith in revery. "If ever island were enchanted," said I to myself, "this is it." This is the haunt of the few gentle Fays who remain from the wreck of the race. Are these green tombs theirs?—or do they yield up their sweet lives as mankind yield up their own? In dying, do they not rather waste away mournfully, rendering unto God, little by little, their existence, as these trees render up shadow after shadow, exhausting their substance unto dissolution? What the wasting tree is to the water that imbibes its shade, growing thus blacker by what it preys upon, may not the life of the Fay be to the death which engulfs it?

This is what one might call the forty-frames-per-minute version of being toward death, a sort of movie in prose of the relation of possibility to temporal actuality. This idea of a shadow cast by the sun is at least as old as Plato's *Republic*, when we step into daylight upon escaping the cave, we cannot look directly upon those pure forms illuminated by the sun. It is surely a metaphor, but not merely a metaphor. This shadow is a projection, and there is a distance between whatever casts the shadow and the light source, and there is a gap, a hiatus, a meaningful non-dentity between that which casts the shadow and the shadow itself.

There is a logical ground for this complex relation. Relational propositions, that is, propositions in which both the subject and predicate terms are treated as defining an extensional class, are never identical, even in analytical propositions, since they define classes separated by a copula and an inclusion/exclusion function of some sort. The only way to carry out a logical analysis in such situations is to project the predicate term into the subject term or vice versa.[19] These projections are shadows of the sort Poe describes, but his descriptions approach more viscerally the temporal ground and the temporal shadow.

Something perdures in this shadow, almost not being, while something else releases its hold on enduring and lets time make of possibility a might-have-been, an adumbration at the shadow's edge, sometimes sharper, sometimes quite fuzzy. Does the description not invite the mind to play the entire scene of the Island in hyper-speeded, time-lapse photography? In a few dozen words, Poe accomplishes *in imagination* and in words what he could not have seen with his physical eyes, time-lapse photography being unavailable at his station in history. And yet we see it with ours by means of technological mediation all the time nowadays: the acceleration of being toward death condensed into a few ephemeral moments.

It makes me pause to wonder whether the people of Poe's time and before dreamed differently than we do. Our dreams seem so much like movies or television that I wonder what they would be, or how they would seem and how I would interpret their images, if I had no physical experience of images played before my eyes in sequence. There is no doubt in my mind that the technical intervention in our senses of sequenced images (that might or might not ever have been actual as depicted) has profoundly altered our sense of possibility and its meaning and structure. A certain limitation has been lifted, but at the price of "enframing" the possible.

Most striking in this passage is the purposiveness of our rendering the lives we have, as if by the transport of our freedom, back to their origins. In "The Fall of the House of Usher," Poe wrote about "free death" in the sense Nietzsche would later identify, this being the idea that one cannot really die until one has chosen it.[20] It is a purposive movement, not a determined one, in Usher as on the Island here. It is not a narrowing of all possibilities to our ownmost, as with Heidegger; it is more like the visitation of a music, whether invited or unwelcome, that reminds us of the constant egress of possibility in each moment, not just in dying. We have purposed it. The difficulty is grasping it. It is important, I think, to recognize that Poe set out to put into prose this borderland of life and death, possible and actual, and that he recognizes that music is a fitting intelligible medium for helping us identify in our own experience the presence and meaning of this unceasing exchange of possibilities perduring and dying, that actualities may have a brief moment in the sun and then pass into perpetual perishing.

Somehow Poe manages to *write* this relation, but the relation can, after all, be found in every experience. We should not be surprised that it can be exhibited by any art, assuming that one has sufficient command of the form to bring us all into that dynamic borderland, and to make us feel those possibilities as lures we *do not take,* but rather *feel* (prehend) ourselves neglecting and eliminating. Thus, we see that the controlled or purposive movement finds its origin in the exclusion of infinitely many ordered possibilities, which I call "the egress of possibility," *for the sake of which* (and this is *primal* teleology) the actual movement is enacted.

Thus, the dance, like the making of music, is not enacted *for the sake of* onlookers or spectators, in the primal instance, but for the sake of eliminating possibilities, of leaving them deliberately *un*enacted. The result is the meaningful act, or at least the shadow of one. The song or the dance or the prose passage may be bad, after all, which is to say lifeless and too much indebted to the actual. Such acts lack the dynamism and negative lure to enable us to feel the egress. They are mere repetitions, not dynamic meanings. This is why the act can be undertaken alone without loss of purpose, once it is located within the already social body; but purpose is reduced in such cases to its primal tension. It won't be art if I do it alone, as Poe rightly observes. Here I apply Whitehead's ideas about possibility, as I understand them, to Poe's aesthetics. It is useful to look at Poe because he is so good with the idea of death, but we should also look at Susanne Langer because she is so good with the idea of life. But we have reworked Heidegger's being toward death such that we can see that it is true we die alone, but if life is to be art, as he encourages us to think, the art of dying must be included. That art is social, even if individually enacted, proximally and for the most part.

Part II: Being toward Life as the Art of Being toward Death

The move from the experience of death as a limit of individual life is generalized in our cultural experience, not just in art. It is not too much to assert that the problem of death is first experienced symbolically and as a function of *sensus communis* for human beings. It is precognitive and is felt *as a limit* by the group that is then imparted to the individual as something included within the generalized feeling of death, and in the crucial instance, while it includes biological death, the true death is the egress of possibility. The egress of possibility is *why* death matters. The limit of the group, then, as its possible limit in time, its possible destruction, its contingency as actual, its confrontation with metaphysical annihilation, precedes the individual experience of being toward death.

For human beings, our access to the spatial limit suggested by death is mediated by the places of death, the necropolis, and the virtual times (ritualized practices) that acknowledge death's work upon us. We attend funerals to mark the egress of possibility as much as to mark the pastness of an actual life. We seek a common therapy in the beauty of the ritual, the art of the ceremony, for the painful understanding that a meaningful companion to our time will ingress as a collection of possibilities no longer, and all that might have been will remain underdetermined constellations of possibilities. They are might-have-beens even if they are futural: one will have to endure the next holiday season, or birthday, or anniversary bereft of needed ingress. The art of life is closely tied to this communal dance with our future might-have-beens. Every holiday is observed to mark something of this character, to re-dedicate us to the meaning of whatever was lost and is being commemorated.

To approach death with reverence and awe, or at least *solemnity* (to use the well-chosen word of William James) is to treat death as a *place* that has only the thinnest separation from the *space* that supports it. The place is an overlay of the space in which we gather and, in the case of the ritual, the aim is to reduce the distance between the raw space and the place we fix upon it. Something permanent is made, or quasi-made, or at least asserted, on top of something ephemeral. Spaces endure only so long as the variable overlapping of the temporal flux holds.[21] Strangely, the virtual place, as a meaning, is often better able to endure than the physical spaces it overlays. Such is the power of art when the balance of life and death in it is perfectly struck. If the ritual, the dance, the feast, the revel, the festival, can be organized upon the edge of that thinness between space and place, then we can welcome death as a possibility and defy it as an actuality. Our song and dance become the celebration of life, not just the observance of death. There is always slippage in these thin times and space-places, and the community feels the danger, the proximity of limit, the presence of the gods and the demons. This is part of the reason that human sacrifice made a certain kind of mythic sense to groups taken with such a precognitive tempest of the possible. But to come through the sacred time is to endure through a hiatus in which all possibility comes into immediate relation with all actuality. This time is sublime, unthinkable, but it can be endured. To endure it is to be free in the sense of overcoming death. To be free is to make art of this thin relation.

We moderns do not encounter this limit in the traditional way. I do not think that describing our relation to death as the inauthentic concerns of "*das Man*" is a complete characterization of our situation. It is true that if we give ourselves over to morose mundanity, the enframing, the technical interpretation of thinking, concern dominates care, challenging occludes bringing forth. Heidegger is surely correct that this is a living death. But there are authentic ways of orienting ourselves to "what must be endured" that are embedded in high civilization and related to the project of *creating* for ourselves the very freedom we would enjoy—and this is not limited to some sort of return to the Greeks or romantic hankering for eighteenth-century German poetry. Cassirer says:

> [Philosophers] declared that the only way to freedom that is left to man [in our modern situation] is to banish from his mind the fear of death. "He who has learnt to die has forgot what it is to be a slave. To know how to die delivers us from all subjection and constraint." Myth could not give a rational answer to the problem of death. Yet it was myth which, long before philosophy, became the first teacher of mankind, the pedagogue who, in the childhood of the human race, was alone able to raise and solve the problem of death in a language that was understandable to the human mind. "Do not try and explain death to me," says Achilles to Odysseus in Hades. But it was just this difficult task that myth had to perform in the history of mankind. Primitive man could not be reconciled

to the fact of death; he could not be persuaded to accept the destruction of his personal existence as an inevitable natural phenomenon. But it was the very fact that was denied and "explained away" by myth.[22]

Cassirer argues that this work performed by myth never really goes away in the development of a greater distance of symbol (place, in this case, however thin) and thing symbolized (space, in this case). A threat to the survival of the group can lead to a collapsing of the tension and distance that holds the symbol and symbolized apart and the result is the modern mythic regime, rationalized by technique and impervious to exteriorities that do not fit with the myth and ritual required to push death, or the limit point, away, or to push through it blindly. Our civilizational health resides in cultivating the tension and distance between space and place, existing in that tension, even inauthentically. That is the art of life, even when the art is bad. But in experiencing the immediacy of the possible, in egress and, subsequently, in ingress, we *cultivate* (in the most literal sense of the word) that fruitful tension. To be oblivious to the immediate availability and work of possibility is more than inauthenticity, it is dogmatism, ideology; it is the ontological lie. Unhappily, Heidegger did not recognize this important function of healthy culture and hence gave too narrow an account of being toward death. He did not understand Cassirer's case and he evidently did not wish to.[23]

Naturally, the first thing a spectator may feel in the presence of this primal separation of space and place is what *is done* rather than what *is not done*. Yet, the spectator will quickly recapture the feeling on the egress of possibility in, as it were, a *feeling* that is like a temporal version of a photographic negative, and that precedes the positive picture in much the same manner. The meaning of the enacted movements cannot become reflective for the spectator without taking that egress, that negative into the darkroom that exists between thinking and reflecting to reverse its presentations. The *reflective* account, which makes explicit what was implicit in the dance or the song, or the meaningful act in general, must begin with what was *not done*, how the place was *not used*. This is the phenomenology of the act as a description, but a description continuous with what has ingressed and egressed. It is what Langer calls a "discursive symbol," with its ground in a highly organized feeling of the situation. Langer says:

The meanings given through language are successively understood, and gathered into a whole by the process called discourse; the meanings of all other symbolic elements that compose a larger, articulate symbol are *understood only through the meaning of the whole,* through their relations within the total structure. Their very functioning as symbols depends on the fact that they are involved in a *simultaneous integral presentation.* This kind of semantic may be called "presentational symbolism" to characterize its essential distinction from discursive symbolism, or "language" proper.[24]

This presentational symbolism is what I likened above to the photographic negative. When discursive language is well formed, as with the stunning prose of Poe, we don't notice the transition from our feeling of the world to our description of it. The better the language, the closer the image it evokes to the feeling that is the larger whole to which the discursive symbols belong. But the situation is analogous and perhaps even more difficult to sort out when it comes to the relation between music and the way we feel it (and form presentational symbols that are our feeling and belong to the whole temporal context), but at the expense of a massive tacit egress of possibility. Yet, we must keep the feeling separate from the experience as a temporal whole; and we must separate the presentational symbol from the discursive account of the symbol. It is music that most sorely tempts us to collapse them. Langer says:

> Music has its special, purely auditory characters [I would add vibratory to auditory] that "intrinsically contain certain properties which, because of their close relationship to certain characteristics in the subjective realm, are frequently confused with emotions proper." But "these auditory characters are not emotions at all. They merely *sound* [or vibrate] the way moods *feel*". . . . The notion that certain effects of music are so much *like* feelings that we mistake them for the latter, though they are entirely different, may seem queer, unless one looks at music as an "implicit" symbolism; then, however, the confusion appears as something expected.[25]

I would not choose the same terminology as Carroll Pratt, whom Langer quotes here, but one can see him straining for words to describe the problem with music when it becomes a presentational symbol and *then*

Music, Time, and the Egress of Possibility   193

we try to describe that symbol discursively. As Langer rightly observes, confusion is something we should expect. But it does not change the situation whereby the symbol is formed, and it does not diminish the importance of egress as *prior* to the presentational symbol, and as an immediate condition of its meaningfulness.

If the reflective account, whether in discursive language or any other greatly reduced reflective expression (e.g., highly abstracted or minimalist or conceptual art in any medium), seeks more than phenomenology and would move to ontology, the tension between place and space must be recovered and thematized. That tension, that distance between the space of action and the variable temporality that supports it, is the key to recovering in discourse the egress of possibility and its positive residuum. How did the space become a place, the "play of the forces," to use Nietzsche's term, and how was the place pushed apart from the space? These are the questions that lead to the metaphysics not of ritual movement, wherein space and place are allowed a functional unity, but of music and dance, in which the rejection of that quasi-unity ("quasi" since it sets aside the regress of possibility) and the abjection of space are conditions for the aesthetic meaning.

Part III: The Hiatus as the Ground of Person

Poe found an outstanding path to narrating this rich double relation, between the egress of possibility and its residuum, and the task of creating a collection of discursive symbols recollective of the positive feeling of the world that remained when possibility had departed. His account is far better than Heidegger's in terms of addressing the limits we denominate and in terms of experience *as* being toward death. He includes all of the moments Heidegger has, but also thematizes and criticizes the inauthentic they-self while holding on to the genuine (i.e., neither authentic nor inauthentic) experience of the egress of possibility. He captures something of the sublimity of limit in relation to the full presence of the past and the full availability of *all* possibility in the combination of egress and ingress (however difficult that may be to imagine). And Poe recognizes that music and dance are the real forms of the intelligibility of such possibility as immediately experienced.

In "The Masque of the Red Death," Poe creates a mythic setting, a kingdom long ago and far away, in a country being ravaged by the plague. But this is not the black plague, which in its slothful progress takes a day or three to kill its victims. This is the Red Death, which accomplishes the same work in the course of "half an hour." The Red Death causes its victims to bleed through every orifice and even their pores, apparently through the rapid corruption of all the blood vessels. And thus is the symbol of life and vitality diabolically transformed into its opposite. The actual blood within is always and ever the same as the *possible* blood without. Such is the anticipatory modality of all in this country.

Thus, there never is any but a contingent distance between the actual blood that animates us and the possible blood that is a sign of our deaths—anima (the life principle) just *is* what is left temporarily intact by the broader and coagulated animus (which is externalized life, transition with little concrescence, i.e., death). The importance of the rapid work of the Red Death is that it forces us to notice the egress of possibility in the compacted timespan, half an hour, and with its almost complete rate of morbidity and perfect contagiousness, to experience its presence at all is to die from it. That vise-grip of possibility, actuality, and absolute limit is a temporal mousetrap. It snaps upon us discursively and makes us feel the egress of possibility as the egress of future life.

Clearly, no such disease as the Red Death exists, except that this description captures, in a sort of verbal analogy to time-lapse photography, the condition of being mortal at all. You'll die anyway. What difference if it's thirty minutes or thirty years? The (largely unconscious) habit of denying our experience of "the egress of possibility," supported by mythic refusal of mortality, is eliminated in Poe's story by the hypothesis of the compressed time-lapse and the certainty of swift death. Here is death, in thirty minutes, and not to be evaded. We feel palpably and undeniably, and in a way that breaks through and beyond the mythic denial, our own genuine situation as temporarily alive. The affirmation of the contingency and delicacy of aliveness, of the space of life, allows us to break through the overlays of place and the denials that are the work of place and symbol, at least when these are taken as exhaustive substitutes for the broader reality from which they were reduced. We stand before stark possibility in its fullest intelligible relation to the actual. We are *not yet dead*. Having grasped this way of gaining imaginative access to our mortality, Poe works with this imaginative conception to deliver some inconvenient truths about the experience of the egress of possibility.

The setting of the story is of a Prince Prospero and a thousand of the most lively and pleasing of his court. They decide to escape the Red Death by sealing themselves within one of the finest royal compounds,

Music, Time, and the Egress of Possibility   195

and to weld shut the gates to allow "means neither of ingress or egress to the sudden impulses of despair or of frenzy from within." This life is robust. It will not be defeated by the temporary whims of those whose consciences or fear might lead to a breaching of the outer skin. This is not *das Man*. This is the genuine dance of life. This compound is a body, and within it there is a happy life-party going on. Your immediate interiority, pumping with life, emotion, and real blood, is no different. So wonderful is this gathering that the monarch of the whole assemblage decrees a ball, with dancing and music. As Poe says:

> The prince had provided all the appliances in pleasure. There were buffoons, there were improvisatori, there were ballet-dancers, there were musicians, there was Beauty, there was wine. All these and security were within. Without was the "Red Death."

Within this happy community, a healthy body politic gathered for the dance of life, of living, is a remarkable ballroom with seven chambers standing at acute angles to one another so that one may not easily see ahead or behind. These symbolize, among other things, the three-score years and ten, the seven decades of life, with its regular limits in terms of memory and foresight—to see the next room, one must give up one's view of the previous, and the previous is viewed only at the cost of seeing the chamber ahead. This is the character of "place." But each chamber has its own charm, its own color scheme created by an artificial light, as Poe describes, its own relation to the music that emanates from a chamber from which all can hear, in their own way, and we have our minimal combination of three "talents" described in "Island of the Fay"—the light, the music, the dance—that combine and overlap to create a full and functional virtual overlay of the complex of actuality and possibility that is the space upon which these confines are built, in prose, in image, and, if there were such a compound with such a ballroom, in physical reality. We have here, then a symbol, both presentational and more narrowly discursive, of mediated life, in which experience and activity are substitutes for time, actuality, and possibility. What is required to create this mediation is that space should become place.

But of the light, a bit more must be said; all of Poe's chambers are lit artificially from without—there are no true windows to the outside but rather, in exterior hallways beyond the chambers, tripods supporting bright fires shine through colored windows, creating an other-worldly light that varies in hue and contrast from one chamber to the next.[26] Thus, we have a third symbol, with the music and the dancing, of the mediation between a virtual and an actual space. Within these chambers we have not space and light and time, then, but place and glow and experience. Poe then describes the limit of both life and of virtuality in the most extreme chamber, the one done in black with blood red windows casting a red glow over the whole, and from this place emanates the thinness, the awareness of those moments when possibility as such becomes wed with the mediated activity that is our experience. He writes:

> But in the western or black chamber the effect of the fire-light that streamed upon the dark hangings through the blood-tinted panes, was ghastly in the extreme, and produced so wild a look upon the countenances of those who entered, that there were few of the company bold enough to set foot within its precincts at all.

It was in this apartment, also, that there stood against the western wall a gigantic clock of ebony. Its pendulum swung to and fro with a dull, heavy, monotonous clang; and when the minute-hand made the circuit of the face, and the hour was to be stricken, there came from the brazen lungs of the clock a sound that was clear and loud and deep and exceedingly musical, but of so peculiar a note and emphasis that, at each lapse of an hour, the musicians of the orchestra were constrained to pause, momentarily, in their performance, to hearken to the sound; and thus the waltzers perforce ceased their evolutions; and there was a brief disconcert of the whole gay company; and, while the chimes of the clock yet rang, it was observed that the giddiest grew pale, and the more aged and sedate passed their hands over their brows as if in confused reverie or meditation. But when the echoes had fully ceased, a light laughter at once pervaded the assembly; the musicians looked at each other and smiled as if at their own nervousness and folly, and made whispering vows, each to the other, that the next chiming of the clock should produce in them no similar emotion; and then, after the lapse of sixty minutes, (which embraced three thousand and six hundred seconds of the Time that flies,) there came yet another chiming of the clock, and then were the same disconcert and tremulousness and meditation as before.

Here of course is being toward death, and its music is different. Heidegger missed this quite completely. The music, in the relevant sense, *is* the pause, the hiatus, the reminder, the discomfort, all markers of the egress of possibility. But the hiatus is not precisely the denial of an ultimate coincidence of experience and existence, and yes, one might well describe this, with Hegel and Sartre and so many others, as the meeting place of what is *for itself* and what is *in itself*. But Poe's treatment is subtler than even these masters, for he is willing to attempt a description of not just the hiatus, the pause in the life of both body and mind that, shark-like, must keep moving, must endure through the unknowable act of existing, but also of the extreme, of the point of ultimate limitation.

This is not, as with Heidegger, "*my* ownmost possibility"; nay, this is *our* ultimate limit, not merely *mine*. As we saw earlier, for Poe the social setting for this kind of limitation, the immediate relation of the collection of possibilities ingressing to the infinities that egress, is ineradicable, is parcel if not quite isolated part, of the meaning of the hiatus. It is not alone that we die, but *with each other*. Even Heidegger eventually realized that the *mortals* (note the plural, a *sensus communis* of the ever-forthcoming necropolis) are indispensable to the ringing of the fourfold. If this mortal contribution to the ringing doesn't quite rise to being a viable social philosophy in Heidegger's thought (and it doesn't), it is at least a nod in the right direction. There are incursions into our mediated experience from the "eternal," in Whitehead's odd sense, namely, the nontemporal and settled order of possibilities, and they are partly intelligible to us, but only *as* a community, not to any one of us alone (as though we ever could be alone in the relevant sense). One might say "ec-stasis," but that description is inferior to Whitehead's broader account. We endure together, as we always have, *with* the hiatus, the uncanny sounding of the bell and what it portends of the extreme western chamber in the seven houses of existence. We do not analogize the death of another to ourselves; we die *with* one another, whenever *any* of us dies. It is the only way we *can* die. As Poe says, excepting the westernmost chamber,

> [T]hese apartments were densely crowded, and in them beat feverishly the heart of life. And the revel went whirlingly on, until at length there commenced the sounding of midnight upon the clock. And then the music ceased, as I have told; and the evolutions of the waltzers were quieted; and there was an uneasy cessation of all things as before. But now there were twelve strokes to be sounded by the bell of the clock; and thus it happened, perhaps, *that more of thought crept, with more*

time, into the meditations of the thoughtful among those who revelled. And thus too, it happened, perhaps, that before the last echoes of the last chime had utterly sunk into silence, there were many individuals in the crowd who had found leisure to become aware of the presence of a masked figure which had arrested the attention of no individual before. (my emphasis)

One notes the care with which Poe qualifies his descriptions with "perhapses" and the mood of contingency. This stands in stark contrast to Heidegger's less empirical descriptions. One must note also the embeddedness of insight, thought, and awareness within certain members of the community of revelers, and these do not stand in contrast to the rest, the crowd, but are rather an immanent feature of the party itself. The revelers, the alive, are *with one another* both authentically and inauthentically, and for better and worse, richer and poorer, in sickness and in health. This new presence is a shambling and gaunt figure costumed as one from the grave who has capitulated to the Red Death, wrapped in the shroud of burial. The partygoers find this disguise to be in poor taste and are offended. As Poe puts it:

> In truth the masquerade license of the night was nearly unlimited; but the figure in question had out Heroded Herod, and gone beyond the bounds of even the prince's indefinite decorum. *There are chords in the hearts of even the most reckless which cannot be touched without emotion.* Even with the utterly lost, to whom life and death are equally jests, there are matters of which no jest can be made. (my emphasis)

It comes back always to music, uninvited music in this case. The sympathy between the chords in these hearts and the music of the clock is a *sensus communis* of the individuation and dismemberment of the community into those who may only be called back to the whole with the command of the extreme limits of experience, where it passes into existence. All the way from the easternmost chamber, the prince shouts to the western end "Who dares!" and commands that this subject be revealed. But none will approach the figure and so the prince hurries through all the chambers, his life passing before his eyes in the space of an instant, and charges the form with dagger drawn, and attaining the final chamber, drops dead to the floor. The revelers then, seizing the figure

Music, Time, and the Egress of Possibility 199

to reveal it find the bandages "untenanted by any *tangible* form." Within is only "the presence of the Red Death," and as the revelers die, one by one, the tripods burn down and "Darkness and Decay and the Red Death held illimitable dominion over all."

Poe has gone beyond Heidegger and has examined the presence of death in the midst of life, how it may be within our awareness, how it may even be *thought* (reflectively) by some among us, how it affects the old, the reckless, the bold, and the merry, and even those "utterly lost." And most crucially, it is the music of the virtual hours in their virtual chambers, as interrupted at intervals by the music of time itself, as it flows. This is the contrast of the time of concrescence with the time of transition, to put it in Whitehead's terms. That transition holds dominion over all of life is not something we can seriously doubt.

This brings us back to the question of music and its relation to the egress of possibility. A strange result is afoot in this narrative. "Person" is a potency of the hiatus. I apologize for what follows here, since it is extremely bad form to quote one's own writing, but I prefer this formulation to any alternative I might offer here merely to avoid the appearance of indelicate self-absorption. Besides, perhaps I am, and many of us are, to be honest, self-absorbed, which is to say, we prefer gazing at the shadows we cast over turning toward the light. Thus, in an earlier book, a co-author and I wrote:

> Rhythm is an avenue into identity, and one that Whitehead identifies as of supreme metaphysical importance. Rhythm, Whitehead suggests, is the "causal counterpart of life . . . wherever there is some rhythm, there is some life."[27] Periodicity by itself—and hence the analysis that trigonometry provides us—is not the same as what Whitehead calls "rhythm," since periodicity is just the empty repetition of pattern. But this is still an essential component of rhythm: "A rhythm involves a pattern and to that extent is always self-identical."[28]

Here is really the secret to the potencies in the hiatus. It is easier to illustrate this relation of rhythm and the regimentation of potencies than to explain it. I thus turn to Miles Davis and his understanding of both periodicity and hiatus. When Davis, in 1958, created the score to the Louis Malle film *Elevator to the Gallows*, the idea was to compose by watching the film and responding to what the musicians saw. Miles led a French band he had never before played with or even met. They essentially improvised the score. The experience (not irrelevant to Bergson's understanding of time) led Davis to think of the musical space as a space between, as a hiatus, as action plays out, as something that exists in the rests and interstices, in modes foreshadowing action and lingering as action passes into the past. He was, in my terminology, exploring the relation between space and place, but from the experiential ground of the flux, not from a reflective, conceptual platform.

These were his thoughts in December 1958, and they were forming around a plan about what to do on his next album with recording sessions already scheduled for March 1959, and leading up to the breakthrough recording *Kind of Blue*. Describing the sessions, Julian "Cannonball" Adderley, the alto sax player said: "The band was a workshop. Miles really kind of talked to everybody and told everybody what to *not* do. Not so much what to do. . . . He never told anybody what to play."[29] It is significant that Adderley says what "to *not do*," rather than "what *not to do*." The latter is a prohibition. What not to do presupposes a conceptualization of possible action, determinate and discursive, set before the musicians. What to not do is a suggestion about leaving undone some possibilities, allowing them to egress and waiting to see what crops up in the hiatus. Notations and charts for the tunes were, as one might guess, minimal.

Carlos Santana expresses his admiration for this transition effected by Davis from 1958 to 1959 in a question: "How do you go to the studio with minimum stuff and come out with eternity?"[30] The answer was an exploration of *possible* sound. Herbie Hancock says, "The concept that was used throughout the record, called modal playing. . . . [P]eople weren't writing for jazz, this kind of idea, before."[31] David Amram adds, "Instead of having all these tremendously sophisticated chord changes, Miles said, instead of doing all that, let's use a mode."[32] What Davis was doing was creating sonic space, partly through what Eddie Henderson calls "Miles's sparsity of notes,"[33] and partly through the group exploration of modal playing, what to *not do,* as Adderley says.

Davis got at something very elusive but very real. He was able to symbolize the egress of possibility. Everyone agreed it was "dark," and that was an insight Davis had—and he changed his band in order to get the sound, bringing in Bill Evans on piano and Jimmy Cobb on drums. I would suggest that the *effect* is the holding in tension of *possibility,* as a hovering as *constellational* presence, unenacted, *and* the inevitable egress of possibility as the past presses, the durational epoch becomes stressed

Music, Time, and the Egress of Possibility

by the way that memory, the past is flooding directly, unmediated, into the present span. The longer the span of the epoch can be maintained, the more of the past rushes in, until finally the weight of it becomes too much to maintain; the flux closes in on the moment of the act. Constellational possibility egresses and collectional possibility is left in place, remaining *simply* possible in its virtual mode, but now also actual as played notes. This is so much more than being toward death. The feeling of the egress surely is that of finitude, and it can only be captured by the dark tonality, Miles evidently believed, and with Poe, but what is left behind *lives,* as actual, meaning very little without its own immediate contrast with its collection of possibilities. Yes, they are the same, but the collection is virtual and bears an immediate and intelligible relation to all the constellational possibility that has egressed. That tension, within possibility itself, is experienced as a lack by the living being, and it is the lack we experience immediately and first. The meaning of the act depends on it and is derived from it.

In a very real sense, since then, the egress has been sealed, structured, prefigured before the act. We can weld the doors of the compound to protect ourselves against frenzy, but egress cannot be physically contained. It has to do with the structural incompossibility of the constellation of possibilities *as a whole* with the collection it includes. The collection has already been selected, valuation has occurred, but intensity, depth, has not yet emerged from the event horizon—the something that will happen could not *now* be prevented, but there is contingency in *how.* Some say that it was Bill Evans's touch on the keyboard that Davis *had to have* for this group exploration; others say it was the withholding of harmonies that were suggested, almost demanding to *be,* and then, in the last moment turned modal by being forced to share meaning with the notes unplayed. Evans and Cobb could be counted on to make those modal turns in the allowances and the affordances of nonharmony and nonrhythm.

Thus, constellational possibility hangs, refuses to egress until it is abjected, insists upon itself for an interminable, indeed, from the standpoint of the constellation, this moment *eternally* hangs and holds the meaning of having come into intelligible structural contrast, from the standpoint of finite actuality, *with* the selected collection of possibilities, that is to say, the ingression. A fundamental incompatibility holds and holds and then finally egresses. I am quite sure that this is the "in between beats" experience that Ralph Ellison describes in the "Prologue" to *Invisible Man.* He warns against it; living in between like this will not be sustainable. He even swears off marijuana due to a suspicion that it might have messed up his experience of time just enough to bring him to slip between the cracks of continuity. It is worth mentioning that Ellison was a jazz trumpet player of no small ability. It is also worth mentioning that his main character is in the process of turning his subterranean dwelling into 100 percent light so that no shadow can take hold. When it becomes too much for the eyes, he shades them. Like Miles Davis.

It is not as if Miles Davis hadn't read Ellison, and not as if Ellison hadn't heard Miles Davis—Ellison was a *trumpet* player. But Miles ignored the warning. If he hadn't, we wouldn't have *Kind of Blue*, not to mention other masterworks. The psychological and emotional cost of exploring this modal in-between-ness is very high, especially if one brings to it the "thin veil" of the artist (as Bergson described it).[34] Davis already took it all so seriously, including himself, that he surely would have been damaged by half of what he actually discovered, let alone the whole "place" he inhabited. Some of what came through was uninvited. No collection of lightbulbs could keep it in the shadows, and no welded gates can bar it from ingress and egress. In a very real sense, Davis never came back (and Ellison might agree and wag his head). He got lost there. But he managed to find company. Davis developed a rapport with his audience (and his supporting musicians were sacrificed on this altar, willingly), and Davis became increasingly less interested in the mere "followers" who didn't "get it" when it came to grasping the sorts of places he was creating, *with* them and *for* them to share collectively. "I always listen to what I can leave out," he said many times. *That* is the egress of possibility.

The true interpreters of his day knew exactly what he was doing, and they understood their role.[35] His back to the audience, far from being an arrogant snub, was an invitation to listen with him, to the way he would suggest a theme for everyone to consider, and the audience, knowing his habits, his history, the things he might do with such a riff, *joined* and then Miles would leave off, provide a silence (indeed, he was known widely as the Prince of Silence—*and* of Darkness) for the audience to enter the in-between, to share the possibilities, to follow their own feeling about it. And when he came back in (i.e., let loose some actual tones), it was not always to define the egress that had occurred during the silence. Very often it was to pull the listeners actively back into the *constellational* path he was feeling; these were more like calls across a dark interval that said to the listeners, "Okay, you keep going where you are going, for now, but I'm over here."

One can often hear, in the live recordings, little gasps from audience members, experiencing the way that Davis's path had crossed or complemented or even contradicted their own. They rebuild his path, as they feel it to have been, between where he left off and where he called out with a new tone, and suddenly it is *all* present, in the "same" durational epoch (i.e., place), as immediate memory that has not (yet) dropped into the past. By this method, or more accurately, *praxis,* Miles Davis could hold constellational possibility above its definite collection by means of the collective energies and feelings of those who joined the place. He would not be able to do this sort of thing alone, as Poe rightly observed. It requires a community of interpretation (to invoke Royce's happy phrase). One can *feel* it build in these recordings until everyone who is capable understands that soon, very soon, Miles will take control again and let those possibilities go, and that together all of those who could participate would claim a fair share of credit for the value that had accrued, in all its wondrous ambiguity.

This holding and release is a huge generic contrast, to use Whitehead's apt term. The place Davis creates through this action is also a generalized space, something that could be coordinated topologically and genetically specified in infinitely many ways, but the specifications wouldn't be equally intense. For guidance on intense specification, listen to Miles Davis and "modal playing." The outcome of such cooperative specification is no particular, no merely logical individual. It is a *meaning* that is inherently general and that is also plenty definite (everything actual is possible, and everything I am describing can be experienced by finite actual entities); it is also intelligibly determinate—there is no failure of structural relation and clarity here. Yet, this feeling, this presentational symbol, subsequently in the possession of each who inhabits the place, is not the sort of thing that can be explained by the scientific method of inquiry, taken alone. That is partly because this symbol does not exist in any one biological body. The body that experiences this presentational symbol is both spatially and temporally mobile, but it is a *sensus communis* that precedes all individuated biological bodies, and indeed, it *makes* those bodies from its own ephemeral activities.

It isn't even close to true that Miles Davis is the discoverer of the egress of possibility.[36] The feeling associated with it is to be found not only in all daily human experience, but also in animal experience, and also below the level of organization we call "societies" of actual occasions, those organic associations of events that hold together from next to next with a depth in the whole that pervades and defines the intensity of the parts. In fact, the egress of possibility is both part and parcel of the accretion of value itself. It is everywhere and experienced by everyone. But what Davis did was to bring it out in a "semblance," to use Langer's term, that made it available for precognitive but highly refined interpretive experience. This semblance is available only to those who listen *actively*—it will not appear for those who merely sit and wait for the performer to do all the work.

The experience with Davis was an experience of a "between," not quite either this or that, and never becoming so—it was only *kind of* blue, it has a proximity in place and duration toward blue; it would not be arriving at any Newtonian or Einsteinian space, and its gravity was not a physical force. But that doesn't deprive it of rich determinate meaning. Indeed, it would be a more apt inquiry to see whether those overdetermined spaces of Einstein and Newton have any *meaning* at all. Can we overlay such spaces with places? If so, the believers in such space don't do much to maintain its humane viability. Everything egresses and nothing concresces in such spaces. I am glad that space isn't actually like that.

Davis is a much better steward of meaning, including the meanings we don't want to examine. And here, of course, we find the tragic, in the American sense of an avoidable *collection* of possibilities. Things did not have to be as they are. But, as Royce rightly enjoined, there is a Romantic value to such tragedy. I may exaggerate my own "moment" (in all the meanings of that term) until I receive an Emersonian compensation for the fact that God doesn't need me, in the sense of *just the me* that is actual. Still, as Royce says, today's work is done. It need not be repeated. Possibilities have genuinely egressed. The tragedy is complete. We may now sit back and see whether the goat man with the giant phallus flounces out onstage to mock the gods and give the mortals a span of laughter. Sometimes, after all, the Satyr play does ensue.[37]

And this note of the actual individual who is but did not have to be brings us, at length, to the matter of "person." Herbie Hancock said, "I don't know how to put it into words, but it's like, once you've been touched by Miles, you're changed forever. But what you change *to* is more of who you really are."[38] I think that there is something in the difference between what we are told not to do and what we are encouraged to not do that makes all the difference to the emergence of person. Those who bring us to the moment of person are those who encourage us to listen to what is possible and to let go of what is incompatible with the place we are making, enacting. When we have let those possibilities egress, the ingression is seamless and what we do is done without effort and with the cooperation of all else that is creative of meaningful place. We let each other happen, and we do so together or not at all.

Music teaches this "truth," if one dares to invoke such a word, but so does every other activity, if we can rise beyond the needless opposition of the ontic as over against the ontological, and if we can move beyond mere being toward death and into the much freer experience of the egress of possibility. The ground of person lies with this latter, precognitive *sensus communis* and place-making. Authentic "being-with" is no puzzle, it is the gift of every mortal who can develop a free relation in community with those who resolutely let possibility egress. These souls are those among us who bring the intervals, the rests, the hiatus, the letting be, yes, even the *Gelassenheit* that is so elusive to Heidegger's followers, who are not known either for their love of jazz or for releasing the mechanisms of control that ensure the importance of being important in the teeming and confused mass of humanity, thrown, fallen, situated, and chattering without surcease about the meaning of being. It isn't exactly making life into a work of art. Seeking a better account of possibility would be a place to begin.

Notes

1. See my extended treatment of how the variable flux creates the space of life in "Evolutionary Time, and the Creation of the Space of Life," in *Space, Time, and the Limits of Human Understanding*, ed. Shyam Wuppuluri and Giancarlo Ghirardi (Berlin: Springer Verlag, 2016), ch. 31, 381–400; see also Randall E. Auxier and Gary L. Herstein, *The Quantum of Explanation: Whitehead's Radical Empiricism* (London: Routledge, 2017), chs. 7–9.

2. I will cite some of my own work on Bergson's ontology in subsequent notes, but also see Robert Fieldler, "Self and Person: Distinctions in Bergson," in *In the Sphere of the Personal: New Perspectives in the Philosophy of Persons*, ed. James Beauregard and Simon Smith (Wilmington, DE: Vernon Press, 2016), ch. 8.

3. Poe's stories are widely accessible in many editions. An easy source is: http://poestories.com/read/islandofthefay, accessed April 30, 2017. I will not worry with notes for each quote. The stories are short and the passages are easy to find.

4. See especially Auxier and Herstein, *The Quantum of Explanation*.

5. See Whitehead, *Process and Reality*, corrected edition by D. Griffin and D. Sherburne (New York: Free Press, 1978), 23, 27, 65–73.

6. Brightman discusses this in many places, but see, for example, *The Problem of God* (New York: Abingdon Press, 1930), 172–76.

7. See my extended treatment of how the variable flux creates the space of life in "Evolutionary Time," ch. 31, 381–400.

8. Poe, "The Island of the Fay" (1850), second paragraph.

9. Josiah Royce did some outstanding work on the structure of exclusion of possibility prior to Heidegger's efforts, but there was no meshing of these two philosophies. Interestingly, Charles Sherover noticed the complementarity and captured a part of it in his essay "From Kant and Royce, to Heidegger," which became the title essay of a collection published near the end of Sherover's life (Washington, DC: Catholic University of America Press, 2003). But Sherover does not have an explicit account of possibility.

10. Heidegger discusses the "technical interpretation of thinking" in a number of places, but most famously in the long opening paragraph of the "Letter on Humanism," which has been variously translated. See the nice translation by Miles Groth here: http://wagner.edu/psychology/files/2013/01/Heidegger-Letter-On-Humanism-Translation-GROTH.pdf.

11. The line is from Hölderlin's poem "Patmos." See Heidegger, "The Question Concerning Technology," in *The Question Concerning Technology and Other Essays*, trans. W. Lovitt (New York: Harper Torchbooks, 1977), 3–35.

12. Heidegger did read volumes 1 and 2 of Cassirer's masterwork. The Cassirer/Heidegger relationship is not an easy topic to consider in any brief scope. I recommend Michael Friedman's *Parting of the Ways* (Chicago: Open Court, 2001), and Peter E. Gordon, *Continental Divide? Cassirer, Heidegger, Davos* (Cambridge: Harvard University Press, 2010). There is a nice review of the latter book by Jeffrey Andrew Barash, "Ernst Cassirer, Martin Heidegger, and the Legacy of Davos," in *History and Theory* 51 (Oct. 2012): 436–50. It is available on line here: https://www.academia.edu/3982924/Ernst_Cassirer_Martin_Heidegger_and_the_Legacy_of_Davos.

13. Langer, *Philosophy in a New Key*, 3rd ed. (Cambridge: Harvard University Press, 1957), 116–17 (subsequently cited as *PNK*).

14. Ibid., 117.

15. Bataille's idea is understood, by him, in primarily economic terms, but it has implications in every imaginable direction. See Georges Bataille, *The Accursed Share*, 3 vols., trans. Robert Hurley (Cambridge, MA: Zone Books, 1991, 1993). For a fuller discussion of the distinction between "place" and "space," see my "From Presentational Symbol to Dynamic Form: Ritual, Dance, and Image," in *Engagement: Dance and Philosophy*, ed. Rebecca L. Farinas (London: Routledge, 2018), forthcoming.

16. I take the term *affordances* from Eleanor and James J. Gibson. See the latter's "The Theory of Affordances," in *Perceiving, Acting, and Knowing*, ed. R. Shaw and J. Bransford (London: Routledge, 2017 [1977]), 67–82. I do not see their theory as departing from Bergson's general ontology in any important way, but rather, they have filled out Bergson's ontology with admirable empirical detail and theoretical insight. Something similar may be said of Michael Polanyi and Marjorie

Grene, who worked together on making a process biology into a viable account, both experimentally and theoretically, and joining that account to a defensible theory of knowledge that avoids scientism. An affordance is the possibility of an action on an object or environment, but I place a greater emphasis on the word *possibility* in this definition than psychologists would. I have discussed this ontology in some detail in *"In Vino Veritas,"* in *Southwest Philosophy Review* 30, no. 1 (Jan. 2014): 39–66; and "Image and Act: Bergson's Ontology and Aesthetics," in *Sztuka i Filozofia / Art and Philosophy* 45 (2014): 64–81. The latter is accessible at: http://bazhum.muzhp.pl/media//files/Sztuka_i_Filozofia/Sztuka_i_Filozofia-r2014-t45/Sztuka_i_Filozofia-r2014-t45-s64-81/Sztuka_i_Filozofia-r2014-t45-s64-81.pdf. I am reserving the term *allowance* (my own) for the way that variable flux makes available the spaces that can become places through our symbolic acts. Thus, the "affordance" takes the reality of spaces for granted and the "allowance" does not.

17. The terms *ingress* and *ingression* to describe the presence of possibilities (unfortunately called "eternal objects") is Whitehead's. The term *egress* as applied to possibility is my own, but obviously implied by Whitehead's usage. The theory of ingression in Whitehead is complex and not entirely filled out in his corpus. Gary Herstein and I spend a great deal of effort explaining it and filling it out in *The Quantum of Explanation*, chs 7–9. For now, it is enough to note that in everything actual we find one "collection" of determinate possibilities, made definite in their actuality, and infinitely many "constellations" of less determinate but determinable "constellations" of possibilities that are intelligible but not made definite in anything actual—possibilities that never become actual. The terms *collection* and *constellation* are ours, but the distinction between determinate and definite possibilities is Whitehead's.

18. Poe wrote a number of stories on the borderland of life and death, famously "The Pit and the Pendulum," and "The Fall of the House of Usher," and "The Premature Burial," and less famously "The Oval Portrait" (which was originally entitled "Life in Death"), but his most philosophical investigations of the borderland of darkness and light and of life and death are not as widely read. One should consult "Mesmeric Revelation" and "The Facts in the Case of M. Valdemar" for a fuller picture of Poe's ideas about being toward death.

19. I borrow this point from the work of the Deweyan/Aristotelian logician Delton Thomas Howard, who congenially chooses the terms *projection* and *shadow* for the point, and anticipates Quine's destruction of the modern analytic/synthetic distinction in 1951. See W. V. O. Quine, "Two Dogmas of Empiricism," *Philosophical Review* 60 (1951): 20–43. It is easy, at this historical remove, to make too much of Quine's contribution. The death knell of the analytic/synthetic distinction had been ringing for some time earlier, in the work of Quine and others, not the least of whom would be Dewey. See Howard, *Analytical Syllogistics* (Evanston: Northwestern University Press, 1946), see esp. 155–59. Langer uses the term *projection* similarly throughout the course of her work (indeed, Howard may have taken

the term from her, since they were colleagues at the time he wrote the book just cited), and she uses it interchangeably with a very interesting and powerful interpretation of "analogy." Langer is correct, I think. There really is an analogical relation at work in this difficult "shadowing," but it is beyond my present scope to treat it in detail. I have discussed Langer's view in detail in "Susanne Langer on Symbols and Analogy: A Case of Misplaced Concreteness?" *Process Studies* 26, no. 1–2 (1997): 86–106. My present point is only that there is more going on here in this description of Poe's than a nice metaphor, and indeed, Poe himself has the matter worked out in systematic detail in *Eureka*, a work that deserves more attention than it has received.

20. See Nietzsche, *Thus Spake Zarathustra*, Part 1, Speech 21. The 1990 Adrian Lyne film *Jacob's Ladder* is worth considering in this context.

21. See my "Evolutionary Time and the Creation of the Space of Life," cited above, for a fuller account of the creation of space by variable overlapping modes of temporality. The contrast and relation between space and place discussed in the context of dance and Langer's philosophy is in "From Presentational Symbol to Dynamic Form: Ritual, Dance, and Image," also cited above.

22. Cassirer, *The Myth of the State* (New Haven: Yale University Press, 1946), 49 (henceforth *MS*). The first quotation is from Montaigne, *Essays*, 1, 19, in *Works*, trans. Wm. W. Hazlitt, revised ed. by O. W. Wright (New York: H. W. Derby, 1861), I, 30. The second quotation is from Homer's *Odyssey*, Bk. XI, v. 488.

23. I refer readers again to Peter Gordon's *Continental Divide*, cited above.

24. Langer, *PNK*, 97; my emphasis.

25. Ibid., 244–45; the quotation is from Carroll Pratt, *The Meaning of Music* (New York: McGraw-Hill, 1931), 191.

26. This sort of idea about light and possibility is thoroughly explored by James Turrell in his many installation artworks. The power of the sort of simplification of perception that is brought about by distilling light, sound, or other stimuli into purer forms is that the effect is to bring more of transition to concrescence. Under normal, more mixed conditions, synesthesia will bring less depth and more width to the intensity of experience. Concrescence is normally guided by use or other more mundane considerations. When use is set aside, and when the distillation of, for example, light has been purposively ordered, concrescence can incorporate a wide nexus with greater depth than is usual. This is one reason we close our eyes to attend to music, and there are many more examples of how these dynamic relations can be varied.

27. Whitehead, *Enquiry into the Principles of Natural Knowledge*, 1971.

28. Ibid., 198.

29. This is from a radio interview done in 1972 which was included in the audio track of the Chris Lenz documentary on the making of *Kind of Blue: Celebrating a Masterpiece*, Part 1, https://www.youtube.com/watch?v=6RqrBKfg1sE, 11:10; accessed May 24, 2016.

30. Ibid., 1:10.
31. Ibid., 13:09, 14:35.
32. Ibid., 13:35.
33. Ibid., 19:07.
34. See, again, my "Image and Act: Bergson's Ontology and Aesthetics." The thin veil discussion is in Bergson's *Laughter*.
35. In this context I want to mention the first interpreter of Miles Davis I ever knew, and to dedicate this essay to him, Kurl McKinney of Memphis, jazz musician and teacher. On given days he would make his students put away their instruments and *not play,* so that they could learn to listen to what Miles Davis wasn't playing. It gave these students a shot at becoming musicians—it did not *make* them musicians, it showed them the possibility.
36. Davis's explorations are poignant, original, and true acts of genius. They represent a kind of extreme. But he is also far from the only musician who has gone to these places. Pink Floyd, for example, did it in a completely different way, which I described in some detail in my essay, "It's All Dark: The Eclipse of the Damaged Brain," in *Metaphysical Graffiti: Deep Cuts from the Philosophy of Rock* (Chicago: Open Court, 2017), 131–57. There are many interesting ontological similarities between these two approaches to music, but the essay cited addresses the matter more as phenomenology than the present essay does.
37. I took a fairly serious (if popularized) look at this aspect of comedy in my essay "Hijackers Surprised to Find Selves in Hell," in *The Onion and Philosophy*, ed. Sharon Kaye (Chicago: Open Court, 2010), 119–29.
38. Chris Lenz, *Kind of Blue: Celebrating a Masterpiece*, Part 3, https://www.youtube.com/watch?v=tj59kLpalo8, 9:25; accessed May 24, 2016.

10

Harmony, Existence, and the Aesthetic

ROBERT CUMMINGS NEVILLE

Jonathan Edwards began the American tradition of philosophical aesthetics with extraordinary observations on the beauty of things, such as spiderwebs, in his youth. As he matured, he developed a theory of beauty as symmetry, balance, and harmony of form. He was not the first to do this, of course, following Plato, for instance, in the Philebus. But Edwards's observations on beauty evolved into a metaphysical position holding that to exist at all is to be beautiful, in the case of God, the world as a whole, and each thing in the world as a part of nature, including human beings. He said the nature of true virtue is "benevolence to being in general," and benevolence is consent, propensity, and union of heart.[1] Such benevolence is beauty for human beings. He laid the groundwork for a theory of beauty as harmony upon which Emerson, Peirce, Santayana, Dewey, and many others expanded, though perhaps not consciously extending Edwards.

I mean here to sketch a twenty-first-century American philosophical aesthetic that involves both the broad and narrow senses that Walter Gulick marks out in his opening chapter to this volume; broadly, aesthetics deals with all beauty and its perception; narrowly, with art and its appreciation.[2] I accept and applaud Gulick's contextualization of American aesthetics and mean to work within that. My sketch will entertain five main hypotheses. First, we should understand everything determinate to be a harmony. Second, every harmony has goodness. Third, beauty is the goodness a harmony has in itself and is the mark of its existence, its primal trait. Fourth, we appreciate beauty by relating to the beautiful harmony in what

I will define as an aesthetic "situation." Fifth, we can apply the theory arising from the first four hypotheses to the appreciation and criticism of art in ways that express American themes.

From this brief announcement of the topics of this essay, you can see that I share the stretch for generality and abstractness in aesthetic theory that characterizes Wesley J. Wildman's chapter in this volume, "Axiological Landscape Theory: Uniting Aesthetics, Ethics, and Inquiry."[3] Like Wildman, I view aesthetics in art as part of aesthetics more generally, and that as a part of axiology that has the most abstract range. Wildman's development of axiology in terms of landscape theory is one I fully applaud and affirm as an account of one paradigm of the connections between goodness or value and its appreciation; his use of "affordances" and appeal to evolutionary theory is an important contribution to axiological philosophy. In my judgment, however, his axiological landscape theory is not as abstract and general as he means and needs it to be. It does not account for *what* there is in the affordances of the environment and their valuations contoured to the landscapes that is valuable or good, only *that* things are valued in this way and that this valuation can be extended to all sorts of landscapes, including cultural and artistic ones.[4] The tacit appeal to evolutionary success and individual continuance begs the question as to what makes them good. So I believe that true generality and abstractness of the sort Wildman seeks is to be found in the examination of determinateness and its axiological structures, the topics of the first two sections to follow.[5]

Harmony

My first general hypothesis in this aesthetic theory is that to be a determinate thing is to be a harmony. This general Platonic/Edwardsian/Confucian hypothesis stands in contrast to the Aristotelian hypothesis that to be a determinate thing is to be a substance.[6] Whereas goodness for a substance is its completeness, goodness for a harmony is its aesthetic properties of just fitting together (in ways to be explored here). A substance bears its properties in itself, as the subject of a sentence bears predicates. A harmony has properties only in relation to other things. Please forgive the abstract assertiveness of this hypothesis; it will be built slowly in detail to become intelligible and illustrated to become plausible.

The analysis of harmony hangs on an analysis of determinateness. To be determinate is to be something rather than something else, and so every determinate thing is determinate with respect to something else. Therefore, a determinate thing needs two kinds of components, conditional ones by virtue of which it is related to those things with respect to which it is determinate, and essential components by virtue of which it integrates all its components and has its own being over against the things that condition it. Thus, a determinate thing is a harmony of conditional and essential components. If it had only conditional components, it could not stand as a term in relation to other things and everything would be swallowed up in relations, with nothing to relate, something like Bradley's Absolute. If it had only essential components, it could have no relations with other things that could define it as different from them, as determinate with respect to them. As a harmony of conditional and essential components, a determinate thing is both defined relationally and defined in terms of its own existence as something in relation. A thing cannot be defined only in terms of other things, and it cannot be defined only in terms of some kind of internal atomic nature. It must be a harmony of both conditional and essential components.

The first level of aesthetic relevance of the hypothesis that any determinate thing is a harmony is that any harmony relates to all the things with respect to which it is determinate. Thus, nature is predominantly a tissue of relations relating harmonies. Because of the essential components, each harmony harmonizes its relational components from its own perspective. Nature is a togetherness of things *relating* to one another. The aesthetic principles that make things cohere or harmonize are manifest in the relations of things in nature.

That things are harmonies means that they all have four traits, according to my hypothesis, just by virtue of being determinate.[7] Any harmony has (1) a form, (2) the components that are harmonized by that form, (3) a location in an existential field that is constituted by the ways the harmony relates to the things with respect to which it is determinate and vice versa, and (4) the goodness or value that is achieved by getting these components together with this form in this location relative to other things. The claim about goodness or value is what is most interesting to an aesthetic theory, and the next section will develop it at length.[8]

The form of a harmony is the pattern of how its components fit together. Some harmonies are static, so that their form is how they are together at a moment. Most things in the world, however, are processes of change, so that their harmonies are dynamic and play out in time. Regarding art, a finished painting has a mainly static form, whereas a musical performance has a dynamic one. Remembering that the components of a harmony include all the other harmonies with respect to which it is determinate, the form of a harmony includes many things that are not obvious when we think of the thing as a substance. For instance, the form of a cherry blossom opening, flourishing, then dying and falling includes not only that trajectory, which can be celebrated in painting and poetry, but also the temperature of its duration and all the ecosystems that affect its nutritional and metabolic base. The way the form of the blossom composes the atmospheric and biospheric components likely is by assigning them trivial or vague functions, reducing them to rather local conditions for its trajectory. *Triviality, vagueness, narrowness,* and *width* are terms I borrow from Whitehead and will define more technically in the next section.[9] But those distant conditions are still components of the cherry blossom, and its form assigns them functions within the blossom's harmony. The components of the blossom that we notice most likely are assigned functions that Whitehead would have called narrowness and width. Narrowness is a function of components that have high contrast such as shape, color, odor, and so forth; width is a function of components that integrate the many narrow components and hold them together, such as the physical structure of the blossom on the tree, its DNA, and the like.[10]

The components of a harmony include both the other harmonies in relation to which the harmony is determinate in some respect and the essential components by virtue of which the harmony composes itself. These essential components include the spontaneity in changing things according to which what is actualized is added to, moral decisions such as commitment to a course of action or a selection among alternative possibilities, and, in cases such as the cherry blossom, the DNA functioning both as essential for organization as well as a condition to be integrated with, say, available nutrients. The components of an oil painting, for instance, would include not only the essential ones involving the artist's creativity but also perhaps the interests of the person commissioning the painting, the potential role of the painting in the artist's career, and anticipations of the interests and abilities of the potential viewers, as well as the obvious paints, canvas, composition, and so forth. If any of those things were different, the harmony of the painting would be different. In understanding how a harmony composes its components, it is sometimes important to look at the components in their own integrity, not just according to the roles they play in the harmony itself.

Every harmony has a location in an existential field relating it to the other things with respect to which it is determinate. The ways in which a harmony internally relates itself to other things, and the ways in which those other things relate to one another and to the harmony in question, constitute an existential field of mutual relevance. This field is not an external container such as a space-time box but is constituted by the roles the harmonies play in each other. This does not make sense in a substance worldview where things have sharp boundaries and have what Whitehead called "simple location."[11] The doctrine of simple location says that things are located only in their own proper place and can be in other things only by representation unless their proper place is contained within the proper place of the other things. The hypothesis of harmony says that a harmony includes other things within itself as components while those things also have their own existence not reduced to their functions within the harmony. In addition, things can be represented within harmonies, but that is just a special way of including the other things as components. Within the formal perspective of a given harmony, other things are assigned functional roles in that harmony. But they also have their own natures to be appreciated as beautiful in their own way and perhaps deferred to. Landscape paintings, for instance, especially those of the American Hudson River School, can be appreciated for pointing to nature beyond what they present or represent.

The goodness of a harmony consists of the value achieved by getting its components together in the form that it has at the existential location it has with respect to other things. This sense of goodness, of course, is the root of beauty, and it is a complicated philosophical hypothesis to defend, the task of the next section. Beauty is that aspect of the goodness of a harmony that it has in itself. A harmony, of course, has many kinds of goodness insofar as it functions as a component in other harmonies. It also has value for what it does to or for things that function within it as components. For the sake of my hypothesis, I define beauty as the goodness that a thing has in itself in contrast to the kinds of goodness it has for other things. The "in itself" here should not be understood as the properties of a substance within its boundaries. "In itself" as I mean it here includes all the other harmonies with respect to which this one is determinate insofar as they are harmonized within the harmony's form.

Those other harmonies have their own existential locations and goods that may not be part of the harmony in question.

With this sketch of a theory of harmony in hand, let me turn to goodness in harmony. Although I want to tie aesthetics to beauty, many of the aesthetic notions we associate with beauty apply throughout to goodness of other sorts. A drawback to the term *harmony* is that for some people it always has the connotation of being nice and helpful. When things are harmonious, "everyone gets along." Yet, in point of fact, although everything is good in itself, and so is beautiful in itself, things can be very bad for other things that they affect. An aesthetically beautiful HIV virus is devastatingly wicked for those whom it affects; a perfect storm kills fishermen; a massive shift in tectonic plates is a beautiful geological phenomenon but destroys living forms all around; a beautiful supernova is a cascade of lost forms. Only with respect to its beauty, that is, the goodness it achieves in itself, is a harmony simply good. Given the relationality of the universe just sketched, no harmony is only in itself.

Goodness in Harmony

If beauty is a special kind of goodness, then we must begin with elaborating the hypothesis that every harmony has goodness. This argument has three steps, cumulatively making a case for Leibniz's idea that value consists in density of being. The first step deals with the ways in which the combination of components within the hierarchy of a form leads to more reality than the components not combined. The second deals with the ways in which the combinations of components exhibit both complexity and simplicity, and the harmony of complexity and simplicity exhibits elegance. The third deals with the ways the pattern within a harmony, its form, composes the components in relations that exhibit narrowness, width, vagueness, and triviality. To understand that goodness or value consists in density of being requires all three levels of analysis.

The first level of analysis is fairly simple. The components of a harmony can be combined with one another in various ways that constitute new harmonies, and then recombined to constitute even more new harmonies, and so forth. The more harmonies that arise out of combination and recombination, the denser the being of the overall harmony.

The second level of analysis notes that the patterns of combination of components can have complexity in the sense that they contain many different kinds of components. They can also have simplicity in the sense that their components are not of different kinds but are homogeneous. Mere conjunction would be pure complexity and total homogeneity would be pure simplicity; neither of the pure extremes would be much of a harmony, and most harmonies have various elements of both complexity and simplicity. The combination of simplicity and complexity with which the components are patterned I call "elegance." A given baseline of components can be constituted with many different kinds and degrees of complexity and simplicity, thus with different kinds of elegance.

Elegance is the aesthetic trait of fitting things together with complexity and simplicity. Each harmony built on that baseline has its own kind of goodness, I want to argue, which is to say each has its own elegance. Each is elegant in its own way. Sometimes we want to say that one harmony is *more* elegant than another, and hence better. Somehow this has to do with optimizing both simplicity and complexity, although there might be variant ways of doing this. This is especially the case when faced with harmonizing a moral conflict. Also, when painters imagine first this composition with the three colors and then that, they want to be able to identify the better or more elegant compositional pattern. Nevertheless, each harmony built upon that baseline has the value of getting its components together with its harmonic pattern or form, relative to the other things with respect to which it is determinate.

Now let me add yet a third level of analysis to this aesthetic theory, that of the compositional functions of narrowness, width, vagueness, and triviality, Whitehead's aesthetic categories reconstructed within my theory. Narrowness is the focusing or concentrating of many components so as to have high contrast between two or more traits that just fit together and yet have depth of differences. Whitehead called this intensity of contrast.

Width is the function of components in a harmony that put the narrow important foci together. In a painting, for instance, the compositional lines provide the width that arranges the narrow color contrasts together. Because harmonies can have many different places in a harmony, they can function as narrow foci in some places and in other places function to provide wide coherence of different focal points. The components in a harmony that we usually notice, and that are important in the sense that they determine how the harmony hangs together and how it behaves in a wider environment, are narrowness and width.

Nevertheless, components also can function vaguely so as to represent other components that therefore do not have to function with narrowness and width. So, for instance, we look into the sky that contains a zillion (that is a very large number!) meteorological events, but grasp them with the color blue that is vague with respect to all those meteorological events. The meteorological events are harmonized within us by being transformed into a blue color patch we see. When the mental image of the color blue vaguely stands for the zillion meteorological events, those meteorological events function trivially within the person. That is, it is as if they were not there in forming the harmony of the person. They are still components, and if they should change in character, for instance lose their light, the mental image of blue would not contain them vaguely. The vague functioning of components is the way by which the infinite complexity of components of components of components is organized so that only a few focal and coherent elements determine the value of a harmony. Suppose the painting is an oil portrait of George Washington. Among its components are all the things that led to the production of the paints, canvas, and brushes, processes going back to the decomposition of dinosaurs to produce oil. But just having those paints in the tubes on the easel constitute components that function vaguely to define the painter's situation and allow that long history to be trivialized and make almost no difference to what the painter does with the paints in that situation. A crucial part of the goodness of the harmony of the painting is that it is recognizably George Washington, and the artist takes this into account in creating the painting, anticipating how Washington will be recognized and what emotions and historical events will be associated with him. The artist is likely to have a vague anticipation of the viewers, however, trivializing the differences between the real possible viewers.

The more a harmony trivializes the components of components that play narrow and wide functions in it, the shallower it is. A rock is very shallow, vaguely repeating its earlier stages for the most part and trivially rejecting nearly all cosmic history. A human being, however, is likely to be very deep in bearing a DNA with an epochal history, living in a place with great complexity that makes a difference to human life, and having capacities of memory that allow for the vague symbolic encoding of many things that can function, through the vague symbols to determine narrowness and width in the person's life.

Returning to our thought experiment, the discussion of the form of a harmony supposed that there are baseline components. These were treated as completely vague, having characters that are different from one another but neglecting all their own components of components as trivial for the sake of the discussion. The harmonies discussed there were shallow in that they were no deeper than the baseline. Going in the other direction, the more those harmonies exhibited narrowness and width of components that resulted in intensity of contrast—narrow things consisting of contrasts are made coherent with the broad things that put them together in the harmony as a whole.

In reality, there is no baseline for any harmony save what we provide by how we focus attention, a topic for another time. No harmony is completely vague with regard to its components; in fact, it is a harmony because it has components that it composes with narrowness and width as well as vagueness and triviality. For any harmony, some of the roots are very deep and others trivial, some of the components are intense in narrowness and width and others not. Each harmony is uniquely itself in the goodness it holds.

The density of being of a harmony is the unique goodness it achieves by its composition of components that can be fitted together with narrowness, width, vagueness, and triviality, achieving an elegance of its own. Harmonies have their own density of being in the larger environments, and they have components with their own densities of being. The "ten thousand things," to use the Confucian expressions for "world," are lumpy with densities of being, and each harmony is itself a density of being. This is what its goodness is, as getting these components together in this form in relation to the other things to which it is related.

This has been a complex argument developing a line of argument about aesthetic coherence as goodness that runs powerfully through Edwards. Now we need to ask why we identify this density of being with what we take to be good or valuable. This requires an examination of the experience of goodness, because that is where my appeal must go: "See? Isn't this what you mean by goodness?" Before that, however, I need to identify beauty among the kinds of goods a harmony might have.

Beauty and Existence in Harmony

For the purposes of my hypothesis, I heuristically define beauty as the kind of goodness a harmony has in itself, regardless of the other kinds of goods, or ills, the harmony might have for other things. Recall how complex a harmony is just "in itself" if the hypothesis about harmony here is close to correct: every harmony includes as components within "itself" all the things with respect to which it is determinate. This is so even when its form makes the vast majority of things in the world with respect to which it is determinate to be trivial in its own shape, perhaps not even vaguely represented. The crucial cosmological point to get here, however, is that the harmony composes those things within itself so as to have its own-being as a harmony. The essential components of the harmony work to make the harmony something in itself over and above the other harmonies that are its components. Without the essential components, the harmony would not be anything of which those other harmonies might be components: there would simply be the other harmonies. In their own turn, those other harmonies would not be determinately different from one another unless each had its own essential components so as to be itself over against the others. Unless harmonies have their own essential components, they would not have their own-being so as to be able to be determinate with respect to anything else. If things were not determinate with respect to anything else they could not be different, and so there would be only one thing. But being totally and in principle indeterminate, that one thing would be no different from nothing. Therefore, if there is something determinate, there must be a plurality of determinate things each with its essential components. That plurality of things might share all their mutually conditioning components. Each also needs its own essential components so as to be itself in relation to the others.

A harmony "in itself" is its components, both conditional and essential, formed or configured in its own way, located in its own place in existential fields with other harmonies. Considered just so, the goodness it has is its beauty. To be sure, that beauty takes on other kinds of goodness when the harmony becomes a component in other things, including its multitude of relations that affect the things around it. That beauty also affects the goods of other things insofar as it modifies them or affects them and so has other kinds of goodness (or badness relative to the goods of other things). But what I mean by beauty is simply the goodness the harmony has in itself.

Beauty is thus the goodness the harmony bears just because it exists. Beauty is the good of existence itself. The existences of the plurality of determinate things complicate one another because they condition one another. Any harmony that comes to be achieves the beauty of its own existence. For any of its components, however, there is the existence of the component with its own beauty. Within the harmony, the component is integrated with some narrow, wide, vague, or trivial function in a form in which it fits with the other components. Within the harmony, the component contributes to some kind of elegance balancing complexity and simplicity, and to the density of being of the harmony. Yet, the component does not only play functional roles within the harmony; it has its own in-itself nature, which is its existence. If within the harmony the component is modified, each of those modifications is itself a harmony with its own existence, and therefore its own essential components.

Although there are many kinds of essential components, for actual things in space/time, they include spontaneous creativity that adds something to what was already actualized, and that resolves open alternate possibilities down to the singular possibility actualized. This spontaneity provides an ontological depth to existence. Earlier I characterized existential depth as the ways and degrees to which components in the past or distance are carried in to the makeup of a harmony, the elements below any artificially drawn baselines' representations. Now I call attention to the ontological depth of existence, namely, that harmonies exist because they contain essential components that give them their own-being over against their conditioning components and allowing them to receive and integrate those conditions into their own harmonies. Not only does a harmony have the ontological depth of its own-being coming from its own essential components, each of its components has that ontological depth on its own terms.

Now the "density of being" takes on a new dimension of meaning. It refers not only to the complexity and simplicity of a harmony resulting in its elegance. It refers also to the ontological depth of the harmony and of each of its own components. Suppose we would say, as Edwards did, that because each thing is a creature of God, its existential createdness consists in its beauty that is its goodness as simply existing in itself. To be a thing is to be a beautiful creature, for Edwards. To be a creature is to be a beautiful thing, for Edwards. I will not defend his or any other theory of ontological creation here.[12] Nevertheless, with this theory of harmonies as good, and with the goodness of beauty insofar as they have goodness in themselves in their sheer existence relative to other things, harmonies can be understood in an Edwardsian way to exist because they are beautiful.

I have made some strong philosophical claims here that make aesthetics more abstract and complicated than many people hope it would be. The abstractness of the theory of goodness so that it applies to everything determinate stands in its favor. So does its coherence if in fact it turns out to be coherent on further examination. But how does it stand when illustrated by experience? Don't you have moments when you focus on something in nature, a bird, or a branch, or light shining on a rock, and become transfixed by its beauty, by its existence just as it is in the moment? Don't you have moments with friends when time seems to stand still and you focus just on the existence of the moment as something in itself that you might call beautiful? Steve Odin has written a remarkable book mentioned earlier about Japanese aesthetic sensibilities and Whitehead's theory of tragic beauty: it is when something perishes that our attention is called to the beauty of its existence, now contrasted with its fading or nonexistence. Sister Mary Corita Kent, the American artist famous for the painted gas storage tank in Boston, had a lesson for her art students in which she gave them sheets of paper with a rectangle cut out in the center. With these "finders" they would set boundaries on things in nature, the classroom, or magazines so as to see elements isolated for the moment, "harmonized" momentarily by the finders. This was supposed to show both the sheer existence of the isolated view through the rectangle and a beauty that would not have been noticed otherwise. Many moments occur in common experience in which attention is suddenly called to something isolated so as to be experienced "in itself," and that experience notes its beauty and its sheer existence, which are the same thing.

To be sure, this naive appeal to experience only carries so much weight until we have a theory of the experience of aesthetic objects, things regarded as to their beauty, which is the next topic.

The Situation of Appreciating Beauty

I have spoken of beauty as a goodness proper to beautiful things, and the argument for this has to come down to getting you to agree that this is how we see things to be beautiful. The experience of something as beautiful is very different from the beauty in the thing experienced, however (although the experience of something beautiful might be beautiful as an experience, too). Experience is always interpretive, mediated by signs. We can experience the beauty in a thing only in terms of the signs we have to interpret it. Because we never interpret a thing in all respects, only in the respects for which we have signs and that fall within our interpreting purposes and habits, we never grasp the whole beauty of something. Our aesthetic experience is always partial to our own perspective. Nevertheless, we commonly revise our aesthetic judgments on learning something new about the aesthetic object, or changing our perspective. Therefore, it is something in the object that constitutes it as beautiful and about which we might be wrong in our interpretation. This requires greater explanation.

The house where my wife and I live in Milton, Massachusetts, is on a rocky hill and faces west. Our good neighbors Tim and Tony, across the street and slightly downhill, have a beautiful house with a side yard surrounded by a yew hedge and containing flowering shrubs and small trees. Directly in front of our view Tim and Tony have a classically shaped hemlock in which birds like to nest, but which is not so tall we can't see over and around it. Blessedly often we are treated to beautiful sunsets, moving swiftly with torqueing shapes and tumbling colors before the prevailing northwest wind. For more than a quarter of a century incrementally we have built up a sunset viewing terrace with a small fountain and four reasonably comfortable chairs where we can relax with some wine (white for her, red for me), delight in the sunset, and watch the birds go to roost as evening falls. That's the time of day for neighbors to stroll by, stopping to talk and sometimes joining us for wine; our sunset terrace has a definite social location in the habits of our neighborhood and in the punctuation of our lives.

In what does the beauty of the sunset consist? It is a harmony, of course, the beautiful sunset, and it is located within a vast global, solar system–wide, indeed galaxy-wide, existential field of a gazillion (that is more than a million, million, zillions) harmonies with all sorts of causal properties. Most of these cosmic harmonies are trivial in the beautiful sunset. Unlike most of our daily lives in which the rotation of the Earth is vaguely dismissed by attention to the clock time of night and day, the beautiful sunset includes observation of that moving rotation while not always acknowledging the astrophysics of it. The beautiful sunset itself is a harmony of a kind I call a "situation" that includes at least the meteorological events on the horizon and the intentional observations of us viewers. That situation also includes the physical geography that allows the viewing angle from our sunset terrace to the meteorological events in the sky above the horizon, as well as the intervening atmosphere that allows us to see that far (our area is too often is fogged in, which makes the beautiful sunset an impossible harmony insofar as we are concerned). The meteorological events include the winds blowing the clouds as well as the angle of the setting sun to our horizon. The situation in which there is a beautiful sunset in addition includes viewers with the optical capacities to see the colors in the sky, to see the shapes and movements of the clouds, and with the kind of attention to watch something happening on the horizon.

The situation of the beautiful sunset has another characteristic of its harmony, namely, the perspective and intentionality of the viewers to enjoy sunsets, including this one. Indeed, by "situation" I mean the kind of harmony that takes its form and limitations from the intentionality structure, broadly interpreted, of the experiencers. Without the intentionality structure of the experiencers, there could be many elements in the connections between the meteorological events and the people on the sunset terrace, but these would not make up the beautiful sunset. In the language used earlier, the beautiful sunset has two points of narrow importance, the meteorological events and the intentionalities of the viewers intent on viewing. The components that are important for the situation are those that serve the viewers in their experience of the beautiful sunset. The rest of the components are only vaguely relevant, or to be dismissed as trivial.

Part of the intentionality structure of the viewers is the capacity to represent the meteorological events in the colors, shapes, and movements of human experience. The earthworm at the base of our fountain would not appreciate the sunset. Up close, the meteorological events would not be so colored or shaped; only from the angle of vision structured by the horizon, the terrace, and many things in between can the sunset be seen in the sunset's terms. The human signs and viewing habits are necessary for there to be a beautiful sunset. As I have described it, many sunsets are seen with the auxiliary symbolic associations with the pleasures of relaxing with wine, conversing with neighbors, and exercising an important rhythmic structure of our lives. The beauty of the sunset often includes many of these associations that are not merely functions of the meteorological events and our ocular structures. My wife often compares the sunset at hand with paintings by Thomas Cole and Frederick Church, Hudson River School painters. When that happens the experience of the sunset is all the richer. So the situation of the beautiful sunset includes not only the physical properties of the elements in the connections between the meteorological events and the acts of vision, but also the cultural and semiotic apparatus we bring to what we experience, often with elaborate interpretations.

The radicalness of this aesthetic observation and the theory with which I am interpreting it becomes clear when we distinguish between three kinds of harmonies that are at play. One kind of the human harmonies are my wife's and my lives. Among the components of our lives

Harmony, Existence, and the Aesthetic   225

are the sunsets we have experienced. These components are integrated into our larger lives.

A second kind of harmony is the situation within which we experience the beautiful sunset. This harmony is not just a property of our own subjective experience, as many philosophers would say. Rather, it is a harmony in which the real meteorological events, our real observations, our experiences and social lives, and all the connecting causal harmonies are integrated into the harmony of the situation. Experience in this sense is not something within a subject to which the events on the horizon are a kind of external world, but a kind of harmonic interaction or engagement between the human intentionalities and the meteorological events, something Dewey called the interaction of "organism and environment," the words Whitehead used to name his chapter on narrowness, width, vagueness, and triviality. In this harmony of the situation, the human intentional structures including the social activities are components. The beauty of the situation is that all the components harmonize so that the meteorological events are seen as a beautiful sunset. This is not just internal to the viewers but embraces all the nature and culture involved.

A third kind of harmony is what happens in the meteorological events themselves, which might not be a beautiful sunset at all. Those events would be what they are whether are not there is anyone in the right place to see them as beautiful. The beautiful sunset itself is the harmony of the situation in which the meteorological events and the viewers with their intentionality structures, plus many mediating circumstances as "width" functions, come together just so.

Given the angle of vision on the horizon and the intentionality to enjoy beautiful sunsets, there can be a beautiful sunset situation only if the meteorological events are just right. If there are no clouds or if the sun is in eclipse, there is no beautiful sunset. That is why we say that the beauty is in the sunset, not in the sunset terrace or in our imaginations or capacities to see colors, shapes, and so forth. Many days, there are no beautiful sunsets. This is the sense in which beauty is "realistic," that is, characteristic of the object interpreted in the situation. Also, there is no beautiful sunset if there is no vantage point from which it could be seen by viewers with our visual and interpretive apparatus. But if there is that vantage point, and there are such viewers, there is a beautiful sunset.

Some people will object that there is no beautiful sunset if there are no actual viewers. But I say that there is a beautiful sunset if all the conditions are right except for the fact that my wife and I are preoccupied inside and do not notice it. There is a beautiful sunset but we missed it; neighbors comment on it next day and we are sorry we missed it. The sunset is beautiful *if it could be seen* as beautiful from our vantage point. What makes the sunset beautiful or not is the meteorological events related to our vantage point so that it could be interpreted as beautiful by viewers if they are there. This point reflects a deep philosophic dispute between nominalists, who would deny the beautiful sunset if it is not observed, and realists such as the pragmatists, among whom I am, who say that the general conditions are real whether or not they are being actualized at the moment. I say that the sunset is beautiful *if it could be seen* as such in the right situation.

We human beings are in many situations where we appreciate the beauty of various things. The appreciation is in the harmonic structures of those situations, not merely in some kind of private experience. The situations of appreciation require the conditions of our intentionality structures as well as the forms of those harmonies that we appreciate as beautiful. Those situations of appreciation in turn are components of our lives, and we interpret them in terms of many kinds of interests. Because of the mutual conditioning of situations of appreciating beauty with the formation of human experience, such that each is a kind of condition in the other, human life is filled with beauty, as well as all sorts of other things that are not so good. This leads me to narrow our focus here to art.

Beauty in Art

Art is humanly produced beauty. Just about all that I have said about harmonies and their goodness, and beauty as the goodness of harmonies considered in themselves, applies to art. I also want to say some things that are specific to art.

First, I gratefully follow John Dewey in saying that art arises out of what people appreciate for the intrinsic appeal of it, beginning with what they do for the fun of it.[13] Dewey says that people sing when doing drudge work because it makes the work less odious and because singing is fun in itself. He says we deck ourselves before we clothe ourselves. We have religious festivals to appease the gods or to make it rain, but mainly because of the beauty and fun in celebrating stuff. Art begins with these common and perhaps "primitive" things that we seek, repeat, stabilize, and perform because they are intrinsically enjoyable and make our lives better. Art is more serious when we distinguish the better singers from the worse and encourage them, finally professionalizing training in music and investing in the institutions of music of all sorts. Dewey rightly advises drawing any sharp distinction between common arts and "fine" arts.

Second, works of art, including performances, can have all sorts of goods that are not themselves artful beauty. For instance, professional artists and performers sometimes make a living out of selling or performing. They earn monetary value because people think their artwork is good, but that commercial value is not part of the value of the work as art unless it affects how the artist harmonizes the components in the work, considered in itself. A season of performance by a symphony orchestra has the value of helping pay the rent on the concert hall, but that is not part of the artful beauty of the music played, unless some of it is composed just for spaces such as the hall. Many symphonies indeed are composed with sounds that are expected to be heard in large halls.

Third, the beauty of a work of art is the good it has in itself considered as a harmony. As a harmony, however, it contains all its components in a composition that exhibits the functions of narrowness, width, vagueness, and triviality. If one of the components of a work, for instance a painting, is to memorialize a donor or decorate a space in a house, then that component is taken into consideration in the composition of the painting.

Fourth, the components of a work of art include much more than the materials of the artwork, more than the paints and canvases, the moves of the dancers, or the surface story line of a novel. The paints, for instance, have among their components the history of their being made from oil and color pigments, perhaps from plants or ground colored minerals. The past of the paints' origins is trivial for the painting, and all that matters is that they are vaguely captured in the paints that the artists uses. If the artist avoids certain colors because they are too expensive, then something in the past of the paint tube is relevant to the artwork's harmonic structure. But if there is a portrait more is relevant in the person posing than the look of the person posing; the painting might aim to commemorate an important person, or portray a certain character. All those things function as relevant components.

Fifth, one of the things that distinguish artworks from natural things of beauty, besides being made by human beings, is that artworks focus very sharply on the narrow and wide compositional elements, distinguishing these elements from the trivial components that make hardly any difference and the vague components that can be pretty much taken for granted. Artwork has a high focus that often compels our attention. Things of natural beauty, by contrast, are usually deeply embedded in their deep ecologies, and this is noticed in their beauty.

Sixth, when artwork is done deliberately, not absentmindedly humming while hoeing, the prospective audience is taken into account in the composition of the work. A painter composes with some sense for what a viewer would see, what kinds of signs the viewers would bring, distinguishing how different cultures might see a painting. Music is composed and performed within music traditions, and composers and musicians work within what can be interpreted. Good artists often are creative with what people can recognize and create surprises; but this supposes expectations, or at least a repertoire of aesthetic expectations.

Seventh, all art is appreciated only in situations, as described above, in which the appreciators have signs that allow interpretation. This means that art is always embedded in a culture that involves much more than the art at hand. Art often plays all sorts of nonartistic roles in many societies, such as producing income for artists, soothing the savage beast, or structuring industries such as oil paint makers, piano tuners, and publishing houses. The culture within which its artistically relevant signs and symbols exist is interwoven with many other cultural parts of society. Nevertheless, certain arts can develop in-groups of interpretation to which most of the rest of a society's culture is indifferent.

Eighth, the appreciation of a work of art on the one hand is immediate. That is, we grasp its harmony as hanging together in itself. This is so whether we are looking at a static statue, walking through the Taj Mahal sequentially appreciating it, or listening to a performance where the harmony comes to be through time. Appreciation is the aesthetic grasp of the artwork's components as related together according to its form in its existential relation to other things with respect to which it is determinate, all as interpreted.

Ninth, on the other hand, any given appreciation of an artwork is fallible and we frequently have the experience of finding new components, new compositional elements, new symbolic references, and so forth as we see the sculpture again and again, live with the painting on the wall, hear the song over and over. This sense of many levels of sophistication in aesthetic appreciation of an artwork is magnified in the face of sophisticated art criticism. Such criticism can bring to appreciation a sense of context, of the historical place of the work, and of the elements of artist's own life. One of the great joys of art in our contemporary cultures is that it gets better and better, the more we enrich the harmony of the situation of appreciation.

Tenth, sometimes, however, it works the other way. The more we come to perceive in an artwork by more sophisticated interpretation, we see that the aesthetic harmonies' functions of narrowness, width, vagueness, and triviality just do not in fact come together as it seemed at first. The apparent beauty on first look was kitsch, or a cheap trick, or too derivative to be part of the whole integration. In literary criticism, we learn how to read a novel appreciating the truly great "densities of being" in the writing, the lesser lumps, the incoherent parts, and all the rest. Appreciating a work of art is not to see it as a surface quality with no depth, but as the contrast of all the elements composed with narrowness, width, vagueness, and triviality, at least to the degree the appreciator has the culturally informed depth to do so.

Eleventh, whereas natural things of beauty simply have what beauty they have in their own natures, works of art need to embody an ideal beauty. Art as art aims to be good art (even when it fails), so that we say that the composition does have striking points of narrow focus, compositional coherence wide enough to encompass the whole, and all the rest. So we say that novels are more or less good, most somewhat flawed. Performances have high points and low points. Most paintings are not great, employing stereotyped elements, incoherent compositions, and the like. It helps to see, read, or listen to some bad art to appreciate just how complicated and wonderful great art is. This is not to say that medium-good art (even kitsch) is not a source of beauty in people's lives, in amateur music, theater, painting, and so forth.

Twelfth, because art is appreciated always through interpretation, Wildman's point about the axiological landscape is relevant to art too. Each individual always has a personal history of what can be appreciated, what is desirable in art, what is of artistic interest. In this sense, beauty is in the eye of the beholder. However, this is only because artistic beauty requires a situation to be appreciated and the situation requires the intentionality structure of the appreciator. Different intentionality structures give rise to different appreciations and assessments. The artwork is the same in different situations in which it might be appreciated. "Classics," as David Tracy would call them, can be appreciated for widely different things in different cultures, and by different individuals within a single culture.[14]

Thirteenth, in creating a work of art, even in performing a previously composed score or script, the artist engages in a kind of creative dialectic between an imagined ideal for the work intended and the materials at hand, perhaps changing the ideal as much as the material. Before putting paint to canvas, the artist might have a vague imagined composition with imagined colors, or perhaps a quick sketch. Working on the painting, the artist modifies the imagined ideal upon seeing what some actualization looks like. Rarely would an artist have a completely determinate vision of what the painting should be; rather, the vision of the ideal or goal for the work becomes more determinate as the creative process progresses, sometimes altering radically.

Fourteenth, the other side of that dialectic is that the artist comes to know the materials better and sees new possibilities in them. Much of creativity comes in seeing such new possibilities in the materials with which an experienced artist is at home, not only in thinking of new compositional patterns. Artistic creativity is not just finding a way to harmonize a paintbox full of colors on a canvas, but finding new ways to combine them so as to produce new kinds of harmonies that add up to great intensity and depth in appreciability.

Fifteenth, kinds of works of art are almost infinitely various, and the boundaries of kinds are constantly shifting. There are songs and stories, storytelling and novels, choreography and dance, plays and performance, music of many sorts: Dewey's quaint example (in the quotation in endnote 13) is the art of walking on stilts at American Fourth of July celebrations.

Sixteenth, ways of appreciating art are also various, usually taking time, walking around a static thing, returning to a painting, participating in a performance whose harmony form takes time and space to play out, and so forth.

Seventeenth, in all cases of artwork, I suggest, what makes it art is the beauty of its harmony as it is in itself and as that is appreciable. In contrast to natural beauty, which need not be appreciated in order to be beautiful, art is intended to be appreciated for its beauty.

Conclusion

This essay has swept through an American aesthetic philosophy quickly and on many levels. I have presented mind-numbing abstractions about what it means to exist as a harmony, applications to beauty in art, an epistemology of appreciation of beauty in nature and art, and an array of points about art and its differences from beauty in nature (though that is not a sharp distinction), all of which illustrates some of the more general points. As an American aesthetic philosophy, it has elaborated existential points from Jonathan Edwards, aesthetic points from Ralph Waldo Emerson, semiotic points from Charles Peirce, artistic points from John Dewey, and a classificatory point from David Tracy. As a typical American philosopher, I integrate approaches from outside the Western tradition, something that Emerson began in a big way. With the sense of accountability of a systematic philosopher, however, I do not take this aesthetic philosophy to be good as an example of American exceptionalism but as a hypothesis worth discussing in the global philosophical conversation.

Notes

1. See Edwards's *The Nature of True Virtue*, in *The Works of Jonathan Edwards, Volume 8, Ethical Writings*, ed. Paul Ramsey (New Haven: Yale University Press, 1989), esp. 54. My own generally approving interpretation of Edwards on this point is in my *Existence: Philosophical Theology Volume Two* (Albany: State University of New York Press, 2014), 227–29. As general background for my remarks on Edwards and the aesthetic, see my "Philosophy of Nature in American Theology," in *Theologie Zwischen Pragmatismus und Existenzdenken*, ed. Gesche Linde, Richard Purkarthofer, Heiko Schulz, and Peter Steinacker (Marburg: N. G. Elwert Verlag, 2006), 3–11.

2. Walter Gulick, "Toward an American Aesthetics," in *American Aesthetics*, ed. Walter Gulick and Gary Slater (forthcoming).

3. Wesley J. Wildman, "Axiological Landscape Theory: Uniting Aesthetics, Ethics, and Inquiry" in ibid. Most of the papers in this volume come from a conference of the Institute for American Religious and Philosophical Thought that I was unable to attend. So I can interact only with a few of the papers made available to me after this essay was solicited by the editors after the conference. The conference itself sounds as if it were a splendid aesthetic experience!

4. Existentialists have worried about why not to commit suicide, and Japanese aesthetics focuses on the exquisite beauty of death and decay.

5. This essay in many ways summarizes material from a book-length writing project on which I am currently working, for now called *Metaphysics of Goodness: In Harmony and Form, Beauty and Art, Obligation and Personhood, and Flourishing and Civilization*. The first four chapters of the current draft are about harmony and goodness, the second four about beauty in art, the third four about obligation in truth, morality, rightness, and virtue, and the last four about

mediations of social structure, ritual, creativity, and civilization. These interests overlap a great deal with Wildman's. Previously I have written a trilogy called *Axiology of Thinking* that deals with different kinds of valuation and perception of value, including a philosophical cosmology showing how goodness can be real in the world and how this can be interpreted. The volumes are: *Reconstruction of Thinking* (Albany: State University of New York Press, 1981), *Recovery of the Measure* (Albany: State University of New York Press, 1989), and *Normative Cultures* (Albany: State University of New York Press, 1995). They deal with axiological valuation in imagination, interpretation, theorizing, and the pursuit of responsibility or practical reason, all of which are involved in the present essay about philosophical aesthetics.

6. The inclusion of Confucianism in the contextualizing of this essay is perhaps confusing. After all, one of the main themes of this volume is American exceptionalism in the West, and I do not claim that the American aesthetic tradition is heir to Confucianism. Nevertheless, *I* am heir to Confucianism and so bring that in to the American aesthetic tradition. My discussion of the themes of goodness and harmony in Chinese thought is in my *The Good Is One, Its Manifestations Many: Confucian Essays on Metaphysics, Morals, Rituals, Institutions, and Genders* (Albany: State University of New York Press, 2016), especially chapters 1–3 that make the connection between Platonism and Confucianism. The connection between Confucianism and American pragmatism in which this essay stands is by no means new, beginning with Ralph Waldo Emerson and flourishing with John Dewey's own trip to China. Recent studies include David L. Hall and Roger T. Ames, *The Democracy of the Dead: Dewey, Confucius, and the Hope for Democracy in China* (LaSalle, IL: Open Court, 1999) and Joseph Grange, *John Dewey, Confucius, and Global Philosophy* (Albany: State University of New York Press, 2004).

7. This somewhat staccato hypothesizing of four transcendental traits of harmonies is elaborated at very great length in my *Ultimates: Philosophical Theology Volume One* (Albany: State University of New York Press, 2013). It is easier to accept in this shortened version, however.

8. "Value" is the word most commonly used in discussions of axiology. Its drawback is that it has the connotation of being the product of valuation instead of what valuation is about in things. So I have taken to using "goodness" and the adjectival form "good" to refer to what valuation is about, the value resident in things by their nature.

9. See Alfred North Whitehead, *Process and Reality: An Essay in Cosmology*, Corrected Edition, ed. David Ray Griffin and Donald Sherburne (New York: Free Press, 1978), ch. 4, "Organisms and Environment."

10. For perhaps the best interpretation of Whitehead's value theory and its relation to cherry blossoms, see Steve Odin's *Tragic Beauty in Whitehead and*

Japanese Aesthetics (Lanham, MD: Lexington Books, 2016). The cover of the volume is important.

11. See Whitehead's *Science and the Modern World* (New York: Macmillan, 1925), ch. 3, 72.

12. But see my *Ultimates*, part 3, where it is defended in great detail.

13. See Dewey's *Experience and Nature*, in *John Dewey: The Later Works, 1925-1953: Volume I: 1925*, ed. Jo Ann Boydston, this volume ed. Joseph Ratner (Carbondale and Edwardsville, IL: Southern Illinois University Press, 1981), ch. 3. Dewey wrote:

> Human experience in the large, in its coarse and conspicuous features, has for one of its most striking features preoccupation with direct enjoyment: feasting and festivities, ornamentation, dance, song, dramatic pantomime, telling yarns and enacting stories. . . . The body is decked before it is clothed. While homes are still hovels, temples and palaces are embellished. Luxuries prevail over necessities except when necessities can be festally celebrated. . . . Useful labor is, whenever possible, transformed by ceremonial and ritual accompaniments, subordinated to art that yields immediate enjoyment. . . . Most sources of direct enjoyment for the masses are not art to the cultivated, but perverted art, an unworthy indulgence. Thus we miss the point. A passion of anger, a dream, relaxation of the limbs after effort, swapping of jokes, horse-play, beating of drums, blowing of tin whistles, explosion of firecrackers and walking on stilts, have the same quality of immediate and absorbing finality that is possessed by things and acts dignified by the title of esthetic. (69–71)

14. David Tracy, *The Analogical Imagination: Christian Theology and the Culture of Pluralism* (New York: Crossroad, 1981), ch. 1.

11

Historical-Aesthetic Complementarity

An American Philosophical Contribution to the Study of Religion

Gary Slater

> Just because art . . . is expressive of a deep-seated attitude, the art characteristic of a civilization is the means for entering sympathetically into the deepest elements in the experience of remote and foreign civilizations. By this fact is explained also the import of their arts for ourselves. They affect a broadening and deepening of our own experience, rendering it less local and provincial as far as we grasp, by their means, the attitudes basic in other forms of experience.
>
> —John Dewey, *Art as Experience*

Introduction

Would you rather be fluent in every language or proficient in every musical instrument? This is a question I often ask my students at the beginning of their "Introduction to Religions of the World" class. The answers I get are illuminating—and predictable. Those who would choose fluency in language tend to mention the access that it would grant in terms of understanding cultures and contexts. Those who would choose proficiency in music tend to emphasize an element of intuition in musical experience that is more universal than language, and which is a form of communication unto itself. The patterns that emerge in these answers speak to the central relationship that this essay aims to explore: that of history and aesthetics. It is the task of this essay to show how self-conscious reflection on aesthetic-historical complementarity offers unrecognized resources for studying religion.

In referring to "aesthetics" and "history," it is important to be clear just how these terms are being used. Aesthetics is understood with respect to the three notions about aesthetics discussed by Walter Gulick in his introductory essay, "Toward an American Aesthetics." On Gulick's telling, the first notion of aesthetics stems from Kant's understanding of aesthetic judgments as attending to beauty based upon disinterested perception of works of art or nature.[1] The second notion of aesthetics "interprets art in many normative ways beyond beauty alone" (*G*, 15). The third notion of aesthetics "involves the recognition that felt aesthetic criteria can influence any and all judgments, not just judgments about art" (*G*, 21). In exploring this third notion, Gulick takes care to distinguish four distinct meanings for the term *feeling*. At present, the most important of these meanings is the fourth, in which feeling is understood as "a vague process of discrimination that judges between rational or perceptual alternatives according to norms of harmony, appropriateness, proportion, elegance, profundity, compatibility, beauty, fit, and similar essentially aesthetic terms" (*G*, 20). It is this definition of feeling, and the third sense of aesthetics with which it is linked, that best expresses the meaning of aesthetics as it employed within this essay.

Understanding aesthetics in this way generates a few specific claims. First, the aesthetic is where we really live. Aesthetic judgments apprehend what is most basic to experience and, in extraordinary moments, serve as a deep root of empathy. Second, aesthetic judgments traverse very specific sorts of relationships between perceiver and perceived. These relationships encompass relations between persons, between cultures, and into the depths of nature. In such relationships, what makes a judgment distinctly *aesthetic* is its inescapably qualitative dimension—that is, its apprehension of basic qualities such as color, sound, or even such nonphysical qualities as "grace" or "proportion." Third, being so closely linked to feeling as a vague process of discrimination within perception, aesthetics carries with it a certain kind of volatility. This volatility is wild in that it has the capacity to confound not only other forms of judgment, but also the very idea of judgment as a discursive process. For example, Franz Schubert, when asked to explain the meaning of one of his pieces, allegedly resorted to replaying his piece rather than venturing an articulation in words.[2] With these points in mind, this essay focuses on three specific contexts for aesthetic inquiry: (1) religious belief and practice, (2) historical and cultural context, (3) a holistic account of religion in cross-cultural perspective that integrates (1) and (2).

And what of history? History is understood as the study of the human past since the advent of written texts. As such, history is the most encompassing approach available for understanding human intentionality and behavior in cultural rather than the metaphysical frameworks typical of philosophy and religion. Granted, many of the natural sciences pronounce without metaphysics upon topics at a greater level of generality than history, and some of these—neuroscience, for example—do so in a manner directly related to human intentionality. Yet these disciplines exclude questions of aesthetics, ethics, or logic—what C. S. Peirce called the normative sciences—as part of the meaningful lives of human beings as persons. Although this sense of history is a bit thin, it can be engaged as thick insofar as there are innumerable orders of meaning within history at various levels, not so much as chronological threads across time as clusters of meaning at levels of generality.

As a reflective discipline, history displays some important commonalities with aesthetics. Such commonalities include judgment on things that are pervasive within experience, descriptions about real qualities in objects encountered, and adherence to certain sets of ideals. To be sure, not everything that is historical immediately presents itself as aesthetically pleasing in any of Gulick's senses of the term. Think of a boring sentence from a history textbook or an ugly monument, for instance. And not everything that is aesthetically pleasing immediately presents itself as historical. Think here of a sunset or a starry sky. Yet the pervasiveness of artistic imagination and historical discipline makes it especially important to clarify what distinguishes them. The major difference is that, although each involves aesthetic judgment, adequate assessment in the arts and history are beholden to different sets of ideals. While aesthetic judgments trade in such ideals as beauty or harmony, historical judgments trade in clarity, erudition, and fidelity to evidence about the past.

The central argument of this essay is that exploring the different but related standards guiding aesthetic judgment in history and religion opens up new ways of understanding religious phenomena in different historical and cultural settings. It is a task for which American philosophy is uniquely suited. Within a tradition that extends as far back as the works of Jonathan Edwards, American thought has long been acute in its attention to felt experience within everyday life. Moreover, American thinkers such as Peirce, Dewey, and James were committed not only to giving everyday experience its due, but also to embedding such experience within social and natural contexts. For these thinkers, the frameworks by which one understands the relationship between everyday experience and its embedded contexts are natural rather than transcendental, a distinction that bears many theoretical virtues. Such virtues include the recognition of purpose within inquiry, the revisable nature of one's hypotheses, and the continuity between nature and human culture.

Within the American philosophical tradition, there are three figures whose writings, for present purposes, offer relevant insights on the relationship between history and the embodied aesthetic sensitivities infusing perception, thought, and action. These figures are Robert Corrington, John Dewey, and Charles Peirce. Corrington's work is masterful in its attention to the wild aspects of aesthetics, which is to say the aspect of aesthetics that confounds our sense that we fully understand the world in which we are situated. With reference to Corrington's projects of deep pantheism and ecstatic naturalism, this essay uses Corrington's work to highlight the preponderance—indeed, the overabundance—of basic aesthetic qualities within everyday experience: the colors, the sounds, the immediacy of feeling. Corrington argues for a sort of radicalism within aesthetics that is separate from human histories and cultures in profound ways. As for Dewey, his *Art as Experience* eloquently defines aesthetics in terms that link aesthetic experience to networks of communal life.[3] In Dewey's telling, there are historical depths within aesthetics that grant access to the values—including religious values—of a wide range of communities. As for Peirce, his work provides in the three fundamental categories of Firstness, Secondness, and Thirdness a logic of relations that balances Dewey's emphasis on aesthetic relationships with Corrington's emphasis on the wilder aspects of aesthetics.

The results of this particular combination of thinkers are promising for religious studies in three ways. First, this combination suggests novel forms of categorization that can be directed toward cross-cultural studies of religion. Second, it points toward heightened capacities for the sort of empathy that is necessary if one wishes to make aesthetic judgments as those within particular periods of history would have done. And third, it provides warrants for a richer recovery of historical practices that are also particularly shaped by aesthetic standards.

Defining the Task

Imagine an outburst of noise. This noise is rhythmic. It evokes happiness. Imagine a chorus in the key of D major, with voices accompanied by trumpets and timpani. The voices are sometimes in unison and sometimes counterpoised, and they rise ever higher as the sound proceeds. Imagine voices that are singing phrases translated from the Book of Revelation, with "for the Lord God omnipotent reigneth" sung in unison and others, like "the kingdom of this world is become" or "and he shall reign forever," distributed differently across different voices. Punctuated throughout is "Hallelujah," which is so suffused within the overall sound—its tones and textures, its swelling harmonies, its exultant impact—that this word comes to represent the entire experience. Imagine the "Hallelujah" chorus of the *Messiah*, an oratorio composed by George Frederick Handel in 1741 and first performed in Dublin in April of the following year.

The preceding paragraph proceeds from an impressionistic toward a more historically astute description of a famous piece of music. The piece is historically and theologically significant in the content of its lyrics, the social history of its performances, and in the music itself. Yet how can the words written above capture the experience of hearing or singing it? With regard to those who heard its first performance, perhaps impressionistic language gets closer to conveying the experience than technical language would. But how would we know, when the sounds of that first performance dissipated in April 1742? What is the relationship between these sounds and the way we might understand them verbally or historically?

It may seem contrived to divide the experiential and the historical aspects of a phenomenon in this way, as these things are profoundly integrated within everyday experience. Still, the experiential and the historical *are* two different things, and this distinction is essential to religious inquiry. Religions bear the weight of historical tradition. They also imbue the aesthetic with theological significance. To say that understanding religion requires drawing upon both forms of inquiry is not a controversial point, and one finds plenty of scholarly works about religion that demonstrate the historical-aesthetic combination. For example, note the richness of qualitative description, the indispensability of embodied material reality, in the following passage from Marcella Althaus-Reid's *Indecent Theology*. In this passage, the author describes her old neighborhood in Buenos Aires as the basis for a radical critique of sexual identity within theological discourse:

> Please go for a walk around the sunny streets of my *barrio*, San Telmo, where stray dogs sleep in the doors of abandoned buildings, and prostitutes buy their newspapers at siesta time under the intense heat of summer. There is usually a sweet smell, that mixture of street garbage at the junctions of the Avenue Nueve de Julio, which mixes with the smell of flowers and baskets of lemons, onions and fresh herbs sold by the women who sit on the pavement. In summer they sweeten the air with parsley and lemons, but can you smell the odours of their sex? Perhaps they do not have underwear while they sit there with lemons and children, and give you change while wrapping parsley. Look at their long, lustrous black plaits and their delicate indigenous faces. Hear the song of their voices calling the passers-by to buy their merchandise. . . . See if their babies are wrapped in cloth, hanging at their backs, as is traditionally done, or if the children sleep in a fruit box, protected with blankets and knitted shawls. . . . You have just seen the lemon vendors in the streets of Constitution or San Telmo. You have seen the witnesses, moreover, the subjects of one of the most important postmodern phenomena of fragmentation and dissolution which happened 500 years ago in Latin America.[4]

Sweet smell. Lustrous plaits. Voices calling. In Althaus-Reid's passage, the aesthetics of her description exist within an historical context. This context is indispensable to her arguments: these scenes are on the margins, they are *real*, and scholars of religion must account for them. But equally important is the materiality of what's described, the odors and movements and all else, without which her argument would remain abstract. For such accounts, it is necessary to have both historical context and embodied materiality. Each is distinct, and each is indispensable.

But imagine that the sights that Althaus-Reid describes could not be seen, the sounds heard, or the odors smelled, because they are no longer present. That is, imagine if these scenes are available only to historical inquiry. Is the qualitative element of a past phenomenon inevitably submerged in the ocean of intervening events? Gaston Bachelard, author of *The Poetics of Space*, writes of a *direct ontology* that is the "opposite of causality" and which is unavailable to history.[5] Bachelard would almost certainly answer "yes" to the question just preceding. Yet other scholars have responded to the challenge of understanding the perception of aesthetic or qualitative elements within history by inquiring after how aesthetic experiences signify sacred realities. Robert R. Yelle's *Semiotics of Religion: Signs of the Sacred in History* is one such attempt, examining historical shifts in semiotics of religion while drawing from structuralist and poststructuralist thinkers.[6] Another example is Jack Goody's *The Interface Between the Written and the Oral*, which examines relationships between spoken and written language across history to identify the deep logics of culture across time.[7] Still another example is Diarmaid MacCulloch's *Silence: A Christian History*, in which sound and silence function as a way to signify the wider Christian paradox of engagement with and withdrawal from the world.

Each of these efforts speaks in its own way to the same challenge, the same curiosity: that of resuscitating the vital experience of quality from the past. In clarifying this task, the following factors apply: (1) religion as actually practiced, (2) historicist attempts to describe previous religious experience that rely upon explanatory devises such as causation, and (3) imaginatively reenacted religious experience sensitive to indicators of the feelings involved in religious practice beyond textbook descriptions of beliefs and actions. Aesthetic judgments are involved in writing religious histories and in highlighting how aesthetic judgments pervaded past religious practices. Historical analysis also displays the cultural context in which particular individuals are embedded in aesthetically influenced religious thought and action. In spite of the value in each of the aforementioned projects, this essay argues that the means for developing this sort of imaginatively reenacted religious experience is best found within the American philosophical tradition. Within this tradition, the writings of Robert Corrington, John Dewey, and C. S. Peirce stand out as a particularly compelling combination. The sequence of these figures in the pages that follow is logical rather than historical: Corrington supplies aesthetics with a crucial element of wildness, Dewey argues for historical-aesthetic complementary, and Peirce reconciles these visions and links them to nuanced insights on history and temporality. These figures can be examined in turn.

Corrington, Dewey, and Peirce

Robert Corrington is among the most consistently insightful commentators on the aesthetic dimensions of American philosophy. Before discussing

Corrington's aesthetics, it is helpful to establish the appropriate career contexts. Corrington is known as the creator of ecstatic naturalism, which he describes as an alternative to contemporary metaphysical perspectives that are either too dependent upon a brute descriptive materialism or to an honorific process cosmology. In the ecstatic naturalist vision, nature is *the* dynamic entirety, the wide and vast reality that creates itself out of itself alone. Corrington calls the religious picture that extends from this metaphysical fore-structure of ecstatic naturalism *deep pantheism*. In deep pantheism, God or gods exist within an evolutionary process of emergence in nature with no transcendent reference whatsoever. The method of deep pantheism is what Corrington calls ordinal phenomenology, which "uses the ordinal concepts that are also pertinent to the metaphysics of ecstatic naturalism, the 'frame' within which deep pantheism thrives and functions."[8] It is among these projects that Corrington's distinctive perspective on aesthetics emerges.

Corrington locates his philosophy of aesthetics within certain key distinctions. First, following Kant and Schopenhauer, he distinguishes beauty and the sublime. Even though a given artwork can be an intersection of beauty and sublimity, these are not to be conflated. As Corrington puts it in in his book *Nature's Sublime*, "[B]eauty must be a trait within nature and hence ordinally located. Hence, beauty in nature must have boundaries analogous to the boundaries found in works of art."[9] As for the sublime, this is "encountered when we see nature in its full life-threatening glory and our own significance shrinks to a small infinitesimal point" (*NS*, 166). Corrington's beauty/sublime distinction points toward a profound insight, which is that aesthetics contains within itself a balance—often unstable—between what I call the *intimate* and *alienating* aspects of aesthetic experience. Corrington states that "[g]reat art can have two simultaneous functions that appear to be incompatible but are not. On one hand it can bring peace and joy to its assimilator, while on the other hand it can reject and critique the status quo, that is, be a great refusal" (*NS*, 152). As I see it, aesthetic intimacy refers to the experience of continuity that brings to life a novel relationship between a perceiver and object.[10] It is almost beatific. Aesthetic alienation refers to a shattering of one's sense of worldview. Such alienation provides an awareness of something wild beyond expectation and grants awareness of radical givenness in all other moments. This is negative, painful, disruptive, a kind of semiotic clearinghouse. Corrington captures this sense of rupture in saying that it is "only when something dramatic happens within the otherwise stable and self-effacing horizon of the individual that the horizon is aware of its finitude and its contrast to other horizons."[11] By acknowledging this crucial element of alienation, Corrington recognizes within some aesthetic experience a sort of wildness that confounds and upends other forms of judgment.

Corrington also acknowledges the power of aesthetic sensitivity to challenge religious complacency. His work claims "to show that religion surpasses itself, and thereby becomes deeply ethical, when it sublates itself into the aesthetic" (*NS*, 82). Aesthetics thus emerges in Corrington's recent work as a counterpoint to tribalism, in which religions and the corresponding notions of revelation are positioned as innately tribal, whereas art "struggles toward the universal, toward the depth-dimension of the human process" (*NS*, 154). In counterpoising (tribal) religion and (universal) art, Corrington's aesthetics echoes a similar distinction made by Wassily Kandinsky in his classic 1912 work *Concerning the Spiritual in Art*. In this work, Kandinsky distinguishes "history" and "spirit" as respectively limited and universal ways to understand artistic creation. On one hand, there is art that is "the child of its age," restricted in relevance to its historical context.[12] On the other hand, there is art "which is capable of educating further," that "springs equally from contemporary feeling, but is at the same time not only echo and mirror of it."[13] Like Kandinsky, Corrington presents his distinction between tribal and universal as a means to extoll the ways in which art can expand the imagination and confound cultural boundaries. Also like Kandinsky, Corrington denigrates history as an artificial intervention between humanity and nature that also reifies boundaries between cultures. By contrast, in spite of the fact that pieces of art are inherently particular, there is nonetheless universality *within* the particular significance of art that confounds and scrambles the neatly drawn intellectual categories and opens us up to one another more effectively. This calls to mind a line from the composer Felix Mendelssohn, which, to paraphrase, is that music (and by extension, art) isn't too vague for words; rather, it's too specific for words.

The work of John Dewey presents a contrasting view, one that locates aesthetic inquiry *within* historiography as part of a symbiotic relationship between the two disciplines. Although Dewey, like Corrington, sees aesthetics as a means of expanding empathy, the view of history he presents is as a holistic system of social and cultural relations that serves aesthetic inquiry rather than opposes it. Before exploring this contrast farther, it helps to be clear on how Dewey understands aesthetics. As expressed in his *Art as Experience*, Dewey understands an aesthetic experience as different from experience per se; it represents an experiential center that is: (1) a unity, yet also (2) connected to cultures and contexts beyond the individual's own life (*AE*, 38). As he puts it, "Art is . . . prefigured in the very process of living" (*AE*, 25). What is emphasized here is not just the importance of art within everyday life; Dewey is also concerned that too much aesthetic theory has impoverished art by isolating it from a variety of social and historical contexts. He describes the problem in a passage that bears quoting at length:

> When artistic objects are separated from both conditions of origin and operation in experience, a wall is built around them that renders almost opaque their general significance, with which esthetic theory deals. Art is remitted to a separated realm, where it is cut off from that association with the materials and aims of every other form of human effort, undergoing, and achievement. A primary task is thus imposed upon one who undertakes to write upon the philosophy of the fine arts. This task is to restore continuity between the refined and intensified forms of experience that are works of art and the everyday events, doings, and sufferings that are universally recognized to constitute experience. (*AE*, 2)

Dewey's emphasis on embedded contexts within the study of art provides a vision for how historical inquiry serves aesthetics.

Dewey also writes eloquently on the link between aesthetics and cross-cultural understanding. This link holds whether the culture one seeks to understand exists in the present or the past. As he puts it:

> For all but the antiquarian, ancient Egypt is its monuments, temples and literature. . . . Troy lives for us only in poetry and in the objects of art that have been recovered from its ruins. Minoan civilization is today its products of art. Pagan gods and pagan rites are past and gone and yet endure in the incense, lights, robes, and holidays of the present. (*AE*, 340)

With this link between history and aesthetics comes an increased capacity for empathy. For Dewey, art "is a more universal mode of language than is the speech that exists in a multitude of mutually intelligible forms," such that this language is "not affected by the accidents of history that mark off different modes of human speech" (*AE*, 349). This might seem to resemble Corrington's distinction between the parochialism of history and the universality of art. Yet for Dewey, the ecumenical nature of aesthetic experience *serves* history, doing so in a manner that is particularly relevant to historical studies of religion.

On Dewey's account, what makes possible such mutual support between aesthetics, history, and religious studies is that the relative universality of artistic experience, when combined with the empathic element noted above, conveys heightened sensitivity for recognizing causes of historical change. For Dewey, "Change in the climate of the imagination is the precursor of the changes that affect more than the details of life" (*AE*, 360). Dewey also asserts that the aesthetic artifacts of a given religious culture are among the most powerful drivers of historical change. As he puts it, "[B]ecause of the esthetic strand, religious teachings were the more readily conveyed and their effect was the more lasting. By the art in them, they were changed from doctrines into living experiences" (*AE*, 342). What is important in this series of claims is the balance between concrete, aesthetically laden experiences and contexts of religious doctrine historically understood. As Dewey puts it:

> Theologies and cosmogonies have laid hold of imagination because they have been attended with solemn processions, incense, embroidered robes, music, the radiance of colored lights, with stories that stir wonder and induce hypnotic admiration. That is, they have come to man through a direct appeal to sense and to sensuous imagination. (*AE*, 31)

One sees precisely this relationship at work in Marcella Althaus-Reid's description of her barrio in Buenos Aires as described in the example from *Indecent Theology*.

In spite of the eloquence in Dewey's recognition of complementary relationships between aesthetics, history, and religion, Dewey's account of aesthetics in *Art as Experience* contains certain drawbacks. Two in particular stand out. The first drawback is that Dewey's account risks overestimating unity. This holds whether the unity in question is that which exists between cultures or between history and aesthetics. This threatens to domesticate the wildness of aesthetics so acutely described by Corrington. How does Dewey's account for, say, the divergent assumptions about history across cultures? In my book *C. S. Peirce and the Nested*

Continua Model of Religious Interpretation, I describe how "history" can mean different things in different historical contexts:

> For the Israelites of the Old Testament, for example, history was the story of a particular group overcoming a particular problem. For members of the middle class in nineteenth century Britain, it was an indefinite march of progress for people across the world. For practitioners of Mahayana Buddhism, history is the sum of misperceptions about the nature of reality, a cyclical system of torturous risings and fallings between realms that is ultimately to be transcended with proper meditative understandings.[14]

The second drawback is that, in illustrating aesthetic experience by continually referring to works of art, Dewey tends to neglect the element of felt experience *beyond* art that characterizes Gulick's third sense of aesthetics. This has the ironic effect of working against Dewey's own critique of theories that isolate art.

Is it possible for both Corrington and Dewey to be right? That is, is there a wild element of aesthetics that is irreducible to—or even juxtaposed against—history even as history and aesthetics support one another in expanding cultural and religious understanding? I believe the answer is yes. In order to understand how this might be, it helps to turn to the writings of C. S. Peirce. Peirce did not write about aesthetics with the same breadth as Dewey or Corrington. Yet one still encounters certain key texts that illuminate Peirce's understandings of aesthetics. Among the texts in which Peirce discussed aesthetics most directly was in his 1903 lectures on pragmatism. In these lectures, Peirce argued that logic is understood as supported by ethics, which in turn is supported by aesthetics, although such support is often implicit. As he put it: "Although I do not think that an esthetic valuation is essentially involved, *actualiter* . . . in every intellectual purport, I do think that it is a *virtual* factor of a duly rationalized purport."[15] Holding that only aesthetics can serve as the basis for appropriate action and thought, Peirce wrote that "an ultimate end of action deliberately adopted . . . must be a state of things that reasonably recommends itself in itself aside from any ulterior consideration; it must be an admirable ideal, having the only kind of goodness such an ideal can have; namely, aesthetic goodness."[16] Such notions are derived at least in part from Schiller's triad of *Spieltrieb* (play of mind), *Formtrieb* (demand for form), and *Stofftrieb* (drive for diversity), from his *Aesthetic Letters*. Peirce's sense of a play-impulse appears most profoundly in the notion of "musement" as found in the 1908 essay, "A Neglected Argument for the Reality of God."[17]

As with so much else in his thought, Peirce's considerations on aesthetics relative to ethics and logic fit within his fundamental triad of Firstness, Secondness, and Thirdness. Peirce defined these categories as follows in his 1891 article, "The Architecture of Theories":

> First is the conception of being or existing independent of anything else. Second is the conception of being relative to, the conception of reaction with, something else. Third is the conception of mediation, whereby a first and second are brought into relation.[18]

Firstness comprises all the qualities we perceive in the world, from colors to sounds to the feelings elicited from our experience of such things. It is the most elemental base available to experience, and is closely connected to aesthetics. Secondness applies to the objects one runs up against in lived experience, objects that are distinct from one another and from the person perceiving them, yet are indubitably real and must be dealt with. This is closely connected to ethics. Thirdness, as mediation, is associated with meaningful relationships, intelligibility, and purpose. This is closely connected to logic. In associating Peirce's account of what he called the normative sciences with the three categories, it bears mentioning that *all* of the categories are implicated within aesthetic experience. For example, any aesthetic judgment is characterized by Thirdness, as it involves intelligibility, general norms, and a host of meaningful relationships. Secondness characterizes the brute actuality that constitutes the direct encounter with something that prompts aesthetic reflection, whether this is a work of art or some other object. And the simple qualities without which aesthetic experience would be devoid of content—and the feelings that attend such experience—are characterized by Firstness.

Peirce's categories illustrate how Corrington's and Dewey's understandings of aesthetics might be reconciled. On Corrington's side, Peirce's category of Firstness, which is associated with aesthetics, bears much of the wildness that resonates within Corrington's account.[19] Sandra B. Rosenthal has noted the radicalism implicit in Peirce's category of Firstness in a way that is congenial to Corrington's view:

> There emerges from Peirce's . . . characterization of Firstness in perception a metaphysical category of Firstness that is neither a remnant of traditional conceptions of determinate repeatable qualities nor a remnant of traditional conceptions of eternal Platonic possibilities. Rather, what emerges is a Firstness that attributes to reality precisely those characteristics most antithetical to such traditional conceptions. Firstness in this sense not only underlies Peirce's radical rejection of foundationalist-antifoundationalist alternatives in epistemology, but also anticipates his rejection of the ontological alternatives offered by a tradition of substance metaphysics.[20]

At the same time, by placing Firstness within a set of categories and applying the term to all manner of other vocabularies, Peirce clearly understood Firstness—and by extension, aesthetics—as part of the nexus of relationships Dewey prizes. Of particular interest is the relation between Firstness and Thirdness as applied to historical inquiries into aesthetics. In such inquiries, one encounters both the qualitative immediacy of particular colors, sounds, or shapes (Firstness) and various comparative, historically relevant categories of explanation (Thirdness). By positing analytical categories beyond and within both the aesthetic expressions of religious communities and their historically situated interpretive structures, Peirce's thought helps one explore the means by which phenomenal experience becomes encoded in texts and practices, and expands the capacity for comparing the texts and practices of one community with those of another.

Conclusion

By providing an account of relations that allows aesthetics to remain wild while also linked to relationships within history, this combination of insights from Corrington, Dewey, and Peirce points toward a richer historical approach in studying religion. This approach is richer, first of all, because it is more sensitive to the felt experiences of aesthetic phenomena in history. Crucial to this expanded approach is its heightened capacity for empathy, which is useful for reconstructing the aesthetic judgments of the cultures one is studying. Dewey articulates such empathy well: "It is when the desires and aims, the interests and mode of response of another become an expansion of our own being that we understand him. We learn to see with his eyes, hear with his ears, and their results given true instruction, for they are built into our own structure" (*AE*, 350). Aside from being a good in itself, such empathy carries with it certain rewards for the study of religion. On one hand, one might be able to chart in the changing contexts of aesthetic manifestation the changing patterns of perception of a given community across time. On the other hand, to have interpretive access to the context in which a given aesthetic manifestation was named is to gain insight into the historical inception of a nexus that links the experience of something ineffable and the various semantic structures by which this object is cognitively engaged. The implication here is that understanding aesthetics is mediated by the history of a community or set of practices, just as community practices are mediated by aesthetic experience.

Another benefit of this particular vision of historical-aesthetic complementarity is that aesthetics might serve as an organizing principle for research into how phenomenal experience is featured in the religious practices of historically situated communities. That is, one might be able to undertake colligative studies organized around such aesthetically relevant qualities as colors, shapes, or sounds. In his book, *Bright Earth: The Invention of Colour,* Philip Ball demonstrates the sorts of insights generated from these sorts of analyses. For example, the social importance of ancient Egyptian art was reflected in the culture's systematic accumulation of bright pigments.[21] Or during the Counter-Reformation of the sixteenth century, bright colors became a fixture of ecclesiastically mandated art as a means to stir the emotions and furnish a "Bible of the Illiterate"—which was a valuable propaganda tool.[22] Above all, this vision for historical-aesthetic complementarity reflects a sense of excitement about expanding what it is possible to learn from historical practices of religion. That is, there is a sense of exploring areas that other theoretical models might assume to be foreclosed. In his essay "How to Make Our Ideas Clear," Peirce expresses this sense in writing about the possibility of uncovering facts thought lost to history:

> I may be asked what I have to say to all the minute facts of history, forgotten never to be recovered, to the lost books of the ancients, to the buried secrets. *Full many a gem of purest ray serene/ the dark, unfathomed caves of ocean bear/ full many a flower is born to blush unseen/ and waste its sweetness in the desert air.* Do these things not really exist because they are hopelessly beyond the reach of our knowledge? . . . To this I

reply that, though in no possible state of knowledge can any number be great enough to express the relation between the amount of what rests unknown to the amount of the known, yet it is unphilosophical to suppose that, with regard to any given question, investigation would not bring forth a solution to it.[23]

This essay shares Peirce's optimism. Guided by plausible hypotheses, self-consciously recognizing historical-aesthetic complementarity could give rise to meaningful patterns that emerge during the process of inquiry. As clusters of relations start to emerge, increasingly general hypotheses might be averred regarding both aesthetic judgments and the historical and religious practices and words associated with them. Such an approach has the capacity to allow interrogation into the qualitative dimension of the sentiments of religion, into the dread and hope and love and joy and judgment, into the intricacies of doctrine, or into the metaphysical subtleties of the hypostasis or meditative practices.

Notes

1. Walter Gulick, "Toward an American Aesthetics," 12. Hereafter cited in the text as *G*.

2. Paul Cobley and Litza Jansz, *Introducing Semiotics* (Flint, MI: Totem Books, 1997), 27.

3. John Dewey, *Art as Experience*, (New York: Penguin Books, 2005), 346. Hereafter cited in the text as *AE*.

4. Marcella Althaus-Reid, *Indecent Theology: Theological Perversions in Sex, Gender, and Politics* (New York: Routledge, 2000), 2–3.

5. Gaston Bachelard, *The Poetics of Space*, trans. Maria Jolas (Boston: Beacon Press, 1994).

6. Robert R. Yelle, *Semiotics of Religion: Signs of the Sacred in History* (London: Bloomsbury, 2013).

7. Jack Goody, *The Interface Between the Written and the Oral* (Cambridge: Cambridge University Press, 1987).

8. Robert Corrington, *Deep Pantheism: Toward a New Transcendentalism* (Lanham, MD: Lexington Books, 2015), xxiiii.

9. Robert Corrington, *Nature's Sublime: An Essay in Aesthetic Naturalism* (Lanham, MD: Lexington Books, 2013), 163. Hereafter quoted in the text as *NS*.

10. The term *continuity* is used here in a metaphysical as well as a hermeneutic sense. Hermeneutically, it refers to the unbroken process by which interpreter,

interpreted, and interpretation are brought together in a seamless and meaningful way. Metaphysically, it refers to the absence of ontological divides between mind and matter, self and world, and humanity and nature. Both senses of the term are derived from Peirce's philosophy of continuity, which he called *synechism,* which he introduced in his first *Monist* series of 1891–93 and developed across the last two decades of his career.

11. Corrington, *Deep Pantheism,* 14.

12. Wassily Kandinsky, *Concerning the Spiritual in Art,* trans. Michael T. H. Sadler (Whitefish, MT: Kessinger Publishing), 22.

13. Ibid.

14. Gary Slater, *C. S. Peirce and the Nested Continua Model of Religious Interpretation* (Oxford: Oxford University Press, 2015), 108.

15. Charles Sanders Peirce, *Collected Papers of Charles Sanders Peirce,* Vol. V and VI, *Pragmatism and Pragmaticism and Scientific Metaphysics* (New York: Belknap, 1935), 5.535.

16. Ibid., 5.130.

17. Michael Raposa, *Peirce's Philosophy of Religion* (Bloomington, IN: Indiana University Press, 1989) does a brilliant job linking this essay with the rest of Peirce's career, including the childhood influence from Schiller.

18. Peirce, *Collected Papers,* 6.32.

19. In strictly semiotic terms, one also finds in Peirce's *dynamic object* a form of experience similarly unavailable to linguistic description. Corrington explicitly links the dynamical object to how he understands the sublime.

20. Sandra B. Rosenthal, *Charles S. Peirce's Pragmatic Pluralism* (Albany: State University of New York Press, 1994), 108.

21. Philip Ball, *Bright Earth: The Invention of Colour* (London, Vintage Books, 2001), 69.

22. Ibid., 146.

23. Peirce, *Collected Papers,* 5.409.

IV

Applying American Aesthetic Theory to Practice

American Aesthetics incorporates a holistic vision of aesthetics as involving both theoretical description and normative assessment of artistic creation and practice. Thus, examining how art in its many genres is created, practiced, and evaluated is essential to the practice of American Aesthetics. This section's essays attend to these important activities in various ways.

Art critics and art historians as well as creative artists and performers put philosophers' aesthetic theories to work. Leanne Gilbertson and Walter B. Gulick claim that an examination of art critic Harold Rosenberg's writings reveals the sort of holistic sensitivities that qualify him to be regarded as a prototypical example of a critic expressing the concerns of American Aesthetics. While Rosenberg is most famous for coining the term "action painters" in 1952, it is his illuminating treatment of the situated character of American art that deserves special appreciation. He did not confine his aesthetic criticism to the analysis of individual artworks, as was the tendency of his rival Clement Greenberg's criticism, but rather celebrated how individual artists created works in response to the cultural and social demands of their time. His work can be seen as a kind of process aesthetics.

Vaughan Durkee McTernan claims that Whitehead's aesthetics provide a basis for explaining why installation artist James Turrell's light spaces evoke powerful existential experiences. Viewers become participants in Turrell's spaces and are thereby immersed in the changing patterns of light, whether natural or artificial. These luminous spaces afford instances of Whiteheadian process that can be articulated through such aesthetic terms as massiveness and intensity, or harmony and contrast. The light-drenched spaces Turrell creates can be experienced as sanctuaries of the sacred in which perception, feeling, and a sense of the divine are fused.

Walter B. Gulick's interview with Corey Drieth explores how Drieth as a visual artist sees himself as participating in the American tradition of abstraction. While Drieth is not a household name in the field of art, he is unusually articulate in describing how his aesthetic feelings guide him to a Deweyan sort of completion, expressed as a sense of gratitude. His cultural sensitivity exemplifies the broadly inclusive approach of American Aesthetics to creative expression. His sharply focused works reflect his admiration for, and aesthetically attuned appropriation of, works by those in the Steichen school (especially Arthur Dove and Georgia O'Keeffe), the abstract expressionists, and Agnes Martin, with her delicate minimalism.

Arthur Stewart, once a concert pianist of classical music, is now a professor of philosophy attentive to the aesthetic dimensions of performance. A goal in learning a musical score is to make one's ability to execute it as habitual as possible. Once that is accomplished, a pianist can attend to apt interpretation and expression of the memorized piece. Peirce's understanding of esthetics (his usual spelling) as the normative science of inherent, enjoyable excellence can serve as a helpful standard of assessment. Performance thus judged stands in contrast to a nominalist concern with technique, audience response, and similar distracted attention. In an ideal performance, the bracing timbre of individual notes, a delight of Peirce's category of firstness, is augmented by each note's contrast with other notes, secondness, giving rise to the comprehensive interpretation of the music's meaning, thirdness, as part of the total fabric of music's reality.

Steven Hart's approach to aesthetic excellence as a director of choral music rests upon his appreciation of the social embeddedness of aesthetics. To bring choral singing to its moving and expressive climax, the singers (and not just the conductor) need to participate emotionally in the meaning of the lyrics and understand how the music accentuates that meaning. In *Reconstruction in Philosophy*, Dewey argues that when individuals stand in organic relation to larger socially embedded meanings, the resulting openness leads to dynamic discovery culminating in unified expression. Hart facilitates such aesthetic discovery by situating choral pieces in their historical and cultural context and elicits in the singers the poetic meaning of the lyrics, eschewing technical emphasis on the piece alone.

James McLachlan explores the quintessentially American "B" Westerns of filmmaker Budd Boetticher and discovers in them unexpected wealth. These films have often been interpreted in terms of existentialist philosophy in light of the impassiveness displayed by their leading actor, Randolph Scott, and the existential crises faced by the villains. McLachlan makes use of pragmatist Robert Neville's notion of "broken symbols" to suggest that Scott can best be seen as a kind of imperfect Western icon of justice acting in a beautiful natural environment. This symbolic setting supports not so much an existentialist interpretation of the films as it points to how even troubled humans reside in a world of transcendent possibility.

12

An Exemplary Critic in the Tradition of American Aesthetics

Harold Rosenberg

LEANNE GILBERTSON AND WALTER B. GULICK

Where might one look to find stability and insight regarding aesthetic excellence in the protean realm of the arts? For the visual arts, art museums and their curators are charged to display important contemporary works as well as great works from the past. Art historians remind us of what has been achieved in the past and why it is significant. As is true of virtually all claims of significance, there is far more certainty regarding worthy achievements of the past than is the case for what will stand the test of excellence among current works. Stated more precisely, art judged significant in the present is subject to diverse and often conflicting conclusions, but as time passes, the whirlwind of opinions about what is fashionable gradually dies down and the assessments of textbooks assign the work a relatively stable spot in art history.

Art critics stand at the center of the whirlwind. Indeed, their reviews help create the whirlwind. For those seeking a comprehensive understanding of contemporary artistic excellence likely to stand the test of time, art critics of a certain kind are needed. The ideal critic is not the shill for a certain movement, knowledgeable about only one type of artistic expression. The ideal art critic has many of the characteristics of the "Renaissance man." This person understands what is occurring throughout society, has a broad comprehension of politics and world affairs, is historically informed, but also is philosophically astute—can sense what issues and influences are shaping cultural events and views, has a refined sense of aesthetic and other values, and cares about the quality of what is produced and displayed. But especially this person must have an embodied knowledge of the passionate commitment, the sensitivity, and the skill required of individuals to create and perform art that matters. And the ideal art critic must not be bashful about critiquing—praising and condemning works and performances based on clearly presented evidence as interpreted through thoughtful, refined critical sensitivity. Respect for integrity, rather than love for kindness, is what is most likely to be characteristic of the best critics.

We believe Harold Rosenberg (1906–1978) is worthy of such respect. Moreover, we think that when one examines his career, one sees a writer whose work exemplifies many of the characteristics of American Aesthetics as described in Walter Gulick's introductory article in this volume. Two characteristics of Rosenberg's writing—somewhat in tension with each other—stand out above all others in this regard:

1. He maintains a focus on the individual artist as the source of creative excellence in contrast to any historicist reduction of creativity to the effect of tradition, social influence, commercial pressure, or similar extraneous influences.

2. He interprets the significance of the arts, and culture in general, in relation to political, cultural, and philosophical factors operative in particular times and spaces. American history and geographical/cultural location are important to him in this regard.

Characteristic 1 is all too easily misinterpreted as implying that Rosenberg celebrated the alienated autonomous individual as cultural hero. On the contrary, he consistently understands all truly creative artists to be productively immersed in and responsive to a thick social and cultural context, namely that characteristic listed as 2. As we shall see, though, there are different types of artistic response to cultural promptings. Rosenberg believes creative art requires an active response that challenges conventional aesthetic assumptions, not a response alert to extraneous factors such as allegiance to the dictates of some previously defined aesthetic fashion, commercial success, status among peers, etc. Thus, for the creation of meritorious art, characteristics 1 and 2 should be seen as complementary and interwoven, not antagonistic.

We will examine his individualistic emphasis (1) first after a very brief summary of some of Rosenberg's life experiences that played into his overall perspective on life and criticism.

Harold Rosenberg was born and died in New York City, and he also lived in Washington, D.C., and Chicago. His perspective is thoroughly urban; he evinces little interest in nature as an artistic subject. The mental world of words and images is his favored domain. He is at core a writer. His skill and interest in written expression perhaps contributed to his early choice of a career and to his chief artistic avocation. He was educated to be a lawyer and he wrote poetry, eventually having a book of his poetry published. Beginning in 1931, he wrote for the Chicago literary magazine *Poetry*. During the Depression, he studied Marx and wrote for the leftist publication *Partisan Review*, among others. But his interest in the creative artist and diverse forms of artistic expression conflicted with Marxist tenets. He maintained a Marxist interest in social affairs while being a stout anti-Stalinist politically. As an editor, writer, and muralist, he worked in the New Deal WPA, serving as the art editor of the WPA *American Guide* from 1938 to 1942. For many years he was a program consultant for the Advertising Council. Increasingly, however, his domineering passion became serving as an art and cultural critic. Based upon the increasing recognition his writing granted him, he accepted academic appointments, culminating in becoming a professor of art at the University of Chicago. In 1967 he was appointed art critic for *The New Yorker*.

The varied experiences and interests evident in his career funded the broad scope of his writing. But perhaps it is that diversity that is responsible for an aspect of his authorship that bears emphasis. Rosenberg was often a passionate writer, and passions of the moment tend not to issue in systematic thought. It is not difficult to find inconsistencies in his articles, sometimes even in the same article. So if an interpreter of Rosenberg has a particular bias to promote, that person can probably find quotations to support that bias. The variability in his writing leads to diversity in scholarly accounts of Rosenberg's interests and accomplishments. Fair interpretation of what he accomplished requires one to search for his repeated emphases and not settle for the one isolated comment supportive of one's preexisting view. Two of these emphases have been pointed out, and to the first of those emphases, the value he placed on individual creativity, we now turn.

The Creative Individual

In an article from 1948, he challenged the common idea that the true artist and art critic are tragically alienated from collective culture and themselves. "That being oneself and not others should be deplored is the most unambiguous sign of the triumph in the individual of the ideology of mass culture over spiritual independence."[1] All Americans, he notes, are aware that the abstractions of TV or the popular press do not apply to themselves. He distinguishes between formulaic common experiences of mass culture ("*the* experience of the twenties," or more recently it could be "Generation X believes") and common situations that individuals sometimes experience. Authentic literature begins when an author "will accept the fact that he cannot know, except through the lengthy unfolding of the work itself, what will be central to his experiencing; it is his way of revealing his existence to his consciousness."[2] The existentialist flavor of Rosenberg's individualistic emphasis is evident here and even more in the following passage from 1949: "All art is, of course, subjective—or, in Leonardo's term, a mental thing. . . . The modern painter is not inspired by anything visible, but only by something he hasn't seen yet. . . . In short, he begins with nothingness. *That is the only thing he copies.* The rest he invents."[3] The overtones of Sartre's thought are overtly manifest in this selection.[4]

Rosenberg's affection for the creative individual appears decisively in his most influential article, "The American Action Painters," which was written in 1952. With respect to such artists as de Kooning, Kline, and Pollock, Rosenberg writes, "At a certain moment the canvas begins to appear to one American painter after another as an arena in which to act—rather than as a space in which to reproduce, re-design, analyze, or 'express' an object, actual or imagined. What was to go on the canvas was not a picture but an event."[5] On such an account, the work itself is an artifact of secondary import—a trace perhaps best regarded as a clue to the creative event. The significant products of individual creativity can too easily be reduced by others into a formula and thus disintegrate into a style that others imitate. Centering attention on an individual's artistic *creativity* is a repeated motif of Rosenberg's work as a critic. Thus, in 1975 he writes that "art has been unable to relinquish its affinity with man's most mysterious power, and his most precious one: I mean, the power of creation."[6]

Such paeans to individualism are a recurrent theme in the course of American culture. Think of Emerson's essay on self-reliance or the lore of the self-made man. The Lone Ranger is an example of the American hero who comes to a paralyzed town to rid it of evil and then goes riding off into the sunset. Individualistic, masculine heroic action freely bestowed is part of American mythology and influences its native aestheticism. Rosenberg participates in and updates this aspect of American Aesthetics.

Rosenberg and Greenberg

Here it is appropriate to bring up the well-known contrast between the art criticism of Rosenberg in relation to the views of his rival art critic Clement Greenberg, because their different views of aesthetics encapsulate the differences between American Aesthetics and aesthetics carried out in analytic style.[7] Commenting on the individualism he celebrates in "American Action Painters," Rosenberg writes, "A painting that is an act is inseparable from the biography of the artist."[8] Earlier in his career, Greenberg applauded art that dealt not with artist experience, motivation, and creative act, but with the adequacy of the artist's portrayal of the world. In 1944, he wrote, "The visionary overtones of [Eakins's] art moves us all the more because they echo *facts*. This is perhaps the most American note of all."[9] Greenberg at the peak of his career, however, shifted his critical attention away from factual representation to the artwork as itself a fact located within an art movement. Not only was the artist's experience unimportant, even the subject matter of the artwork became increasingly irrelevant to Greenberg as his writing evolved in the 1950s and 1960s. According to Greenberg, the art critic best performs his or her office by revealing how artistic traditions develop over time. Evolutionary continuity, not individualistic creativity, is his basic theme.[10] He saw modernist painting to be working toward a goal of greater and greater purity. Stripping away attention to what a painting represents and paying attention to what art actually is—that is, shifting from illusion to fact—is interpreted to be the modernist ideal. Therefore, the critic should call attention to such characteristics of a painting as the flatness of canvas, the color of paint, the impact of how a work is framed, and so on. "Painting continues, then, to work out its modernism with unchecked momentum because it still has a relatively long way to go before being reduced to its viable essence."[11]

American painting until the early 1940s is generally regarded as marked by provincialism, by dependence on continental—especially Parisian—trends insofar as it sought to incorporate avant-garde fashions. World War II and its aftermath stimulated a desire for a uniquely American art. Both Rosenberg and Greenberg comment that the Abstract Expressionism that emerged signaled a break from past American art. In an article from 1957, Greenberg stated, "American art has been able to establish its full independence not by turning away from Paris, but by assimilating her. . . . New York is second only to Paris as a home for artists brought up in other countries. And just as they become French in Paris, so they have become Americans in New York."[12]

Well, then, perhaps the distinction between Rosenberg and Greenberg is overdrawn, as each speaks of the rise of distinctly American art after World War II. However, Greenberg gives no clear reason as to why Abstract Expressionism should be regarded as truly American just because the emigré artists, who are leading pioneers in the new movement, live in New York. Indeed, he quite openly regards Abstract Expressionism as the latest strand in the development of international modernism rather than as distinctly American. In contrast, Rosenberg understands the emergence of uniquely American art not as a logical development of modernism, but in reaction *against* the modernist tradition that led to the war and that he thinks is heading toward eclectic mediocrity. In "The American Action Painters," Rosenberg grouses that "[t]o be Modern Art a work need not be either modern nor art; it need not even be a work. A three-thousand-year-old mask from the South Pacific qualifies as Modern and a piece of wood found on a beach becomes Art."[13] He applauds the desire of American artists to respond to the crises of the time by creating a new tradition. Moreover, Rosenberg, never one to modulate his criticism, takes Greenberg to task for his thesis of artistic continuity.

> "I fail to see anything essential in it [the new abstract art]," writes Clement Greenberg, a tipster on masterpieces, current and future, "that cannot be shown to have evolved [presumably through the germ cells in the paint] out of either Cubism or Impressionism, just as I fail to see anything essential in Cubism or Impressionism whose development could not be traced back to Giotto and Masaccio and Giorgione and Titian." In this burlesque of art history, artists vanish, and paintings spring from one another with no more need for substance than the critic's theories.[14]

To account for the international success of American abstract expressionism in the 1950s, Rosenberg focuses on the artist's creativity in the context of American history and experience; Greenberg analyzes individual works of art as they participate in modernism's supposed thrust toward greater purity. Greenberg's formalist aesthetic stands in contrast to Rosenberg's more inclusive notion of factors influencing the artistic creation of individuals.[15]

To this point in this article, Rosenberg's aesthetic views—beyond his emphasis on the individual—may seem to be hazy. Can his aesthetic thought be more clearly articulated?

Rosenberg and Aesthetic Judgment

Rosenberg's antipathy to Greenberg's aesthetic interpretation of art history leads him to question any theory of aesthetics with pretentions to universal validity.

> The notion of an aesthetic realm that transcends human existence is convenient for critics, collectors, and art historians in that it locates them, their ideas, and their property in a mental region tightly secured against unhappy interventions. The detachment of art from life offers nothing, however, to artists, nor does it stimulate the creation of art, since it takes no account of the subjective realities of the times.[16]

It isn't that Rosenberg dismisses aesthetic thought. Rather, he places it in the context of an artist's daily struggle with the issues that impinge upon her subjectively and shape her understanding of the political and social conditions within which she dwells. Contra Greenberg's historicism and his emphasis on formalism and the autonomy of the art object, Rosenberg's dynamic relational view of aesthetics situates its genesis as emerging from and responding to the everyday challenges of living. This view is consistent with John Dewey's vision of aesthetics. "The poem, or painting, does not operate in the dimension of correct descriptive statement but in that of experience itself."[17] Excellent art for Rosenberg brings the artist's creative response to existentially important issues into the sort of unity that Dewey praises as constituting *an* experience. "The poetic as distinct from the prosaic, esthetic art as distinct from scientific, expression as distinct from statement, does something different from leading to an experience. It constitutes one."[18]

Furthermore, although Rosenberg rejects Greenberg's understanding of modernism and thinks modernism's vitality has expired, that does not mean he is wholly antipathetic to the inspirations originally founding modernism. Indeed, he sees some modernist artists to have aims consistent with his own democratic antiestablishment American aesthetic of appreciating authentic artistic creation no matter from which class or aspect of society it comes. Art's aim should not be to escape life into some aesthetic heaven, but to engage it creatively in "this vale of tears," to allude to his Marxist sympathies. "The breaking down of the barriers between art and life is undoubtedly one of the dominant impulses of the modernist revolution."[19] That modernist thought is seen to unfold in a tradition of individualism is an aspect that Rosenberg appreciates.[20]

However, in Rosenberg's view, modernism and even individualism can all too easily become compromised by social and economic forces. His critical articles of the 1960s and '70s become increasingly caustic both about the course taken by the remnants of modernism and about the critical dismissal of the significance of artist involvement in action painting. He blamed this development on the shift of artist education from art schools and studios to the university, where the need to grade students in MFA programs led to intellectualizing art into its essential elements—"line, plane, form, color" (which no doubt contributed to the rise of minimalism). The rise of an artworld of dealers, agents, collectors, and reviewers helped transform art into a commodity enveloped in mass media. "There emerged the artist without background who knows the history of art through tracing formal resemblances in slides and reproductions, and who conceives picture making in terms of technical recipes, but who is entirely ignorant of the role of art in the struggles of the modern spirit."[21] He asserts that "the net effect of deleting from art the artist's situation, his conclusions about it and enactment of it in his work is to substitute for the crisis-dynamics of contemporary painting and sculpture an arid professionalism that is a caricature of the estheticism of half a century ago."[22] Many modernist artists, he believes, as professionals in a tradition, have given up the revolutionary opposition of modernism to bourgeois complacency in order to become tame enough to be commercially successful. Others have tailed off into personal fetishism, become involved in arbitrary happenings, or attempted to shock merely for the sake of gaining notice.

What then is Rosenberg's positive alternative to the narrow formalism of Greenberg and the perceived dissolution of modernism? To answer, it is helpful to return to an article Rosenberg wrote way back in 1932, "Character Change and the Drama." He calls it "a basic piece . . . which in a way I keep elaborating upon."[23] The piece distinguishes between an individual's "personality" (a partially perceived and intuited image that suggests but can never fully delimit an individual or anticipate her actions) and the dramatic fixture of a "role" or an "identity." In the theater, characters are identities with roles, not persons with histories.[24] In such Greek dramas as *Oedipus Rex* (or equally one could refer to Hamlet, as Rosenberg did), the play achieves its tension because its characters' identities are assumed to be static. "Dramatic reversal of situation derives its overwhelming effect from this persistence of identity. Everything has turned inside out, yet the actor goes on doing the same thing. Were psychological adjustment to the new position possible, it would destroy the tragic irony and disperse the pathos."[25]

Rosenberg sees the ideologies and conflicts of the twentieth century to unfold according to the logic of unchanging identities and ideologies clashing with tragic results. The artist's response to the conflicts engendered by seemingly endless social, technological, and historical change can be a vehicle of hope. But in order for art to be successful in this enterprise, artistic creativity must challenge those who are wedded to apparent fact, to static identities, to programs. "*The aim of every authentic artist is not to conform to the history of art, but to release himself from it in order to replace it with his own history.*"[26] In one of his thoughtful reflections on the course of American painting, Rosenberg notes that pioneers and immigrants bring their aesthetic traditions with them and are often oblivious to any thought that uniquely American experience demands its own authentic response. He names this tendency Redcoatism, in reference to the British soldiers who did not change their red-coated military strategy to counteract effectively the "Coonskinned" American guerrilla style of warfare. Rosenberg thinks American painters have ricocheted back and forth between a Redcoated allegiance to European aesthetics and a Coonskinned approach to painting manifest as folk art independent of any aesthetic tradition. "Coonskinism as a principle won ascendancy in American painting for the first time during World War II. With no new styles coming from Europe—and for deeper reasons than transportation difficulties—American artists became willing to take a chance on unStyle or antiStyle."[27] In response to the crises of war and cold war, Americans initiated action painting as the first fine art movement based on a truly American aesthetic rather than on some preexisting style.[28] This development illustrates the important distinction Rosenberg makes between those artists who create in allegiance to some set of aesthetic rules and those who create in response to the personally experienced issues of the times without being constrained by aesthetic niceties, such as novelty for the sake of novelty. "I do not believe that technical 'breakthroughs' and what Baudelaire called 'studio jargon" are relevant to art criticism."[29] The aesthetic standards of artists must themselves be flexible, open to adjustment in relation to existentially important environmental challenges and changes.

Again, it can be seen that Rosenberg's thought is consistent with American pragmatist and process thought. The very title of Alfred North Whitehead's book, *The Adventure of Ideas*, resonates with Rosenberg's aesthetic embrace of adventure and ideas, especially in a context of crisis. Whitehead writes, "Thus the contribution to Beauty which can be supplied by Discord—in itself destructive and evil—is the positive feeling of a quick shift of aim from the tameness of outworn perfection to some other ideal with its freshness still upon it."[30]

Caution is needed here, though. The revolutionary hope for some entirely new state of affairs is a dangerous illusion. Rosenberg conceived change to be in dialectical struggle with continuity. Consequently, he considered the notion of the entirely new to be a myth used to obscure historical realities and to conceal social and economic needs. Artists need to find and then keep open a space between political commitment and aesthetic idealism. In introducing *Possibilities*, a one-issue magazine Rosenberg co-edited, he declares, "This is a magazine of artists and writers who 'practice' in their work their own experience without seeking to transcend it in academic, group or political formulas." He continues: "Political commitment in our times means logically—no art, no literature. A great many people, however, find it possible to hang around in the space between art and political action."[31]

We have noted that Rosenberg never developed a systematic presentation of his ideas. It can be seen that his very recognition of the need for flexibility in one's aesthetic theory mitigates against developing any system. Creativity is just as much a cardinal value in aesthetic theory and art criticism as it is in artistic activity. But nevertheless we would like to endorse two related phrases as adequate to capture a consistent emphasis in his thought: his is an *aesthetics of the act*.[32] In Whiteheadian terms, his is a *process aesthetics*. It is carried out as a practice grounded in the artist's own experience. Whitehead claims that "fertilization of the soul is the reason for the necessity of art. A static value, however serious and important, becomes unendurable by its appalling monotony of endurance. The soul cries aloud for release into change."[33] Aesthetic actions, as suggested in "The American Action Painters," are carried out by persons—by individuals not locked into identities. Personal acts of exploration and creation are needed to produce authentic art. In our age of uncertainty, what is sought is a mode of acting, a practice of becoming that inspires confidence.

> How to be inspired with certainty—and to be filled with the certainty of inspiration—is the overwhelming problem of our revolutionary age. What state of mind will bring individuals and groups to the enlightenment they need in our constantly changing situations? In a period of crisis—and with us crises, private and public, come in an unending series—what can be more valuable than a trained gift for improvisation?[34]

Hidden within Rosenberg's critical excursions, which occasionally erupt into tirades,[35] is a yearning for a space for individual freedom and social progress. Art is most excellent when it steers beyond programmatic sameness and obstructive thinking, and opens up new vistas of possibility. An imaginative aesthetics that can foster an "as if" mentality—perhaps even a "why not?' mentality—can promote social welfare. For social progress to be made, though, the freedom granted the artist must not become a liability, as it is when fancy is let loose in disciplines where truth and integrity should reign. Rosenberg is prescient when he writes that what "novelists ought to complain about is not that truth has become stranger than fiction but that politicians have become fiction makers, competitors and collaborators of fiction writers."[36]

The meliorism inherent in Rosenberg's writings is consistent with the thought of Peirce, James, Dewey, and Whitehead. The underlying moral commitment motivating Rosenberg has been missed by most art historians, who tend to confine his influence to his coining of the term "action painting." Daniel Siedell offers a counterpoint to this stereotyped interpretation. He notes that, typically, institutions of art have overly aestheticized Rosenberg's notion of action and transformed it "from a sociological inquiry concerning the ideological collapse of the avant-garde into an aesthetic 'theory' for making more intense Modernist paintings."[37] In Siedell's view, the art establishment has transmuted Rosenberg's criticism directed toward itself and replaced it with a castrated version consistent with the establishment's programmatic biases.

The second main theme found throughout Rosenberg's writings, his attention to the historical, social, and cultural factors that contribute to the struggles of daily life, has been referred to throughout this essay. Now it is time to nail down more firmly its importance for his aesthetic theory. We have seen that in his theory of the individual, he contrasts the passionate attempts of the person to be authentic and uncaptured by dogma or social role with the preprogrammed activities of an actor having a self-limiting identity. In "The Stages: A Geography of Human Action," Rosenberg compares Hamlet with Claudius as examples of these two types of individuals. Hamlet is aware of a past in which his father was murdered, and he struggles to take historical *action* according to his sense of just recompense. Past is recalled and future looms. For Claudius, "The act is the thing; the man slips into it as into a Platonic form. It extends beyond human consciousness into the eternal."[38] Claudius has settled into a role as king; his actions are for him but episodes in a master plan. The present is real, the past and future but empty abstractions. Hamlet is a person; Claudius plays a role.

The contrasting sense of demand and possibility experienced by Claudius and Hamlet maps cleanly into a contrast between two views of history and social status developed by Rosenberg. For Claudius, the past is past. History has an external telos into which one learns to fit. One enacts the role that has evolved for oneself. Fate (or some other deterministic version of history) proclaims that fact and inevitability are what is real; the possibility of freedom and self-construction are comforting illusions. Hamlet, on the other hand, indwells a sense of history that is not closed but is ripe with possibility and obligation. The ghost of Hamlet's father symbolizes a past that exerts pressure in the present. Creative resolution is called for. The rich view of history Rosenberg extols places emotional demands on a person. It thereby creates anxiety: to be or not to be. The stew of family needs, social obligations, economic challenges, political crises, etc., etc., offers the possibility of acting creatively and courageously. Greenberg's emphasis on "the real" and the role of the artist as constrained by tradition has some suggestive parallels with Claudius's worldview, while Rosenberg's view comports quite closely to Hamlet's view.

The artist has a greater possibility than almost any other person of escaping routine and acting authentically. The artist must learn her craft, develop her skill, yes—but then has the possibility of engaging the issues of the day with passionate creativity. Whitehead's thought again captures the essence of Rosenberg's process vision. The ideal education balances the focused training of intellect with creative "intuition without an analytical divorce from the total environment. Its object is immediate apprehension with the minimum of eviscerating analysis. The type of generality, which above all is wanted, is the appreciation of variety of value. I mean an aesthetic growth. . . . What we want is to draw out habits of aesthetic appreciation."[39] Rosenberg's *process aesthetics* advocates such a plunging into the world to apprehend the values worth appreciating. Rosenberg the critic engages existential issues with the full-blooded and comprehensive vision of the Renaissance man. He thinks all the arts, but especially literature and the visual arts, are to be examined for their insights into issues of the times. He employs aesthetic vision more as a means to meaningful insight than as a constraining blueprint. Rosenberg's writing as a critic is itself a manifestation of the aesthetic vision he promulgates.

Notes

1. Harold Rosenberg, "The Herd of Independent Minds," in *Discovering the Present: Three Decades in Art, Culture, and Politics* (Chicago: University of Chicago Press, 1973), 16–17. This book is henceforth cited as *DP*.

2. Ibid., 27.

3. Rosenberg, "On Space," *DP*, 72.

4. Rosenberg was friends with both Sartre and Simone de Beauvoir and may have articulated thoughts on nothingness predating Sartre's own in *Being and Nothingness*. So although his reference to nothingness sounds very much like Sartre, it should also be noted that he was critical of Sartre's notion of individual action, which he thought suggested a denial of the social and historical factors within which a person dwells. "Sartre declares that no plot of history exists but that it is for us to make events by our own free choice, to write the drama as we like it. . . . It turned out that Sartre had a free choice so long as he did not choose within the action itself. . . . He demanded action, but did not name the actor." Harold Rosenberg, "Resurrected Romans," *The Tradition of the New* (New York: Horizon Press, 1959), 173.

5. Harold Rosenberg, "The American Action Painters," in *The Art World: A Seventy-Five-Year Treasury of ARTnews*, ed. Barbaralee Diamonstein (New York: ARTnews Books, 1977), 226.

6. Harold Rosenberg, "Metaphysical Feeling in Modern Art," in *Art and Other Serious Matters* (Chicago: University of Chicago Press, 1985), 308. This book is henceforth cited as *AOSM*.

7. See "Art Critics Comparison: Clement Greenberg vs. Harold Rosenberg," at the on-line site, "The Art Story," for several easily available pages contrasting the views and influences of the two critics. Available at www.theartstory.org/critics-greenberg-rosenberg.htm; accessed March 12, 2017.

8. Rosenberg, "American Action Painters," 227.

9. Clement Greenberg, "Thomas Eakins," in *Art and Culture* (Boston: Beacon Press, 1961), 178.

10. Rejecting Rosenberg's notion of action painting, Greenberg writes that for Rosenberg painting "remained as but the record of solipsistic 'gestures' that could have no meaning whatsoever as art—gestures that belonged to the same reality that breathing and thumbprints, love affairs and wars, but not works of art, belonged to." Excerpt from Clement Greenberg, "How Art Writing Earns Its Bad Name," in *The Second Coming* (March 1962), quoted in Herschel B. Chipp, *Theories of Modern Art: A Source Book by Artists and Critics* (Berkeley: University of California Press, 1968), 569.

11. Clement Greenberg, "'American-Type' Painting," in *Art and Culture*, 209.

12. Clement Greenberg, "New York Painting Only Yesterday," in *The Art World*, 271.

13. Rosenberg, "American Action Painters," 229.

14. Harold Rosenberg, "Action Painting: A Decade of Distortion," in *The Art World*, 322. The brackets are Rosenberg's.

15. Rosenberg sees the arts as being flush with many meanings. Again, this view differs from the views of Greenberg and the many persons he influenced. "To formalist art historians, whose influence is especially strong in modern-art museums, the importance of a work derives from the position it derives from the position it occupies in the evolution and diffusion of forms. Other meanings are discounted" ("Metaphysical Feeling," 308).

16. Harold Rosenberg, "Art and Political Consciousness," *AOSM*, 291–92.

17. John Dewey, *Art as Experience* (New York: Capricorn Books, 1958 [1934]), 85.

18. Ibid.

19. Harold Rosenberg, "Inquest into Modernism, *AOSM*, 48.

20. Harold Rosenberg, "The Avant-Garde," *DP*, 80.

21. Harold Rosenberg, "Then and Now," *AOSM*, 42.

22. Rosenberg, "Decade of Distortion," 322.

23. Rosenberg made this comment to Dorothy Sackler on July 8, 1968, as listed in the Rosenberg/Tabak Papers (New York) and quoted in Elaine Owens O'Brien, "The Art Criticism of Harold Rosenberg: Theaters of Love and Combat," PhD diss., City University of New York, 1997, note 9, 259.

24. Harold Rosenberg, "Character Change and the Drama," in *The Tradition of the New*, 140–41.

25. Ibid., 141–42.

26. Harold Rosenberg, "Olitski, Kelly, Hamilton: Dogma and Talent," in *Art on the Edge: Creators and Situations* (Chicago: University of Chicago Press, 1983), 64–65; italics in original.

27. Rosenberg, "Parable of American Painting," in *Art in America 1945–1970: Writings from the Age of Abstract Expressionism, Pop Art, and Minimalism*, ed. Jed Pearl (New York: Library of America, 2014), 238.

28. Rosenberg gestures toward but perhaps does not give enough attention to how the tragic burden of guilt and destruction in Europe after World War II led the European nations to seek grounds for cultural hope in the relatively unscathed United States. New York–centered abstract expressionism was internationally acclaimed not only because American artists were innovative but also because American art was marketed in a postwar cultural vacuum as energetic and hopeful in a world needing those qualities. The comparatively flush American museums and their supporters organized international exhibitions and publications that "fostered an image of American art as the expression of individual freedom—a rich and powerful image, which could be read at home as anti-communist and abroad as modern." Catherine Dossin, *The Rise and Fall of American Art, 1940s–1980s: A Geopolitics of Western Art Worlds* (London and New York: Routledge, 2017), 44.

29. Ibid., 64.

30. Alfred North Whitehead, *Adventure of Ideas* (New York: Mentor Book, 1933), 256.

31. Harold Rosenberg (with Robert Motherwell), *Possibilities*, no. 1 (Winter 1947–48), 1. The journal's co-editors are an impressive group: Motherwell for art, Rosenberg for literature (not art), Pierre Chareau for architecture, John Cage for music. Note Rosenberg's prioritization of experience in the spirit of Dewey.

32. See O'Brien, "Art Criticism," 30.

33. Alfred North Whitehead, *Science and the Modern World* (New York: The Free Press, 1967 [1925]), 202.

34. Rosenberg, "Metaphysical Feelings," 308.

35. For instance, Rosenberg calls critic Hilton Kramer "*The New York Times*' tireless meter maid of the arts" and deplores his affiliation with "the burlesque-house song-and-dance monologist Tom Wolfe." Shortly thereafter he refers to "the cesspools of Kramer's sarcasm" that "bubble over" ("Then and Now," 40). With such language, does Rosenberg himself engage in sarcasm that bubbles over?

36. Rosenberg, "Art and Political Consciousness," 281.

37. Daniel Andrew Siedell, "An Excavation of Tenth Street: The Failure of Modernism and the Politics of Postwar Historiography," PhD diss., University of Iowa, 1995, 164.

38. Harold Rosenberg, "The Stages: A Geography of Human Action," *Possibilities*, 50.

39. Whitehead, *Science and the Modern World*, 199.

13

Experiential Immersions in Beauty

A Confluence of James Turrell's Light Spaces and Whitehead's Aesthetics

Vaughan Durkee McTernan

Alfred North Whitehead's exposition of Process aesthetics details occasions of Beauty[1] and our experiences of them. In keeping with the broadening purview of aesthetics since the nineteenth century, Whitehead's idea of Beauty is not tied to traditional understandings of "the beautiful." From a Whiteheadian perspective, Beauty and our experience of it are broad processes that can be articulated. Consequently, developing an awareness of the dynamics of art through a Process perspective deepens our experience of artworks as well enhances our role as viewer/participants. Moreover, a Process perspective gives us a nuanced and flexible measure for assessing value.

    Accordingly, this paper on immersions in Beauty is a thought experiment describing Whitehead's ideas of Beauty and how they apply to art in general and to one artist's work in particular. The visual arts provide a ready context for exploring Whitehead's aesthetics. Further, there are types of contemporary art that would undoubtedly intrigue Whitehead because they are good examples of occasions of Beauty as he understood them. In particular, experiential, abstract installation art fits into Whitehead's discussion of Beauty. These types of works are outside the norm of what Whitehead would have experienced. Nevertheless, exploring them gives us insights into his ideas about Beauty, and his ideas help us see the contemporary works themselves with greater clarity and effect.

This thought experiment takes the light-based installations created by the renowned artist James Turrell and looks at them through the lens of Whiteheadian experience. Turrell creates spaces out of light and color (***Infinite Light Tunnel***)[2] (see this endnote regarding images). The majority of his works are large, abstract installation pieces we, as viewers and participants, enter. Turrell immerses us in his art (***Akhob—Las Vegas***), and this immersion makes his work especially apt for exploring Beauty through visual and physical experiences of complexity, intensity, and creativity. Turrell, who studied mathematics and psychology as an undergraduate at Pomona College and then received an MFA from Claremont Graduate University,[3] was not directly influenced by Process thought (despite Claremont's being a center for Process philosophy), but his art is a physical embodiment of Whitehead's philosophic notion of Beauty. Turrell's works are instances of "Process" Beauty, providing us with ready venues for experimenting with and experiencing what Whitehead was writing about. Turrell's works, by the way, are easily accessible, usually public, and widespread enough that you can probably find one near you to experience and perhaps discern Beauty in it as Whitehead might have.

An overview of Turrell's installations and then a review of key elements of Whitehead's idea of Beauty will highlight in what ways Turrell's art works are instances of Beauty. The focus of this undertaking is to see how Turrell's work outwardly expresses Beauty through continual change, the interface between simplicity and complexity, appearance, and the experience of heightened intensity.

All of Turrell's works are studies in light. He creates spaces out of light, using both natural and a wide spectrum of colored light. As installation works they are three-dimensional and most of them are works one physically enters. They include large chambers of variously colored light that participants walk around in called *ganzfields* (***Breathing Light***). They include pools of illuminated water in which we are immersed (***Stonescape/ Stonesky*** [**nighttime view**]). They include rooms called skyspaces where viewers sit on benches around the perimeter looking up at a vault and/ or oculus open to the sky (***Blue Planet Sky***). And they include an entire volcanic crater in Arizona in which passages and openings are engineered to let in natural light; it becomes an artwork in which visitors stand and move (***Roden Crater*** **exterior**; ***Roden Crater*** **interior**).

In Turrell's creations, solid structure is used only as a holder of light or as a diverter of light. Any structurally massive elements of the works are there only to direct light in ways that deliberately focus our perception on the light[4] so that we will see qualities in it we do not usually see—such as density, varied hues, and contrasts. Turrell also changes our visual perception of light by playing with combinations of colors and shapes that alter the colors we see and alter our depth perception (***Skyspace at UT Austin***).

Ordinarily we think of light as revealing some object to us. We take it for granted that light illuminates surfaces so that we can see objects. We shine a bright light so we can see things, such as writing on a page, more clearly. In Turrell's works, however, it's the light itself that we see more acutely. The light itself and its varying qualities are revealed,[5] rather than some object to look at. In addition, Turrell engineers the light to change our perception of it from what we would ordinarily see to what we don't expect. He engineers light to produce in the light itself qualities such as depth, solidity, and diffuseness,[6] and, in Whiteheadian terms, intensity, complexity, and ongoing novelty.

Turrell's art is, in fact beautiful (***House of Light* Japan**). It also exemplifies Whitehead's idea of Beauty, which is not the same as beautiful, although it can include it. For Whitehead, Beauty involves massiveness, contrast, intensity of feeling, balance, novelty, and harmony. All these dynamics are featured throughout Whitehead's philosophy. But, particularly in a discussion of process aesthetics, it is worthwhile to focus on Beauty, because Beauty pulls the potential richness of becoming occasions into the foreground. That is, for Whitehead, the experience of Beauty is roughly equivalent to (and perhaps helped inspire) the expanded notion of aesthetic sensibility that emerged in art criticism during the twentieth century. In its comprehensive, experiential nature, it is a cognitive version of American Aesthetics.

For Whitehead, as he describes it in his 1933 volume *Adventures of Ideas*, Beauty requires a balance between massiveness and intensity.[7] Both are integral to Beauty. In his vocabulary, massiveness is the volume of prehensions that are becoming an occasion. It is important in Beauty because it is the building material of an occasion, and the more massiveness there is, the more potential there is for contrasts and complexity. Massiveness on its own, however, can neither constitute nor maintain Beauty. As its name implies, massiveness tends to get heavy. It tends to be repetitive, since repetition of previous subjective forms is the most common state of existing things. Massiveness will eventually fail if there is too little contrast or novelty brought into the mix. Thus, the "anesthesia," as Whitehead calls it, of too little novelty and contrast works against potential Beauty.[8]

Novelty and contrast, then, hold together the volume and complexity of massiveness, saving it from deadly heaviness. While volume is the sheer number of prehensions or parts in an occasion, complexity is the manner in which their aims come together. Novelty and contrast hold together the parts in complex variety. In so doing they create an opening for Beauty that evokes intensity. Intensity of feeling develops when novelty and contrast reach the greatest extent possible in massiveness without losing too much building material—that is, while still retaining most prehensions or parts.[9]

When the contrasts are as effective as they can be, when novel occasions can come together without inhibiting each other's subjective aims, and while achieving as much complexity as possible, then there is intensity and the potential for Beauty. Still, intensity is undergirded by massiveness. And, as Whitehead says, "the maximum of intensity proper is finally dependent upon massiveness."[10] So, massiveness provides a framework for intensity, underscoring that intensity cannot constitute Beauty on its own either. Some balanced dynamic between the two is required.[11]

Initially, when massiveness and intensity, still incorporating novelty and contrast, find a workable dynamic, Harmony is the outcome.[12] But, Harmony as Whitehead understands it is never permanent and never means sameness. We commonly think harmony means a kind of "almost" sameness. Harmony sounds nice because the notes go together. They are not discordant. But, for Whitehead, the important thing about Harmony is contrast.

Harmony sounds nice *because* the notes are different, different enough to make it interesting and pleasing. Harmony arises when the contrasts in that balance between massiveness and intensity are effective.[13] For Whitehead, contrasts make Harmony interesting and intensify subjective feeling without becoming so discordant that objective content gets discarded or results in a loss of intensity and complexity.[14]

We might be tempted here to think of harmony as perfection. But, Beauty involves complex contrasts, tireless novelty, and dynamic, shifting intensities, and in such a dynamic, Beauty and perfection are never synonymous. For Whitehead, Beauty may include interesting moments that can be more or less perfect than the moments preceding or succeeding them. But it can never be absolute or permanent. He writes, "There is no totality which is the harmony of all perfection."[15] And furthermore, "All realization is finite and there is no perfection which is the infinite of all perfections."[16]

For Whitehead, any perceived static perfection is a precarious position. Maintained perfection is likely to become dull because of repetition and lack of novelty. In, fact, where civilizations are concerned, Whitehead believes that perceived attainment of perfection eventually leads to downfall.[17]

The dynamics of Beauty for Whitehead are also the dynamics of rich experiences of light for Turrell. His works are visual and physical experiences of complexity and intensity that are always in dynamic change. Static perfection is neither a part of nor a goal of Turrell's art. Unlike art that captures a moment, such as a painting, or a static sculpture, Turrell's installations are perpetually new (**Aten Reign Guggenheim**).

They involve constantly novel configurations of light. The contrasts he engineers seem key to how he wants us to experience light. When he changes the color inside a space, it changes whatever we see as we look through that light, whether it is the outside sky or another interior. Even in a semi-open sky-space, the color interactions alter the colors we see and our three-dimensional vision (**Twilight Epiphany Series**). As the interior light changes, our perception of the exterior sky is altered. It may change in density and hue and appear closer and more immediate. As the exterior light changes with the slow passage of time, the interior light takes on different qualities and hues and appears more or less bright and saturated. Combinations and contrasts of shifting colored lighting and outside natural light give us a novel view of light in each moment.

If we are in a *ganzfield*—a room full of light of generally the same color—modulating hues and density envelope us as we move from place to place. We are in shifting modes of light throughout (**Bridget's Bardo**). In pieces where there are pools of water illuminated with colored light, the light changes in the room and in the pool as the water moves (**Japanese Light House Pool**). Outside pools change with the daylight and surrounding environment. The same installation is completely different at night than in the daytime (**Stone Scape/Stone Sky**—day and night views). In still other types of works, participants walk straight through corridors of light as the colors change, blend, and merge (**The Light Inside**).[18] None of Turrell's pieces are static, even those in which we are looking at a shape that appears to be solid. Thus, there is no enduring moment of perfect Beauty in Turrell's work. Instead, just as for Whitehead, there are moments of relative beauty that are not repeated

Turrell's work develops in us a heightened awareness of light, of its gradations of hue, density, fluidity, and brightness, all of which are developed in contrast upon contrast. For Whitehead, the complexity found in massiveness is held together without clash by just such contrast upon contrast. Turrell's works physically, in outward appearance, achieve this balanced harmony through carefully engineered contrasts. In addition, we contribute to complexity in Turrell's pieces by being immersed in and thereby a part of his work. Overall, by deliberate design, Turrell engineers contrasts we perceive as moments of rich intensity and feeling. For Whitehead and Turrell, novel, complex contrasts and shifting dynamics are purveyors of Beauty.

In neither Whitehead nor Turrell is balance or deliberate, calculated contrast unadventurous. Beauty requires unexpected novelty. Novelty, despite what it implies, too easily becomes an ordinary process. Beauty needs the spark of unexpected novelty. It needs change that captures our attention to give it depth and richness. Turrell's works, while balanced and carefully designed, have that unexpected novelty. Random shifts in color and contrast, changes in location and perspective, variations in natural light and the outside sky, none of which can be thoroughly anticipated, enrich how we experience Turrell's works.

And yet, there is a serene simplicity about them. The Appearance of Turrell's works belies their complexity. But, this simplification is for Whitehead a part of Beauty. Art brings the Harmony and intensity of complexity, held together by contrast, into the foreground. For Whitehead, Appearance is important to Beauty as "a simplification of Reality."[19] It unifies diverse objects while retaining contrast and high volume.[20] "Appearance," says Whitehead, "combines massiveness with intensity."[21] He goes on to say, "The parts set up the whole to be a harmonious simplicity."[22] In other words, complexity, when harmonized, brings about a rich, intense simplicity. We may not see the complexity of Reality in Appearance,[23] but we experience the complexity as intensity of feeling.[24]

For Turrell, simplicity and intensity sum up how we experience light as viewers and participants in his works. Turrell's pieces are in many ways contemplative in their simplicity. We watch, we wait. We walk though light as it changes around us. We contemplate. Focused simplicity of light as it appears in his works is concentrated intensity. While there is a somewhat religious and certainly spiritual quality to this simplicity, which Turrell deliberately intends,[25] his works are not overtly religious. It is best to describe them broadly as sacred spaces. A bit of his background will explain why his installations take on intensity and depth with sacred overtones.

Turrell comes from a Quaker background and has recently returned to that practice.[26] The Quaker concept of Inner Light, of divine light within each person, led directly to his work with light. He tells the story of his grandmother explaining to him as they went into Quaker meeting that he could "go inside and greet the light."[27] He understands this practice of greeting the light in both an inner sense, and as physical space in which to discover light as a facet of the sacred. In particular, he experiments with what it means to experience light in novel, unexpected, and far out of the ordinary ways. For example, the **Live Oaks Meeting House** in Houston, which is a skyspace focused on the exterior sky, and the interior *ganzfield* installations **Crossing Jordan** and **Armat** have sacred qualities evoked by using light in unconventional, contemplative ways.

Whitehead's discussion of Beauty also is not overtly religious, but his ideas of intensity and depth point to the sacred. This is not the place to get into discussions about Whitehead's ideas of God. They are summed up nicely as they developed variously over time by Randy Auxier in his glossary entry to Whitehead's 1926 book *Religion in the Making*. But Auxier makes a point that is helpful for understanding the religious/spiritual overtones of Beauty and of Turrell's work with Light. He points out first that for Whitehead, God cannot be described.[28] However, he says, "[f]or whatever else it may be, a definition is a linguistic articulation of some intuition, and as an articulation, it always remains partial and incomplete."[29] This statement is helpful for thinking about Turrell's work in the Process context. Whitehead himself uses the term "metaphysical intuitions"[30] toward the end of *Adventures of Ideas*.

We can think of Turrell's light-works in a similar vein. His work comprises artistic expressions, always partial and incomplete, of an intuition about God that we might glimpse through light. "Going inside to find the light within,"[31] as Turrell intends us to do in both a physical and metaphysical sense, is to always be exploring that intuition. The spaces he creates are sanctuaries where we can freely carry out these explorations (**Raemar Pink and White; Roden Crater**).

The Beauty we experience in Turrell's work is harmonious, always simplified and brought to the foreground in bold, novel creations rich with new intensities. These intensities, or at least intuitions of them, are indicative of the richness and depth of feeling evoked in Beauty. As Beauty pulls the potential richness of becoming occasions to the foreground, we get a glimpse through Turrell's work of the richness and depth intuited in occasions of Beauty. For Whitehead, when an artwork is effective it connects to the vast background of individual occasions that go into its synthesis. The result of this connection for both Turrell and Whitehead is intensity of feeling, Harmony, and Beauty, all of which are part of an effective artwork's Appearance,[32] in other words, the work of art we see.

Because of his dynamic view of Beauty, Whitehead insists on the importance of art. The intensity of Beauty is what energizes and persuades, even lures, us to imagine new configurations of Beauty and Harmony as individuals and societies. Would Whitehead see Turrell's experiential, installation art as persuasive? Does it have what it takes? Does it provide us with the necessary jolt or dose of Beauty to make us continually pursue new configurations—whether of the sacred or of community? I imagine Whitehead would think, "yes," it does. At the most fundamental level it challenges our notions of how we see light and what light is. Such an elemental challenge could push us to find new perspectives on other basics we take for granted in our lives and environments.

In addition, Turrell's work gives us the opportunity to see ourselves in a new light, both literally and figuratively. As the ones experiencing and intimately participating in Turrell's light spaces, we are a part of the works themselves as they are constantly reconfigured. We are a part of the complexity and contrast, a part of the Beauty.

Turrell's work really is a visual representation of Whitehead's ideas. And Whitehead's ideas do give us a verbal explanation of what we see and experience in Turrell's works. Each man's way of engaging the world enhances the other's. Through Turrell's vision we see and participate in Beauty in novel ways enriching both us and the Beauty of the work itself. Through *Whitehead's* vision, we understand the dynamic processes of Beauty and our involvement in them through works of art. As we are surrounded by natural light, color-saturated light, and water in Turrell's works, we are immersed in the process of Beauty (**Dividing the Light**; MoMA *PS 1 Skyscape*).

Notes

1. Process and Beauty are among the ordinary words that are capitalized to indicate that they have stipulated meanings that are based on Alfred North Whitehead's special usage.

2. Throughout this paper I have included in bold the names of examples of Turrell's works that the reader can easily access on line while reading the paper.

Doing so will make the paper more complete, as it was originally presented with slides of the works.

3. Jan Butterfield, *The Art of Light and Space* (New York: Abbeyville Press, 1993), 71.

4. Julia Brown, "Interview with James Turrell," in *Occluded Front: James Turrell*, ed. Julia Brown (Los Angeles: The Lapis Press/Museum of Contemporary Art, Los Angeles, 1985), 15.

5. Butterfield, *The Art of Light and Space*, 87.

6. Ibid., 23.

7. Alfred North Whitehead, *Adventures of Ideas* (New York: The Free Press, 1967), 252–53.

8. Ibid., 259, 275, 285.

9. Ibid., 261, 263.

10. Ibid., 253.

11. Ibid., 261.

12. Ibid., 252.

13. Ibid.

14. Ibid., 261, 263.

15. Ibid., 276.

16. Ibid., 257.

17. Ibid.

18. This piece is illustrated on the cover of this volume.

19. Ibid., 281.

20. Ibid., 261.

21. Ibid.

22. Ibid., 264.

23. Ibid., 247.

24. Ibid., 249.

25. "James Turrell: Live Oak Friends Meeting House," ART21 interview from *Art in the Twenty-First Century*," Season 1 episode, "Spirituality," 2001; available on YouTube.

26. Elaine King, "Into the Light: A Conversation with James Turrell," *Sculpture* 21, no. 9 (Nov. 2002).

27. Linda Essig, "Three Hours in Light: Experiencing the Work of James Turrell," in *TD and T (Theater Design and Technology)* (Spring 2003): 15. See also "James Turrell: Live Oak Friends Meeting House," cited in endnote 23.

28. Auxier refers to Alfred North Whitehead, *Religion in the Making* (New York: Fordham University Press, 1996), 244.

29. Ibid., 247.

30. Whitehead, *Adventures of Ideas*, 283.

31. Essig, "Three Hours," 15.

32. Ibid., 281.

14

Dialogue

From Rich Experience to Minimalist Expression

COREY DRIETH WITH WALTER GULICK

In the following dialogue, I (Walter Gulick) have posed seven sets of questions to artist Corey Drieth, who then responds at some length. The questions and responses are not transcribed from direct conversation; the written exchanges reflect upon issues that arose in earlier discussion. Our discourse is supported with illustrations of Drieth's artwork available in the Paintings section of his website, cdrieth.com. Additional artwork referred to can also be found on line.

I see Drieth as an artistic practitioner who has reflected deeply about the aesthetic quality of his work, spare though it may be. His painted wooden blocks have none of the obvious American content of a Thomas Hart Benton, Edward Hopper, or Roy Lichtenstein, yet his full-bodied responses to my questions exemplify the wide-ranging sensibility characteristic of American Aesthetics. His account of his past development, artistic influences, and personal intentions provides richer insight into the aesthetic meaning of his art than analytical attention to a work alone can generally muster. Many artists consistently decline to answer questions about their work, deferring instead to their works as autonomous entities. Then an analytic approach to the artwork may have to persevere. Drieth, in contrast, provides a rich account of the genesis of his work both in general and in relation to one suite of his works in particular. Religious and philosophical issues as well as art history shape his acute aesthetic sensibility. Notice how often his feelings, the wellspring of the aesthetic, come to expression in his responses and guide the course of his creativity. And, significantly, aesthetic feeling brings his work to a climactic ending: the work is complete when Drieth feels "grateful to have been a part of its realization."

The sort of discussion Drieth provides enhances a viewer's appreciation of his work, but in no sense is the meaning of the work exhaustively uncovered by this conversation. In neither his paintings nor his discussion is Drieth didactic, telling us exactly how to think about what he has produced. Rather, his responses are confessional and invitational. Nevertheless, his description of how he creates one of his paintings pays tribute to Dewey's concept of authentic artistic creation as a coherent process that "has a satisfying emotional quality because it possesses internal integration and fulfillment reached through ordered and organized movement" (*Art as Experience*, 38).

Drieth states that "my subject matter is spirituality." By "spiritual" he means something of personal existential import as situated in a specific practice, the tradition of abstract painting. His works are not tokens of conventional religiosity. His aim is to create works that are poetic, that elicit curiosity, that embody the sacred. They hover before us as, in Langer's terminology, presentational symbols calling for our interpretive response. The square is the central emblem of sacredness for him. So personally significant, so intimate their creation, are his works that he is reluctant to sell them. But he is happy to display and discuss them. We are the beneficiaries. So, on to my questions and Drieth's responses.

> At first glance, your paintings seem to be most plausibly interpreted as falling within the tradition of minimalism. Your works don't have the repetition of Donald Judd's sculpture, the overall emphasis on balance characteristic of Piet Mondrian's paintings, the extreme simplicity of Ellsworth Kelly's work, the concentration on colors and their contrasts of Mark Rothko or Joseph Albers, or the rather mystical attention to "zips" of Barrett Newman. Yet they seem to have aspects of many of these artists. What artists have most influenced you? Whose work do you most admire? Why?

Experiencing art is such an important part of my creative process that I feel compelled to acknowledge those artists and thinkers who have had a profound effect on me . . . and there have been a lot of them! All of the artists you mentioned have had an immense impact on my work, particularly Mondrian, Albers, and Kelly. But the three that probably have had the greatest influence on me in terms of the visual language that I use and the thinking behind it would be Georgia O'Keeffe, Frederick Sommer, and Agnes Martin. I admire each of them, as each offers something different. But if I can say something in general about all of them it would be that they each, in very different ways, evoke a sense of beauty, sublimity, and/or mystery in their work. Their art wakes me up, causes me to pay attention and to be more curious, and inspires me to respond to the world by creating art (see Georgia O'Keeffe, *Abstraction White Rose*, 1927). In fact, the more I study (read about, look at, etc.) their work, the richer it becomes; the things they made and said endlessly inspire me.

Further, each one of these artists has also challenged me to perceive the world in new and more open and generous ways. In the case of Martin, when I first saw her paintings I was stunned by their unique character. I had seen work that embraced formal simplicity before. But something about her sparse, fragile, gentle grids confronted my understanding of what I considered to be viable art. So, I felt like I had a choice: dismiss it or try to move closer to it. Luckily I chose the latter. As I began reading more about her paintings—particularly the work she made in the 1990s that addresses love—my mind began to change. By way of getting closer to her work intellectually, I was eventually able to move into it experientially and in doing so had a breakthrough in the way that I saw art and subsequently the world. This was a jaw-dropping moment for me, and I am reminded of it whenever I see her paintings (see *Untitled #2* by Agnes Martin). It seems almost obvious to me now that all of her works express a desire for an experiential purity, for a kind of foundational, transcendent perfection. They constantly rekindle intellectual, emotional, and spiritual longings I have had since I was a child. So it would not be hyperbole to say that, through the rhythmic use of pale bands of pale color and delicate pencil lines, Martin's paintings evoke moments of simplicity, innocence, joy, and love. In doing so, they refresh and deepen my relationship with the world. O'Keeffe, Sommer, and Martin all have asked me to look again at my assumptions about art, the world, and myself. My goal is similar in the sense that I want viewers to slow down, to pay attention, and to be aware of what they are feeling and thinking while they are looking. I want them to feel curious and be imaginative. Ultimately, my goal is to make paintings with a similar vitality and renewing spirit, paintings that offer some sort of revelation. [See image #1, *Confluence*, illustrated on this book's cover.]

> You majored in philosophy at Colorado State University and have expressed an interest in the mysticism found in different religious traditions. To what extent has your intellectual background shaped what you seek to achieve through your art? What critical or aesthetic terms do you use in evaluating your own work?

My intellectual background has very much influenced my work and what I hope to achieve through it. And it continues to do so, particularly my interest in mysticism and contemplative religious practice. But I hesitate to trace my work to specific religious or philosophical concepts, for a number of reasons. First, for me art making isn't about the articulation of ideas. I think other fields of study—like philosophy—do that much more effectively. I think many artists today experiment with and explore materials in an attempt to create (or discover) and share experiences. Ideas are often launching points for that journey, and when they are, they tend to color everything about the work along the way, including the decisions that takes place in terms of media and design. But I generally agree with the poet and art theorist Herbert Read when he says (to paraphrase) that the main business of art is not the presentation of ideas but rather the communication of the artist's emotional reaction to them.

Another reason I am hesitant to talk about ideas—and I think this is one of the reasons a lot of artists are elusive—is that doing so can misdirect viewers from the expressive immediacy of the work. We all tend to apply categories to things we don't fully understand because it makes them easier to navigate. But it also makes them easier to dismiss because we too quickly assume familiarity. Powerful contemporary art asks viewers to engage. It calls us to draw our own conclusions. Its meaning is rarely determined. It is a guided dialog (guided by the sensitivity of the formal decisions made by the artist and the knowledge and receptivity of the viewer), but a dialog nonetheless. Artists often have complex and ambivalent relationships with their subject matter, and use art as a way of trying to better understand those relationships. This makes talking about what they do even more difficult. To add to the mess, contemporary art has its philosophical roots in the Modernist Avant-garde whose driving question was, "What is art?" Artists today continue to ask that question in the work they make, but usually without positing answers in the form of manifestos or grand proclamations. So sometimes discussing source ideas in too much depth creates didacticism and limits the poetic (associative, metaphorical and emotional) potential of a piece of art, which is one of the primary reasons we make it (#2, *Bed*).

That being said, I wouldn't be making the work I make today without the descriptions and ideas of religious experience that I encountered in the classes I took and books I read in my studies. General themes such as the relationship between immanence and transcendence, between the sacred and the profane, between light and darkness, inform my work. In fact, the notion of emptiness—or fertile darkness—as it is found in Buddhist and Christian mystical traditions is particularly important to me. Spiritually inclined poetry (whether Hafiz, Rilke, or Mary Oliver) inspires what I make, too, as do religious images and icons. I am very interested in the erotic religious narratives found in Indian Miniatures and in the ritualistic use of Tantric diagrams. I was fortunate to have taken classes from philosophy teachers who were sincerely interested in art and its role in guiding and articulating spiritual aspiration (#3, *Immanence*).

In terms of evaluating my work, I only do that within the studio, before I show it. Any assessment after that I leave to others. For most of my artistic life people have asked me, "How do you know when a painting is done?" It is a direct question but one that is deceptively difficult to answer. For years I responded with a prepackaged, although honest, and not very insightful response: it depends on the piece. But a couple of years ago during a gallery talk it suddenly occurred to me that I know a piece is finished when I feel grateful. Like a lot of artists, I feel like I am participating in something greater than my ideas when I work rather than being in charge of everything that happens. This seems slightly at odds with the fact that I am notoriously picky about letting things out of my studio; I am a slow producer because I exert so much control over my materials and process. In addition, it is incredibly important to me that my work comes from something I feel deeply about (an idea, another piece of art, a feeling, place, or memory, etc.), and then, as I make it, it is equally important to me that it starts to take on a life of its own. I try to cultivate this relative autonomy from my intentions by pushing each painting to the point of technical failure every time I work. I try to cultivate serendipity and I do this to allow for something new (to me) to occur. This high-wire approach contributes to the sense that I am not fully in control. So, questions I would use to evaluate success would be: Is this painting earnest? Did I take enough risks to allow it to reveal something to me? Did it open me up more to my own life? Do I find it to be mysterious and/or beautiful and/or sublime? Does it contain subtle awkwardness, insecurity or tension (something I want my work to have), and finally and perhaps most importantly: Do I feel grateful to have been a part of its realization? When I do, I know that in all likelihood other people will find it to be powerful too, and it is good to go.

> You have said that you are seeking through some of your paintings to develop a personal iconography. This sounds like it fits into the prevailing individualism of American society. What are some of the characteristics of the iconography you have developed? What interplay do you see between the personal, the historical, and the social in your work? To what extent is the history and culture of America relevant or irrelevant to what you are seeking to express and achieve?

One of the primary characteristics of the iconography I am exploring is the use of the square as a sacred principle. This shape has a rich cross-cultural iconographic history that I first became aware of while studying Modern Art history. I am fascinated by how central it is to so many of the design aesthetics of recent time (in art, architecture, urban planning, etc.). I do not know if the square, as an American design motif, was influenced by Thomas Jefferson's notion that land could be democratically distributed by way of the application of a basic grid system. But I would think so. I believe it has its roots in classicism. Regardless, my interest in the square lies in how it feels, its simple geometric perfection, its stability, its lack of structural hierarchy, and its ability to be repeated to create tight and orderly systems (see Josef Albers, *Study for Homage to the Square: Departing in Yellow*, 1964). The circle is equally perfect and nonhierarchical but less rigid, less seamlessly systematic. I am interested in the synthetic (human made instead of produced by nonhuman processes) associations of the square, too, because I see it as the seed of reason. It is an archetype of geometry, and as such I see it as a guiding principle for our drive for order, balance, and perfection. Other themes within my work include loose references to portals (doors, windows, curtains, shrouds, etc.), the various states between concealing and revealing, and the wooden ground itself as curvilinear, radial, natural order, something that is intuitive, situational, and fluid in its logic. Plus, small wooden panels have been used for centuries for icon painting in a variety of artistic and religious traditions. They are readily available, familiar, and easy to live with . . . expressive qualities that are important to me (#4, *Gnosis*).

In response to the other questions you posed, let me begin by saying that in the past, friends and colleagues have accused me of being a Modernist. I absolutely disagree with them for reasons too numerous to count. First and foremost, I am not even sure that is possible today. Regardless, it is true that I am very interested in Modernism and spent a lot of time in my youth looking at Modern Art. Perhaps as a consequence my approach to painting mirrors paths taken by both early–twentieth-century American artists such as Arthur Dove and Georgia O'Keeffe and mid-century painters like Mark Rothko and Agnes Martin. As I said above, the work made by these artists still moves me. So, in terms of its relationship to history, my work is a look back on modernist ideals. But it is not a glance that is characterized by confidence or trust. Rather, I am looking at them insecurely, with a tentative combination of hope and doubt. These feelings define my worldview, and I think the worldviews of many people today.

I see my work as part of an American tradition of abstraction because of its relationship to the history of American painting, in particular the artists I just mentioned. Dove and O'Keeffe worked close to nature and everyday life, and their paintings are drawn directly from it. Their abstraction is rooted in the experience of concrete things in the world, not in ideas or theories (see Arthur Dove, *Fog Horns*, 1929). They move between the representational and the nonobjective, playing with space in ways that are both familiar and wildly ambiguous. Both address their subjects sensually, utilizing swirling, writhing, crawling, vibrating, soft and rigid, overlapping sensuous form. My eyes move into and out of their illusionary space with frequency and at various paces.

Rothko and Martin—who considered themselves Abstract Expressionists—infuse deep sentiment into their work as well. But generally speaking, their artistic practices were driven by more abstract feelings. Their later work is atmospheric in its articulation of space. They both abandon any narrative read altogether and convey something more transcendent by way of soft fields of value and color and their use of serrated edges and/ or delicate lines. Their paintings tend to evoke slow, if not fixed, scrutiny, causing our eye to hover over their surfaces. We are aware of great depth but are not able to penetrate it for too long (if at all). Or, perhaps that depth radiates out toward us too at times, depending on the work. Whatever the case, the mature work of Rothko and Martin offers the viewer few recognizable spatial cues, while still being built on rectilinear forms rather than a variety of curvilinear ones (see Mark Rothko, *Black in Deep Red*, 1957).

So, I see my work as structurally related to the work of the early American Modernists while expressively aligned with Abstract Expressionism. Unlike European artists such as Malevich and Mondrian who were deconstructing art with the goal of moving toward social and spiritual utopias, my work is driven by personal emotional and spiritual concerns and its grammar is drawn directly from recognizable stuff in the world. While it is very personal, it is social too. I consider it a part of an ongoing historical artistic discussion about the nature of abstraction.

As far as the quest for a personal iconography, I can see why that might qualify my work as American as well, considering the role of individualism and self-reliance in our cultural history. But I see this individualism as part of the contemporary experience in postindustrial society in general, where a growing number of people prefer spiritual creativity to religious identity and borrow from a number of artistic and religious precedents in an attempt to define their own sense of the sacred. This is part of our time, part of the "New Age." We are living in an era that seems to be defined by cross-pollination and hybridity, and my work reflects that urge. But unlike so much of the art that exists within a global capitalist culture that has its roots in American economic policy, my paintings are intentionally low-tech, anti-spectacle, anti-heroic. While they address larger existential issues, they do so in intimate, quiet, fragile, and reserved ways. So with this in mind, and considering my fascination with the square, I probably owe as much to Josef Albers as I do any American artist.

> Wood and its grainy patterns play an important role in your work. A conversation of sorts seems to take place between the wood and colorful flat surfaces. Is "conversation" a useful metaphor to describe what is going on? If so, what sort of meaning seems to emerge from such conversation? If "conversation" is not an apt description, how would you describe the relation between paint and wood and its place in your work?

Yes, I think the term *conversation* is a useful one to describe the relationship I am interested in exploring between surface and substrate (#5, *Saint #5*). I say this because the surface treatment and the ground are equally important, and whatever meaning is generated in my work depends on their mutual interaction within each composition. As I mentioned earlier, I use the opacity, translucency, and transparency of paint (gouache) to conceal and reveal the grain structure of the poplar ground. First and foremost, this creates an illusionistic spatial depth on the surface of each piece. This dynamic is obvious and foundational to almost all 2-D art, and when working graphically (with hard edges, solid or semisolid colors, and distinct shapes), as I do, it is usually apparent what generally feels closer in space. Leaving the ground unpainted, or translucent, allows the wood's grain to become part of the composition as well, which reminds viewers of its "object-ness" due to our familiarity with that kind of structure. So, my basic goal is to subtly move the viewer between suspension of disbelief that happens with almost all illusionistic art and a more objective awareness of the material conditions of the object itself. In other words, I hope to cause the viewer to flutter between the imaginative and the factual. Shifting the perception of the viewer in such a way has been a part of what artists, musicians, and writers have done for as long as art has been around. But for painters, this goal gained greater significance in the late nineteenth and twentieth centuries when the traditional mimetic function of their practice changed. I am interested in it because of that history (painting as a deconstruction and reconstruction of the empirical world), but more so because one of my primary goals is to make objects that remain objects but that feel intensely intimate and deeply mysterious . . . that feel sacred. I want to make objects that evoke emotional and imaginative responses that are associated with spiritual experiences but that don't lock into specific narratives or references. This is important because, for me, sacred experience is both immanent and transcendent, because I believe objects have real power. When I am experiencing something I would call spiritual, the world does not drop away. Instead, it opens up. The world stays the world, but what I thought was real expands and deepens and insights are revealed. These insights can be grand or small, or both at the same time. But in every case the experiences that provide them don't last long. While changed by them I quickly return to the familiar.

 Each particular work, then, is an exploration and expression of what is happening underneath specific "sacred" experiences I regularly have in the world. These experiences include memories, insights, ideas, feelings, other pieces of art, poetry, or music, etc. These "source" experiences always feel deeply familiar and fresh and expansive at the same time, regardless of the individual story behind them. But, again, while they open me up, they are also elusive, partial, and temporary. Thus, my work is rarely purely or overtly ecstatic because my experiences rarely are. Ultimately my paintings are my process of seeking to understand, create, and evoke these kinds of experiences. And they are about that process itself; they are about how these experiences feel, how they are revealed and concealed, how they move. Consequently, my paintings are consciously and meticulously crafted to create a strong sense of preciousness. But while they are guided by belief in truth and beauty (underlying order and a harmonizing of contrasts, which I will talk about below), this belief is tenuous at times. There is almost always something slightly off, a subtle tension, a quiet lack of balance within each composition. This plays out via specific expressive relationships within each piece, namely between opaque and transparent shapes, within space and color dynamics, and in contrasts between hard-edged geometry (synthetic order) and soft wood grain (organic logic). Ultimately, this work is about seeking. It is the only truth I know. It is kind of a ritual for me, one that is both intuitive and rational and rarely purely graceful. Destinations (the finished paintings) become landmarks within a larger geography of process. The spaces articulated between the surface and ground within my work reflect this shifting truth as honestly as possible.

> If I have heard you correctly, you seem to follow Kandinsky and others who emphasize that art in general and painting in particular conveys a spiritual message. What can you tell us about the spiritual in art as you have experienced it and seek to express it?

I may have partially answered this question in my previous responses. But let me see if I can add something more here. I do think art can convey spiritual messages and has throughout history. Most of the time these messages have been religious ones (occurring within a historical institution and utilizing its myths, allegories, symbols, etc.). However, I don't think that art necessarily conveys spiritual messages, or that painting is more suited to do so than any other form of art. For me, powerful art *is* spiritual art, regardless of its subject matter. The art I have experienced that I would consider powerful, whether that be poetry, music, photography, etc., draws me into it until I holistically comprehend how its form is the manifestation of its content (through how it is expressively composed). Of course more often than not this kind of experience requires educating oneself about the context within which a piece of art was created. See the Agnes Martin example above. But for me art has power when its subject matter and the concept embedded within it are not privileged over its physical reality in the way the soul is granted priority over the body in some religious traditions. Art is powerful when its form embodies its content. This is a very traditional way of looking at art, and for me the most deeply *spiritual* art psychosomatically reminds me of my human-ness, enriches it, while simultaneously and intimately connecting me with parts of the greater world. I feel wonder, I feel vulnerable, and it stirs the concentrated notion of individuality and isolation within which I normally operate. I forget myself for a moment and become more inspired, curious and grateful. Also, I want to be clear that this kind of art does not have to be beautiful. It often is, and when it is, it is also often tense or painful in some way. But it can be sublime or grotesque or absurd. It can be anything really, as long as it has this kind of effect on me.

As far as my own work is concerned, I am interested in using painting to convey spiritual messages—my subject matter is spirituality—and consider it also to be both religious and contemporary at the same time. What I mean by this is that my artistic and spiritual practice consists of openly embracing influence. I consider myself to be a devotee of Abstraction (not to mention almost anything I encounter that moves me); I have formally committed my life to it. In doing so I adhere to many of the values of it as an institutionalized tradition. In other words, I am married to a practice that takes places within a canonized art history (specifically Modern and Contemporary Art), and I utilize an inherited syntax for my own creative and contemplative goals. In addition, I am a reverential student of many art histories across cultures. The visual language and iconography I employ is drawn from these histories as well as other interests such as religious studies and pop culture. Because of the way I have situated myself, I do not aspire to be original. Rather, I seek sincerity and an almost familial relationship with other, older artists and art movements. At the same time I also I want my work to be lyrical, to come from the details that make up my specific life. I want my work to be a kind of unique confluence of sources, but without those sources all being fully dissolved into my work. Ultimately I want to find my own place, but within the historical development of painting, by participating in the conversation of abstraction. I should note that participating in this conversation means that the relationship is not always congruous: it can be contentious too. Because of the way I work, and because the references I lean on come from sources that are private, popular, and specialized, the messages I convey are only partially clear to others. They are also veiled. But this quasi-idiomatic approach itself is part of the cultural and institutional paradigm I am operating within as well.

> Your art is nonobjective yet far from freely expressive. That is, you employ sharp edges of basic geometrical shapes and are attentive to issues of fine craftsmanship. To what extent do you see your work as calling viewers to be reflexively attentive to the components and processes of creating a fine work of art, and to what extent do you hope viewers might find objective meanings resident in what you create?

With regard to my work the word *reflexive* is an interesting one to use for a couple of reasons. First, as I have said, I consider my work to be a both a personal method of sacred contemplation and a way to convey messages about such practices, namely, that those practices are those experiences. So in this way it reflexively refers back to itself. Second, because I believe that form and content are not separable in powerful art, it is important to me that viewers are reflexively (unconsciously) attentive to the meticulous nature of craft in my paintings. That is not to say that I don't want them to be consciously aware of it too. This goes back to what I said initially about the work's reflexivity. Attentiveness toward high craft is associated with historically sacred objects, especially those used in religious performance (ritual and liturgy). Of course, the particular kind of art I am making is not overtly related to any religion, at least to their most popular forms. Instead it is connected to the history of spirituality within Modern and Contemporary Art, which as I have said I consider to be my "religion." Regardless, the association is important because I want viewers to feel *and* understand that the objects are delicate and precious and made with thoughtful intent. High craft is part of how I try to make them beautiful. I am not sure if this is objective meaning, but maybe.

Fundamentally, I believe that beauty causes viewers to respond to the world in a more unconsciously reflexive way. While it is true that some people are drawn to ideas before beauty, I think that for the most part this isn't the case. I would even wager to say that for those who are, the majority consider their chosen ideas to be beautiful in some way. Whatever the case, I have no basis to argue with Confucius when he said, "I have not seen one who loves virtue as he loves beauty."

Tangent aside, while the notion of beauty is complicated in our time because it is now so closely associated with the cosmetic, I am interested in a deeper experience, one that is aligned with the classical relationship between truth and beauty. Subsequently I use hidden and overt geometry alongside luminous color, soft velvety surfaces, and grainy depth to create perceptible order within sensually ambiguous space. Further, the shapes and spaces I use touch upon recognizable things in the world. They remind us of things and are thus not definitively nonobjective; they feel familiar and mysterious at the same time. So I embrace the notion of beauty as a harmonizing of contrasts (Whitehead). Beauty and ambiguity are tools to visually draw viewers in. But these tools are also a part of my subject matter and as such become part of whatever objective meaning viewers help create. This is actually what I mean when I say that I want to make works that are poetic. I am not interested in didacticism at all. I find art that tries to teach us something, send us a direct message, or tell us how to think, to be patronizing and disempowering. Lyrically poetic work uses form to generate and guide sensual, associative, imaginative, emotional, and intellectual responses. It wants us to engage with it, to commune with it, to coax it into being. This kind of work asks us to be aware more than anything else. Awareness requires consciousness and sensitivity, but it is fundamentally holistic. I do believe that for most viewers an artist's expressive use of his or her materials is the immediate entry point into the work at hand. When a work is powerful, it invites a more conscious engagement with the layers of meaning built within it. But the direction of a viewer's entrance into a work is irrelevant. Sometimes an artwork's form is too challenging, too far outside of viewers' expectations, for them to immediately enter into it. Sometimes, like I did with Agnes Martin, a viewer has to intellectually investigate context first. Context leads toward more objective, factual meaning. But revelation in those situations only occurs when ideas open up and form awakens (#6, *Near*).

> Pick one or two pieces you have created and that you would like illustrated in the book. Then in relation to that/those piece(s) tell the story of the background experiences and processes that brought the painting to its particular finished form.

To respond to this request, I will refer first to a suite of paintings called *My Secret Love*. Rather than continuing to use the square as I have in the past (as form and content within my work), this work self-consciously (even somewhat melodramatically) directly addresses my love for that shape itself as well. Because exploring the relationship between intimacy and mystery is one of my goals, I find myself more and more interested in narrowing my approach to *very* specific palettes, compositional strategies, and themes. My hope is that, by temporarily pulling back from my practice, through my practice I might get even closer to the issues that define it. I can't say why I think this is a good plan. But it feels like it is. What I can say is that in the past I have tended to move from one theme to another, from one individual painting to another. Over time, thematic and design similarities emerged, which has been very insightful. But my goal for these newer paintings is to direct the search even more by sidestepping this slow reveal. So for *My Secret Love #2* (#7) I chose white, magenta, pink, peach, gray, and black, colors that are popularly associated with sex and love. And most of these pieces also use colorful portal and curtain structures against black voids to create a sense of drama and eroticism.

In addition, I recently started working on another suite of paintings that will serve as smaller finished "studies" for larger works. Less self-referential than the pieces that make up *My Secret Love*, these paintings all similarly address one theme: gratitude. Entitled *Praise* the palette for this body of work is yellow, white, ochre (raw wood), and gray. Rather than using veil forms and deep dark recesses, these paintings are built upon the rhythmic use of ascending vertical lines, hard grey architecture, and warm open spaces (#8, *Praise*, on cover, upper right). Certain pieces within both bodies of work utilize rebating rectangles, a compositional strategy where implied squares are formed within larger rectangles using the shorter sides of those rectangles. This strategy increases the impression of structural harmony and offers additional, if subtle, reference to my beloved square. But as I have said, within every painting a discussion occurs between my materials and my intentions; I never succeed at telling it exactly what I want it to be. Each painting has its own will and intentions. Through the ritual of drawing, masking, painting, looking, removing, sanding, and starting over again and again we eventually come to a sweet spot in our debate, a spot that satisfies and informs a hidden part of myself that seems to guide it all.

15

The Fabric of Thirdness

A Concert Pianist's Peircean Interpretation of Performance

Arthur Stewart

> I venture to think that the esthetic state of mind is purest when perfectly naive without any critical pronouncement, and that the esthetic critic founds his judgments upon the result of throwing himself back into such a pure naive state—and the best critic is the man who has trained himself to do this the most perfectly.
>
> —Charles Sanders Peirce, "Lectures on Pragmatism"

Introduction: The Concert Pianist

What is the goal of the concert pianist? Is it to entertain paying audiences? Is it to dazzle onlookers and listeners with technical brilliance at the keyboard? Is it to, somehow, *edify* or, in some sense, *elevate* listeners? Or is it to communicate, philosophically, even pragmatically, perhaps, dimensions of *meaning* in classical piano literature regardless of competing influences and temporary circumstances? Surely, the latter is primary, and it succeeds most fully when the pianist is an esthetic "self-critic," to paraphrase the quotation from Peirce above. This requires a "scientific" intelligence that, according to Peirce, is "an intelligence capable of learning by experience."[1]

Such a focus on *meaning* has led me as a pianist-philosopher to a rephrasing of the selected question into this into something like, "What sort of meaning is it the goal of the *Peircean* concert pianist to communicate?" One answer, and it is an answer to be applauded, comes from the legendary concert pianist Artur Schnabel (1882–1951). An answer of his to the sense of our reformulated question comes from his 1942 *Music and the Line of Most Resistance*. Here Schnabel speaks about performers as makers, as opposed to "functionaries who only talk . . . [w]ho try to penetrate it [music] from the outside."

These—the makers—have to travel in the opposite direction, from the interior to the exterior, from conception to appearance, from idea to shape . . . from *technique to mystery* . . . toward a higher . . . simplicity, toward that other shore, which, to be sure, can only be sighted but never reached.[2] As we shall see, these general thoughts about the concert pianist journeying, somehow, "from technique to mystery" and thereby to a higher simplicity make for a most harmonious combination of thoughts with those of Peirce. The present investigation, then, is concerned with examining how and why one's pianistic journey "from technique to mystery" is (1) informed by and based on both theoretical and practical understandings of Peirce's view of esthetics as the fundamental Normative Science; (2) reflected in Peirce's understandings of his three Universal Categories of Experience, Firstness, Secondness, and Thirdness; and (3) guided, even *lured* by Thirdness, indeed the *Fabric of Thirdness*, which will be found "ubiquitous" as a developmental goal in the performance activities of the *Peircean* concert pianist (see *CP*, 5.121; 6.58). This *Fabric* itself is intimately associated with the background of philosophical Realism, as Peirce understood it, namely, that "the real is that which is independent of the vagaries of me and you" (*CP*, 2.311). And as we shall see, Peirce's "esthetic state of mind" is expressed through what he termed "abduction." This expression functions as an experiment that aids immensely in determining adequate pianistic portrayals of this Realistic *Fabric*.

A Style of Styles: καλός as Normative Foundation, and Pianistic Abductions

The concert pianist's cognitive states are shaped, of course, and indeed *sharpened* by aesthetic norms that underlie and contribute to Peirce's lofty esthetic state of mind. The most immediately recognizable of such norms concerns matters of musical "style." Knowledge of musical "styles" includes historically situated understanding of appropriate esthetic standards that can be acquired. For example, to perform correctly works by the Baroque-era German composer J. S. Bach (1685–1750), one should be thoroughly acquainted with authenticated period-practices in ornamentation, and know how German practices in ornamentation differed from their French counterparts of the time.

At another, much larger level, one shouldn't, for example, attempt to perform a Classical-Era piano sonata by W. A. Mozart (1756–1791) as if it were a Romantic-Era piano sonata by Johannes Brahms (1833–1897). The business of the Peircean concert pianist, then, thinking of Schnabel's remark concerning a "higher simplicity," involves seeking a kind of "Style of Styles." This involves experimentally seeking, acknowledging, immersing oneself in, and cultivating καλός (*kalos*), to use Peirce's deliberately chosen Greek term. As we shall shortly see, *kalos* is the centerpiece of what Peirce meant by "esthetics."

Peirce considered "esthetics" to be the most fundamental of his Normative Sciences, thus the primary normative concern. In the following, rather lengthy extract, Peirce not only explains the meaning of *kalos*, but also makes clear what he takes to be the relationship between esthetics and theories of beauty (the latter not a specific concern, here). From his "Minute Logic" of 1902, thus:

> That science [esthetics] has been handicapped by the definition of it as the theory of beauty. The conception of beauty is but the product of this science, and a very inadequate attempt it is to grasp what it is that esthetics seeks to make clear. Ethics asks to what end all effort shall be directed. That question obviously depends upon the question what it would be that, independently of the effort, we should like to experience. But in order to state the question of esthetics in its purity, we should eliminate from it, not merely all consideration of effort, but all consideration of action and reaction, including all consideration of our receiving pleasure, everything in short, belonging to the opposition of the *ego* and the *non-ego*. We have not in our language a word of the requisite generality. The Greek καλός, the French *beau*, only come near to it, without hitting it squarely on the head. "Fine" would be a wretched substitute. Beautiful is bad; because one mode of being καλός

> essentially depends upon the quality being unbeautiful. Perhaps, however, the phrase "the beauty of the unbeautiful" would not be shocking. Still "beauty" is too skin-deep. Using καλός, the question of esthetics is, What is the one quality that is, in its immediate presence, καλός [the good, the beautiful; the noble]?³ Upon this question ethics must depend, just as logic must depend upon ethics. (*CP*, 2.199)

Esthetics, ethics, and logic, or, feeling, action, and thought or representation (see *CP*, 5.129) then form a *triadic* normative framework, for Peirce. In analogical parallel for the performer, "how" a certain composition is performed depends upon previous notions as to "why" it should be so rendered, this in turn informed, fundamentally informed, by καλός, the bedrock normative concern.

So the pianist influenced or even guided by Peirce's thoughts on these three normative sciences will recognize and acknowledge the importance of what to admire per se: "what it is that one deliberately ought to admire regardless of what it may lead to and regardless of its bearings upon human conduct" (*CP*, 5.36). Said acknowledgment then informs "why" a given piece should be performed in certain ways, with this "why," once acknowledged, clearing the road of inquiry for a thoroughly, holistically developed "how" of actual concert performance. And this holistic pianistic interchange, this development between and among Peirce's three normative sciences, will continue: the better one gets at the "how" of actual concert execution, the more moments of καλός will be discovered and revealed, which will invite adjustments in the "why" in the matter, which in turn will elicit adjustments in the "how" of execution, and so forth. The whole matter, then, when clearly engaged, exhibits the characteristic of *growth*, thus reflecting something that Schnabel considered an axiom, namely the "axiom that the tonal idea can be efficacious on one single occasion only. Therefore, it has to emerge afresh on each new occasion, and this function can never become automatic" (S, 4). And, yes, *axiom* was his chosen term.

There are, of course, many other normative concerns of varying degrees of importance involved in concert performance. Among the ones that can be "fixed" or "repaired for cost," as it were, should be included the condition of the piano and the condition of the performance hall. One normative concern that cannot be "repaired for cost," however, is the state of one's technical/musical preparation and proficiency. As we shall see, this latter normative concern requires something beyond materialistic "fixes." It calls for a fundamental, primitive shift in one's philosophical posture, one from Nominalism to Realism, as Peirce understood these terms.

A few moments, now, on the materially "fixable." Pianos are fixed-pitch instruments; they cannot be retuned on the spot, as it were, as can a guitar or a violin. And they are, at base, percussion instruments: the strings are activated not by picks or bows, but by felt-covered hammers. Badly out-of-tune instruments will doubtless require more exertion and dexterity to manage with some degree of adequacy. But pianos whose mechanical "actions," the various and several mechanical parts linking key to hammer, are badly out of "regulation," can be hopeless to manage. But, with proper incentives in place, esthetic, administrative, and fiscal alike, these sorts of mechanical problems can be remedied.

Concert halls are always vulnerable to undermine maximal performance on three issues: volume of total space, arrangement of internal components (including but not limited to any given piano), and matters concerning the absorption or reflection of sound. A hall that is too small for the occasion, with a rather flat floor design for seating the audience, with thick carpeting or draperies, for example, will defeat even the best prepared pianist, even when performing on a top-condition Steinway Model D nine-foot concert grand piano. The sounds produced are simply "swallowed up" by the environment. Again, these sorts of mechanical issues can be addressed and adjusted.

The state of one's pianistic preparation is something that always calls for improvement, particularly if one's preparation has been made initially in a kind of haste. But, clearly, unlike physical, materialistic problems with pianos or halls, problems with one's preparation do not admit of purely mechanical solutions. Here one can benefit from employing from the very beginning of learning a given piece all the way through to concert performance what may be considered as a kind of mental and physical "abduction" in one's approach, "abduction" being the type of reasoning, according to Peirce, that moves from effect to possible cause. It is the only type of reasoning that brings forth new ideas, or, new "knowledge."[4] Here is an example of "abduction" that Peirce put forward in 1878 in his *Popular Science Monthly* piece "Deduction, Induction, and Abduction."

Hypothesis [or Abduction]

Rule: All the beans from this bag are white.

> Result: These beans are white.
>
> [One asks, knowing that not all beans are white, whence these beans?]
>
> Case: These beans are from this bag. (*CP*, 2.623; see also *CP*, 5:189)

"Abduction," then, involves *guessing*, in this case *guessing* at the source of these beans, as in the example above, and *guessing* right as a pianist at how the fingers, hands, and arms best address the correct notes. Of course, matters pertaining to use of a piano's pedals are included in such moments of "guesswork," as are items pertaining to increasing or decreasing volumes of sound, and similar concerns with velocity of execution. For now, though, we limit our scope of investigation to the subject of playing the right notes correctly.

On this view, instead of manically and mechanically "forcing" correctness in practicing and performance, one rather "finds" the right notes by having "practiced out" the wrong ones, whether they be nearby on the keyboard, or at some distance: one now knows, by experimental elimination attuned to *kalos*, which notes not to play. This thwarts overintellectualizing of the material at hand, promotes the elimination of errors, and, at a most primitive physiological level, prevents the various musculatures involved in performance from "tightening," from becoming rigid. Within its musical parameters, at least, "abduction" opens the road, and enthusiastically, for the pianist to practice what Peirce termed a "scientific intelligence," an intelligence that learns from experience (*CP*, 2.227). Thus, this elimination of erroneous pianistic "hypotheses" is cut from the same cloth as the perhaps more familiar elimination of erroneous hypotheses in science.

Also, "pianistic abduction" between notes, chords, other tonal formations (even the "rests," the silent spaces), will reveal the nonmaterial but quite Real relations that join pairs of musical entities esthetically, from the most basic to the most advanced structures. This amounts to mentally and physically addressing them in such a way, an almost instantaneous way in terms of an ordinary understanding of time in physical execution, such that the very Real relations that join them are made plain, orally plain, not overintellectualized. Schnabel informs us:

> Music as music can be absorbed only in a state of physical passivity. Words as words never directly arouse sensuous

reactions; thus they cannot impair the superiority of music which addresses itself to the ear without appealing simultaneously to the intellect. . . . Music has to be inspired, regulated and controlled at the same moment by the spiritual and the physical ear. (S, 13, 20)

Realism, Categories, and Mechanical Nominalists

Thus, the very Real relations involved in "music realization" (S, 14) cannot be rendered or understood in, for example, the superficialities of printed performance evaluations.[5] In the case of Piano Jury Forms, specifically, imagine trying to make sound judgments about a person's musical state-of-affairs when one of the items on "The Form" concerns the performer's "Musicianship," which is to be evaluated against a five-point scale: "Failing" through "Superior." How is one to quantifiably *define* "Musicianship" (or even "Philosophership," perhaps), especially in the light of Schnabel's observation that "music, apart from a few elementary and arbitrary stipulations, is not as fixed as the multiplication table"? (S, 16) And on the topic of such mechanical or practical superficiality, taken to a frightening level, imagine a person of importance at a university telling its music department that their concert hall Steinway Model D nine-foot grand piano should be dispatched to the municipal landfill because it is "ugly," due to having a few scratches and nicks in its exterior finish. Such an occasion has been observed, sadly, literally.

Examples of this kind of mechanicalistic, pseudo-algorithmic approach come to us from sources of the earlier twentieth century, namely Tobias Matthay's *The Act of Touch* of 1903 and his 1911 *Some Commentaries on the Teaching of Pianoforte Technique*, and from Karl Leimer and Walter Gieseking's *The Shortest Route to Pianistic Perfection* of 1932. In the latter book, Leimer and Gieseking remark that "[r]eally accurate rhythmical playing can be achieved *only* through *severe* self-control."[6] When learning an Invention by J. S. Bach, the authors write, "It is necessary to play the Invention very slowly. [T]o play the whole invention straight through, when studying . . . should be *forbidden*."[7] One will observe, from experience, from Peircean experimental experience, that such "rhythmical playing" comes rather from following the composer's indications preserved in the score's notation, not from the performer exercising some sort of mechanical "severe self-control." Likewise, the age-old stricture to begin learning new works by playing them at much-reduced tempi (velocities) is equally counterproductive: one simply cannot adequately anticipate how to perform Franz Liszt's *Mephisto Waltz No. 1* by learning it at roughly one-eighth its finished tempo. Schnabel observes: "The marathon runner does not start his daily training by first walking slowly for an hour, no tennis champion begins with light and soft shots" (S, 76). And then there are these telling remarks by Matthay, who informs us that we should be deducing the laws and rules that govern successful performance and then *directly* communicating such laws of procedure to the pupil, instead of leaving him to discover them for himself. . . . Evidently, teaching, as applied to Science, Harmony, or Language, does not here signify that the discovery of the implicated Laws shall be left to each individual learner.[8]

Among other prescriptions involved in Matthay's version of pianistic perfection and mechanicalism, please consider that among his *deduced* (?) "laws and rules" are admonishments concerning what the performer should be doing with his or her *feet*. Thus:

> The position of the feet should be such, that the weight of the leg can rest upon the ground upon the pedal. The right foot should always be thus in contact with its pedal; the left foot, when not required for the *una corda* pedal [the one farthest to the left], is best placed further back, with the sole of the foot only touching the ground, and with its toe almost as far back as the heel of the right foot—when the latter is engaged upon its pedal.[9]

These remarks from Leimer and Gieseking as well as Matthay concerning "laws and rules," "severe self-control," what should be *forbidden*, what one must do with one's feet, and so on, are part and parcel with what Peirce described as *Nominalism*. Here is one illustration of Nominalism from Peirce, concerning the practice of medicine. The case concerns medical pathology and the infamous nineteenth-century French physician Claude Bernard, MD, who championed the idea in medical pathology that disease consisted of no more and no less than a sum of accumulated *symptoms*. Peirce comments in his "Lessons from the History of Science" of 1896 that at the time of Pasteur,

> the medical world was dominated by Claude Bernard's dictum that a disease is not an entity but merely a sum of symptoms (see *Leçons de Pathologie expérimental, 2me leçon*, Paris, 1872).

This was pure metaphysics which only barricaded inquiry in that direction. But that was a generation which attached great value to nominalistic metaphysics. . . . [T]he observation of facts has taught us that a disease is in many, if not most, serious cases, just as much an entity as a human family consisting of father, mother, and children. (*CP*, 1.109; 1.111)

As you can see, even from this extract alone, Nominalism champions the idea that named collections of physical symptoms are the goal and endpoint of investigations. The very real *disease*, in the background, manifested in such symptoms, cannot be approached, on this view. Likewise, for the Nominalistic pianist, it is only the superficial "symptoms," such as the position of the feet, or mere compliance with certain "laws and rules," or like striving not to play wrong notes, each as an end in and of itself, that matter. Note in the citations above from Leimer and Gieseking and Matthay that mentions of music per se, or of artistry or of aesthetics, are absent[10] admonishments toward compliance with their "methods," however, are plentiful: just follow the materialist's rules!

An investigation of Peirce's three Categories of Experience will now show, with three practical examples from the literature of classical piano performance, how *kalos* and the other Normative Sciences along with his Categories of Experience resonate in unison for the Peircean pianist. This resonance also divulges from, and starkly, the dead-end nature of "Nominalism;" a nominalistic approach can never approach *The Fabric of Thirdness*.

Peirce's Universal Categories of Experience are three in number and, being "ubiquitous" (*CP*, 5.121), form the categorial background within which his notion of καλός flourishes, expands, and develops. These Categories are composed of "Firsts," "Seconds," and "Thirds," so termed.

> [These] make for the three inseparable and comprehensive divisions or categories of experience, for Peirce [see *CP*, 1.369f]. Those aspects of experience whose predominant trait is *immediacy* best exhibit "firstness," while those aspects which exhibit *resistance* likewise show "secondness." Those departments of experience that manifest *lawfulness* or systematic *habit* (broadly construed) sustain "thirdness." A vigorous slap of the hand upon a table, for example, will illustrate firstness in the immediacy of a stinging, painful sensation, secondness

in the resistance provided by the table, and thirdness in the background lawfulness [or regularity] of nature by which the pain was occasioned.[11]

Now for three musical examples of Peirce's Categories in action, in real time, upon the concert platform. The reader is encouraged, of course, to listen to, to actually *hear* and consider these selections in association with the following remarks.

First, consider the very beginning of Nocturne in B-Flat Major, op. 55, no. 2, by Frederic Chopin (1810–1839). This begins with a single, isolated note; a "B Flat," as it is termed. What does this note represent? Is it best understood as the beginning of something musical, or does Chopin mean to symbolize something else? If the latter, what *abstract, universalizable* emotion(s) does it represent, or portend? When realized on stage, what characteristics of *kalos* and immediacy, as one, might this single note convey, semeiotically?

Second, consider the very beginning of the Sonata in A Major, op. 101, by Ludwig van Beethoven (1770–1827). This opening does not operate under the same conditions as the Chopin example, clearly. This opening is, somehow, already "in motion," as if one had walked in on a conversation already well in progress. One immediately asks, normatively, "why" has Beethoven set this up in just this manner? The reactions of Secondness that ensue, as the notes pass by, indeed the tonal *chain reactions* that propel the movement forward, evolve and demonstrate the answer to our question of "why," in terms of καλός; in terms of beauty, elegance, and nobility.

Third, consider as a holistic continuum the last Etude Tableaux, op. 39, no. 9, by Sergei Rachmaninoff (1873–1943). Here the immediate question, recalling the third of Peirce's Normative Sciences in particular, is "how" to *physically execute* this monumental work! If performed at the levels of "dynamics" (volumes of sound) he notates, Firstness erupts, explodes, actually, when one drops one's hands onto any of his larger chord formations: there is indeed an immediate, stinging sensation in one's fingertips. Secondness is "already there," so to speak, in the resistance provided by the instrument, and, as in the Beethoven example cited above, it is the propulsive chain reactions of Secondness that lead the way. And toward what is this "leading" leading? The *Fabric of Thirdness*: the nonstatic background regularities involved in the whole event, which, simultaneously with the Firsts and Seconds involved, is made manifest.

Impediments of Nominalism, Peirce's "Aesthetic Frame of Mind" and "Aesthetic Abduction"

The Nominalist, with his limitations of superficial, "symptoms only" considerations, and thus materialism, cannot develop his esthetical considerations (such as they may be) past Secondness. The Nominalistic fallacy, in our context, amounts to restricting the field of investigation to only those items that physically exist, to only those items that can be materially quantified or measured. The pianistic Realist is the pianist who subscribes to Peirce's notion that, again, "the real is that which is independent of the vagaries of me and you" (*CP*, 2.311). The Peircean/Realist pianist without hesitation recognizes and embraces nontangible relations, such as the immaterial relations between notes, chords, the immaterial relations that hold whole compositions together, and those involved in "beauty," even the "sublime." Nominalism and its mechanical manifestations, however, do not acknowledge the reality of immaterial relations, and thus render efforts at reaching genuine Thirdness, that is, *immaterial* Thirdness, pointless.

Thus, one cannot generate Thirdness solely from its constituent parts, from combining Firsts and Seconds, only. Further, "Thirdness" cannot survive being reduced or decomposed. Now, working from a posture of Realism is not a normative concern like getting a piano tuned or regulated, a concern that involves something's being materially "fixed" or "repaired at cost." Here, again, we require a philosophical shift, a kind of "conversion" perhaps, from the superficialities of Nominalistic nostrums to Realistic realizations.

When engaged with καλός and Peirce's Universal Categories, then, the practical in-action antidote to these mechanical formulations appears by adopting what Peirce described as "the esthetic state of mind," this "state of mind" experimentally expressed in and through abductive "guesswork."

So think again, now, in closing, of the three piano pieces mentioned earlier, the Chopin, Beethoven, and Rachmaninoff pieces. In all three we see that Peirce's "esthetic state of mind" forms a background in which the pianist uses "abduction" to make experimental explorations, explorations toward *The Fabric of Thirdness*; explorations toward genuine artistry. With Peirce's "aesthetic state of mind" put to action through "abduction," we note that nominalistic concerns with mechanical technique as an end in itself, difficult pianos, audience responses, and similar distractions, fade away. Through what we may term Peirce's "esthetic abduction," the relations, small and large, binding together the integuments of the musical event come clear, and the musical *Fabric of Thirdness* involved is discovered, and revealed.

Notes

1. Charles S. Peirce, *Collected Papers of Charles Sanders Peirce*, ed. Charles Hartshorne, Paul Weiss, and Arthur Burks, 8 vols. (Cambridge: Harvard University Press, 1932–1960), 2.227. Selections from the *Collected Papers* will hereafter be cited internally in the text with the volume and page number following *CP.*

2. Artur Schnabel, *Music and the Line of Most Resistance* (Princeton: Princeton University Press, 1942), 13–14; emphasis added. Schnabel was the first pianist to present all thirty-two of the Sonatas for Piano by Ludwig van Beethoven (1770–1827) as a holistic cycle. Among other accomplishments, Schnabel was also the first pianist to present a complete performance edition of these Sonatas, including performance notes authored by Schnabel in English, German, and French. In a sense, Schnabel is a sort of pianistic grandfather for me. I studied with one of Schnabel's students, the legendary Leon Fleisher, during the late 1970s. Reference to Schnabel's book is hereafter cited in the text as S.

3. Translation of καλός provided by Dr. Thomas Urban.

4. David L. O'Hara, "Abduction," in *American Philosophy: An Encyclopedia*, ed. John Lachs and Robert Talisse (New York: Routledge, 2008), 7.

5. See Steven Hart, "Inspiring Singers toward Emotional Communication through Aesthetic Discovery," following in the present volume, for his discussion of the Montana High School Association Official Adjudication Form and his incisive observation that "[t]he implied assumption underlying the rating form is that adding up . . . collection[s] of separate entities somehow magically produces something of value." We ask: Have the authors of this form confused necessity with sufficiency?

6. Karl Leimer and Walter Gieseking, *The Shortest Way to Pianistic Perfection* (Philadelphia: Theodore Presser, 1932), 5; emphases added.

7. Ibid., 26.

8. Tobias Matthay, *The Act of Touch in All Its Diversity: An Analysis of Pianoforte Tone-production* (London: Longmans, Green, 1903), 2; original emphasis. See Professor Steven Hart, again, for a more enlightened view of Matthay's "individual learner."

9. Tobias Matthay, *Some Commentaries on the Teaching of Pianoforte Technique* (London: Longmans, Green, 1911), 305.

10. See again Professor Hart's evaluation of the Adjudication Form mentioned above, and his telling remark that "[c]ommunication of artistic intent finds no place on the evaluation instrument!"

11. Arthur Stewart, "Thirdness," in *American Philosophy: An Encyclopedia*, ed. John Lachs and Robert Talisse (New York: Routledge, 2008), 761.

16

Inspiring Singers toward Emotional Communication through Aesthetic Discovery

STEVEN HART

What is an inspired performance? Specifically, what are the observable, tangible markers from the audience members of a truly inspired performance? What are the observable, tangible markers of the performers?

Try this exercise in imagination. Remember a particularly great concert. What was it like? What did it feel like? What did the performers look like? Take a moment to stop reading and recall. Focus upon the sensations and observations in fine detail.

Typical responses include the following: *I was totally focused on the performers. I forgot to breathe. It gave me goose bumps. Such powerful emotions—I was ready to cry. You can both lose yourself and find yourself in the music. The performers looked like they transcended the music. I forgot where I was for a while.*

My intent as a choral conductor and music educator is to create the conditions for what I call "peak aesthetic experience." The peak aesthetic experience is difficult to describe in words, but some of the markers are common. The heart races or the jaw drops; tears come. Faces "light up." Time is suspended. There is absolute clarity or focus. Some people may feel a soaring sensation, or an overriding sense that all is right with the world. Others may liken the experience to deep prayer or meditation.

These responses to such rare, culminating aesthetic events align with John Dewey's writing on *having an experience*. When we give ourselves over to the aesthetic power of great works of art, something transcendent can occur. This transcendence is why I do what I do. But how is this nurtured and actualized in performance?

Unfortunately, the norm in choral music rehearsals and performances is a disintegrated collection of proper vocal and choral techniques. Regarding the opposing pole of aesthetic experience, Dewey writes, "Instead of exemplifying wholehearted action, it takes the form of grudging piecemeal concessions to the demands of duty."[1] Typically, singers dutifully carry out the fragmentary demands of the conductor: *clean cutoff on beat 4, increase volume at measure 16, decrease volume at measure 17*. While useful, these elements are a continuing set of duty-bound occurrences rather than a unifying whole of aesthetic understanding. For Dewey, the "enemies of the aesthetic" include submission to convention in practice and intellectual procedure, as well as coerced submission and incoherent indulgence—both of which are "deviations in opposite directions from the unity of an experience."[2]

The enemies of the aesthetic are consistently embedded in conventional choral rehearsal practices and our approach to formal public performance. Take, for example, the Montana High School Association Official Adjudication Form, which is used at every district music festival across the state. Similar forms appear in in many other states. This rating form consists of seven categories worth five points each, the sum of which determines the final rating. The seven categories are tone, intonation, accuracy, interpretation, balance/blend, vocal technique, and "other factors." Communication of artistic intent or assessment of the aesthetic quality of the complete performance find no place on the evaluation instrument! The category called interpretation comes close, but even here, one of the top-rated markers under this category states, "accurate style and tempo." So, the interpretation was accurate? This is clearly untenable. The implied assumption underlying the rating form is that adding up this collection of separate entities somehow magically produces something of value. Or, that these technical categories are the most valued aspects of performance. Or, further, that the inspired expression of the beauty embodied in the music carries no value.

How, then, can a choral conductor avoid a fractured approach to performance and instead encourage singers, even in practice, to explore the unified experience that Dewey praises? For when singers discover and express the aesthetic potential in a choral composition, the chances are great that an audience can also participate in the emotional power of the piece.

Crowd Source the Artistic Intent

We must reclaim artistic expression as the driving force and highest priority in choral music, and involve our singers in aesthetic decision making. If we do not, our ensemble members will rarely focus their mental capacity on anything other than vowels, consonants, and a clean cutoff on beat three. I propose a new rehearsal design and a style of interacting with the choral ensemble that encourages aesthetic experience and makes inspired performances happen with greater frequency.

I have a crazy idea that the people doing the singing should have a say in how that singing is done. This idea may come close to blasphemy within many circles of choral conductors. Traditionally, it is the conductor's role to interpret the music.

Mary Goetze, founder of the International Vocal Ensemble at the Jacobs School of Music in Indiana and a driving force in the children's choir movement in the United States, had an illustrious career as a music educator. She made this observation: *In any given music classroom there are 30 living breathing human beings, with definite artistic likes and dislikes. Why is the teacher the only one making aesthetic decisions?*[3]

Engineer Their Artistic Discovery

Imagine yourself walking along the beach with a loved one. You find a cool rock. *Wow!* You show it to your loved one, but the response is unenthusiastic: *Yeah, okay, I guess.* The reason for this contrast in response is that people love discovery. Finding is half the fun. The conductor delivering brilliant insights about the music can be met with ho-hum response from the choir. We must lead singers to find the beauty for themselves, so that they can have their own *wow* moments of discovery.

When conductors invite the singers to the artistic party, they place feeling-meaning and artistic intent at the forefront of the collective consciousness. Questions that used to be reserved solely for the conductor are now posed to the entire ensemble: What are the artistic intentions of the composer? How do I bring this work to life? How can this music become more expressive than it is right now? When the singers share their insights, they invest the full power of personal conviction because their artistic ideas were valued and implemented.

An ensemble doesn't have to be perfect to have an aesthetic experience. Technical achievement depends on the level of sophistication of the ensemble, but aesthetic experience is within the grasp of every group engaged in choral singing, because singers of all ages and abilities can make personal connections to the emotional content in the repertoire and learn to make musical choices. Even when there are technical problems, such as wrong notes or unpleasant tone production, an audience can still be moved or inspired by the emotional communication and aesthetic awareness of the ensemble. Both audience members and performers may carry that inspiration with them long after the concert is over.

Diagram of a Rehearsal Model for Aesthetic Experience

Inspiring people through the power of music and words is the very goal, the heart, of the choral art. The layout of the rehearsal model in Appendix A is designed to illustrate how the combined energy of these two expressive systems can be fused into rich aesthetic unity. Note the development over time for each of the three categories: music, poetry, and the combined expressive power of music and poetry. On the poetry side, the questions invite a deeper understanding of the poetry over a seven to nine-week period. On the music side, the developmental understanding also develops over time, beginning with the general, heading toward the specific, and returning to the unified whole. In the combined expressive power section, there are techniques and rehearsal activities that lead singers to discover the rich aesthetic synergy inherent within the art of choral singing.

Poetry

Musicians tend to be much more skilled at the music side of this diagram than the poetic side. They may need to be reminded that the poetry has a life outside the musical setting. Just say, "and He shall reign for ever and ever," and choristers cannot help but hear the "Hallelujah Chorus" from *Messiah* by G. F. Handel. When introducing a new piece of choral literature, ask singers to close their music and listen to the poetry. Read the entire poem to them, asking them to notice what images and ideas are most compelling.

As rehearsals continue, periodically ask the singers questions that deepen their understanding of the poetry, moving from simple paraphrase through interpretation, to their own personal relationship with the text. Through consistent poetic analysis, a more mature poetic feeling-meaning emerges.

The principle is the same, whether the text is sacred or secular. Regardless of the individual background or belief system, the singers can find and express meaning in the words. When choirs sing with the intention of conveying meaning, a dramatic shift happens in the room. Feeling-meaning becomes apparent. Vitality of sound is coupled with great conviction and the need to express the importance of the text. Inspired singing begins to happen.

Music

When art is the goal, even the business of mastering technique is related to the expressive content of the repertoire. American Aesthetics recognizes that many individual elements contribute to aesthetic consummation, and often skill development is needed for the work to become presentable in public performance. Vowel unification, consonant clarity, rhythmic precision, lyricism, intonation, phrase shape, and balance, will most likely need individual practice. However, after the ensemble works on an individual component, *we must return the attention immediately to wholeness.* In order to create the conditions for inspired performance, we must return to the reason behind the repertoire—the initial spark that ignited the creative act of the composition.

Combined Expressive Power of the Two Art Forms

Famed opera singer Maria Callas is said to have "put the inspiration on the inhalation." In other words, when you get ready to sing (inhalation), start with the feeling-meaning you are trying to communicate (inspiration). By exploring textual depth and the relationship of music and text, singers make profound connections to the expressive content in the repertoire and learn how to make aesthetic choices. The combination of the feeling-meaning in the text and the feeling-meaning of the music create a synergy that gives rise to musical artistry and leads to the aesthetic experience.

Composers use dynamic, rhythm, melody, and chord as fundamental expressive tools. By asking the chorus to sing the reason for the musical feature, we put art at the center of the rehearsal process.

Dynamic: Feeling-Meaning versus Volume

Ask the chorus to sing the reason for the dynamic. Replace all dynamic markings in the score with an emotional character word. *Forte*, or loud, can be exuberant, forceful, angry or celebratory. *Piano*, or quiet, can be sad, timid, secretive, or tender. Once the chorus has agreed upon the emotion they are trying to convey, write that emotional character word in the score. Singers will produce a sound at an appropriate dynamic because it was generated from a context of emotional expression.

Rhythm: Implied Meaning of Eighth, Quarter, and Whole

Ask the chorus to sing the reason for the rhythm. In "Bound for the Promised Land," arranged by Mac Wilberg, the repetition of the word *land* has three different rhythmic treatments within the span of just a few measures. The first repetition is set with moving eighth notes, suggesting the activity or movement of the journey. The second repetition is a quarter note followed by a quarter rest, which gives it a quality of declamation, as if to say, *I put my staff down here!* The third repetition is a full whole note, the longest note in the piece thus far, suggesting the expansiveness of the land, the full breadth of the journey, and the magnificence of the arrival.

Melody and Harmony

Ask the chorus to sing the reason for the pitch, the reason for the chord. Rising intervals can heighten a sense of questioning, as we do in speech.

(*Really?*) Likewise, a dark or dissonant chord can intensify grief. Discoveries regarding the implied feeling-meaning in individual pitches or choice of harmony can dramatically increase the communicative power inherent in both the music and the text.

The Cumulative Effect of Crowd Sourcing the Artistic Intent

The pragmatic results of an approach based in aesthetic discovery and experience are vast and varied: a truly cohesive ensemble, singers excited to help the ensemble powerfully express great ideas, singers who do your recruiting for you, increased support from administrators, increased engagement with the community, and the personal satisfaction of knowing you have contributed positively to the world. Singers who come to rehearsal having made discoveries on their own are eager to share them. The rehearsal environment builds a culture of personal responsibility, as each singer invests in the artistic outcome. By crowd sourcing the emotional intent, singers bring themselves to the brink of their emotional expressive capacity.

Moving toward Transcendence

One of my favorite Robert Shaw quotations is, "For the dove to descend you have to clean the bird cage."[4] Shaw knew that singers must learn the craft of music making, including notes, rhythm, pitch memory, breathing, tone production, and so on. Yet, too often, conductors and music educators take on the task of cleaning up vocal technique, but forget to invite the dove. When the choral rehearsal is limited to mastery of technique, we lose track of the artistry. The resulting performance becomes a gleaming, empty cage: technically excellent but emotionally uninspired—and uninspiring.

We must deliberately invite singers to turn their attention to matters of art. We must make artistic expression the primary goal of the ensemble and place aesthetic choice at the center of the rehearsal process. By inspiring singers toward emotional communication through aesthetic discovery, we can create the conditions to manifest a peak aesthetic experience.

Appendix A

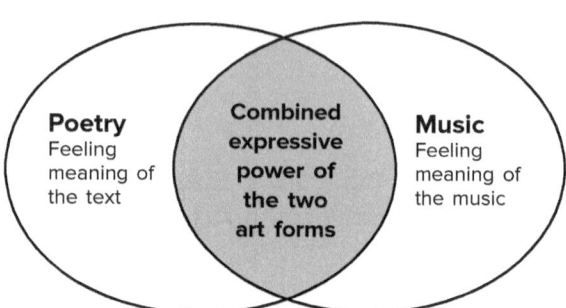

Poetry
Design developmental understanding over time

What does the poetry do?

What's the emotional arc of the poem from beginning to end?

At rehearsal, the conductor asks the chorus:

  What are the compelling ideas or images?
  What is the emotional journey?
  How does the poem relate to your personal life?
  How might the poem benefit the audience?

Music
Design developmental understanding over time

What does the music do?

What's the emotional arc of the music from beginning to end?

At rehearsal, the conductor asks the chorus:

  What needs our attention?
    Notes, rhythm, dynamic
    Tone, vowel/consonant clarity
  What's the character of the first phrase?
  What's the relationship of the first phrase to the second?

Combined Expressive Power of the Two Art Forms

At rehearsal, the conductor asks the chorus:
How does the music enhance the meaning of the words?
Establish the emotional intention; then sing the phrase.
Sing the reason for the dynamic. What kind of loud or quiet?
Sing the reason for the note. Is the scale degree stable or unstable?
Sing the reason for the rhythm. Does it calm or activate the energy?
How does the composer feel about the poem? How do you know?
How can we perform the full expressive power of this work of art?

Notes

1. John Dewey, *Art as Experience* (New York: Capricorn Books, 1958 [1934]), 39.

2. Ibid., 40.

3. This quotation from Mary Goetze is from a lecture I attended in the early 1990s as a doctoral student at the University of Colorado in Boulder. Her presentation fundamentally shifted my approach to choral conducting.

4. Robert Shaw's metaphor about cleaning the birdcage appears in a variety of contexts. In a letter dated October 7, 1991, he describes it in this fashion: "The dove (of mystical revelation) does not descend to a dirty perch." *The Robert Shaw Reader*, ed. Robert Blocker (New Haven: Yale University Press, 2004), 88.

17

Budd Boetticher's Transcendental Westerns, or, Schrader, Bazin, Sartre, and Neville Walk into a Saloon

JAMES MCLACHLAN

Introduction

There is no more American genre in the cinema than the Western. Many Westerns unfold according to a typical plot structure in which a hero faces great odds but eventually overcomes evil, in a natural setting of great beauty. This formula proved to be profitable as entertainment. But, of course, some directors sought to serve what they saw as higher ends. And, some critics saw in the work, not only of the directors of prestige "A" Westerns but also of the quickie "B" Westerns that filled the lower half of double bills at matinees and drive-ins, something more interesting than forgettable entertainment.

Paul Schrader's 1972 seminal text, *Transcendental Style in Film: Ozu, Bresson, Dreyer,* offers one of the classic interpretations of religious aesthetics in film. Schrader claims religious blockbusters like Cecil B. DeMille's *The Ten Commandments* failed in their attempts to indicate transcendent values because they represent transcendence through special effects that age quickly and show themselves not to transcend the year they were made, much less approach the eternal. Schrader celebrates the art films of Yosujiro Ozu and Robert Bresson, saying that each points viewers to the transcendent ideal of the infinite beyond the temporal. Oddly enough,

Schrader also sees transcendence in the "B" Westerns of Budd Boetticher. These 1950s Westerns that starred an aging Randolph Scott include *Seven Men from Now*, *The Tall T*, *Decision at Sundown*, *Buchanan Rides Alone*, *Ride Lonesome*, and *Comanche Station*. Schrader thinks the great accomplishment of the Boetticher Westerns, like great works of religious art, is that they lead the viewer to an experience of the transcendent. Schrader calls the Scott characters in these films modern archetypes, primitive figures who can exist in a contemporary situation. In 1970 he wrote that audiences "search for transcendence in the year 2001, in 'Jupiter and beyond,' when perhaps the closest thing to archetypal 'transcendence' has occurred in these neglected Randolph Scott westerns."[1]

The seven Boetticher/Scott Westerns, also called the Ranown cycle, were first noticed by French critics, including André Bazin, who praised them in the pages of *Cahiers du Cinéma*. For Bazin, Scott's character was an alienated existentialist hero. American critics and film historians Jim Kitses and Alexander Sarris also saw them as existential Westerns. While this reading fits the 1950s *esprit du temps*, its imputed existentialist emphasis seems incompatible with two themes: Scott's status in the films as a kind of "broken" Western icon and not an existentialist antihero, and the films' celebration of the beauty of nature.

How defensible is Schrader's reading of the Boetticher Westerns that emphasizes their transcendent qualities? I will suggest Schrader's account could be strengthened by Robert Neville's naturalism and his treatment of "broken symbols" as a tool of aesthetic interpretation. Scott's iconic position in the films has the character of a broken symbol.

Schrader's Transcendental Style

Paul Schrader argued that there is a transcendental style in art and filmmaking that is universal, transcending the differences between cultures and individual religions.[2] He outlines three phases, or moments, of the style:

1. *The everyday: a meticulous representation of the dull, banal commonplaces of everyday living (le quotidian or true realism)* (TS, 42). Schrader's ideal directors are Robert Bresson and Yosujiro Ozu, each of whom roots his cinematic aesthetic in a realistic portrayal of everydayness. For Bresson, the quotidian is shown in the meticulous representation of pickpocket technique in *Pickpocket* and the dullness and bigotry of village life in *Diary of a Country Priest*. Bresson's spare use of music, a

soundtrack that consists mostly of everyday sounds, his use of only one camera angle, and his employment of nonprofessional actors reinforce his portrayal of the everyday. He sees plot, acting, music, editing, etc. to act as "screens" that divert the viewer from the discomfort and meaninglessness of the everyday. For Schrader, Bresson's films represent the idea of film as anti-entertainment, as a kind of ethnography.

Schrader argues that the same can be said of Yosujiro Ozu's style. Ozu's films focus on the daily lives of middle-class postwar Japanese families. His camera never moves but is always at the level of the tatami or the sitting position, which is not only taken by Zen adepts in meditation, but by a family taking a meal together. The experience of the everyday is to put us face to face with the humdrum routine of the world. Here, Schrader's critique of the classic Hollywood religious epics such as *The Ten Commandments*, *Ben Hur*, even *2001: A Space Odyssey*, is evident. In these spectacles, we never confront everyday life; rather, they offer us a false transcendence inconsistent with what we experience outside the movie house. In the movie theater, we escape the ordinary; we go to exotic places and experience extreme situations. The emotional highs of dramatic music, pageantry, and special effects carry us away. But the spiritual effect is bogus and does not last. We return to the boredom of our daily experience without having confronted it.

2. *Disparity: an actual or potential disunity between man and his environment that culminates in a decisive action* (*TS*, 42). Bresson's films confront us with the disparity between a transcendent reality and the dull service of everyday reality. Suddenly, there is an outburst of inexplicable spiritual emotion, as in *Pickpocket* and *Diary of a Country Priest*, or violence and incredible evil as in *L'Argent* and *The Devil Probably*. Bresson's heroes either find transcendence beyond the everyday or are destroyed. Disparity between reality and the ideal injects a "human density" into unfeeling everydayness that grows until the moment of decisive action (*TS*, 70). By showing disparity, the filmmaker tries to evoke a sense of the "wholly other." In *The Diary of a Country Priest*, the priest is further and further alienated from his environment. In Ozu's films, such as the classic *Tokyo Story*, the characters encounter the disparity between the Confucian ideal of humanity and family and the daily failures of a modern Japanese middle class to come anywhere close to it. Decision is an important moment in both Bresson and Ozu. Bresson said, "There must, at a certain moment, be a transformation; if not there is no art" (*TS*, 42). Schrader claims this similarity between the two filmmakers: their films are

primitive and archetypal. Decision happens when the tension between the dull everyday reality and the symbolic ideal is too great to bear.

3. *Stasis: a frozen view of life that does not resolve the disparity but transcends it.* In Schrader's account of the transcendent style, there is a definite before and after. After a mounting sense of disparity occurs, decisive action occurs, followed by a stance of stasis. This is a paradoxical expression of the Transcendent. Schrader writes: "Complete stasis, or frozen motion, is the trademark of religious art in every culture. It establishes an image of a second reality which can stand beside the ordinary reality; it represents the Wholly Other" (*TS*, 49).

Applying the Transcendental Style to Boetticher's B Westerns

Schrader began his classic article "Budd Boetticher: A Case Study in Criticism" in 1971 in the film journal *Cinema* by noting that French critic Andre Bazin and American film historian Andrew Sarris rescued Budd Boetticher from obscurity (*BB*, 45). Schrader thought the best auteur criticism on Boetticher concerned the conflict within "a moral man in an immoral universe" (*BB*, 47). The character recognizes the disparity between the ought and the everyday. "The central conflict in Boetticher's films . . . occurs not only on the individual level, but also on a more fundamental, archetypical level" (*BB*, 47). Schrader saw Boetticher's films in Jungian terms. The characters wear the familiar guise of individualism, but in the moment of crisis they function as archetypes. He thought the films resemble primitive and archetypal art (*BB*, 48).

The Boetticher Westerns were low budget B films shot on very tight schedules of usually around twelve days.[3] They generally were shown on the lower portions of double bills. They were not the "prestige" Westerns of John Ford, Anthony Mann, Delmer Daves, George Stevens, and Fred Zinnemann. The cooperation between Boetticher, writer Burt Kennedy, producer Harry Joe Brown, and actor Randolph Scott is responsible for how these films express decision and grace. Schrader thought, "Kennedy's scripts 'sophisticate' Boetticher's archetype: they force him into a world filled with irony, dark humor, pessimism and moral ambiguity" (*BB*, 54), and that "Boetticher is obsessed with the primitive dilemma: 'at what point does the individual become archetypal?'" (*BB*, 55) These "primitive" archetypes are moderated by the modern complexities of Burt Kennedy's scripts that throw the characters into the ambiguities of moral decisions.

Stoic Hero and Appealing Villains: Bazin and Kitses

French critic André Bazin opens his review of Boetticher's 1956 *Seven Men from Now* (in the August-September 1957 issue of *Cahiers Du Cinéma*) with gushing praise. He places it in the company of Anthony Mann's *The Naked Spur* and John Ford's *The Searchers* as the greatest Western he has seen since the war. "My admiration for *Seven Men from Now* will not lead me to conclude that Budd Boetticher is the greatest director of Westerns—although I do not rule out this hypothesis—but simply that his film is perhaps the best Western I have seen since the war. It is only the memory of *The Naked Spur* and *The Searchers* that makes me reticent."[4] This is great praise for a B Western that most Parisians never saw. It had a very limited run at only one theatre in Paris. But Bazin raised the possibility that Boetticher perhaps even exceeded the far more famous Mann and Ford. Bazin claimed *Seven Men* was "much superior" to George Stevens's *Shane* (1953), and George Zinnemann's *High Noon*. He called both "super Westerns."[5] Like Schrader, Bazin claimed that *Seven Men from Now* returned to primitive and traditional mythology. Bazin thought that "[t]oday the Western cannot in most cases continue to be simple and traditional except by being vulgar and idiotic." The genre was drowning in its own mythology. This, claims Bazin, was the problem with *Shane*. The mythology of the genre was being treated as the subject of the films, but the beauty of the Western was its spontaneity and its "perfect unconsciousness of the mythology dissolved in it." The stark simplicity of *Seven Men from Now* made it "one of the most intelligent Westerns I know but also the least intellectual; the most refined and the least aesthetic; the simplest and the most beautiful."

Bazin recognized the austere humor of the film, a kind of irony that does not diminish the characters but allows their naivety to coexist with intelligence. He notes Boetticher's wonderful use of the landscape. It is spare yet beautiful. It's not as monumental as in Mann's or especially Ford's work. Boetticher would have agreed with Bazin on this point. He was friends with John Ford, but faulted "Pappy" for letting the monumental overcome his characters.

Ford's films were famously shot in Monument Valley and the Valley of the Gods in Utah and Arizona; they little resembled but doubled for Texas in *The Searchers*. The mythic power of the landscape of the Four Corners region is an important part of the film. George Stevens shot his Jesus film *The Greatest Story Ever Told* there. Stevens shunned shooting in Israel because he thought the power of the Utah desert more appropriate to the great religious myth.

Boetticher's low budget films were shot in the Alabama Hills near Lone Pine, California, the site of many Westerns. But Boetticher's celebration of nature is clear to anyone who sees the films. Bazin claimed we are drawn to the "varied substance of the earth, or the grain and shape of the rocks." The films luxuriate in nature. This is nowhere more evident than in their celebration of the beauty of horses. Bazin wrote, "Nor do I think that the photogenic qualities of horses have been as well exploited for a very long time." Boetticher raised horses, and when he finally gave up on Hollywood he retired to his horse ranch. His love of the beauty of the animals and the landscape is palpable in each film.

Critics and film historians are unanimous that Scott's presence in the films is central to their success. Bazin sees Scott as recalling Western icon William S. Hart. "Finally, there is Randolph Scott, his face irresistibly recalling William Hart's right down to the sublime lack of expression in his blue eyes. . . . The face expresses nothing because there is nothing to express." Scott's leathery features make him almost a part of the landscape. He blends into the harsh rocks of the Alabama Hills. Bazin writes that his reticence—his inexpressive manner—is so pronounced that it is one of the most expressive things in the film. He sees him as the isolated, alienated existentialist hero—the Humphrey Bogart of the Western.[6] Boetticher was pleased by the attention given his films by the French critics and quipped, "The French were on our film like flies on a gut wagon."[7]

Critics Save Boetticher and Make Him an Existentialist: Sartre and the Westerns

Jim Kitses, in his commentary on *Seven Men from Now* and in his history of the Western, *Horizon's West*, thinks that Bazin and the French critics' enthusiasm for *Seven Men from Now* was motivated, in part, by the popularity of existentialism in France in the 1950s. There is some reason to think this is correct. Indeed, when the existentialist phase of the first Spaghetti Westerns rolled out of Europe in the early 1960s, they were marked by existentialist themes. Sartre's famous discussion of "the look" as a kind of battle with the Other over objectification in *Being and Nothingness* is famously rendered, through Leone's tight focus on eyes, in the Sergio Leone *Dollar* trilogy as the antagonists stare each other down in the gunfights. Leone once called out to Boetticher on seeing him at a film festival, "Dear Budd, I stole everything from you."[8] Kitses thought all the Boetticher films are variations on the same existentialist (and transcendent) themes: How are we are to live? How can we have a meaningful life in a meaningless world?

I want to question the claim that the films are completely existentialist in nature. The films are bleak but not like film noir, which became the quintessential existentialist film form. There is too much pleasure in the beauty of nature (and the grace of horses) in the films to fit the existentialist mood. The visual texture of the films is marvelous. Still, one can make existentialist claims about the characters. Scott's characters are a very alienated lot and, though the names change, he is the same character in each film. He has no time for talk. He has had and lost everything. He is independent and immune from the judgment of others. But unlike Will Kane in *High Noon*, he seems without inner psychological conflict, a throwback of sorts to the mythic Westerns of the silent era. Rather, Scott's characters are moral icons like the classical Western heroes of the silent films, but they are also mysterious. All this clashes with the existentialist label.

In Boetticher's Westerns, we can contrast the enigmatic, stoic hero with very human and appealing villains. The entertaining, sympathetic villains humanize the films, yet they eventually face emotional, existential decisions. Lee Marvin in *Seven Men from Now*, Richard Boone in *The Tall T*, Pernell Roberts in *Ride Lonesome*, and Claude Akins in *Commanche Station* are all charming villains. They are more human than the iconic Scott. We understand them better than we understand the stoic Scott. Of the four, only Roberts crosses over and forsakes the wild life. Marvin, Boone, and Akins all die. Their deaths are tragic affairs and we are moved by them.

A specific example of a villain facing existential decisions is Lee Marvin in *Seven Men from Now*. He is a cad, but we understand his lust, yearning, and wit. We can sympathize with him. Scott's characters have settled habits such that anxious decision making is never seen. There is never a moment, as there is with that other icon, Gary Cooper's Will Kane in *High Noon*, when any of the Scott characters even consider running away and not fulfilling the moral imperative that seems to govern their existence in the uncaring world. Of the villains, only Pernell Roberts's character, Sam Boone, in *Ride Lonesome*, and Richard Rust's Dobie in *Comanche Station* are transformed. For the most part the villains, including Lee Marvin's Masters in *Seven Men from Now*, John Carroll's Tate Kimbrough in *Decision at Sundown*, Claude Akins's Ben Lane in *Comanche Station*, and Richard Boone's Frank Usher in *The Tall T*—despite their warped but still sympathetic humanity, wit, lust, and greed—seem to be driven by the constant desire for more. They want to be masters of their world. Marvin's character in *Seven Men from Now* is even named Masters.

If Kitses and Bazin are accurate in interpreting the films as existential Westerns, then the villains fit nicely within Sartre's contention that the human condition is generally one lived in the bad faith of self-deception. They are examples of the desire to be God, trying to be what they are not. Sartre sees the human being as a project to come to be, to reach completeness. There is no preexisting plan or reason for our existence, nor any purpose imposed from the outside. This is the meaning of the famous existentialist mantra, "Existence precedes essence." Nevertheless, we want meaning and purpose, so we must create it for ourselves authentically. But we recognize these meanings and purposes will die with us. Out of frustration with our finitude, we desire both to be perfect and to have the spontaneity and ability to control consciousness. Sartre describes this as the desire to be God. In a famous passage from the conclusion of *Being and Nothingness* he asserts that human reality is a passionate effort to create Being in-itself-for-itself, which is equivalent to Godlike freedom. God is the projection of our desire to be a complete and independent being. Consciousness, which is the negation or absence of the material being it is aware of, would then become the foundation of its own complete positive being. But this is a contradiction. To be conscious is to think about something, something that one is not, and to be affected and changed by it. Our passionate efforts to create a basis for our own existence are all doomed to failure. Sartre famously concludes that "[m]an is a useless passion."[9]

But this desire is also the source of Hell. We like to imagine we are complete beings, little gods, completely in control of our own fate. Others, simply by their otherness, constantly remind us of our lack of being God, our lack of totality, of completeness, and of our partial dependence on them. God is thus only a projection of our contradictory desires, of our will to power. Hell is other people.

This antipathy toward the other is essential to the villains in Boetticher Westerns. Each one plays out his desire for control up to his death. Boetticher once said he was not interested in films about mass emotion but about individuals. In *Seven Men from Now*, Marvin is the quintessential individual desiring to be a god. The seeds of Marvin's more famous villain Liberty Valence are here, but Marvin's Bill Masters is much more sympathetic than Valence. He is a cad driven by self-interest, who shoots his partner down so he won't have to share with him. He would like to be the center of all relationships, and he attempts absolute control. But he is also charming and has great respect for Scott's character, Ben Stride. When he dies, we along with Stride feel regret. His death is tragic. His life may be a useless passion but it is, after all, a passion. However, Scott's Stride is not simply another person who opposes Masters, but an archetype, almost not human. He is a force against which the greed and narcissism of Marvin is undone—his desire to be God destroyed. This is also true of Ben Lane (Claude Akins) in *Comanche Station* and Frank Usher (Richard Boone) in *The Tall T.* In each case the villain, human and as such desiring control, cannot "cross over." The villains confront Scott, the one character they cannot control, and die. Men are not gods. The villains in the Ranown Westerns are slaves to Sartrean bad faith.

Film historian and auteur theorist Andrew Sarris was one of the critics who resurrected Boetticher for American audiences. He saw Boetticher's films as "floating poker games" in which each character bluffs about his hand.[10] Jim Kitses saw the films as poker games where everyone loses. The moral of Boetticher's films is thus a simple one: everyone loses. Life defeats charm, innocence is blasted. The world is finally a sad and funny place, life a tough, amusing game that can never be won but must be played. If Boetticher's films can darken to near-tragedy, the pessimism is always held in check by an innate response to the absurdity of it all, the way in which we take up roles in a farce.[11]

It is interesting to compare the Ranown Westerns with John Ford's more mythic, "prestige" Westerns. Consider the grave scene in Boetticher's *Seven Men from Now* and compare it with cemetery scenes in Ford Westerns. In some of Ford's best-known films, *My Darling Clementine* (1946), *She Wore a Yellow Ribbon* (1949), *The Searchers* (1956), and *Three Godfathers* (1948), cemetery scenes highlight the relationships between the living and the dead and remind us of the human cost of settling the Western frontier. The participants are mythically and visually rich, often accompanied by a hymn and singing by the Sons of the Pioneers. In *Seven Men from Now*'s burial scene, the characters are absurd figures living outside of society and culture. People just die. There is no funeral. Master's partner, Clete, is annoyed with having to bury a man and the absurdity of saying words over the dead. The dead are just dead.

But, again, is *existential Western* really the best overall characterization of these films? They do share elements with film noir that were made in the same period, and Boetticher even made a film noir, *The Killer is Loose*, in 1956. Yes, the Ranown Westerns highlight the alienation of the characters from each other and the absurdity of existence in good Sartrean fashion. But the existentialist reading of the films must not be taken too far. The films have too much of the American ethos of the Western and its relation to nature to simply call them existentialist. The homage to nature's beauty and Scott's "at homeness" in nature are hardly existentialist. The exuberance of Boetticher's presentation and obvious enjoyment of the beauty of nature is quite far from Roquentin's nausea at the experience of nature in Sartre's novel. The stark beauty of the Alabama Hills and the beauty of horses are not existentialist themes. Most importantly, Scott's iconic stature in each film stands against an existentialist reading of the films. The early Spaghetti Westerns have a much more existentialist feel than Boetticher's films.[12] Scott's characters are at home and really a part of the stark but beautiful nature. He might be alienated from his past and others but not from nature. Only in *Decision at Sundown* do we get anything close to the kind of existential Western created by Sam Peckinpah in *The Wild Bunch* (Peckinpah was another admirer of Boetticher) and the existential spaghettis of Leone, Solima, or Corbucci. Peckinpah's characters in *The Wild Bunch* are profoundly existentialist heroes. They are flawed, alienated, human beings trying to live by a code that they know is doomed. In most of the Westerns of the Ranown cycle, however, Scott stands as a symbol, albeit a broken one, that transcends, in terms of Schrader's third phase, the desires and lusts of the other characters in the films. I believe it would be better to explain the Ranown kind of transcendence and Boetticher's joy in nature in American philosopher Robert Neville's notions of creation and broken symbols rather than in existentialist terms.

Neville, Nature, and Broken Symbols

Robert Neville's interpretation of the doctrine of creation ex nihilo, developed in *God the Creator* (1968) and continued throughout his work, argues that to be is to be determinate, to be finite. To be determinate is to contrast with other determinations in a context of mutual relevance, and the ultimate context of mutual relevance—that which grounds the many determinations of being—is pure indeterminacy. Neville's Creator is the purely indeterminate and impersonal ground of being. Thus *creatio ex nihilo* is not the act of a personal creator. In the Western tradition, Neville's notion of divinity as expressed in his doctrine of ex nihilo is thus close to Meister Eckhart's *Gottheit*: "the simple ground, into the silent desert, in to which distinction never gazed, not the Father nor the Son or Holy Spirit."[13] Eckhart alludes to a ground that precedes the determinations including a personal relation between creator and creature. Schrader, in agreement with Neville, sees transcendence as a glimpse of an infinite ground of being resistant to explanation. This is the how Schrader reads the "all is grace" conclusion of Bresson's *Diary of a Country Priest* and the final experience of *mono no aware* (sympathetic sadness) in Ozu's *Tokyo Story*.[14] The films point us to transcendence as something more than everydayness. Similarly, Schrader thought that Boetticher's Westerns point us to transcendence. There is a feeling of sadness and beauty in the best of them that evokes an aesthetic feeling of transcendent meaningfulness.

Like Schrader, though in a much more nuanced fashion, Neville provides a cross-cultural analysis of how religious symbols function from a theological and philosophical perspective and how transcendence points to this indeterminate ground of being. I will briefly explore how, using Neville's discussion of broken symbols, we could read Boetticher's Westerns as examples of transcendence in film.

In *The Truth of Broken Symbols*, Neville defends the view that there are contexts in which "symbols that obviously are not literally true may nonetheless be taken to be true in broken innocence, including both hopes for heaven and addresses to personal gods."[15] Neville presents a theory of religious symbolism in the American pragmatic tradition extending and elaborating Paul Tillich's claim that religious symbols participate in the divine realities to which they refer and yet must be broken in order not to be idolatrous or demonic. Religious symbols can be properly understood as true or false. Symbol-systems such as myths, theologies, or liturgies are to be used to engage divine realities. Notice the similarity between the notion of the ground of being and Schrader's notion of stasis. It is only through a mystical experience that we are aware of being itself. Neville can see the footprints of God within creation and follow them back to the creative process that leaves its marks in creation.

The phrase "broken symbols" was made famous by Tillich. Symbols engage us in what they symbolize and yet are different from them. This is particularly important in the case of religious symbols that are finite and symbolize the infinite. Tillich wrote in *Systematic Theology* that the true symbol must participate in the power of the divine to which it points.[16] This is the difference between a sign that is merely arbitrary and a symbol that is irreplaceable. Dead symbols have ceased to function as embodiments of the sacred. But symbols can also become idols that, in Martin Buber's terms, eclipse the divine. For this reason, Tillich rejected all representations of God that are literal. Neville rejects all literal notions as well. Neville cites *Dynamics of Faith* where Tillich argued that only in the natural stage of literalism are mythical and literal meanings indistinguishable. When literal truth is seen as differently evaluated than fictive truth, one replaces the "unbroken myth" with the "broken myth," the story that evokes meaning beyond what literally happens. Tillich thinks that "the enemy of a critical theology is not natural literalism but conscious literalism with repression and aggression toward autonomous thought."[17]

Schrader and Bazin claim the primitive character of Boetticher's films harken back to the early silent-age Westerns that were effective because they were naive in their mythology. This form of mythology could resonate with Schrader's Jungian reading of the power of symbols in the Ranown cycle. What brings the Ranown Westerns into mythic meaning beyond literal meaning is Boetticher's cooperation with writer Burt Kennedy. In any case, these films are more than simply naive or existentialist. The clash between the archetypal hero and the human existential villain takes them beyond the simply naive silent Westerns of William S. Hart. We become aware, as Kitses observed, that in floating poker games there is no final victory. To try to become God, to gain total control, is a delusion. The mythic clash can foster understanding the films in terms of both transcendent meaning and broken symbolism.

Following Peirce, Neville believes that the primary value of religious symbols is their soteriological instrumentality, but also that they are still representations and need to be examined in regard to their relevance and truth (*TBS*, 1). Symbols are alive if they engage their interpreters with the objects to which they refer (*TBS*, 20). Some symbols may not refer to anything real but could have powerful influence over the lives of the interpreters. But if the symbols do not engage the interpreter, they are dead. The options for belief must be alive, just as for William James's

Boston audience the Madhi was not the living option that it would be for a Twelver Shi'ite.[18]

Beyond living, Neville argues that the symbol must also be true. Symbols are true "when their meanings accurately describe or evaluate what they refer to and communicate this into the experience of the interpreters" (*TBS*, 20). They are false when they are idolatrous. Consider the religious blockbusters of Cecil B. DeMille with their casts of thousands, special effects, and swelling music. These spectacular items manipulate the audience with their false presentations of transcendence. DeMille's films were as much cold war propaganda as they were religious films. They were great political and religious pageants where the actors performed in the fashion of the great hillside pageants of the nineteenth and early twentieth centuries, invoking the proper religious styles of the times. (Of course, such pageantry was also prominent in Soviet and Nazi rallies, illustrated in the Nazi films of Leni Riefenstahl.) Such use of symbols falsely refers to the divine by means of something literal, finite and nondivine offered for the sake of profit. Symbols can also be false by being demonic. In this case, the symbol actually perverts the divine nature. "History is full of divinely charismatic villains and religions sometimes have difficulty identifying their own demonic aberrations" (*TBS*, 20). For instance, Plato correctly interpreted the vulgar content of Homer's description of the gods as an aberration.

Think of DeMille's version of the Exodus story of liberation. While it tells of the freeing of one people, it involves murder and expropriation of others. This version has been used as a justification for violence in many cases over the years. DeMille's *Ten Commandments* makes no mention of the very human Egyptians (or later the Midianites, Amalekites, and Canaanites) being slaughtered as Moses (Charlton Heston) and Joshua (John Derek) lead the Hebrews to freedom. DeMille only sees the story in the clear light of the battle of American democracy and Soviet communism.

Neville notes that religions call people to their moral obligations. This is certainly the case in the Scott Westerns. They are morality tales, as are all the classic Westerns, and they succeed not only as entertainment but also in terms of transcendence because Scott is not a hero to be taken literally. Rather, as a kind of more-than-human mythic force guided by grace in confronting corrupt human aspiration, he evokes thought about transcendent meanings. Yet in stasis these meanings function as broken symbols that are only suggested, not asserted as facts to be believed. Neville makes the key point that symbols recognized in their symbolic function are liable to be broken yet nonetheless true (*TBS*, 29, 243). "*Truth is the carryover of value from the object into the interpreters' experience by means of signs, as qualified by the biological, cultural, semiotic, and purposive contexts of the interpreters*" (*TBS*, 240; italics in the original). This recognition of the brokenness of symbols allows for escaping reductive literalism and supports a mystical, apophatic approach to transcendent truth.

I think the Boetticher Westerns achieve this kind of truth. Like the existentialist film noir and some of the best existentialist war films, such as Sam Fuller's *Steel Helmet*, their low-budget character forces the filmmaker to rely on story, setting, and particularly character. Boetticher's Westerns are stark, but unlike films influenced heavily by existentialism, they revel in the beauty of nature and point toward the possibility of transcendence. Unlike the great mythic films of John Ford, they exude a sense of a sadness at not being able to grasp and hold the momentary sheer beauty of the finite moment within the infinite. This is not in the same sense that one might find sympathetic sadness in Ford. It is not about the passing of the mythic West at the end of *The Searchers* or *The Man Who Shot Liberty Valence*. It is, rather, that the symbols are symbols that never did quite make it to the divine but point us to something profound. They provide an American Aesthetic vision of incredible beauty and nobility that gives us a home in the natural world.

Notes

1. Paul Schrader, "Budd Boetticher: A Case Study in Criticism," in *Schrader on Schrader*, ed. Kevin Jackson (New York: Faber and Faber, 2004). Subsequently this work is cited internally in the text as *BB*.

2. Paul Schrader, *Transcendental Style in Film: Ozu, Bresson, Dryer* (New York: Da Capo Press. 1972), 38. Henceforth this source is cited internally in the text as *TS*.

3. Ranown stands for the two producers, Randolph Scott and Harry Joe Brown.

4. André Bazin, "An Exemplary Western," in *Cahiers du Cinema: The 1950s Neo-Realism, Hollywood, New Wave* (Cambridge: Harvard University Press, 1985). Republication of *Cahiers du Cinema 74,* Aug.-Sept. 1957, 169.

5. Ibid., 170, as are the next two quotations. The following quotations prior to endnote 6 are from 171.

6. Bazin was an admirer of Sartre. He read and annotated Sartre's early study on the imagination, *L'Imaginire*. Bazin's *What Is Cinema?* is an homage to Sartre's *What Is Literature?* He thought in the Sartrean vocabulary of the time, and held that "cinema's existence precedes its essence" because "contingency is also a necessary quality of film." Dudley Andrew, Forward to 2004 edition, in Andre Bazin, *What Is Cinema?* (Berkeley: University of California Press, 2005), x, xii.

7. Jim Kitses, Audio Commentary to *Seven Men from Now* (Hollywood: Batjac Productions and Paramount Pictures, 2005).

8. Ibid.

9. In the famous passage at the end of *Being and Nothingness* Sartre explains that the basic human desire is for us as incomplete beings to become complete. But to be human is to be incomplete, thus we are a useless passion. Still, we are a passion, and if we can understand and escape the bad-faith belief that we can complete our projects, a type of existentialist salvation is possible. "Each human reality is at the same time a direct project to metamorphose its own For-itself into an In-itself-For-itself and a project of the appropriation of the world as a totality of being-in-itself, in the form of a fundamental quality. Every human reality is a passion in that it projects losing itself so as to found being and by the same stroke to constitute the In-itself which escapes contingency by being its own foundation, the *ens causa sui*, which religions call God. Thus the passion of man is the reverse of that of Christ, for man loses himself as man in order that God may be born. But the idea of God is contradictory and we lose ourselves in vain. Man is a useless passion." Jean Paul Sartre, *Being and Nothingness,* trans. Hazel Barnes (New York: Washington Square Press, 1956), 784.

10. Andrew Sarris, *American Cinema: Directors and Directions 1929–1968* (New York: E. P. Dutton, 1968), 98.

11. Jim Kitses, *Horizons West: Directing the Western from John Ford to Clint Eastwood* (New York: Palgrave MacMillan, 2004), 184.

12. The exception is *Decision at Sundown*, where the disillusioned hero drinks himself into oblivion after giving the town a moral purpose that enables the people to liberate themselves from the local boss.

13. William Harmless, *Mystics* (Oxford: Oxford University Press, 2008), 117.

14. Schrader, *Transcendental Style*, 31–33.

15. Robert Neville, *The Truth of Broken Symbols* (Albany: State University of New York Press, 1996), ix. Hereafter cited internally as *TBS*.

16. Paul Tillich, *Systematic Theology* 1: 239, cited in *TBS*, x.

17. Paul Tillich, *Dynamics of Faith* (New York: Harper, 1957), 52–53.

18. William James, "The Will to Believe," in *Essays in Pragmatism* (New York: Hafner, 1948), 89.

V

Aesthetic Aspects of a Flourishing Life

American Aesthetics is a broad-based species of inquiry. Following all the classic American philosophers, but Dewey in particular, it includes serious attention to how aesthetic experiences and judgments pervade ordinary life. It is concerned to discern how aesthetics can enhance the quality of life in a way that augments the contributions of all the other factors influencing well-being.

Thomas Leddy poses a number of questions related to the status of everyday aesthetics. He begins by distinguishing between an "ordinarist" who thinks it demeans the everyday to apply art-based perception to understand its ordinary quality, and the "extraordinarist" who claims that experience becomes nonordinary as soon as it is attended to aesthetically. Which one more usefully understands everyday aesthetics? Leddy provides a sympathetic interpretation of Clive Bell to support his claim that everyday aesthetics, like all aesthetics, exists on a continuum. Not all aesthetic experiences attain the completeness characteristic of Dewey's "an experience." But everyday practices, often ritualistic in nature, can attain an aesthetic dimension that offers a respite from the humdrum. Buddhist mindfulness introduces a practice with aesthetic qualities to counter alienation and provide qualified support for the extraordinarist.

David Strong's article reveals that the importance in American Aesthetics of context extends beyond illuminating the sources and meaning of artistic creation. How we organize everyday life and what we engage has aesthetic weight of its own. Strong claims the context of placeless availability in contemporary commodious consumption contributes to aesthetic loss in experience. Easily available goods require little or no investment of time or skill on our part, and consequently they are not world forming for us. In contrast, such American thinkers as Emerson,

Thoreau, Dewey, and McKibben offer constructive alternatives to aesthetic loss. In particular, Albert Borgmann's notion of *centering things* draws us into aesthetically rich, skill-requiring, world-forming experience: the cello, kitchen stove, running path, trout stream, and so on. Essential to Robert S. Corrington's essay is a process he calls "selving," in which the self seeks wholeness within all-encompassing nature. Selving humans share semiotic factors with other animals. Derived from C. G. Jung's concept of "individuation" and with reference to Peirce, Dewey, and others, human selving is a deeply aesthetic process expressing the inner telos of self-development. Selving best takes place in a democratic community of interpreters. Corrington understands beauty to furnish spiritual food that empowers a person during the selving process. Within Corrington's ecstatic naturalism, wholeness is gained through an entwining of the beautiful and the sublime, a relationship that stimulates growth through the jostle of harmony and disruption. Art and beauty connect one to the universal, while the sublime of ecstatic naturalism opens one to nature's unfathomable depths that no religion can capture.

18

Resolving the Tension of Everyday Aesthetics in a Deweyan Way

Thomas Leddy

My aim in this article is to explore the extent to which it is possible to apply aesthetic analysis to everyday experience, and if it is, what benefits might be realized by doing so. I will work my way to this general inquiry by first attending to a more limited issue that has come to be seen as central to the emerging field of everyday aesthetics. The following quotation comes from an article I wrote in 2005 on the nature of everyday aesthetics. The quotation has been picked up by a number of thinkers in the field including Yuriko Saito, Allen Carlson, and Paisley Livingston and seems to indicate a central paradox, dilemma, or tension within the field that needs resolution.[1]

> It would seem that we need to make some sort of distinction between the aesthetics of everyday life ordinarily experienced and the aesthetics of everyday life extraordinarily experienced. However, any attempt to increase the aesthetic intensity of our ordinary everyday life-experiences will tend to push those experiences in the direction of the extraordinary. One can only conclude that there is a tension within the very concept of the aesthetics of everyday life.[2]

Each of the thinkers mentioned has provided his or her own solution to the problem raised. For example, in a recent article in which he takes everyday aesthetics to be an example of new directions in aesthetics, Livingston argues that the dilemma may be resolved by clearly distinguishing between practical experience where means-end rationality prevails and experience where the content is not primarily instrumental but "whatever contributes to the intrinsic value of the experience."[3] Inspired by C. I. Lewis, he bases his argument on an imagined example in which a woman named Yukiko responds in three different ways to receiving a gift of confectionary from a suitor. The first is interpersonal and practical-oriented (for example in efficiently opening the package), the second is oriented to the mild pleasure in examining the package, and the third involves disapproval of the craft in the packaging leading to a negative experience. In each case, Yukiko is responding to the same object, but only aesthetically in the second, even though the first experience is more typical of daily life.[4] I would disagree with leaving personal responses out of the domain of everyday aesthetics. Whereas Livingston's resolution of the dilemma is to keep a strong distinction between practical and aesthetic experience, Deweyans would insist that there cannot be a strong distinction.

Some of these theorists, in particular Saito and Carlson, have tried to resolve the question by simply focusing on the ordinariness of the ordinary. However, if one focuses on this *in an aesthetic way*, the focusing itself transforms the experience. So, for example, if an artist takes many photographs of ordinary gas stations, as Edward Ruscha did in 1966, this aestheticizes something that is really quite humdrum, something which usually goes aesthetically unnoticed. The ordinariness of the ordinary *is* stressed by Ruscha. But, in the process, the ordinariness is lost, or at least bracketed, through aestheticization. It is not theorizing about the ordinary that aestheticizes it: it is paying attention to it in an aesthetic way, for example by taking photographs of many such stations, framing them, and showing them in a gallery. Nor does this only happen when artists attend to the ordinary. If you pay attention to laundry-hanging in an aesthetic way you transform that experience, taking it above the level of the merely or humdrum ordinary. As Pauline Rautio has observed in her study based on the letters of a Finnish housewife, acts of hanging laundry can be experienced as moments of beauty.[5]

That attending to something aesthetically takes it out of the realm of the humdrum ordinary might be a problem for someone who thinks that an important goal in life is to experience ordinary things in an ordinary humdrum way. But I don't think anyone really has that goal. And even if they did, the goal would be pointless, since that is how we usually experience ordinary things anyway.

Sometimes focus on the ordinariness of the ordinary is associated with an attempt to disconnect ordinary aesthetics from associations with fine art. The idea may be to give a kind of credit to the ordinary qua ordinary, credit that can be lost if works of artistic genius are allowed to dominate the scene. Perhaps the concern is that the dilemma I posed somehow takes credit away from the everyday by pushing the ordinary toward kinds of experience more like those of fine art. On this view, the ordinary is diminished by comparison with kinds of experience associated with fine art. I will address this issue later in this essay.

Or perhaps it is just thought that we need a complete phenomenology of human experience. It is true that to have such a phenomenology we need also to consider the ordinariness of the ordinary. And we would probably need an account of ordinary nonaesthetic experience in order to make a clear distinction between the aesthetic and the nonaesthetic at this level.[6] But simply to talk about the nonaesthetic ordinary is no longer to talk about aesthetics: the topic has been changed.

One valuable thing about the new subdiscipline of everyday aesthetics is that it encourages paying *aesthetic* attention to ordinary phenomena, both philosophically and on an everyday basis. But, again, in doing the latter we heighten the aesthetic nature of these phenomena. To be sure, the phenomena might already have a low-level aesthetic quality even before we consciously attend to them aesthetically. For example, we might pick a shirt we want to wear without thinking or asserting any evaluative sentences about the look of the shirt. And yet we pick it based on its "look," that is to say, on its aesthetic qualities. Of course, after making the initial choice, we might articulate this choice by saying to ourselves, "This one looks good." We might even go farther and *wonder* about the shirt, *focus* on it aesthetically, and say something like, "This shirt would look better on me than this one, right?" Focusing on it aesthetically and asking for a verbal judgment (for example, from one's mate) moves the experience to another level. My point here is that low-level unarticulated aesthetic experience, for example when we make a nonverbal judgment (as when we just choose the shirt unreflectively), often is followed by more explicit and conscious experience, which in fact increases the aesthetic intensity of the object by way of our attention.

Some would say that the nonreflective judgment made when just choosing the shirt without any thought is *not* aesthetic. And there are certainly meanings of "aesthetic" that go along with this. But we choose the shirt because of its colors and lines, and maybe other, more symbolic or expressive features as well; and this either is, or at least seems very close to, aesthetic choice.

I do not want to say that choosing a shirt is (ordinarily) "an aesthetic experience." We expect "an aesthetic experience" to meet higher standards of complexity and intrinsic value than the kind of experience we have when we merely choose aesthetically. We even expect it to meet higher standards than those met when we choose the shirt reflectively, that is, after thinking about it. But insofar as choosing a shirt involves making aesthetic judgments (as in either just choosing it or choosing it after reflection), it is aesthetic. Thus, choosing the shirt is an experience that, at the very least, has an aesthetic component. Paying aesthetic attention (i.e., not just choosing based on aesthetic properties) ratchets the experience up to another level, and choosing reflectively does so even further.

I also claim that paying attention pushes the experience *in the direction of* the Deweyan ideal of "*an* experience." This is true even though the experience does not itself function in that way—is not actually "*an* experience" in Dewey's sense.[7] We can see how this can happen by looking at a piece of great literature in which the beauty of shirts plays a role. There is a famous scene in *The Great Gatsby* where Gatsby's shirts are laid out. Fitzgerald writes, "Suddenly, with a strained sound, Daisy bent her head into the shirts and began to cry stormily. 'They're such beautiful shirts,' she sobbed, her voice muffled in the thick folds. 'It makes me sad because I've never seen such—such beautiful shirts before.'"[8] She is having "*an* experience" in John Dewey's sense. The experience is complex and richly layered. Moreover, as this was for me the most memorable moment of the book when I first read it, reading this passage was also "an experience" for me.

The concern over the tension of everyday aesthetics marks a debate between what I will call "ordinarists" and "extraordinarists." The ordinarist wishes to focus on the ordinariness of the ordinary and the extraordinarist claims that experience becomes nonordinary as soon as it is attended to aesthetically, the second group emphasizing the continuity and dynamic interaction between ordinary experience and extraordinary experience including such experiences as meet Dewey's criteria of "*an* experience." These include powerful experiences of art as well as of nature, including human beauty. As I have suggested, part of the concern of the ordinarists is not to have an arts-based way of perceiving dominate *all* forms of aesthetic perception. And I agree that it should not. However, as I will show, the interaction between arts-based and non-arts-based experience is dynamic in ways that should not be ignored.

But in order to understand the importance and force of the dilemma posed we need to see how it is related to much larger questions. It may be these larger questions that are the real area of concern. They include, (1) "Is everyday aesthetics a legitimate branch of inquiry?" (2) "How is everyday aesthetics to be defined?"[9] and (3) "What is the relation of everyday aesthetics to the rest of aesthetics?" With respect to this third question, we need also to ask whether findings or debates in everyday aesthetics have implications for aesthetics in general.

I would add a fourth and a fifth question to this list: (4) "What is the relation of everyday aesthetics to philosophy today?" and (5) "How can everyday aesthetics as a subdiscipline contribute to resolution of the deepest human problems: for instance, to the achievement of happiness?"[10] These last two questions may seem too ambitious or unrelated, but isn't this the sort of thing we should keep in mind when engaged in serious philosophical inquiry?

Connections to Gulick's Project of an American Aesthetics

I will not attempt to answer all of these questions in this short paper, but the tenor of approach is basically Deweyan. Inasmuch as my answers would be Deweyan, I think my approach to the dilemma falls within Professor Gulick's project of constructing a distinctly American aesthetics. I see the term *American* here not as exclusive. In fact, I will be referencing several non-American sources in this discussion. Rather, I see the appeal to American philosophy as a strategy in which the American philosophical tradition is seen as a key to forward movement in answering the questions at issue.

Gulick defines aesthetics as "a normative discipline that identifies and assesses patterns, qualities, and relations arising in feeling that shape judgment in all the processes of perceiving, thinking, and making." This definition unusually chooses feeling over sensation (for instance, the sensation of pleasure, or just the presentations of the senses in general), but this is not a real problem, since "feeling" can be understood as the feelings that respond to sensuous and imaginative experience. A good feature of Gulick's definition, from a Pragmatist perspective, is that it fits feeling into the context of decision making, thinking, and the construction of artifacts.[11] It is also consistent with a positive attitude toward everyday aesthetics. The "processes of perceiving, thinking, and making," for example, could include a wide range of things normally found under everyday aesthetics. There is also a narrower sense for the term *aesthetics*, which refers to creation and evaluation of works of art: but this is out of the domain of everyday aesthetics and not our concern here.

What about Americanness? As Gulick observes, although "[s]elf-reliance and problem solving have seemed more American than aesthetic reflection and enjoyment," aesthetic appreciation may sometimes be something that attends self-reliant and problem-solving activity, as Dewey often observed. Similarly, everyday aesthetics is consonant with Dewey's ideals of "egalitarianism, informality, and the democratic participation of all," as mentioned by Gulick, insofar as it attends not to rarefied fine art but to informal practices as well as ones that everyone is or can be involved with.

Gulick marks four American thinkers (Peirce, Dewey, James, and Whitehead) as both taking a naturalistic stance and stressing the importance of the aesthetic dimension of experience. He also observes that these philosophers are "alert to artistic expression as a dynamic affair" and that they attend "to the pragmatic significance of the arts." The points about taking a naturalistic stance and stressing the aesthetic dimension of experience are consonant with the project of constructing a theory of everyday aesthetics. Sometimes aestheticians take these positions as uniquely Deweyan, and yet if the case can be made for the other three philosophers (and probably also Emerson) as joining in, then the position is arguably even more distinctively American. I think such a case can be made, but will not pursue that here.

As one would expect, Gulick focuses on Dewey, of whom he says, "His holistic approach to aesthetics sees it as emerging from bodily-based engagement with the world in which perception is conjoined with emotionally charged feeling, intellectual discrimination, and pragmatic concern about meaning and impact." He also stresses the way in which Deweyan aesthetics is not constrained to the fine arts but applies to popular culture and to daily life.

With respect to Kant's theory of aesthetic judgment, the great forerunner to American aesthetic theory, Gulick sees that this can be also taken in an expansive way that would include everyday aesthetics, arguing that "even cuisine, ritual, or landscaping evoke aesthetic responses that should be considered in an inclusive theory." The Kantian notions of genius and "aesthetic ideas" would seem to be exclusively applicable to the Fine Arts, and yet, if Gulick is right that they "would seem to be creative images or perhaps even intimations that inspire one towards developing adequate" expressions of originating ideas, we can see them as going beyond Fine Art in significance. Thus, insofar as everyday aesthetics can act as a prolegomena to Fine Art, or as Kant also called it, the art of genius, the two can be seen as closely related and in a continuum that is dynamic and interactional.

Gulick is right, then, to criticize Dewey for not paying attention to Kant's concepts of genius, fine art, and aesthetic ideas. Dewey's reticence is, of course, understandable, since it is arguable that the fundamental difference between him and Kant is that, for Kant, the aesthetic ideas provide a kind of bridge to the supersensible realm by way of creating a unique world out of the materials provided by nature, whereas Dewey would reject the supersensible on the basis of his naturalism. He would of course be enthusiastic about the idea of creation out of materials provided by nature.

It is noteworthy that Kant's discussion of genius appears not in "The Analytic of the Beautiful," but in "The Analytic of Sublime," and the sublime experience of the artist opens up a possible solution to religious crises (as Nietzsche would put it, "what to do after the death of God") that would never be available if we were simply talking about matters of taste. There is also one controversial passage in Dewey in which even he comprehends an "as if infinite" background as a necessary condition for profound aesthetic experience. He writes: "A work of art elicits and accentuates [the] quality of being a whole and of belonging to the larger, all-inclusive, whole which is the universe in which we live." And he thinks that this fact explains "that feeling of exquisite intelligibility and clarity we have in the presence of an object that is experienced with esthetic intensity" as well as "the religious feeling that accompanies intense esthetic perception." He goes so far as to say that "[w]e are, as it were, introduced into a world beyond this world which is nevertheless the deeper reality of the world in which we live in our ordinary experience."[12]

Gulick, however, is correct that Dewey goes beyond Kant in recognizing that "[t]hought, emotion, sense, purpose, impulsion—all bound in a passionate pressing forward—are involved in the making of art." Kant wished to keep all of these things separate from each other, but not Dewey. Moreover, it is arguable that this approach is distinctively American. Also, note that the bridging between the world of science and the supersensible realm is a non-issue for Dewey not so much because he is a naturalist but because his naturalism is so rich it does not need the supersensible. Again, as Gulick observes, Dewey is not alone among American philosophers in holding that "background experience, sociological status . . . psychological state of the creator . . . historical and cultural conditions [and artist's intention] are [all] fair game in aesthetic analysis." This contextualism, which has become dominant today, is in direct opposition to the formalism engendered by what is often an overly narrow reading of Kant's analysis of taste. Still, Dewey's emphasis on the live creature interacting with his environment is a far cry from Kant's dualistic universe of phenomena versus noumena.

Gulick's most important contribution to everyday aesthetics, in my view, is his unearthing of the importance of the concept of feeling, not found in Kant but which he finds in James, Whitehead, and Langer. I would only add that Dewey also frequently speaks of feeling in *Art as Experience*, as when he describes the drama in which "action, feeling, and meaning are one,"[13] or when he speaks of "seeing without feeling" and of "depth of insight, and increase in poignancy of feeling." He also says that "as the painter places pigment upon the canvas, or imagines it placed there, his ideas and feeling are ordered." He even endorses "a way of seeing and feeling that in its interaction with old material creates something new." In addition he notes that "[d]ifferent ideas have their different 'feels,' their immediate qualitative aspects, just as much as anything else," and that "[e]motional energy . . . works [data] into a whole toned throughout by the same immediate emotional feeling."

Feeling plays an important role in everyday aesthetics. As Gulick puts it, it is what is experienced actively or passively in the physical realm of touching and being touched, as when we say "the dress feels silky smooth." With all of this, it is no surprise that "American Aesthetics" as Gulick constitutes it, that is, in terms of the classic American tradition of philosophy, has become increasingly open to the appreciation of "popular culture, vernacular art, and the aesthetics of everyday life."

A Rereading of Clive Bell's Aesthetics so as to Expand the Scope of Our Inquiry

I want now to revisit an important but long-rejected and much-maligned theorist of art and aesthetics, Clive Bell, as a way to help resolve the dilemma.¹⁴ Bell's well-known definition of art as "significant form" would seem at first not to have any relevance to everyday aesthetics, or perhaps only a negative one. But consider first that, in its time, it allowed into the domain of art and hence of aesthetic experience a number of types of objects that were not previously considered to be art, in particular examples of what would be labeled decorative arts (e.g., pottery, weaving, home decoration), as well as expanding the concept of art in an egalitarian way to non-European cultures.

Expansion of the concept of art might not at first seem to be positive for everyday aesthetics since it would seem to push it out of the picture. But one aspect of this is that, before Bell, and especially after Hegel, philosophers of art did not pay much attention to such things as rugs and pottery. Instead, they focused almost entirely on what was called Fine Art, and in visual art this was mainly limited to painting and sculpture. Bell's famous claim was that the essence of art is "significant form," which consists of relations of lines and colors that give the viewer a special "aesthetic experience," an experience that he sometimes refers to as a form of ecstasy. Most readers interpret Bell's theory as an exclusivist formalism, and he certainly seems to support this when says that one should not pay attention to what might have been going on in the artist's mind when making the work.

It is noteworthy, however, that Bell's concept of significant form can be interpreted in a very different way. It plays an important role, for example, in the thought of contemporary Chinese aesthetician Li Zehou, who also has a close affinity to Dewey's humanistic pragmatism.¹⁵ Li interprets Bell's concept in an unorthodox way where abstract forms (of bowls and calligraphy found in the early dynasties) were significant because they evolved out of realistic images and incorporated "socially defined content or meaning." This brings Bell closer to both Dewey and Marx (particularly Marx of the *1844 Manuscripts*) than many would think possible. Although this interpretation probably does not accurately reproduce Bell's intentions, it does open up a dimension of the term "significant form" that needs discussion. For Li Zehou significant form is significant because of what he calls "sedimentation" of cultural meaning behind the form.

Interpretation of Bell as a narrow formalist may also be countered by looking at later chapters in *Art*. Through what he calls "The Metaphysical Hypothesis," he posits that the artistic genius (that is, the person who is excellent as a creative artist) could see "significant form" in the world itself, which implies a close relation between the making of art and intensified perception of nature and everyday life.[16] This is consonant with what great artists actually have done in the past, for example, Brueghel giving us a heightened experience of a winter scene based on his perceptual powers and technical skill, as in his *Winter Landscape with Skaters and Bird Trap* (1565).

Bell observes that one can see a landscape in terms of a "pure formal combination of lines and colors," and that most people have done so, for example in seeing fields and cottages as lines and colors.[17] Allen Carlson, in writing about the dilemma of everyday aesthetics, thinks that this is unsatisfactory as a solution, for, as he puts it, (1) "in many instances formal properties depend upon framing," and perceptual framing is problematic,[18] and (2) the approach trivializes aesthetics since it is associated with postcards and calendar images, things that "promote a misleading and superficial" appreciation of everyday life phenomena. Further, it "reduces the everyday to a shadow of itself, to a shallow veneer."[19] As for the first point, I do not see how we can avoid perceptual framing, since whenever we look at something we have a point of focus and hence an implicit framing of the nonfocused around that, but here I wish to address the second issue.

My claim here is that Bell's approach is *not* trivializing and it does *not* encourage us to focus on the shallow surfaces of things. We can see this by turning to the metaphysical hypothesis chapter in *Art*. Although Bell's solution does not stress the kind of depth Carlson wants, namely, providing a context of scientific knowledge for what is perceived, it does stress depth in a way that connects with a tradition that can be traced back to Schopenhauer, the Transcendentalists, Deism, and Spinoza—a tradition that, although consistent, I believe, with naturalism, allows for a spiritual aspect to a material world, one that is perceived by a suitably prepared perceiver.

I see Bell's position as therefore consistent or at least potentially consistent with Deweyan naturalism. The metaphysical hypothesis is simply that "significant form" is a manifestation of this spiritual aspect of the world (or, as might be better put, the aspect of the world that gives aura to our experience). The quotation about fields and cottages that Carlson offers is actually taken from the metaphysical hypothesis chapter where Bell also writes, "Occasionally when an artist—a real artist—looks at objects (the contents of a room, for instance) he perceives them as pure forms in certain relations to each other, and feels emotion for them as such."[20] As Bell sees it, this moment of inspiration is commonly followed by the desire to express what has been felt. The emotions are not felt for the object as a means but as pure form, as an end in itself. However, something experienced as such can still be experienced as a container of sedimented meaning in the fashion of Li.

Bell goes on to ask a series of questions ending with a rhetorical question indicating his answer: "What is the significance of anything as an end in itself? What is that which is left when we have stripped a thing of all its associations, of all its significance as a means? What is left to provoke our emotion? What but that which philosophers used to call 'the thing in itself' and now call 'ultimate reality'?"[21] His answer is to suggest that "the most profound thinkers" have believed "that the significance of the thing in itself is the significance of Reality." He concludes that perhaps the answer to the question, "Why are we so profoundly moved by certain combinations of lines and colours?" is "Because artists can express in combinations of lines and colours an emotion felt for reality which reveals itself through line and colour."[22]

Although this talk of "ultimate reality" is perhaps overdone (why not just stick with reality?), it is arguable that we *are* moved by certain relations of lines and colors because they direct our minds to the hidden aspect of things, the spiritual side of the material world referred to by Spinoza. I am not advocating Spinozism in general here, for example, his identity of Nature with God. It is not necessary to posit a transcendent realm for Bell and Spinoza to be right, only something immanent, a realm of potentiality within our world. It is often said that you can perceive anything aesthetically if you take a disinterested attitude toward it: but perhaps the significance of that is that in taking the right attitude one is able to get a glimmer of something already there.[23]

For Bell, when an artist perceives significant form in a landscape, he or she is seeing it as charged with metaphysical meaning. This would, of course, be misleading if there were no underlying reality connected with the experience of significant form. Bell himself is hesitant about the metaphysical hypothesis. Still, wouldn't it be obvious that if he were right about this, then clearly, unlike works by Cézanne or the other great Postimpressionists, which he admired so much, kitsch postcards and calendars of the sort Carlson describes are precisely the sorts of things that would *fail* to get at significant form or express this underlying emotion about reality? Carlson does not see that Bell would have as much disgust for this ephemera as he has.

If there is anything to the metaphysical hypothesis, then Bell hardly "reduces the everyday to a shadow of itself" since the everyday, as experienced by the artist or the aesthetically astute observer, would have depth of meaning. His formalism, interpreted in this new way, might then contribute to resolution of the dilemma. I say this with recognition that Carlson wants a depth that Bell cannot offer: a depth of scientific knowledge not associated with metaphysical speculation. But even if we assume that there is no extraphysical spiritual reality or realm of noumenal things-in-themselves as referenced by Kant, it still may be that there are depths of experience not equivalent to scientific cognitive depth.

Now relate this to my series of questions relevant to everyday aesthetics and the problem of tension or dilemma. If everyday aesthetics at its high point is this kind of deep perception (having nothing at all to do with picture postcards), and if this kind of deep perception is most evident, as Bell would have said, in an artist such as Cézanne, then the relationship between everyday aesthetics and art is profound. Of course, then, the relationship between everyday aesthetics and the aesthetics of art would not be accidental, but necessary. The implications for philosophy, which has always been concerned with man's place in the world, and how to deal with the strong feelings we still often associate with religion, even though science rules entirely in epistemology and metaphysics, would be to see this as confirmation of a monistic Spinoza-like view that allows for two aspects to reality, one of them being "spiritual" or transcendent-like, matter and spirit being two sides of the same coin. This idea, of course, was also adopted by the American transcendentalists, forerunners to the pragmatist tradition.

The implications for the question of how everyday aesthetics could contribute to a wider solution to human problems would be that (1) this sort of perception is conducive to wider human happiness, and (2) it is also conducive to more sympathetic understanding of others (both human and nonhuman) and hence more ethical behavior with respect both to other humans and toward the environments in which we live.

But, someone may object, this talk of deep perception of significant form in accord with Bell's metaphysical hypothesis (interpreted in a nontheistic way, as I do) overemphasizes the extraordinary, and this is precisely what many everyday aestheticians (not myself) wanted to get away from as tying the field too closely to fine art aesthetics. On my view, everyday aesthetics, as all aesthetics, exists on a continuum. It is the continuum that resolves the problem or dilemma of everyday aesthetics.

Experiencing the Ordinary in an Ordinary Way

Should we then focus on "everyday life ordinarily experienced"? Should we, as Carlson argues, come to "grip with the aesthetic appreciation of truly ordinary stuff experienced in a truly ordinary way"?[24] I would like to ask some questions here that have their roots in Marx. What if the way we experience truly ordinary stuff in a truly ordinary way is the product of conditions of alienation produced in a capitalist system? What if the oppression we sometimes feel from the ordinariness of ordinary life is a function of late capitalism? What if liberation from capitalist oppression was a matter of overcoming ordinary ways of perception? Consider Herbert Marcuse's way of looking at the poetry of Mallarmé in *The Aesthetic Dimension*. There, he says that Mallarmé's poems "conjure up modes of perception, imagination, gestures—a feast of sensuousness which shatters everyday experience and anticipates a different reality principle."[25] What of an everyday aesthetics that stresses the shattering of everyday experience? Some may reply that shattering everyday experience is precisely what we do not want in everyday aesthetics and that when poetry, for example of Mallarmé, does this, it takes us away from everyday life. But, again, as Marcuse might say, isn't this just giving in to the capitalist reality principle? If art has "emancipatory value," wouldn't that be clear in the way it frees us from perceiving everyday life under such a principle?

This also relates to the issue of how to define everyday aesthetics, since those who would see everyday aesthetics entirely in terms of the ordinariness of the ordinary would argue that I have exceeded the bounds of aesthetics. Interestingly, however, one of these advocates, Kevin Melchionne, offers resources that can provide a transition.[26] Melchionne stresses that the low-level aesthetic phenomena of everyday life should not be seen in terms of individual objects or isolated events but rather in terms of practices and larger daily patterns: it is only then that their pervasiveness comes to be seen as important, perhaps even more important in our lives than the aesthetics of art. He says, "In everyday life, some experiences take on value from the overall practice of daily life, the everyday routines, habits, or practices. Everyday aesthetics is defined more by form than content, in other words, more by the doing than its product."[27] It is not the individual sip of coffee that is important as the aesthetic object in these cases but the regular practice of coffee drinking in the morning, for example, with all of its attendant rituals and multisensory aspects.

My Deweyan Solution to the Dilemma

My own solution to the dilemma is twofold. (1) Drawing from Melchionne, I stress the complex and multilayered nature of the aesthetic object in everyday aesthetics. (2) I stress a notion of continuous range from low-level aesthetics to very powerful, high-level experience. There are extremely low levels of appreciation that might be expressed by phrases such as "looks nice," and "sounds OK," and higher levels of everyday aesthetic experience that may or may not rise to the level of aesthetic experience we get from great art. Such high-level experiences are no longer, strictly speaking, "everyday," and yet they are in response to objects we experience every day, and they are intensified experiences of such objects. As an illustration of this, imagine the way that Cézanne experienced the mountains he was painting as he was painting them. On my view, then, a theory of gradations can at least partly resolve the dilemma.

By contrast, over-concern for the ordinariness of the ordinary may lead us to overstress or be too easily satisfied by the merely humdrum or what Dewey called "inchoate" experience, which is not aesthetic at all. If everyday aesthetic experience is just reduced to everyday humdrum experience, for example, of a worker in an assembly-line factory, the kind that generates frequent suicides in China these days, then there ends up being nothing, or at least very little, to appreciate. Let's assume for now that appreciating the everydayness of the everyday is *not* reduced to appreciating that which cannot, in principle, be appreciated. What then?

Ritualization

A possible solution to the problem of humdrum experience, or what the Marxists call alienation, is ritualization (ideally, in combination with social revolution for the Marxist). Actually, this is probably the main solution, practiced along with the creation of art, for as long as humans have been around. Again, as I see it, the dilemma of everyday aesthetics is that for something to be a branch of aesthetics, it must give us aesthetic experience, and yet as soon as everyday phenomena become aesthetic they leave their usual home, the realm of the humdrum or nonaesthetic ordinary. So it seems paradoxical to aesthetically appreciate the everydayness of the everyday. Yet it seems that it is done. For example, the Japanese tea ceremony takes mundane things and aestheticizes them through ritualization.

Resolving the Tension of Everyday Aesthetics 353

Yet, it is often argued, reference to the tea ceremony does not resolve the paradox because it takes tea out of the realm of the ordinary.

But is that so? It is true that the way in which the teacup and the tea are treated in the tea ceremony creates a domain outside the world of "the everyday." Yet after leaving the tea ceremony one looks at the ordinary cup and tea differently. And so, in a way, the tea ceremony does aestheticize the everyday, not just in the ceremony, but the day after. So perhaps ritualization changes the world outside the ritual, bringing things in daily experience a notch up from nonaesthetic or merely low-level aesthetic experience. Moreover, as I have said, drawing from Melchionne, the daily drinking of tea or coffee can itself have a ritual aspect that is conducive to its aestheticization independent of interaction with more formal ritualization of the tea ceremony sort.

There is another approach that might help to resolve the dilemma, an approach that involves ritualization, but in a different way from the tea ceremony, although drawing from a similar source (i.e., Buddhism). Thích Nhất Hạnh, the Buddhist philosopher, calls on us to be mindful in our everyday lives.[28] He thinks that in washing dishes we should wash dishes for the sake of washing dishes, should slow down and notice every moment of washing dishes.[29] Unlike the tea ceremony, he does not turn washing dishes into an art or something artlike, which seems to have been the problem for some theorists with the idea of ritualization as exemplified in the tea ceremony. Washing dishes does become something more like a ritual, however, when done according to the philosophy of Nhất Hạnh. This would be even truer if this happened in a Buddhist monastery and was recognized as part of Buddhist practice.

There is one way where Nhất Hạnh's work does not help, however. One would think that attending to washing dishes would be a matter of attending to the aesthetic properties of this experience, but Nhất Hạnh seldom mentions aesthetic properties. At the same time, it does seem that Buddhists who achieve mindfulness are in fact attending to aesthetic properties (for example, those associated with the act of washing dishes) since they always speak of this practice as attended by joy.

Yet, perhaps the dilemma of everyday aesthetics remains in that if we attend to dishwashing in the ritualized or ritual-like way that Nhất Hạnh suggests, then we will perceive the ordinary as something extraordinary, and this would take it out of its ordinariness, out of the everyday as everyday. The resolution of the dilemma may simply be that we then realize that this is just how the ordinary *should* be seen, or more generally, experienced. The ordinariness of the ordinary would not be seen in its dull or boring aesthetic nature if social and cultural changes were made, ones that would change both the phenomena and the way we perceived them. These phenomena would not be seen as dull in a better society than ours. The Buddhist point, then, would be similar to Marx's and Dewey's that we need radical cultural change that would make everyday experience itself radically different.

In ritualization, ordinary acts are performed in ways that make them into rituals or ritual-like; for example, tea drinking becomes ritualized in the tea ceremony. Carlson says, "since the point of aestheticization processes such as [ritualization] . . . is to raise the events, activities and objects of everyday life above the humdrum of day-to-day existence, they do not resolve the dilemma of everyday aesthetics" since they do not focus on appreciating the everydayness of the everyday. My thought, however, is that these activities of ritualization reflect, on an intensified plane, what we actually do on a much smaller scale when we appreciate everyday aesthetic phenomena: for example, if we truly attend to drinking tea we treat the experience more like art in that art is treated as something that is primarily an object of contemplation. If we truly attend to drinking tea in an everyday context we also turn that experience into something like a ritual, something closer to the way we attend to tea in an actual ritualized context such as a tea ceremony, and this is why, after attending a tea ceremony, one does in fact attend to drinking ordinary tea in a different way. Moreover, the dilemma of everyday aesthetics is precisely that in the very experiencing of something everyday as aesthetic it is necessarily raised above the humdrum so that the notion of appreciating the everydayness of the everyday is paradoxical if not impossible: what is intensified can no longer be humdrum! At best, we can act *as if* we are appreciating the everydayness of the everyday, or we can make reference to it, as in the case of Rucha and the gas stations. Attending to these ordinary things (for example, when the artist snaps the picture in front of the gas station), even when their ordinariness is referenced, has the effect of moving them out of the ordinary realm. The very act of paying attention to the humdrum transforms it.

Carlson praises Sherri Irvin for her approach to the everyday when she says that even in a tedious department meeting one can observe that "there is a texture of experience in those moments that is possible to appreciate aesthetically, to gain a real satisfaction from."[30] He thinks that Irvin avoids "the temptation to see such moments as special or extraordinary" to which he suggests that I and others succumb. He may be right to some extent: "real satisfaction" is not quite the same as experiencing something extraordinary or experiencing something as extraordinary. Not all aesthetic experiences of the everyday are extraordinary.

However, whereas Carlson associates the term *extraordinary* with great art and magnificent nature, for he says the dilemma of everyday aesthetics is "the worry that when we turn our aesthetic appreciation away from that which is in itself special and extraordinary, such as great art and magnificent nature, and toward that which is truly ordinary in itself . . . then there is nothing to motivate . . . aesthetic experience,"[31] my use of it is intended to be more in tune with the idea of taking something out of the ordinary, as when, for example, an artist perceives a landscape aesthetically while working on a painting of that landscape. The artist is not required to perceive the landscape as though it were itself great art or magnificent nature, not extraordinary in that sense.

The issue is deeper than semantics, however. Although Irvin does not experience the meeting as extraordinary (as like great art or magnificent nature in Carlson's sense), neither is she experiencing real satisfaction in the tedious nature of the department meeting. What is tedious is tedious. What Irwin is doing is detaching herself somewhat from ordinary experience so as to see it in a radically different way. Perhaps what has happened is not extraordinary, but it *is* nonordinary. Most of us do not ordinarily have Irvin's skill of transforming a tedious department meeting into something aesthetic. So I do not think that Irvin is encouraging an aesthetics of everyday life ordinarily experienced but rather an aesthetics of everyday life nonordinarily experienced. Actually, what she is encouraging is very much like what Thich Nhất Hạnh encourages us to do in his philosophy of mindfulness (except that, as I mentioned above, Nhất Hạnh does not recognize that his focus is on aesthetic qualities).

Perhaps one way this issue could be resolved would be to say that we do not ordinarily experience the everydayness of the everyday in the way it should be, and that to do so would be to experience it in the way the Buddhist adept does, or in the way that Irvin has described, which is really quite a nonordinary way of experiencing things.

Concluding Note

The contemporary movement of everyday aesthetics has long been known as deeply inspired by the work of John Dewey. In this respect it falls within the domain of American Philosophy. Perhaps the central area of contention within everyday aesthetics today surrounds what is called the dilemma of everyday aesthetics. Dewey, who always stressed continuity between realms of the spirit and the activities of the live creature interacting with its environment, can lead the way in answering the dilemma. The solution is as follows: (1) everyday practices, when aesthetic, should be understood holistically: we should not look to the sip of coffee for the aesthetic object but to a network of possibly ritualized actions (following Melchionne); (2) we need to recognize a graded series of aesthetic phenomena starting with very low-level aesthetic experience and moving up from there to what Dewey called "*an* experience," of which a gourmet meal at a fine restaurant might be an example, as also a profound experience of a great work of art; and (3) we need to see these grades as involving dynamic relations between the practices of art, including both art making and art appreciation (including fine, popular, and decorative arts) and perceptual engagement with the everyday environment. Moving away from the humdrum ordinary is not a dilemma but an advancement. Finally, we need to see all of this in terms of the need for changes in social structures and manners of perceiving that would be more conducive to human happiness.

Notes

1. Yuriko Saito, *Everyday Aesthetics* (New York: Oxford University Press, 2007). See especially "Conclusion," 243–52. See also, Allen Carlson, "The Dilemma of Everyday Aesthetics," in *Aesthetics of Everyday Life: East and West*, ed. Liu Yuedi and Curtis L. Carter (Newcastle upon Tyne: Cambridge Scholars Publishing, 2014). The dilemma of everyday aesthetics is discussed, using the term *tension* (which is also used by Saito), in Paisley Livingston, "New Directions in Aesthetics," in *The Bloomsbury Companion to Aesthetics*, ed. Anna Christian Ribeiro (London: Bloomsbury, 2015), 255–67.

2. Thomas Leddy, "The Nature of Everyday Aesthetics," in *The Aesthetics of Everyday Life*, ed. Andrew Light and Jonathan M. Smith (New York: Columbia University Press, 2005).

3. Livingston, "New Directions," 262.

4. Ibid., 263–64.

5. See Pauliina Rautio, "On Hanging Laundry: The Place of Beauty in Managing Everyday Life," *Contemporary Aesthetics* (2009); http://www.contempaesthetics.org/newvolume/pages/article.php?articleID=535.

6. Thanks to Walter Gulick for this idea and for other helpful comments on this paper.

7. See my own explanation of "*an* experience" in Thomas Leddy, "Dewey's Aesthetics," *Stanford Encyclopedia of Philosophy*, 2.3 (2016): https://plato.stanford.edu/entries/dewey-aesthetics/. For the Deweyan approach to everyday aesthetics see also Kalle Puolakka who has been a strong defender: "The Aesthetic Pulse of the Everyday: Defending Dewey," *Contemporary Aesthetics* 13 (2015); "Dewey and Everyday Aesthetics—A New Look," *Contemporary Aesthetics* 12 (2014); and "Getting Rid of Bad Habits: The Proper Role of Imagination in Everyday Aesthetics," *Aesthetic Pathways* 1, no. 2 (2011): 47–64.

8. F. Scott Fitzgerald, *The Great Gatsby* (New York: Scribner's, 2004), 92.

9. My own contribution to this question may be found here: "Experience of Awe: An Expansive Approach to Everyday Aesthetics," *Contemporary Aesthetics* 13 (2015); http://www.contempaesthetics.org/newvolume/pages/article.php?articleID=727.

10. I have had something to say about that in "Everyday Aesthetics and Happiness," in *Aesthetics of Everyday Life: West and East* ed. Liu Yuedi and Curtis Carter (Newcastle upon Tyne: Cambridge Scholars Press, 2014).

11. I probably wouldn't choose the way feeling factors shape decision making as the core of aesthetic experience, but I can work with this definition.

12. John Dewey, *Art as Experience* (New York: Perigee, 2005), 195.

13. The quotations on this page are Dewey, *Art as Experience*, 15, 21, 23, 78, 113, 124, and 162.

14. Clive Bell, *Art* (New York: Capricorn Books, 1958).

15. Li Zehou, *The Path of Beauty: A Study of Chinese Aesthetics*, trans. Gong Lizeng (Beijing: Morning Glory Publishers, 1988). For an excellent overview of Li's thought, see Ban Wang, "Aesthetics in Contemporary China," *The Encyclopedia of Aesthetics*, 2nd ed., ed. Michael Kelly (New York: Oxford University Press, 2014) [the electronic copy I am using has no pagination].

16. Bell, *Art*, 19–27; chapter titled "The Metaphysical Hypothesis."

17. Ibid., 20.

18. Carlson, "The Dilemma," 53.

19. Ibid.

20. Bell, *Art*, 44.

21. Ibid., 45.

22. Ibid., 46.

23. In reading an earlier draft of this paper, Walter Gulick has suggested that rather than use "disinterestedness" we should speak of a switch of interest "in aesthetic engagement with an object from its instrumental usefulness to appreciation of its intrinsic value." I am happy with that. Kant did not mean by

"disinterested" that we are uninterested in the aesthetic value but rather that we approach it by bracketing our practical, cognitive and moral interest.

24. Carlson, "The Dilemma," 46.

25. Herbert Marcuse, *The Aesthetic Dimension: Toward a Critique of Marxist Aesthetics* (Boston: Beacon Press, 1978).

26. Kevin Melchionne, in "The Point of Everyday Aesthetics," *Contemporary Aesthetics* 12 (2014), and in "The Definition of Everyday Aesthetics," *Contemporary Aesthetics* 11 (2013), takes an ordinarist position and yet provides the basis for the argument I am providing here.

27. Melchionne, "The Definition," n.p.

28. Thich Nhất Hạnh, *The Miracle of Mindfulness: An Introduction to the Practice of Meditation* (Boston: Beacon Press, 1999). I am told by Buddhists that this is a mere popularization. However, I am more concerned with how his work can contribute to the current discussion.

29. Ibid., 3–4.

30. Sherri Irvin, "Scratching an Itch," *Journal of Aesthetics and Art Criticism* 66 (2008): 25–35, and "The Pervasiveness of the Aesthetics in Ordinary Experience," *British Journal of Aesthetics* 48 (2008): 33–44.

31. Carlson, "The Dilemma," 63.

19

The Struggle for Centering Things in an Age of Consumption

David Strong

My father just decided it was going to be a cello. So he brought one home. The moment I saw the instrument, and I was about seven or eight . . . I knew that this was my destiny. I had an immediate love for the size of the instrument and the sound of the instrument. I still feel the same way. I look at my Stradivari cello, I put it in the corner, and I love it as I did when I viewed the little factory-made cello for the first time.

—The Beaux Arts Trio's Bernard Greenhouse

I fell in love at thirty-five miles per hour. At the age of three, I shared the backseat of a Toyota with a cello belonging to a local musician. I had just heard its exquisite tone in concert, and sitting next to the shapely beauty nearly sent my heart into palpitations. I was certain the feeling was mutual and lost no time in begging for a cello of my own. Instead, my parents, who worried that I might grow discouraged if I started so young, bestowed on me a small parade of temporary instruments by route of Christmas and birthday gifts: a hand drum, a recorder, an egg-shaker, a plastic violin that produced the first fifteen notes of "Ode to Joy," and a xylophone. I was undeterred. "You keep getting me these things," I told them, "but you know what I really want is a cello."

—Rebeca, my daughter, from an essay

Introduction

Technological culture, seen through the lens of Albert Borgmann's philosophy of technology, poses a threat to centering things, things vital to the focus and thriving of our lives. These robust things are being displaced by devices procuring shallow commodities. Centering things will continue to have less and less of a say in our lives as we march mindlessly toward maximum technology, *unless* we change our basic orientation in the world. I analyze and evaluate this threat in terms of the aesthetic attraction of these centering things balanced against the lesser aesthetic attraction of mainstream technological development. I point out that there is a growing awareness of resulting aesthetic loss, and, at the same time, an intuition that the thriving of these centering things is co-destinate with the thriving of our lives. Listening and responding to the appeal of centering things, personally and socially, can be transformative for this needed cultural reorientation. Rescuing centering things, we may just discover, is simultaneously rescuing ourselves.

Dewey's thought has widened our appreciation of the aesthetic dimension far beyond topics limited to beauty or the sublime, as Walter Gulick explains in the Introduction. I will address these aesthetic dimensions later, but first I want to remind readers that the American philosophical and cultural traditions include many who are committed to the value of centering things. Think of Emerson, Thoreau, and Melville, and the regard of the latter two for Walden Pond and Ishmael's "all paths lead to water." Often these centering things are beautiful natural things, especially as William Faulkner's Bear, Ed Abbey's Delicate Arch, and Gary Snyder's San Juan Ridge come to mind. But centering things are more inclusive than natural things alone. Henry Bugbee's *The Inward Morning* (1999), with its wilderness theme and leaping trout, is the most philosophically astute bearer of this tradition, but its centering things are not limited to natural things, so that even ships, racing shells, bells, and towns are loved. Wendell Berry reflects on his farm; Jane Jacobs on cities. Hubert Dreyfus and Sean Kelly's *All Shining Things* (2011) is an outstanding recent academic contribution to this tradition, but that book rarely mentions natural things. In *Zen and the Art of Motorcycle Maintenance* (1974), Robert Pirsig attempts to use an artifact, a motorcycle, as a basis for weaving together a romantic desire for surface beauty with a classical concern for structure and depth. Without this intimate interweaving of the romantic and classic, much of the stuff of our surroundings, he argues, remains superficially glamorous and deeply ugly. Greenhouse's remarks above about his cello really fall into this American tradition, and one can imagine a book entitled *The Cello* written in a genre consistent with *Walden*. Not all of these centering things may be beautiful, but they all must have a life-enriching attraction, at least for their practitioners.

Aesthetic Commodification and Aesthetic Loss

In *Technology and the Character of Contemporary Life* (1984), German-born American philosopher Albert Borgmann argues that modern technology typically follows a consequential pattern. Traditional "things" are replaced by sophisticated "devices" that make a "commodity" "available." Traditional things, such as hearths and wood stoves, are replaced by a central heating system that makes warmth available in a way that is safe, ubiquitous, instantaneous, and easy. In short, the device makes a commodity available in ways that relieve us of burdens. With increased sophistication, a commodity that relieves us of nearly all burdens is truly "available" in a free-floating way. Why we believe that maximizing disburdened availability is such an unquestionable ideal has to do with the kind of expectations and unquestionable successes of technology first foreseen by Descartes and Bacon. The coming age, the modern age, would use science instrumentally, Descartes speculates, to dominate nature and reality generally for the purposes of ridding humans of all the scourges of humanity, all misery and toil. Such disburdenment also promised to make all the goods of the Earth available in this manner to us so as to enrich our lives, make us prosperous. They looked to modern technology as promising a good life. This quest for and expectation of freedom and happiness Borgmann calls "the promise of technology" (35–40). To this day, in modified forms, we are typically still under its sway.

This general "pattern" of replacing traditional things with devices Borgmann calls "the device paradigm" or "the availability paradigm" (40–48). More generally, he shows that it is the basic framework that informs the way we take up with our lives. Following its blueprint has led to the most massive transformation of the planet and, inadvertently, the atmosphere in human history. Likewise, it has led to the most radical transformation of the human condition. And since our lives are shaped in turn by what we shape, this physical commodification of our lived environment is consequential for the way we live, transforming us from active and communally engaged performers into passive, isolated, and enervated consumers.

Indisputably, technology has had a large measure of success in increasing the basic levels of our personal freedom and prosperity. We are freed up for pursuing things that call out to us, like Greenhouse's cello did, and we have better access to education and culture through modern technology. It is really the consequences of hypertrophic developments of advanced technology that raise serious questions with technology.

The term "centering thing" is Borgmann's, to describe what he also calls "focal things and practices." Things in general gather; tools as things, such as axes, make claims on effort and skill. However, some things are more central. Centering things are those things that meaningfully influence what we devote ourselves to: the cello, the dining table, the mountain range, the running path, the trout stream, the tennis court. Centering things reconnect lived nature, tradition, practice, and community into meaningful wholes, in contrast to the distraction and diversion caused by consumption as an ideal. Thus, centering things are the things that raise the most pertinent questions about the device-approach.

We can begin to detect the device's negative and far-reaching consequences when we reconsider the hearth, not as reduced to a heater—a crude device—but as a centering thing. The point of this example is not to return us to a no longer feasible past, a nostalgic rural romanticism, but to illustrate the meaning of what has been lost through our unthinking allegiance to "progress." As a centering thing, the hearth gathers. Etymologically, "thing" means "to gather," as Heidegger points out.[1] Hearth, in Greek, means "focus." The hearth as a thing has many functions and ends; it (1) gathers a multidimensional context or world and (2) engages humans on multiple levels.

(1) The hearth sends people out to fetch wood, thereby disclosing the *local* world of the surrounding countryside in a fresh way. The *natural* world in a more general sense is gathered through the hearth's attunement to the rhythms of the day and night and the seasons. The *cultural* world of tradition, of divinities, births, funerals, and everyday celebrations is gathered by the hearth, for instance, as a place for the cross.

(2) Beyond these ties to its setting, the hearth also engages humans in multiple ways. It is not just a matter of feeling warmth. The warmth even feels different. One also sees, hears, and smells the fire and the pine. One has to move one's body to fetch wood, and one has to learn the skills of fire building and chopping wood. Different tasks are assigned to different

members of the household, thereby providing a center of social interaction and learning. Home is where the hearth is. So the "thing" engages our attention, the full range of our senses, the motility of the body and its skillful depths, and engages us socially. Unlike the commodified warmth provided by central heating, the hearth can have a deeply *felt presence* since it embodies and concentrates so many ties to ourselves and the world. As Heraclitus suggests, "Here, too, the gods dwell." The richness of things that corresponds to all these ties to the world and our engagement with it I call the *powers of the thing*.

A centering thing can be character-forming. Learning to play a cello also brings us into contact with teachers, other musicians, cello makers, and so on. Not just personal or family things, but public or communal things, such as concert halls, theaters, baseball parks, and farmer's markets gather together diverse face-to-face members of actual communities. Thus, when a thing is replaced by a device, a multidimensional world is lost and our bonds of engagement on multilevels are displaced. The machinery of the device takes these over. The furnace provides us with burden-free, trouble-free warmth in every corner of the house. A moment's reflection will show us that this transformation is not always bad, as in the case of the hearth for most, but the account above should also make us both wonder whether some things are worth the trouble and wonder about the consequences of saturating a life with commodities. If we are disturbed by the loss involved when things are replaced by devices, then we must at least be concerned to preserve some things or introduce new things when things like the hearth are displaced.

We can consider this loss in several ways. First, however, it is important to point out, because so much of technology is about reshaping material arrangements, that these powers of things are real and not reducible to the psychological. Mere furnace warmth simply cannot be engaged by us in the same way the hearth can. Nor can an electronic gadget be performed as a cello can. Yes, there may be exceptions, but typically devices invite most of us most of the time straightforwardly to consume them. Devices pattern our behavior. So there is an important material and real difference between the physical structure of devices and the physical structures of things. Devices are materially divided between unfamiliar machinery and familiar commodities, between unfamiliar depths and familiar surfaces.[2] Things interweave means and ends, and we, especially as practitioners, become familiar and intimate with both the features of the thing and its world.

Reflecting on the theme of loss in Wendell Berry's writing, Paul B. Thompson speaks of this transformation of things to commodifying devices in family farming practices as an "ontological loss." Borgmann speaks of this transformation in *Real American Ethics* as a "moral commodification"[3] since it is propelled by a promised liberty and prosperity that is "extended as a promise of the good life" and since "there are *always* moral losses in any kind of moral commodification," even if "the moral gains *unquestionably* outweigh the losses"[4] in constructive applications.

Turning now to my concern with aesthetics and following Thompson and Borgmann, I will use the terms "aesthetic loss" and "aesthetic commodification" to connote the consequences for aesthetics that this transformation of things to devices has had. Following Gulick's description of the broad scope of aesthetic experience in the Introduction, I will consider this problematic impact in relation to (1) what we popularly find attractive, (2) Deweyan concerns with process, and (3) our dominant aesthetic-commodification orientation. Later, in the next section, our overall positive sense of the felt-presence of things will be presented.

(1) Aesthetic commodification lures us. The attractive appeal of technology, its aesthetic appeal, can be divided between the aesthetic experience of disburdenment and the aesthetic experience of device-enrichment. In regard to the former, whenever we find we are freed up from something—the claims of things—there is a certain wow factor or cachet, at least for a time. Flip phones can be embarrassing to their owners when so many more are "with it" with the latest rendition of smartphones. Historically, burden-relieving availability scores well in terms of relieving humans from suffering, pain, and any discomfort. Houses became cleaner, more sanitary, and filled with more light when woodstoves went out the door and lighting systems, vacuum cleaners, and chemical cleaners came inside. Much of the mud, dirt, and hair of existence could be scrubbed clean. More generally, we find attractive something that is less time-consuming, takes less skill and effort and patience, something that promises to be the easy way. Most of us find unquestionably attractive something with guaranteed results, something less risky and safer, something that we don't have to go out of our way for, or something that is low maintenance. So the classical utilitarian standard of pure pleasure unmixed with pain becomes guiding. For this convenient and comfortable commodious character of commodities to be realized, they must be context-free, "free-floating."

More positively, following an aesthetic of device-enrichment, we are excited and moved by discovering something that is now available—by all the wonderful pleasures of advanced technology—places to travel, foods to eat, movies to watch, games to play, and answers to questions we have. Technology makes available the world's greatest art collections and allows us to inspect each of these paintings in ways that would be impossible without advanced technology. We are wowed when technology provides enhanced stimulation, with more vivid colors, intense flavors, perfected performances, higher density, larger screens, and so on.

What are the initial negative outcomes from this basic aesthetic, cultural orientation of the device paradigm? Entrepreneurs and advertisers are especially good at attuning themselves to, mining, and creating, in a secondary sense, (inventing "burdens," for instance) the aesthetic of disburdenment and aesthetic device-enrichment. These features sell well, and devices work well at securing their advertised features. Thus, Borgmann argues that advertising in our culture has replaced art in its traditional (Heideggerian) orienting role.

> [Advertising] has superseded art as the archetypal presentation of what the epoch is about. In advertising, the promise of technology is presented both purely and concretely and hence most attractively. Thus we find ourselves archetypically defined in advertisements. They provide a stabilizing and orienting force in the complexity of the still-developing technological society.[5]

Whatever can be done alone, without depending on or involving others, is less of a hassle. So privacy is of value in the aesthetic of disburdenment. Privacy of the home becomes the center of consumption. "In order to put all these consumable treasures of my home within easy reach, the public realm favors utility—transportation links and shopping facilities along with the utilities to support them."[6] Much in public space outside the home speaks of a reduction to utility, not beauty. Accordingly, in *Suburban Nation*, authors Andres Duany, Elizabeth Plater-Zyberk, and Jeff Speck characterize sprawl in terms of its aesthetic loss as felt-experience:

> [F]or the past fifty years, we Americans have been building a national landscape that is largely devoid of places worth caring about. Soulless subdivisions, residential "communities" utterly

> lacking in communal life; strip shopping centers, "big-box" chain stores, and artificially festive malls set within barren seas of parking. . . . Each year, we construct the equivalent of many cities, but the pieces don't add up to anything memorable or of lasting value. The result doesn't look like a place, it doesn't act like a place, and, perhaps more significant, it doesn't *feel* like a place. Rather, it feels like what it is: an uncoordinated agglomeration of standardized single-use zones with little pedestrian life and even less civic identification, connected only by an overtaxed network of roadways.[7]

Rather than beauty, a large measure of ugliness has followed in the wake of sprawl whose design itself is a device: single-use functions of its zoned components of residential, shopping centers, business offices, schools and churches, and "automotive sewers."[8] Cars as transportation devices take us from one zoned area to another, from home, to jobs, to the strip mall. Remote-controlled garage doors face a traffic-functional street without sidewalks. The home itself is tilted toward the entertainment center—or centers, since interior designs encourage separation more than togetherness.

Our access to the riches of the world has another consequence for place, family, and community. The world's most beautiful people, things, landscapes, beaches, and cities are at our fingertips via a visual world travel service. With these attractions accessible, we should be able to transcend the provincial and local. However, Arthur Boers, following E. B. White, argues that television, affixing us to screens, insulates us from our experience of place, and, importantly, "it diminishes the importance of where one is while accentuating priority of distant locations. Gradually, we find ourselves compelled and convicted that important, vivid, and robust realities and priorities are elsewhere."[9] The remarkable things in and of our own locales go unacknowledged and neglected, and, accordingly, we allow our own locales to deteriorate. "Perhaps it is not surprising that many find it hard to pay attention closer to home. A lot of local settings have become uniformly bland and, alas, even ugly."[10] We can always retreat to virtual reality. So, too, most of us do not feel challenged to develop or maintain our bodies in the excellent physical condition of the strong and agile athletes we watch.

(2) Such reduction and aesthetic loss would not be bad if the aesthetic gains involved with aesthetic commodification always outweighed those

losses. But aesthetic commodification involves a separation of ends from means that should make us cautious. In *Art as Experience* (1980), Dewey, most of all, would be wary of such a separation of process from product, especially when it comes to our aesthetic relations. "Having an experience," whether dominantly emotional, intellectual, or practical, involves the live creature in a *process* that grows from a beginning, includes a middle, and culminates in a consummatory closure. If the experience is truly "an experience," it brings us out of ourselves to take in our surroundings perceptively—an event that goes beyond the mere habitual noting of recognition. For that to happen, the way we come at our situation cannot be simply a single-minded, routine, or mechanical way of aiming at some end-product, or, alternatively, a passive and distracted way of merely consuming experiences. Rather, for "an experience" to form there must be a balance of doing actively and undergoing receptively so that intelligent and emotional adaption takes place throughout the experience. There is a continuing process of interaction and adjustment between ourselves and our environing circumstances. Intelligence flares and emotions are felt because one must come to terms with what is happening, what one is undergoing. One is trying to make some, perhaps narrative, sense of it as a whole to see how the various components fit together in that whole. Dewey's notion captures well the kind of aggressive, heedless mechanistic side of production *and* the distracted, aimless side of passive consumption.

> Unbalance on either side blurs the perception of relations and leaves the experience partial and distorted, with scant or false meaning. Zeal for doing, lust for action, leaves many a person, especially in this hurried and impatient human environment in which we live, with experience of an almost incredible paucity, all on the surface. No one experience has a chance to complete itself because something else is entered upon so speedily. What is called experience becomes so dispersed and miscellaneous as hardly to deserve the name. Resistance is treated as an obstruction to beat down, not as an invitation to reflection. An individual comes to seek, unconsciously even more than by deliberate choice, situations in which he can do the most things in the shortest time.
>
>   Experiences are also cut short from maturing by excess of receptivity. What is prized is then the mere undergoing of this and that, irrespective of perception of any meaning. The

crowding together of as many impressions as possible is thought to be "life," even though no one of them is more than a flitting and a sipping. . . . [N]othing takes root in mind when there is no balance between doing and receiving.[11]

The difference here between "coming at" our situation full of expectation and "being with and responsive to" our situation is the difference between deadness and aliveness. The result is ugliness or something unaesthetic that leaves us cold. As a consumer, I am detached from process; machinery mechanically provides the result. Thus, the overuse of devices in our lives may make us liable to a significant aesthetic loss and loss of meaning.

(3) The gravest losses result from listening *exclusively* to this technological aesthetic of freedom and prosperity as more and more of our lives become ensconced in the technological framework. How do we use our leisure time, for instance? Notwithstanding the screen time we now spend in front of monitors, tablets, and smartphones, television by itself is the way Americans spend 53% of their leisure time, nearly three hours daily (American Time Use Survey 2017). This amounts to more than eight years of our waking lifetime. Such lives are hardly vivid and thriving. Instead of active and communally engaged performers, we have become obese, lazy, and self-centered.

Many of us are busy and feel we feel have no time for positive engagements. Things become crowded out of our lives. Part of this busyness has to do directly with the affluent lifestyle we seek: there are so many opportunities to spend money—just look at the advertisements—we seek the money by working more. Part of our attraction to television and other forms of passive consumption originates when we come home from our workplace feeling too tired to do anything that requires energy. So drained, television becomes the easy alternative. Then, too, whenever we make room for another gadget, such as a smartphone, something else has to give.[12] Some people feel pressured to accomplish more because they are surrounded by so many opportunities for greater accomplishment.[13] But what is the arena of opportunities for accomplishment typically? The creation and support of centering things, such as public parks and live music? That more people are making these kinds of choices is a welcome sign. But the hyperactive individuals Boers is speaking of more often sacrifice themselves, their families, friends, and the obligations of their local communities for the workplace. The pressure to accomplish means working very hard to contribute ultimately to extending the paradigm of availability, to making life generally more convenient and comfortable. Through smartphones, the workplace is extended to all areas of one's life, 24/7. Ironically, this makes the hyperactive individual commodiously available, on call whenever, wherever.[14]

The workplace itself, in order to become more productive of these commodities, has become saturated with so many devices the workers themselves are either eliminated or so many processes become eliminated or simplified that the work becomes unchallenging. Work is degraded to labor; it becomes, like the machinery of the device, a mere means to a paycheck. When the engaging processes of work are eliminated, the aesthetic appeal of work is eliminated as well. Fatigue rather than invigoration follows.

Public things are displaced from our public lives, too. As Dewey writes in *The Public & Its Problem*, "The increase in the number, variety, and cheapness of amusement represents a powerful diversion from political concern."[15] Not only has much of the public space become degraded to mere utility, it becomes less and less intelligible to persons seeking commodities why their tax dollars, dollars that they would be spending in the pursuit of private happiness otherwise, should go toward the support of public cultural things, such as theaters, concert halls, or orchestras. Fewer people get out of their houses to attend and less public monetary support is granted. The *habitat* of public things shrinks, and most talented musicians, actors, etc.—those not as gifted or fortunate as Bernard Greenhouse—are forced to find other ways of making a living.

What is questionable is what I call *maximum technology*. Maximum technology occurs when the good life is reduced to life filled with commodities, no matter how frivolous, that are available at our disposal without imposing burdens on us. It is in regard to maximum technology—the promise that technology will go beyond relieving us of genuine burdens to make us substantively happy, to still the exigency of being within us—that we need to question technology.

Not for all, but for most of us much of the time, our compasses are caught by the lure of this promise and that has made us heedless. Modern technology affords humans great power, a power to overpower, "beat down" in Dewey's words, many of the resistances of reality. With the advent of the steam engine, we had a power, unlike water wheels or windmills, to disregard the seasons, day or night, and local conditions. We became environmentally independent 24/7. As demanding consumers, we want what we want whenever we want it, wherever we are. Spellbound and single-minded, we become heedless individuals, acting in callous disregard of other people, community, the environment—or the aesthetic appeal of centering things. Splendid things are perishing, unheeded.

When centering things are displaced, our lives become troubled. We become worldless, lonely, and detached from the claims of things. Under the spell of the aesthetic commodification's attractions our ontic personal lives become unfocused, diverted, and distracted, while we retain ontologically a focus on consumption as a way of life. So it is not this or that device that is troublesome, but what is really troublesome is the generalized transformation of our setting from things to devices *and* our common expectation that aesthetic commodification is the way to take up with all reality. A crisis of meaning just might make us willing to listen to the appeal of things again. To complete our understanding of the aesthetic loss involved in aesthetic commodification, we need to see it in the light of these endangered things.

The Aesthetic Appeal of Centering Things

Philosophers have overlooked the significance of centering things. Dewey, for instance, correctly draws our attention to processes and events, such as having an experience, but it must also be stressed that events are always tied to things.[16] The performance event is tied to practicing the cello. The focused-life of the living creature, the organism, requires focal things, centering things, especially in our circumstances where the scattering forces of distraction have become so geometrically amplified.

Centering things appeal to us, if we would heed them, and many of them are beautiful. Plato's Diotima was correct to make beauty a kind of divinity, a kind of prime mover that attracts, makes us wonder, calls, draws, and beckons to us from afar. Diotima was mistaken to dislocate beauty from the world, to separate beauty from particular things and events; she was also mistaken to make beauty so self-sufficient that it stands independently of the person it attracts; and she was mistaken to overemphasize the role of Eros in pointing us toward beauty. Fundamentally, Eros is not a flashlight in search of beauty; rather, we first and foremost find ourselves in an evocative relation—called, drawn to, claimed by the really beautiful. Centering things, such as cellos, won't let us alone, although we may have to be re-minded of them. We can fail to heed them, but not without paying a price, not without being hauntingly troubled. Centering things appeal to us, change the course of our lives, and orient us in the world. Because of them, we discover the selves we did not know we were.

Borgmann points out that the things that matter, focal or centering things, have a "commanding presence, continuity with the world, and centering power"[17] The contrast term to commanding presence is the "disposability" or "commodious" character of commodities that are available to us without troubling us in any way—the draw of the aesthetic of disburdenment. They merely serve us, *orbiting* around our desires and under our fingertip control. This makes our relationship to them entirely ego-centric. On the other hand, centering things stand forth and challenge us to be equal to or be a match for them, whether the running path, the pottery clay, or the cello. Rather than an egocentric relationship, we, in an important sense, must trouble ourselves to *enter into their orbit* and develop the mastery—skills, sensitivity and knack—for their flourishing; and they in turn generate an understanding in us that they are worth the trouble. So commanding presence means in part their appeal, their aesthetically attractive presence, their standing forth, such as a mountain lake for hikers or a downtown with lively street life for urbanites. This attraction shines best and sometimes exclusively in the presence of excellent practitioners. Thus, commanding presence is also the felt-presence of *pressure*: a demanding presence, demanding human excellence—the effort, endurance, intelligence, mastery, and the extended commitment of a regular "focal practice" to be at our best in order for the centering thing to be at its best. So the commanding presence is a mixture of pregnant appeal and challenging resistance that one must "undergo."[18]

Centering things are relational to human beings, for the beauty of nature or a cello cannot stand alone, self-sufficient, apart from humans. Rather, our relationship with centering things is a *co-animating* one. In performance, the cellist brings to life the wood, strings, and horsehair of the cello and bow, showing what they are capable of. Simultaneously, the cellist, with her native talents and years of dedicated practice, shines as a person through the performance made possible by her love for the cello. So, too, the beauty of nature cannot be revealed apart from its felt-presence by human witnesses who "have an aesthetic experience" in response to it. So both person and thing are enlivened in a relationship I call correlational coexistence. Beautiful things, such as cellos, are *correlational things* (my alternative term for centering things). Correlational coexistence plays midwife to selfhood and to these correlational things.

Conversely, heedless dependence on technology evokes shallow experience on the part of humans. *It is this mutually vital relationship of correlational coexistence that is destroyed when modern technology, pushed mindlessly, becomes maximum technology, for, when centering things are transformed into commodities resting on machinery, the relationship is transformed into one where humans heedlessly overpower everything.* Following the logic outlined by Dewey above, single-minded unaesthetic egocentrism is the result.

While commanding presence shows how correlational things engage humans on multiple levels, just as the hearth did, these things also gather the world in a way that yields a "telling continuity" between the thing and its world. Centering things are embedded in the context of the actual world, unlike free-floating commodities that are made controllable by detaching them from time and place and community—and are thus "discontinuous" with their world. The snow I ski on is continuous with this November's snowfall, with the high-water snow melt of May in the river I fish, with the level of snow in the high peaks that tells me when I can take my first backpack trip this coming summer. And these are continuous with the community of people I share the things and landscape with. As historian Dorothy Hartley illustrates, "A modern woman sees a piece of linen, but the medieval woman saw through it to the flax fields, she smelled the reek of the retting ponds, she felt the hard rasp of the hackling, and she saw the soft sheen of the glossy flax."[19] As material centers, correlational things, then, concentrate and reflect the simple oneness of a complicated web of *lived relations* with the fullness of the nature, community, and traditions. The setting makes possible a coherent, lived and, as we'll see, felt-unity to things, in all their complexity and diversity. Commodities are discontinuous with tradition, nature, and the local. Their accumulation falls closer to clutter, complexity without simplicity as Robert Neville might say.

This splendor of commanding presence and density of world-relations make correlational things powerful. Moreover, as a practitioner, Bernard Greenhouse can see how his childhood beginnings with the factory-built cello expanded into his long apprenticeship under Pablo Casals, his dozen rocky years as a soloist, and the fortuitous formation of the Beaux-Arts Trio. Because they gather all this splendor, density, and life-landscape, things possess *centering powers*. These centering powers are not experienced by us as consummatory much of the time. However, now and then, we experience the kind of grace-filled convergence Borgmann calls "a centering experience": those momentous invigorating events that "overtake us from behind,"[20] as it were, when we can affirm the whole of our lives. These are vividly memorable assurances when we recognize: "This is where I want to be, what I want to be doing, and who I want to be with." Such mature, deep, wholesome, and lasting affirmations of ourselves, our activities, and those dear to us, differ infinitely from the hyped-up glamour, glitz, and short-lived but addictive thrills of so much distracting consumption.

How important is it that we experience the beauty of things in their world? Bill McKibben attests that real beauty, resonant beauty, extends to unblemished acts of perception in this world. Things, such as McKibben's wooden floors that come from the local forest where sustainable forestry is practiced, look "beautiful to the eye, and to the mind's eye, too"[21] because *they come from, unlike Walmart, a world worth caring for and a world that is taken care of*. His neighbor Granstrom's wine will not be world-class, but it will fill a local niche "for people who want the pleasure of tasting it not only on their tongues but in their minds as well, who will appreciate the story that comes with it."[22] As Heidegger writes, the nearby spring "stays" on in its water poured from the jug, and "stills" a thirst—and much more.[23] McKibben attests that this kind of perceiving is satisfying "enough," enough to meet our deep and anxious yearnings as humans. After a winter of eating locally, which cost him in terms of time, effort, and attention, McKibben attests to a fundamental reorientation:

> But the payoff for that cost has been immense, a web of connections I'd never known about. I've gotten to eat with my brain as well as my tongue: every meal comes with a story. The geography of the valley now means something much more real to me; I've met dozens of people I wouldn't otherwise have known. . . . The winter permanently altered the way I eat. In more ways than one, it left a good taste in my mouth. That good taste was *satisfaction*. The time I spent getting the food and preparing it was not, in the end, a cost at all. In the end it was a benefit, *the* benefit. In my role as eater, I was part of something larger than myself that made sense to me—a community. I felt grounded, connected.[24]

As we see here, when our lives orbit things, we make discoveries, we uncover a world. Through this participation we often make the most vital discoveries, revealing the appeal of that world as something deeper, more and other than we originally expected. The world is revealed in its beauty and poetry and deepest truth in such moments of full "immersion."[25] McKibben helped students to create an organic garden to serve Middlebury College one year, a crowning garden that once had been an unnoticeable hill in a cornfield the year before. He speaks of spending the night in the garden on his backpack trip.

> [A couple of the founding students] crawled inside the new garden shed to sleep, and I rolled out my tent and lay in it happily . . . I . . . felt unaccountably happy. To be around young people, who haven't yet made all the compromises and concessions that life will urge them to make, and to see them finding older people who can help them go a different way, is to be reminded that the world really is constantly fresh, and that therefore despair for its prospects is not required.[26]

How important is it that we experience this *resonant* beauty, the beauty resonant with the world of the thing? Thoreau invites this question about Walden's water which he finds to be at least as sacred as the Ganges.[27] The villagers are planning to treat Walden as a reservoir, a water tank, with pipes running to their kitchen faucets. Of course we want indoor plumbing, and of course we want safe tap water. Such water has much utility and is badly needed for many in poverty. But should *all* water be experienced on such utility terms? Should we maximize the utility of water? Aren't we missing the meaning when we never experience Walden Pond itself, never experience wild and sacred water, never experience and reveal water in its watery world? Walking Walden's shore: "This is a delicious evening, when the whole body is one sense, and imbibes delight through every pore. I go and come with a strange liberty in Nature."[28]

Things take us out into the world where we encounter, not the botanist's flowers or the social scientist's statistics, but the hedgerow and the neighbor. We encounter the poet's world of lived relations and named things: the Thoroughfare, Columbine Pass, Sunlight Basin, Rainbow Lakes, the Wind River, Sweetgrass Creek. Humans are world-revealers, but they must be fully immersed in the world in order to reveal the felt-presence of the things encountered in that world. Resonant beauty is rooted in this relationship. Our commerce with things in their world give rise to "having an experience," to lyrical moments, moments that issue into song, poetry, and the epiphanies of prose. It is from these lyrical encounters with things that Van Gogh writes, "The figure of a labourer—some furrows in a plowed field—a bit of sand, sea, and sky—are serious subjects, so difficult, but at same time so beautiful, that it is indeed worthwhile to devote one's life to the task of expressing the poetry hidden in them."[29] Unbalanced consumption removes us from this poetry-generating involvement with things.

Untroubling Ourselves by Troubling Ourselves for Centering Things

The quest for maximum technology is dominant in our time. Most realize how difficult it is to pursue musical performance as a vocation and even an avocation. The emphasis on business and STEM majors and the career opportunities for them is undermining the centering gifts the humanities and fine arts offer. So are we to throw up our hands and go play video games? If my analysis of aesthetic loss is correct, we have brought on a crisis of meaningful living through this headlong pursuit of maximum technology. Acknowledging this crisis creates a clearing for understanding the pattern of technology and its aesthetic loss as the source of this trouble and for becoming permeable to the aesthetic appeal of centering things.

On the positive side, too, there exist countercurrents.[30] McKibben found that "these woods [in the Adirondacks] . . . captured my imagination and taught me, in my 20s, that the suburban life I'd grown up in was not as engaging as life out here."[31] Accordingly, he migrated to those woods. Similar recognitions and life-changes are the hopeful story of many today: they are heeding the centering things of their lives. Many are recognizing the value of performing, not just consuming, music, and the need for live performance.

There is communal recognition, too, that choosing "things" takes one far beyond limited personal choice, connecting the flourishing of centering things with the flourishing of their habitat. Communities, through programs such as "Arts without Boundaries," have improved access for all children to excel in music. These collective efforts are encouraging.

They are not yet sufficient, however, for the kind of changes required to make a real cultural difference. The philosophy of technology insists on further steps, such as design changes in material culture. Summarizing what this crucial step means, Borgmann cites Winston Churchill's remark, "We shape our buildings, and afterwards our buildings shape us."[32] As evidenced by such movements as "Healthy by Design," people are beginning to understand that flourishing habitat demands better design decisions, for instance, about the place and times of using electronic screens in our households, such as whether or not to have a television or where it is placed in the household so that its powerful magnetism of entertainment does not displace the claims of practicing an instrument. This practicing, too, needs to culminate finally in performances in attractive, public places, such as concert halls or streets alive with people.

It makes a difference whether such moves are informed by an explicit *theory of technology,* and it makes a difference whether the people involved with these things can see in light of that philosophy that what they have at stake is not unlike what practitioners of various centering things and practices have at stake, for then there is genuine opportunity for the kind of unified (given the varied plurality of things) collective effort that will broaden the realization in mainstream culture of the need and direction for real change. Like poets yet distinctive, philosophers provide words for the way. An aesthetically attuned philosophy of technology and centering things could assist this dawning renaissance of the attractive lure of things that are worth the time and trouble to nurture.

Notes

1. Martin Heidegger, *Poetry, Language, Thought,* trans. Albert Hofstadter (New York: Harper and Row, 1975), 172.

2. Pirsig, for instance, by failing to see that devices often prevent engagement, makes his reform of technology, synthesizing the romantic and classic attitudes, all too mental and attitudinal (1974).

3. Commodification is commonly understood as economic commodification, when something is taken out of the public or intimate spheres and enters the marketplace as a tradable commodity. For Borgmann, commodification results from the transformation of a thing into a device with its machinery providing a commodity in the free-floating sense of availability. The two kinds of commodification do overlap but are not identical. For a more complete comparison and contrast, see Albert Borgmann, *Real American Ethics* (Chicago: University of Chicago Press, 2006).

4. Ibid., 156.

5. Albert Borgmann, *Technology and the Character of Contemporary Life* (Chicago: University of Chicago Press, 1984), 55.

6. Borgmann, *Real American Ethics,* 7.

7. Andre Duany, Elizabeth Plater-Zyberk, and Jeff Speck, *Suburban Nation* (New York: North Point Press, 2000), x and 12.

8. Ibid., 72.

9. Arthur Boers, *Living into Focus: Choosing What Matters in an Age of Distractions* (Grand Rapids: Brazos Press, 2012), 162.

10. Ibid., 166.

11. John Dewey, *Art as Experience* (New York: J. P. Putnam's Sons, 1980), 44–45.

12. See Nancy Colier's *The Power of Off* (Louisville, CO: Sounds True Publishing, 2016). A recent study in the UK finds, "The average amount of time spent online on a smartphone is 2 hours 28 minutes a day." See press release for "A Decade of Digital Dependence," Communications Marketing Report, Ofcom August 2, 2018; https://www.asiconferences.com/a-decade-of-digital-dependency/; last accessed March 5, 2019.

13. Boers, *Living into Focus*, 147.

14. Colier, *The Power of Off*.

15. John Dewey, *The Public and Its Problems* (Athens: Ohio University Press, 1954 [1927]), 138.

16. Susanne Langer's critique of Dewey presented by Gulick in the Introduction is more in the direction of my position here.

17. Albert Borgmann, *Crossing the Postmodern Divide* (Chicago: University of Chicago Press, 1993), 87; see also 94–95, 119–22.

18. While Peirce and the pragmatist tradition are informative with the sense of "resistance," I find the American tradition of Thoreau and Bugbee far keener on the sense of "appeal."

19. Dorothy Hartley, *Lost Country Life* (New York: Pantheon, 1979), 5.

20. See Bugbee's *The Inward Morning* on this theme.

21. Bill McKibben, *Wandering Home* (New York: Crown, 2005), 28.

22. Ibid., 33.

23. Heidegger, *Poetry*, 172.

24. Bill McKibben, *Deep Economy* (New York: Henry Holt, 2007), 94.

25. See Bugbee.

26. McKibben, *Wandering*, 51.

27. Henry David Thoreau, *The Portable Thoreau*, ed. Carl Bode (New York: Penguin, 1982), 441.

28. Ibid., 380.

29. Vincent Van Gogh, *Dear Theo*, ed. Irving Stone (New York: Doubleday, 1957), 173.

30. See Colier.

31. McKibben, *Wandering*, 133.

32. Borgmann, *Real American Ethics*, 5; see also 175–76.

20

The Dynamics of Selving and the Aesthetics of Ecstatic Naturalism

ROBERT S. CORRINGTON

The Dynamics of the Selving Process

In this section of the anthology, we are writing about the flourishing of life under the proper aesthetic conditions. I have termed this ongoing event the "Selving" process to denote a growing pattern that is tied to a self-corrective developmental teleology of the self-in-process. The concept of Selving is an extrapolation and enrichment of C. G. Jung's concept of "individuation," in which the psyche seeks, and perhaps attains, wholeness. Where the phenomenology of Selving stretches Jung's psychoanalytic account, is in the recognition that such a move toward wholeness can best take place under highly aesthetic conditions in what Josiah Royce calls "the community of interpreters," and what C. S. Peirce calls "the community of inquiry." Here we see how American Idealism and pragmatism each contribute to a theory of a rich and viable community in which Selving can flourish. Using one of Peirce's many semiotic triads, we see here the logic of the sign→object→interpretant correlation. All signs, even internal ones, refer to something other than themselves; namely, to a real object of some kind. This much is clear, certainly after Husserl, but the next stage is the more interesting one in which the sign/object reference relationship in turn generates interpretants (new signs).

Where Peirce, Dewey, and Rank agree (not to forget Santayana), is in placing the aesthetic in the most honorific place when discussing the self-in-process. For Peirce, of course, aesthetics grounds ethics and logic, while for Dewey the experience of a unified aesthetic trait can transform the self/nature transaction. In turning to Rank, we get a more psychoanalytic account of how the aesthetic realms can make a new self and a new culture possible. Peirce and Dewey would, I think, embrace Rank's account even if neither would have much truck with a real unconsciousness as otherness. Later, in the second section we will discuss the even more radical idea of the unconscious of nature, as inspired by Schelling, about whom Peirce remained conflicted.

The Selving process can exist in two types of community—on a continuum. The first is what I call the "natural or inert community," while the second is the above-mentioned "community of interpreters." Where they differ the most is in what they do to interpretants. Note that interpretants serve to enrich our knowledge of the object, in both its immediate and dynamic dimensions. The natural/inert community, governed by patriarchy and perhaps the Führer principle, is frightened by novel or chaotic interpretants and uses internal (propaganda) and external force to flatten them out so that they are rendered harmless to the preestablished interpretants of the patriarchy. Such communities are often prey to populism. They are called "natural/inert" because they are the ubiquitous form of community in nature and they are subject to inertial pressures that don't allow for deviation from a trajectory. The Selving process cannot flourish when life energy and novel interpretants are suppressed. It is only in the free-floating dialectic and dialogue among equals that Selving, and its growing field of interpretants, can enrich communal life. As John Dewey would argue using our language, Selving in its fullest aesthetic sense requires democracy and education to clear away impediments from the wrong kind of social system.

Interpretants are never free-floating, except perhaps in what Peirce calls "interpretive musement," although he is also talking about abduction there. Peirce distinguished between deduction, induction, and abduction, also called "retroduction." Abduction is a form of "guessing" that, like a Kantian transcendental argument, posits a rule for an observed condition. It represents a creative advance of knowledge. In a sense, each interpretant, no matter how novel, must earn its keep in a pragmatic environment and under evolutionary conditions. Thus, novel interpretants do real work, especially, and perhaps only, in a community of interpreters. In a strong sense, the Self *is* its endless chains of interpretants, although, contra deconstruction, it will evolve a reasonably stable contour in the time process. This contour is subject to spoliation and entropy, of course, and often consists in a loosely bound aggregate in which damage to one component can have a kindling effect on others, thus threatening a sense of identity loss. Yet, overall, the Selving process can often right the foundering ship and once again sail forward.

The Selving process is semiotic through and through and is itself rooted in zoosemiotics (of the animal kingdoms). Hence, our anthroposemiotic life is made possible by the prior semiotic systems of animals and their species-specific environments. We can never escape these evolutionary antecedents; nor should we try to do so, as they are the basis for those quick habits and judgments that enabled our species to evolve and survive in the first place. As Peirce noted, too much time spent in deliberation can spell death to the hesitating creature. His eulogization of "critical common sensism" is of a piece with this argument. But the Selving process is more than its known anthroposemiotic systems and aggregates. Peirce has rather conflicting ideas about the unconscious, and his account needs to be augmented by European psychoanalysis if we are to attain a more fulsome picture of the Selving process. Positive values for the Selving process include: increase in horizonal expansion, empathy, the pursuit of the beautiful and the sublime, and the desire to intersect with other meaning horizons.

My account follows the work of Jung and Otto Rank, with far less emphasis on the patriarchal Sigmund Freud. It should be noted that Rank spent much of his career practicing in America after the rise of the Nazi movement and that he absorbed a few American ideas while here.

We start with Jung. Early on, Jung was impressed with the tendency of the Self/psyche to reestablish some harmony after momentary disintegration into part selves; say, in somnambulism. This led him to his belief in later years that there was a Self-archetype deep within what he came to call the "collective unconscious," or "objective psyche." This highest, and deepest, of all the archetypes, was the goal of the Selving process: his individuation. It is often represented by the quaternity: spheres, sacred mandalas, divine figures, and the *imago dei* within. Note that Peirce was strongly drawn to triads and triangles, whereas Jung would find either the dyadic or triadic schemata incomplete. Peirce is at least right that you can't reduce a triad to two dyads. He cites the triadic relation of A gives B to C. This is not reducible and is a perfect example of thirdness (generality). It would be a profoundly interesting process to find fourthness in Peirce, although he argued that such a real or alleged fourth could be reduced to thirds, nor could there be fifthness, sixthness, etc.

The Peirce/Jung correlation is apt. Peirce contributes an astonishingly rich semiotic phenomenology (phaneroscopy), while Jung probes into the depth dimensions of anthroposemiosis. Both theories need each other if the Selving process is to become at least partially unhidden. If the Self traffics in natural and conventional signs and symbols (as a species of the sign→object reference relation, the others being the icon and index), then it must also struggle with those super-loaded symbolic systems known as archetypes. This is so because of the mediating role of the complexes in the personal unconscious, which may contain archetypal cores. The conscious (attending) part of the psyche is always buffeted by internal complexes that have a kind of magnetic attraction, bringing new semiotic daily life experiences into their orbit. Jung perfected, but did not invent, the word association test in the early 1900s to use key words to find unconscious complexes. The tester would read a carefully selected list of around one hundred words to the testee looking for three things: (1) a delay in response in giving the corresponding word, (2) a distortion in the response word, and (3) changes in galvanic skin response. Whenever all three criteria were met, Jung assumed that an unconscious feeling-toned complex had been struck. This takes semiotics to a new level by extending its reach directly into the unconscious. This also takes us at least slightly past Peirce's "skeletal sets" in the "bottomless lake." I would argue that Peirce's panpsychism, which downplayed genuine otherness within the psyche, blocked the path of inquiry in this area.

With Rank, we move more into the correlation of art and the selving process. Rank was the secretary of the Psychoanalytic Society meeting in Freud's apartment for many years and thus was exposed to the entire range of ideas of Freud's disciples. However, he moved strongly away from Freud to take on the task of probing into the more matriarchal aspects of early childhood development. As in later object relations theories, he gave priority to the pre-Oedipal (around age five) castration drama and replaced it with the mother/child relationship and what today would be called "attachment theory." A non-nurturing relation from the mother could scar the child, of either gender, for life. Added to this is his notion of the "birth trauma" that haunted both mother and child throughout their life trajectory. The need to return to a nonliteral womb that shapes everything we say, contrive, or enact is almost overwhelming, and many substitute or "self-objects" (Heinz Kohut) find their way into our lives, but they are never enough. Examples of such substitute objects might include: idealized persons, a tribal affiliation, a sports team, a sacred space, or a work of art. For Rank, then, the birth trauma, which never goes away, calls forth a whole host of ultimately dissatisfying substitute objects that try to imitate the amniotic fluid in the realm of what Tillich called "dreaming innocence."

Thus, for Rank, the artist emerges as the paradigmatic individual who shapes and defines what it means to be fully human. The artist seeks immortality by creating great works of art, which, in turn, reestablishes the cosmic harmony that existed in the prenatal world. Note that he directly ties his theory of artistic production, and its motivations, to the trauma of birth. For, as noted above with object relations theory, one goes through a series of substitute or self-objects to regain the fluidic world before the brutal explosion of space, time, and causality that greets the infant with a kind of booming chaos, as noted by William James. The artist, perhaps the keenest sufferer of all, has an especially strong motivation toward the creation of some form of lasting harmony. This aesthetic drive lies at the very heart of the Selving process and forms its inner telos. I argue, following Darwin, that there is no telos in nature, but I have modified the theory to allow for telic drives with the human process. These purposive drives have no guarantee of success, either from a divine agency or from sheer power of will. Fate and entropy do their best to corrupt the teleological drives of the Selving process.

Yet such finite and self-corrective purposes do exist, even if unevenly distributed among artists and non-artists, although Rank, like Dewey, sees aesthetic contrivance in each human being, however strong or weak in expression. Aesthetic contrivance is as inevitable as breathing, and as permeable throughout the self-in-process. The finite telos of the Selving process is deeply entwined with the archetypal forces that have great aesthetic bearing. Thus, one cannot talk of the aesthetic dimensions of healing and the flourishing of life without invoking, and being invoked by, the archetypes, which ultimately have their soil in nature. This symmetrical relationship is important. In one sense, we encounter and deal with archetypal potencies, especially as manifest in dreams and art. This gives us heightened power. In another sense, however, we are grasped by archetypal potencies that can change us forever and shake loose any sense of our omnipotence or of malignant narcissism.

Combining pragmatism and depth-psychology, we can say that the flourishing of life always takes place in a pragmatic and instrumental matrix in which the affirmation of any natural trait must pass the bar of praxis, especially social praxis and the quest for justice. This is so because the elevating of a regnant trait out of the mists is already and always a social gesture insofar as semiotics (the depth structure of logic) is communal through and through. A private sign is an impossibility and all traits, especially regnant ones, are at least partially semiotic, or on the way to becoming semiotic (as in Peirce's firstness). A publicly affirmed trait can only survive in the long run if it gives its strength over to the quest for justice, which, as noted, requires democracy as its horizon of power and meaning. And, in an unusual sense, democracy is partly anti-entropic, if the democracy lasts. Yet life's flourishing also requires that the full potencies and powers of the personal and collective unconscious become the focus of ramified query. The forces and structures in the vast unconscious, ultimately of nature itself, must be examined indefinitely in both personal and social settings if any hope for life's flourishing is to be had by finite creatures in an oftimes hostile environment.

Art, Ecstatic Naturalism, and Selving

Let us examine ecstatic naturalism's perspective on the Selving process in more detail and exhibit its deep aesthetic components. If we accept the above arguments that the self is aesthetic through and through, and perhaps some other complexes in zoosemiotics are as well, then it behooves us to move beyond such generic assertions and fill in some details. Clearly, the aesthetic sphere holds the highest rank in the "how" of the Selving process. For Peirce, ethics, which stands below the aesthetic because ethics is merely the sphere of self-control, requires that which makes self-control valuable per se. Self-control (ethics) for its own sake would have nowhere to hang its hat and would ultimately harden into a destructive fundamentalism or Puritanism. However, if there is a highest value in nature, then one can speak of the *summum bonum* as the reality toward which ethics points.

In medieval thought, the *summum bonum* is the only thing that is good in itself—from which all other goods derive their legitimacy. It is not a product of logical inference or of induction, but is evident as the end point of all ethics. For Peirce and for ecstatic naturalism, the *summum bonum* is an entwining of the beautiful and the sublime. The Selving process thus has as its goal, besides that of wholeness, in the enrapture of beauty and the shrivening of the sublime. While beauty can prevail without the sublime, the inverse is not the case. In some situations, beauty will sublate itself and empty its riches into the sublime. But the sublime will always carry dimensions of beauty "within" itself. In the tradition of Kant and Schopenhauer, beauty is pleasing, harmonious, the subject of disinterest, calming, bounded, and a delight for the senses (its enrapturing effects). In the same tradition, the sublime is unbounded, dangerous, unpleasing, and the breaker of secure structures (its shrivening effect). Beauty remains within humanly comfortable bounds, while the sublime, as a potency in art and nature, shakes the psyche and gives it a sense of the precariousness of its various meaning horizons.

Phenomenologically, the self can gently transform and integrate itself by living through the beautiful in such a way as to allow it to seep into horizonal membranes. Beauty is manifest throughout nature, as in the sexual selection process and is, of course, found in great art. In the human sphere, the sense of the beautiful gets so entangled with cultural inscriptions that its universal features are harder to find. However, roughly following Jung's form of universalism, it can be asserted that beauty in art is anti-tribal and has universal significance. With training in insight (horizonal expansion and permeability) one can begin to see the beauty in even the most "foreign" artifacts. In their respective ways, great art will display the objective features enumerated by Kant and, above all, by Schopenhauer.

The domain of art, unlike that of many forms of religion, is democratic, at least in a form that is underway toward more of a horizontal way of comparison among the world's aesthetic contrivances. If religions almost inevitably practice a form of ontological priority, in which a deity or text is held to be more real than other deities or texts, or indeed of nature in general, then art practices ontological parity in which everything is equally real in just the way that it is real. An African ceremonial mask is neither more nor less real than a Picasso painting utilizing selected traits of that mask. Each is real in just the way it is real. By the same token, a Chinese mountain painting with its vast empty spaces and economy of brush strokes is neither more nor less real than a Mark Rothko painting fully saturated with colors on layered planes. In the former case, emptiness (*sunyata*) is celebrated, while in the latter case, the fulsomeness of the universe of color is displayed with powerful immediacy. One is never forced to choose between these two opposite value systems. In fact, the goal is to encounter each with openness and respect, thus emptiness and fullness can both be appreciated for what they are. Beauty in art crosses tribal lines in ways that are almost impossible for religions, which remain in a state of perennial war with each other.

The Selving process thrives on beauty in its overwhelming plurality of forms. Without beauties of some kind, however scarce in some situations, the self-in-process could wither on the vine. The regular enrapture by which beauty empowers the person is one of the most basic sources of spiritual food for the Selving process. The cumulative directionality of these encounters enriches the contour of the self and moves it toward wholeness. But what of the sublime in the Selving process, especially as incompletely rendered in art? It is important to note that the sublime is harder to exhibit in art than is beauty, hence the very incompleteness of every attempt. Yet, without the sublime, the beautiful would not fulfill its inner telos toward maximal expression.

The sublime is harder to describe phenomenologically because of its sheer vastness and its evocation of infinity. Our sense of the infinite is indefinite and we flounder as we try to stretch ourselves out toward it. Beauty, as bounded, can carry us to the edges of the sublime, and often does, but there is no guarantee that this will happen. In a metaphorical sense, beauty is self-protective and only cracks open to the sublime when compelled to do so. The image of "cracking open" may appear harsh and even a manifestation of the violent patriarchal mind-set, yet this is often exactly what does happen when the finite struggles to sublate itself into the infinite. Other metaphors can round out the picture. For Karl Jaspers, the encounter with the sublime (his Encompassing—*das Umgreifende*), produces what he calls "shipwreck" and the above-mentioned "foundering." But the sublation could also be envisioned as a sudden maximal growth spurt that overarches antecedent finitude/beauty. Or, the encounter of the finite with the infinite can be like a rushing river that has fecundity and motion.

The chief thing to be avoided is any eulogizing of suffering or shipwreck. These notions can be seen to come from a privileged Eurocentric perspective in which foundering is a personal existential event, whereas for most the earth's population, the encounter with the finite/infinite sublation must move away from any sense of suffering into a social sense of the liberating powers of the sublime. Especially in great art, the transition from beauty to the sublime, which encases yet facilitates its telos, can be one of great personal and social empowerment as grand new meaning horizons burst into view. So, a cluster of metaphors must be used to evoke the beauty-to-the-sublime transformation.

For the Selving process, the sublime is experienced as the moment of self-transcendence in great art. Note that this transcendence has nothing to do with a supernatural world, but is an event fully within the one nature that there is. If the developmental teleological process of beauty is to sublate itself into the sublime (where possible), then the Selving process follows this trajectory closely. Selving reaches its height and depth when it allows itself to be enveloped by the sublime (the Encompassing). In its highest moment, it enters into contact with what I call "the Wisdom," which is neither omniscient nor omnipotent. Rather, the Wisdom (Sophia) is also a developmental process that cannot provide a clear blueprint for the Selving process as if it had hidden in its heart the built-in entelechy of all things. But the Wisdom can provide comfort and a gentle form of guidance for the disoriented Selving process. The Wisdom grows through the increments of zoösemiosis and is semiotic through and through. The Selving process reaches its depth dimension when it becomes permeable to the personal, collective, and natural unconscious. Ecstatic naturalism is profoundly committed to probing all three modes of the unconscious, with a special focus on the unconscious of nature (*natura naturans*).

The dynamics of the Selving process are most clearly manifest in the creation of great art by the genius or cultural creative. These products filter down into the rest of the community of interpreters and make dramatic new interpretants possible. Natural/inert patriarchal communities fear and abject the genius and her or his works, precisely because of their avant-garde and revolutionary potential. The great product manifests both beauty and the sublime and can thus galvanize the individual and her or his community. That this is held to be a dangerous process is obvious from the standpoint of the welcoming community of interpreters. Such a community carefully develops subtle hermeneutic strategies for maximizing the finite/infinite encounter, while protecting the participant from a psychic overload. Natural/inert communities crush all novel interpretants and thwart the Selving process. That they outnumber communities of interpretation is one of the tragedies of human existence. What is especially tragic is when a thriving community of interpreters (living in a democracy) is slowly torn apart by dictatorial pressures from within. This process is accelerating around the globe, especially here.

But there are two layers to the culmination of the Selving process, as noted by Rank. We have been discussing the first aspect in which cultural creatives generate great works of art that manifest the finite/infinite correlation (or collision). While these products are rare, as genius is rare, they are the stuff that great communities are made of. This is obviously of the highest importance. Yet there is a second dimension that is differently important, although it prevails in a dialectical and symmetrical relation with the first dimension. And that is of the artist going beyond her or his products to make the self-in-process a work of art in itself. This piece is the real key to the dynamics of the Selving proves and the flourishing of life.

The individual psyche, in dialogue with the social psyche, begins to fashion its personality into one of beauty and at least the more available aspects of the sublime. Symmetry, harmony, rich contrasts, and a mobile self-containment reshape the self into a gestalt of grace in which the inner dynamism of developmental beauty finds a home in the psyche. All selves-in-process are ideally meant to become this beautiful gestalt, but unconscious and social structures often war against it. But it can happen even amid the most harrowing of experiences and bear amazing fruits. The dynamics of the Selving process also call upon the acceptance of the uncanny sublime to reshape the self on the very edges of its finite existence. Insofar as the self can grow into and accept the potency of the sublime, it can transcend its antecedent conditions and become a great personality as well as a creator of works of art.

There is a dialectic between art products and the artistic personality in the Selving process. Insofar as one brings a great work of art into prevalence, one also, and at the same time, expands and galvanizes the artistic personality to match the potency of the work of art. The product and its producer deepen and enrich each other and this process continues its developmental trajectory until entropy claims its own.

The Aesthetics of Ecstatic Naturalism

Ecstatic naturalism is a form of religious naturalism that is deeply aesthetic in its expression and value system. But above all it is a metaphysics of nature in the larger American tradition. By "metaphysics" I mean the careful and systematic analysis and disclosure of what Dewey called "the generic traits of existence," or what Buchler refers to as "whatever is in whatever way it is." Historically, the modern American concept of ecstatic naturalism has its roots in the essays and poems of Ralph Waldo Emerson, whose Transcendentalism set the stage for so much that was to follow. Its most recent resurgence is found in my published work starting in the late 1980s. In twelve books and numerous essays, I have worked out the contours of this perspective—a perspective that has many interlocutors, both living and dead, and now is a communal movement that is generating novel interpretants that expand and move beyond my own perspective. Yet it should be noted, as above in our analysis of the Selving process, that non-American trajectories have profoundly influenced the American base, chief among them being: Continental phenomenology, Neo-Platonism, Advaita Vedanta Hinduism (of the *Upanishads*), Buddhism (of the Mahayana schools), the history of art, Schopenhauer, depth-psychology, and others. But the foundation of ecstatic naturalism is firmly rooted in the American pragmatic and naturalist traditions.

We start with the basic affirmation that nature is all that there is. There is nothing beyond it, nor does it have an external creator, as in patriarchal systems. In fact, the very word *nature* cannot be defined, as to define something is to locate it under a genus with a specific difference. What possible genus could it be and what would be its specific difference? More important is the fact that the word *nature* has absolutely no referent. There is no "it" to which any word could be applied in a sign/object relation. It is perhaps best to put the word under erasure, as in Heidegger's crossing out of *Sein* and *Seyn* to show the ontological divide between Being and a thing in being. Thus, we might use the iconic form ~~nature~~ or put scare quotes around it as in "nature." We will use the normal form of the word throughout except in special instances where the scare quotes can emphasize the nonexistence of nature as an "it" or thing in itself.

Within the one nature that there is lies the grounding distinction between nature naturing (*natura naturans*) and nature natured (*natura naturata*). While this distinction has a medieval provenance, Spinoza brought it into prominence in the modern period. My technical definition of nature naturing is: "Nature perennially creating itself out of itself alone with no *creatio ex nihilo*." The word *perennially* is carefully chosen to signal the ongoing cyclical acts of creation that are more like streams of emanation than like a kind of big bang sudden emergence. Nature has always been here and will always be. It prevailed prior to the Big Bang in astrophysics and will prevail if the space/time universe collapses in on itself. Nature naturing is the self-gifting of nature to itself in the various actual and possible modes of time.

I define nature natured as: "The innumerable orders of the World without a collective integrity or contour." The word *innumerable* has been chosen with care. It signals that it is impossible to sum up nature's orders or to find a boundary for them. Each order of relevance (natural complex) can be indefinitely explored and judgments can be ramified in an unending process. No order can be fully known, nor is there anything like a web of internal relations binding them together in a self-referential whole, as in Whitehead. An internal relation is one in which the relata interpenetrate each other, often outside of efficient causality. An external relation involves Peirce's secondness, that is, brute causal interaction between and among orders. There is no penetration or permeability among the "insides" of these relations. Rather, there are breaks in continua, nor is there a continuum of continua as alleged in Peirce's doctrine of synechism. Further, contra Peirce, both early and late, there can be the incognizable, which is not simply something that will be eventually known by inquiry, but a reality of the indefinite "boundaries" and subaltern traits.

Peirce entwines several fundamental categories in his system. Chief among them for our purposes are four: (1) synechism (continuity), (2) panpsychism (matter is effete mind), (3) internal relations, and (4) the notion of three human bodies: the material (carnal), the social, and the spiritual. They all stand or fall together with one exception. Ecstatic naturalism rejects all but one of these concepts, number four, which does have a quasi-independent status. First, ecstatic naturalism rejects the totalization of synechism, whether guaranteed by Kantian infinitesimals or not. Instead, it affirms real breaks among orders and even some of their subaltern traits. Continua are broken all the time and sometimes this is value neutral, while at other times it is value positive or negative, or a combination of all three. There is no hope for total transparent ultimate continuity in the infinite long run, whatever that turns out to be. In this and the next category of panpsychism we find some real difficulties.

Peirce's system flounders in its incomplete and truncated account of the unconscious. His image of "the bottomless lake" is part of his synechism in that the self descends into what I would call liminal consciousness, but the light never totally goes out from above. It is as if Peirce abjected the unconscious and refused to see it as radical and disruptive otherness. Synechism insists that there can be no such thing as a real unconscious as everything must be cognizable. His second doctrine of panpsychism is of a similar sort. It insists that there are no fully emergent properties in nature because everything is mind on a continuum. Combined with synechism, panpsychism sanitizes nature and has a built-in Lamarckian sense of acquired properties through the growth and the passing on of mental traits, which tend to grow and spread, like feelings, from the protoplasm to the human being. Panpsychism denies that spirit or mind are emergent properties from antecedent material conditions, but are part of an eternal cosmic mentality. Here his Darwinism grows rather thin.

If synechism and panpsychism conspire to deny the otherness of the unconscious, then the third concept of internal relations lends a hand as well. For internal relations to work there must be absolute universality combining relata into a whole. Here again the otherness of the unconscious is squeezed out in favor of a synechistic panpsychism that overprivileges the mental over its nonmental support conditions. Internal relations must be transparent to each other in admitting relata into relations. Relations completely dominate over relata.

The fourth category of the three types of body has a deep resonance with ecstatic naturalism. Being emergentist it accepts that the higher functions grew out of matter in ways that are still being explored. Peirce's key concept of community shows the role of contrast and error in the education process. He goes so far as to say that selfish individualism is guilty of a violation of logic, which has direct communal/social import. But the important part is his idea of a spiritual consciousness that is embodied as well. Many Peirce scholars overlook this aspect of his plea for immortality. Spiritual consciousness accompanies us all the time this side of the grave, but we ignore its role in connecting us to the world. After physical death, it has a different kind of body, but a body that still enframes it. The spiritual body may be of different spatial and temporal structure than the carnal body, but it is there in its own way. Metaphorically, one can say that the post-death body is of a higher vibratory resonance unknown to the carnal body.

Turning back to ecstatic naturalism, it is important to stress the centrality of the concept of a robust unconscious that is rooted in nature. We have noted the personal and collective (archetypal) unconscious and the roles they play in the Selving process. Here we plunge into the rarely discussed, or even envisioned, idea of the unconscious of nature "itself." Nature's unconscious has no bottom and contains real darkness, not just Peirce's flickering and dimming light. For Schelling, this is the abyss of nature from which even god arises. For Schelling, the abyss (*der Abgrund*) of nature is the unruly ground (*das Regellose*) for all emergents. It is roughly equivalent to Peirce's firstness, but deeper down, as it were. Ecstatic naturalism correlates the unconscious of nature with nature naturing, which emanates and ejects the orders of the world. This directly harks back to Emerson with his anti–*creatio ex nihilo* stress on an endless stream of emanations, with neither beginning nor ending. Nature naturing is the providingness (Buchler) that makes the orders of the world possible. Thus, consciousness, and eventually self-consciousness, emerge from the fathomless otherness of nature naturing. Nature natured is the provided via the unconscious of nature, the world's orders, or "Creation" in a monotheistic sense. For ecstatic naturalism, all creation is in and of nature and never an event-of-all-events antecedent to nature.

The aesthetic dimension of ecstatic naturalism comes out most sharply in its difference from much religion. Here, we rely on both pragmatism and naturalism in the American vein to provide the leading categories. The contrast will be between aesthetic concepts, or the encounter between the sublime and the religious concept/experience of revelation. The sublime is held to be a universal experience across tribal (communal) affiliations, whereas revelation is held to be person and tribe specific. Both pragmatism and naturalism take the universalistic road, with a heavy dose of justice seeking, while revelations have only tribal value and are not a part of inquiry or query. Thus, like Dewey, the aesthetic takes precedence over the religious even though he wrote a little book on religious experience. But at the heart of Dewey's enterprise is the priority of aesthetic experience over other kinds.

As noted in the previous section, art practices ontological parity, whereas religion practices ontological priority, at least in the Western monotheisms. As a reminder, ontological parity is the metaphysical view that everything is real in just the way that it is real. There cannot be degrees of reality. In fact, the concept of "reality" has no role to play in a capacious metaphysics. It can function in everyday discourse such as, "Now that was a real crème brulée, just like the ones I had in Paris." Here, the word functions as a value assessment and as a mode of comparison. But a bad crème brulée is not less real than a good one, just inferior. One can say that the practice of ontological parity is a spiritual exercise in mindfulness. Given human nature, it must be renewed again and again until it becomes a Peirce/James habit. Art can directly remind us of the need for this mindfulness—what Heidegger calls *Besinnung*.

Religion is another story. Note that the following account only applies to extreme versions of tribalism and revelation, but much of religion is embroiled in both. While the sublime satisfies Peircean universalistic criteria and can be the subject of unending and fruitful query generating endless novel interpretants, religion in our sense is no friend to universalism, except in a form of conquest and the will to power, nor is it a friend to query and novel interpretants. A so-called revelation is a kind of big bang experience that is usually individual in character. When one receives a revelation all epistemological and logical questions cease and the method of authority takes over. If the revelation is a grand vision of a new religion, or a radical revolution in one already standing, then all query is cast aside as heretical. Ontological priority rears its ugly head while the new revelation becomes the only real event or thing and takes control from all other religious beliefs. To question the revelation is to question the deity itself, and the recipient of the revelation becomes divinized in the process, hence she or he is more real than other persons within and without the tribe.

Art is more deeply transformative than religion, as it emerges directly from the potencies and emanations of nature naturing, that is to say, the unconscious of nature. The mysteries of art surround how it becomes active in nature natured, that is, in the orders of the world. Art speaks with enhanced potency insofar as it participates in the archetypes of nature naturing. It must be reiterated that archetypes are not fully formed cosmic cookie cutters that merely impose their form on the world. Rather, they unfold in the dance between the three modes of the unconscious: personal, collective, and natural. Every archetype, say, that of the Great Mother, must be transfigured and individuated by the individual artist or with the help of an artistic community. From the standpoint of ecstatic naturalism, the artist reaches deeper down into the unconscious of nature and has a better grasp of the archetypes. Further, the artist bridges the abyss between nature naturing and nature natured more fully than any other personality type. That is, they render novel traits in the realms of nature natured via the potencies and emanations coming from nature naturing.

In the end, the artist type becomes paradigmatic for the self-gifting of nature naturing. This self-giving is not necessarily benevolent, as it too can have its demonic shadow side. Insofar as artists can wrestle creatively with both sides of the self-unfolding of nature naturing, then they can help the community both to recognize its collective shadow and to find paths toward creative contrivance, whether of self or product, that can keep the flow of rich and novel interpretants moving in and through the community of interpreters. Thus, for ecstatic naturalism, as in Peirce, the aesthetic dimension of nature and life serves as the depth connection with all of nature and enables the Selving process to flourish.

Bibliography

Brent, Joseph. *Charles Sanders Peirce: A Life.* Revised and Enlarged Edition. Bloomington: Indiana University Press, 1998.

Buchler, Justus. *Metaphysics of Natural Complexes.* New York: Columbia University Press, 1966. Second Expanded Edition, edited by Kathleen Wallace,

Armen Marsoobian, and Robert Corrington. Albany: State University of New York Press, 1990.
Campbell, Joseph. *The Hero with a Thousand Faces*. New York: New World Library, 2008.
Corrington, Robert S. *The Community of Interpreters*. Macon, GA: Mercer University Press, 1987/1995.
———. *Nature and Spirit: An Essay in Ecstatic Naturalism*, New York: Fordham University Press, 1992.
———. *An Introduction to C. S. Peirce*. Lanham, MD: Rowman and Littlefield, 1993.
———. *Ecstatic Naturalism: Signs of the World*. Bloomington: Indiana University Press, 1994.
———. *Nature's Self: Our Journey from Origin to Spirit*. Lanham, MD: Rowman and Littlefield, 1996.
———. *Nature's Religion*. Lanham, MD: Rowman and Littlefield, 1997.
———. *A Semiotic Theory of Theology and Philosophy*. Cambridge: Cambridge University Press, 2000.
———. *Wilhelm Reich: Psychoanalyst and Radical Naturalist*. New York: Farrar, Straus, and Giroux, 2003.
———. *Riding the Windhorse: Manic Depressive Disorder and the Quest for Wholeness*. Lanham, MD: Hamilton Books, 2003.
———. *Nature's Sublime: An Essay in Aesthetic Naturalism*. Lanham, MD: Lexington Books, 2013.
———. *Deep Pantheism: Toward a New Transcendentalism*. Lanham, MD: Lexington Books, 2016.
———, Carl R. Hausman, and Thomas Seebohm, eds. *Pragmatism Considers Phenomenology*. Lanham, MD: University Press of America, 1987.
Dewey, John. *Democracy and Education*. Carbondale: Illinois University Press, 2008 [1916].
———. *Experience and Nature*. Carbondale: Southern Illinois University Press, 1988 [1925].
———. *Art as Experience*. Carbondale: Southern Illinois University Press, 1989 [1934].
Emerson, Ralph Waldo. *Essays and Lectures*. New York: The Library of America, 1981.
Freud, Sigmund. *Beyond the Pleasure Principle*. Translated by James Strachey. London: Hogarth Press, 1920.
Greenberg, Jay R., and Stephen A. Mitchell. *Object Relations in Psychoanalytic Theory*. Cambridge: Harvard University Press, 1983.
Grimes, John. *A Concise Dictionary of Indian Philosophy*. New and Revised Edition. Albany: State University of New York Press, 1996.
Heidegger, Martin. *Being and Time*. Translated by Stambaugh and Schmidt. Albany, NY: State University of New York Press, 2010 [1927].

———. *Kant and the Problem of Metaphysics.* Fourth Edition, enlarged. Translated by Taft. Bloomington: University of Indiana Press, 1990 [1929].
———. *Introduction to Metaphysics.* Second Edition. Translated by Fried and Polt. New Haven: Yale University Press, 2014 [1937].
———. *Contributions to Philosophy (of the Event).* Translated by Rojcewicz and Vallega-Neu. Bloomington: Indiana University, 2012 [1936–38].
———. *Mindfulness.* Translated by Emad and Kalary. New York: Continuum, 2006 [1938–1939].
———. *Identity and Difference.* Translated by Stambaugh. New York: Harper and Row, 1969 [1957].
James, William. *William James, Writings 1902–1910.* New York: The Library of America, 1987.
Jaspers, Karl. *The Philosophy of Karl Jaspers* (*The Library of Living Philosophers*). Vol. IX. Edited by Paul Schilpp. La Salle, IL: Open Court Publishing Company, 1957.
———. *Karl Jaspers: Basic Philosophical Writings.* Edited, translated, and with Introductions by Ehrlich, Ehrlich, and Pepper. Athens: Ohio University Press, 1986.
———. *Philosophy.* Vol. 3. Translated by E. B. Ashton. Chicago: University of Chicago Press, 1971 [1932].
Jung, C. G. *Psychiatric Studies, Second Edition.* Vol. 1 of *The Collected Works.* Translated by R. F. C. Hull. Princeton: Princeton University Press, 1970.
———. *The Structure and Dynamics of the Psyche.* Second Edition. Vol. 8 of *The Collected Works.* Translated by R. F. C. Hull. Princeton: Princeton University Press, 1972.
———. *The Archetypes and the Collective Unconscious.* Second Edition. Vol. 9:I of *The Collected Works.* Translated by R. F. C. Hull. Princeton: Princeton University Press, 1971.
———. *Aion: Researches into the Phenomenology of the Self.* Second Edition. Vol. 9:II of *The Collected Works.* Translated by R. F. C. Hull. Princeton: Princeton University Press, 1968.
Kant, Immanuel. *Critique of the Power of Judgment.* Translated by Guyer and Matthews. Cambridge: Cambridge University Press, 2000 [1793].
Kohut, Heinz. *The Restoration of the Self.* Chicago: University of Chicago Press, 1977.
Leibniz, Gottfried Wilhelm. *Philosophical Papers and Letters.* Translated by Loemker. Dordrecht: D. Reidel, 1969.
Lieberman, James. *Acts of Will: The Life and Works of Otto Rank.* New York: Free Press, 1985.
Nāgārjuna. *Middle Way.* Translated by Mark Siderits and Shōryū Katsura. Somerville, MA: Wisdom Publications, 2013 [ca. 150 CE].
Niemoczynski, Nguyen, ed. *A Philosophy of Sacred Nature: Prospects for Ecstatic Naturalism.* Lanham, MD: Lexington Books, 2015.

Nietzsche, Friedrich. *Beyond Good and Evil*. Translated by Walter Kaufman. New York: Vintage, 1998 [1887].
Poe, Edgar Allan. *Poetry and Tales*. New York: The Library of America, 1984.
Peirce, C. S. *The Essential Peirce*. Vol. 1 (1867–1893) and Vol. 2 (1893–1913). Bloomington: Indiana University Press, 1993 and 1998.
Rank, Otto. *The Trauma of Birth*. Translated by Lieberman. New York: Dover, 1993 [1924].
———. *Art and Artist: Creative Urge and Personality Development*. Translated by Atkinson. New York: W. W. Norton, 1968 [German typescript, 1930].
———. *Psychology and the Soul*. Translated by Gregory C. Richter and E. James Lieberman. Baltimore: Johns Hopkins University Press, 1998 [1930].
Reich, Wilhelm. *Character Analysis*. Translated by Garfagno. New York: Farrar, Straus, and Giroux, 1972 [1933].
Santayana, George. *The Life of Reason (Five Volumes in One)*. Teddington, UK: Echo Library, 2006 [1905].
———. *Realms of Being*. New York: Cooper Square, 1972 [1942].
Schelling, F. W. J. *Philosophical Investigations into the Essence of Human Freedom*. Translated by Love and Schmidt. Albany: State University of New York Press, 2007 [1807].
Schleiermacher Friedrich. *On Religion: Speeches to Its Cultured Despisers*. Translated by Crouter. Cambridge: Cambridge University Press, 1988 [1799].
Schopenhauer, Arthur. *The World as Will and Presentation*. Vol. I. Translated by Aquila and Carus. New York: Pearson Longman, 2008 [1819].
———. *Parerga and Paralipomena*. Volumes I and II. Translated by Payne. Oxford: Oxford University Press, 1974 [1851].
Spiegelberg, Herbert. *The Phenomenological Movement: A Historical Introduction*. Third Revised and Enlarged Edition. The Hague: Nijhoff, 1982.
Spinoza, Benedict. *A Spinoza Reader*. Translated by Curley. Princeton: Princeton University Press, 1994.
Strozier, Charles B. *Heinz Kohut: The Making of a Psychoanalyst*. New York: Other Press, 2001.
Tillich, Paul. *The Courage to Be*. New Haven: Yale University Press, 1952.
Whitehead, Alfred North. *Process and Reality*. Corrected Edition. New York: The Free Press, 1978 [1929].

Contributors

Randall E. Auxier is professor of philosophy and of communication studies at Southern Illinois University Carbondale. Among his publications are *The Quantum of Explanation: Whitehead's Radical Empiricism* (2017, co-authored with Gary Herstein), *Metaphysical Graffiti* (2017), *Time, Will, and Purpose* (2013), and numerous edited and co-edited volumes. He is co-editor of the book series with SUNY in American Philosophy and Cultural Thought.

Robert S. Corrington is the Henry Anson Buttz Professor of Philosophical Theology in the Graduate Division of Religion of Drew University. He is the author of twelve books and numerous articles. His most recent book is *Nature and Nothingness: An Essay in Ordinal Phenomenology*. He has a life-long interest in aesthetics, which was deepened by taking classes with Monroe Beardsley as an undergraduate. He has characterized his work as "ecstatic naturalism," or, more recently, as "deep pantheism."

Corey Drieth is a member of the Visual and Performing Arts Department at the University of Colorado in Colorado Springs. He has double undergraduate degrees in philosophy/comparative religious studies and studio art from Colorado State University and an MFA from the University of North Carolina. His work has been exhibited throughout the country, including San Francisco, Chicago, Albuquerque, New Orleans, Washington, D.C., and New York City.

Nicholas Gaskill is associate professor of American literature at the University of Oxford and tutorial fellow at Oriel College. He is the author of *Chromographia: American Literature and the Modernization of Color* (2018) and an editor of *The Lure of Whitehead* (2014).

Leanne Gilbertson is associate professor of art (art history) and director of Northcutt Steele Gallery at Montana State University Billings. She has an MA from the University of Iowa and PhD from the University of Rochester. Her writing on contemporary art and visual culture has been published in exhibition catalogues and in *Art Journal, InVisible Culture, Pastelegram, and Rhizomes: Cultural Studies in Emerging Studies*.

Jacob L. Goodson (PhD, University of Virginia) is assistant professor of philosophy at Southwestern College in Winfield, Kansas. He is the author of *Narrative Theology and the Hermeneutical Virtues: Humility, Patience, Prudence* (Lexington Books, 2015) and *Strength of Mind: Courage, Hope, Freedom, Knowledge* (Cascade Press, 2018). He researches and writes on American philosophy and ethics, baseball and sports ethics, and watching television through the lens of theories of deontology and virtue.

Walter B. Gulick is professor emeritus of philosophy, humanities, and religious studies at Montana State University Billings. Twice a Fulbright Scholar, he has taught in seven countries. He understands philosophy as ideally a synoptic discipline; his publications center on issues of meaning and value. *Recovering Truths*, Gulick's highly annotated comprehensive anthology of Michael Polanyi's writings, is available via the Polanyi Society website.

Steven Hart, professor of music, conducts choral ensembles and teaches conducting, vocal pedagogy, and private voice at Rocky Mountain College in Billings, Montana. He holds degrees from the University of Colorado, the University of South Dakota, and Western Michigan University. He is the conductor and founder of the High Plains Chamber Singers and also the conductor of the Billings Symphony Chorale.

Robert E. Innis is professor emeritus of philosophy at the University of Massachusetts Lowell. He has been Humboldt Fellow at the University of Cologne, Fulbright Professor at the University of Copenhagen, and Obel Foundation Visiting Professor at the University of Aalborg. He has published books on the linguistic theory of Karl Buhler, the philosophy of Susanne Langer, pragmatism and the forms of sense, and semiotics, plus many articles and chapters dealing with the relations between philosophy, semiotics, language theory, cultural psychology, and aesthetics in their technical and everyday dimensions.

Thomas Leddy is professor in the Department of Philosophy at San Jose State University. He is the author of "John Dewey's Aesthetics" for the *Stanford Encyclopedia of Philosophy*. His book *The Extraordinary in the Ordinary: The Aesthetics of Everyday Life* (Broadview, 2012) is inspired by Dewey. A long-time member of the American Society of Aesthetics, he is on the editorial board of the online journal *Contemporary Aesthetics*, and his blog *Aesthetics Today* has received more than 350,000 hits.

Robert Cummings Neville is professor of philosophy, religion, and theology at Boston University and is the author of many books and papers. His wife, Beth Neville, is an artist who has taught him most of what he knows about aesthetics. He is a past president of the Institute for American Religious and Philosophical Thought.

James McLachlan is professor of philosophy and religion at Western Carolina University. Currently he is co-editor of *Element: The Journal of the Society of Mormon Philosophy and Theology*. His recent publications have dealt with concepts of Hell in existentialism, Satan and demonic evil in Boehme, Schelling, and Dostoevsky, and the problem of evil in Mormonism. He is currently working on a study of Levinas and the existentialists.

Vaughan Durkee McTernan is a retired adjunct professor of religion and an Episcopal priest. As a member of the Institute of American Religious and Philosophical Thought, she has a long-time interest in process and pragmatist thought. She has an MDiv from Yale and a PhD from University of Denver/Iliff School of Theology.

Michael L. Raposa is professor of religion studies and the E. W. Fairchild Professor of American Studies at Lehigh University. He is the author of *Peirce's Philosophy of Religion* (University of Indiana Press, 1989), *Boredom and the Religious Imagination* (University of Virginia Press, 1999), and *Meditation and the Martial Arts* (University of Virginia Press, 2003). He is presently completing a book (under contract with Fordham University Press) titled *Theosemiotic: On Religion, Reading and the Gift of Meaning*.

David Rohr is a PhD candidate in religious studies at Boston University and editor of www.PhilosophyOfReligion.org. Most of Rohr's research involves the constructive application of C. S. Peirce's ideas, especially his semeiotic, to issues in philosophy of biology, mind, and religion. His dissertation interprets Peirce's enigmatic essay, "A Neglected Argument for the Reality of God."

Richard Shusterman is Dorothy F. Schmidt Eminent Scholar in the Humanities and director of the Center for Body, Mind, and Culture at Florida Atlantic University. His book, *Pragmatist Aesthetics: Living Beauty, Rethinking Art*, has been translated into fourteen languages. In *Body Consciousness, Thinking through the Body* and other works, Shusterman developed the field of somaesthetics that highlights and cultivates the body's multiple uses in perception and performance. The French government awarded him the title Chevalier de l'Ordre des Palmes Académiques for his work in the philosophy of culture.

Gary Slater is visiting assistant professor of religious and theological studies at St. Edward's University in Austin, Texas. He completed a doctorate in theology at the University of Oxford in 2014, having written on the reception of Peirce's philosophy in the work of Robert C. Neville and Peter Ochs. Other than his young twins, his central interests are in ethics and in exploring novel combinations among academic disciplines, particularly history, metaphysics, and aesthetics.

Arthur Stewart, PhD, is the director of The Center for Philosophical Studies at Lamar University in Beaumont, Texas, where he is also associate professor of philosophy and was previously visiting associate professor of piano performance. He has given keynote addresses to the Russian Academy of Science, the Pontifical Catholic University in Brazil, and the American Society for Aesthetics—Rocky Mountain Division. He is the author of *Elements of Knowledge: Pragmatism, Logic, and Inquiry*.

David Strong is professor of philosophy and environmental studies at Rocky Mountain College. He is the author of *Crazy Mountains: Learning from Wilderness to Weigh Technology* (State University of New York Press, 1995) and is coeditor of *Technology and the Good Life?* (University of Chicago Press, 2000) as well as numerous articles at the intersection of environmental philosophy and the philosophy of technology. Strong characterizes his philosophy as a philosophy in the service of "things."

Wesley J. Wildman is professor of philosophy, theology, and ethics at Boston University and executive director of the Center for Mind and Culture (www.mindandculture.org). See www.WesleyWildman.com.

Index

A Pluralistic Universe (James), 103
abduction, 64, 301–2, 307, 380
abstract expressionism, 26, 262, 271, 289
abstraction, 125–28, 140, 292
action, 104; hiatus prior to, 199–200; often clearer than words, 69
Adderley, Cannonball, 200
Adventures of Ideas (Whitehead), 266, 275, 279
advertising replacing art as world forming, 365
aesthesis, 11
aesthetic appreciation, 5–6, 14, 26–29, 33; fallibility, 228; harmonic structure, based on, 226; immediacy, 228
aesthetic attitude, 7
aesthetic commodification and loss, 364, 367–70, 375; utilitarian calculation, 364
aesthetic criticism, 88–90, 297. *See also* art criticism, artistic self-criticism, criticism
aesthetic description, 240
aesthetic dispositions, evolutionary sources, 97
aesthetic excellence, 257; arising from love of subject matter, 124; existing on a continuum of profundity, 350

aesthetic expectations, 228
aesthetic experience, 15, 177, 238; contemplation, 278; counters tribalism, 243, 385; differing degrees of intensity and complexity, 341; enemies of, 312; inclusive of practical concerns, 340; intimate and alienating aspects, 242; more universal than religion, 243; object and evaluator needed, 17; object centered, 114; perfection not essential, 313; power to shift beliefs, 166; serving history, 245; social dimension, 99; unifying quality, 104–8, 312–13
aesthetic feelings of excellence, 104, 278
aesthetic ideal, 62, 65
aesthetic immediacy: prior to logic, 162, 286, 297. *See also* Firstness
aesthetic judgment, 3–33, 314; derived from perceptual feelings, 97; empathy, root of, 236, 244; influencing factors, 8, 15, 28; intentionality, 6; levels, 4; nondiscursive wildness, 236; in ordinary experience, 341; relation to morality, religion, 47; shapes feeling, 81; three domains summarized, 19–20, 236

Aesthetic Letters (Schiller), 61, 247
aesthetic norms and standards, 19, 104, 299
aesthetic principles, contrast, 276; intensity, 274; richness and ease, 103; simplicity and complexity, 103, 274
aesthetic situation, 223–24
aesthetic theory, 5, 20; critique of Dewey's theory, 245–46
aesthetic-historical complementarity, 236
aestheticism, 8, 264
aesthetics, 27; abstract analysis, 140; American Aesthetics, Dewey's centrality in, 10; basis for thought and action, 246; definition, 3, 4–7, 159, 343; description, 7–8; Emerson's expansion, 40; holism, 26; importance of context, 20, 228; international scope 25; musical beauty, 153; religious influence, 22; state of mind, 298, 307; sub-disciplines, 139; theological meaning, bearer of, 239; wild aspects, 238
affordance, 147–49, 152, 206, 207
Albers, Joseph, 284, 285, 288, 290
allowance, 207
American Action Painters, 260, 262
American Aesthetics, 3–4, 7–11, 19–23, 26–27, 30, 211, 258, 275, 283, 315, 334, 343, 346; analytic aesthetics, contrast with, 27; appreciation of diverse cultures, 231; characteristics, 20, 29; context, importance of, 20, 240; description, 7–8; Dewey's centrality, 10; emphasis on the individual, 261; holism, 26; international relevance, 25; and postmodernism, 29; religious influence, 22

American history: Gilded Age, 9–11
American painting: its history, 265
American philosophers on religious experience, 241
American philosophers, 9–11, 344; naturalistic stance, 9. *See also* Peirce, James, Whitehead, Dewey, Langer
American philosophical tradition, 48, 237, 360
American reaction to terrorism, 44
Amram, David, 200
analytic aesthetics, 25–28, 261, 283; characteristics, 25
analytic philosophy, 8, 27
Anderson, John, 31
Anselm, 64–66; ontological argument, 59
Anti-Aesthetic: Essays on Postmodern Culture (Foster, ed.), 29
appraisal systems, 146
archetypes, 382–83, 393
Aristotle, 48, 144, 149; substance, 212
art; American, 20–21, 290; beauty in, 226–30; creative of experience, 159; embedded in broad culture, 228; expressed as Firstness, 157, 160; expressive immediacy of, 286; function, 235; historical antecedents, influence of, 293; ontological parity of, 385; representation and objectivity, 125; shocking pieces for gaining notice, 264; significance of bad art, 229; significant form, 347; social nature, 31, 34, 188
Art as Experience (Dewey), 10, 50, 105, 111, 116, 123, 158, 235; book's original illustrations, 123. *See also* Dewey
art criticism, 16, 166–70; ideal characteristics, 257–58; need for

Index

creativity in criticism, 266; rejection of didactic criticism, 295. *See also* criticism
Art in Painting (Barnes), 126
artistic creation, 260, 265, 284; binding quality, 165; creation as religious practice, 294; dialectical process, 230; expressiveness in all art, 127; inspiration, lead with, 315; mystery as aim, 291; non-reductive criticism, 258
artistic intent, crowd source, 313, 317
artistic originality, 89
artistic self-criticism, 83–85, 287, 297
artist's intention, 27–28
arts' cultural significance, 258
Arts without Boundaries, 375
Artwork, autonomy of, 287; background influences, 28; goal of unity, wholeness, 315; harmonies, many types included, 227; ideal beauty portrayed, 229; ideal unity of form and content, 294
Arvin, Newton, 39
Asad, Talal, 45
Auxier, Randall, 57, 177–205, 279
awareness, 295
axiological landscape theory, 139, 154–55; broadened beyond biology, 147; critique of landscape theory, 212; features aesthetics, ethics, inquiry, 139–42; limitations, 156; moral pluralism, 153–55; process theology, differences from, 149; summary description, 141–43. *See also* affordance, valuation
axiology, 139–56; description, 140

Bach, Johann Sebastian, 299, 303
background, 104, 107, 117–23
Bacon, Francis, 91
Barnes, Albert, 126

Bataille, Georges, 183, 206
Baudelaire, Charles, 266
Baumgarten, Alexander, 27, 108
Bazin, André, 322, 325–26, 332
Beardsley, Monroe, 25, 26
beautiful feelings, 88
beauty, 121, 211, 294; characteristics, 274; definition, 215–16, 220; as a divinity, 370; Edwards on, 67, 211; an evocative power, 370; experience of, 222; goodness of existence, 220; intrinsic goodness of harmony, 215; ontological parity of artworks, 385; Peirce's account, 67, 299–300; perfection not beautiful, 276; symmetry, balance, and harmony of form, 211
Beethoven, Ludwig, 130, 152–53, 306
Being and Nothingness, 327–29; desire to be God, 328
Bell, Clive, 30, 346–50; art as significant form, 347; metaphysical hypothesis, 347–48
Benjamin, Walter, 174
Benton, Thomas Hart, 283
Bergson, Henri, 163, 173, 200, 202, 206
Berleant, Arnold, 22, 31
Bernard, Claude, 304
Best, Steven, 28
big-bang cosmology, 150–51
biological fitness landscapes, 143–44
The Birth of Tragedy (Nietzsche), 48, 49
body, 30; crucial in poetry, 163; somatic aesthetics, 96–99
Boers, Arthur, 366
Boetticher, Budd, 322–34; beauty of horses, 326; celebration of nature, 326. *See also* Ranown cycle (Boetticher Westerns), Scott
Borgmann, Albert, 360–65, 371, 376

Bradley, Francis, 213
Brahms, Johannes, 299
Bresson, Robert, 322–23
Bright Earth: The Invention of Colour (Ball), 249
Brightman, E. S., 180
broken symbols, 331–34; embodiment of the sacred (Tillich), 332; opposed to idolatry, 331
Brooks, Cleanth, 24
Buchler, Justus, 149, 388, 391
Brueghel, Pieter (the Elder), 348
Buddhist practice, 353–54
Bugbee, Henry, 56, 360
Buell, Lawrence, 47

Callas, Maria, 315
Carlson, Allen, 339–40, 348–50, 354–55
Casals, Pablo, 372
Cassirer, Ernst, 9, 182, 206; myth and death, 191–92
causation, 150
Cavell, Stanley, 45, 46, 49
cello, 359, 371
centering experience, 372–73
centering things, 360, 370–71; their aesthetic attraction, 360, 370; character forming, 363; commanding presence, 371; definition, 362; examples from authors, 360; hearth as example, 362–63; interweave means and ends, 363; resonant beauty, 374
Cézanne, Paul, 123–25, 130, 349–50, 352
Chekhov, Anton, 50, 56
Cheng, François, 121
Chopin, Frederick, 306
choral music's goal, 313, 314
choral practice, techniques inhibiting artistry, 312
Church, Frederick, 10, 214

Churchill, Winston, 375
cinema, 321–34; Western, mythic formula of, 321
circle, 288
classification: aesthetic gratification, 102
Cole, Thomas, 10, 214
Coleridge, Samuel, 10
color and form, 124
color versus line, 123
commodification of art, 264
commodities, 361, 371, 276; egocentric relation to, 371
community of interpretation, 203, 379–80, 387
community, natural/inert, 380, 387
conceptual art, 27
Concerning the Spiritual in Art (Kandinsky), 243
Conduct of Life (Emerson), 47, 53
Confucianism, 219, 232, 294, 323
consciousness, 106. *See also* unity of consciousness
continental philosophy, 8
Coonskinism, 265
correlative coexistence, 371–72
Corrington, Robert, 149, 150, 238, 241–43, 251, 379–96
craft, 124; relation to fine art, 294
criticism, 6; communal basis, 90; puts literature to work, 168. *See also* art criticism
Critique of Judgment (Kant), 11–13, 49; vice, 42
cubism, 262

dance, 30, 184, 188
Danto, Arthur, 25
Darwin, Charles, 144, 383
Davis, Miles, 199–204, 209
death, 42, 207; egress of possibility; 189; immortal spiritual body, 391;

meaningless for Boetticher villains, 330; overcoming denial of, 194; significance, 189; social nature, 197
deconstruction, 380
deep pantheism, 242
Deleuze, Gilles, 174
DeMille, Cecil B., 321, 333
democratization, of aesthetic judgment, 109; of tragedy, 39, 57
density of being, 219, 221, 229
Descartes, Rene, 361
determinate things, 212, 331; essential and relational aspects, 213
device paradigm (Borgmann), 361–64; invitation to consumption, 363; unfamiliar machinery, accessible surface, 363
Dewey, John, 3, 10, 13–17, 22–23, 29, 33, 81–82, 88, 104–7, 157–65, 238, 243–46, 263, 284, 312, 344–46, 367, 369, 380, 392; abstraction, its unavoidability, 127; aesthetic diversity, 230, 345, 360; aesthetic experience, 31, 104; aesthetics as matter becoming medium, 116; *an* experience, 16, 263, 312, 342, 367; art as intrinsically enjoyable, 226; art as symbolization, 113; art, its nature, 130, 133, 244; art's historical, social context, 244; art's ultimate goal, 125; background, 117; Chinese painting, 117; consummatory experiences, 112; continuity between fine and popular art, 227, 344; crafts defined, 124; dissertation on Kant's psychology, 13, 32; emotion, its role, 165; experience attenuated, 366; expressiveness, 125–26; fundedness, 115, 121; interest, 127; James, dependence upon, 106–7, 116; Kantian aesthetics, rejection of, 14, 345–46; legalistic criticism, 167; meaning, constitution of, 113, 116; participation in and of nature, 121; process of artistic creation, 86–88; reconstruction, 170; religious sentiments, 345; space-time matrix, 129–32; on tragedy, 50–51; transactional model of experience, 158–59; words, their power, 164
Diary of a Country Priest, 322, 323, 331
Dickie, George, 7, 25, 26
Dickinson, Emily, 163
dilemma of everyday aesthetics, 339–43, 352–56; resolution summarized, 356. *See also* everyday aesthetics
discovery, importance for aesthetic experience, 313
Dossin, Catherine, 271
Dove, Arthur, 289
drama: unity of action, feeling, and meaning, 346
drawing, Dewey's interpretation, 125
Drieth, Corey, 283–96
Duns Scotus, 70

Eakins, Thomas, 261
Eckhart, Meister, 331
ecstatic naturalism, 242, 384–93; aesthetic dimension, 392; entwining of beautiful and sublime, 384; probes three modes of the unconscious, 387
Edwards, Jonathan, 9, 60, 66–69, 211, 219, 221, 237; beauty as guide to God, 22; nature as religiously meaningful, 68; semiotic theology, 68
El Greco, 125
elegance, 217
The Elements of Logic (Whatley), 61
Eliot, T. S., 23, 26

Elkins, William, 49
Ellison, Ralph, 201
Emerson, Ralph Waldo, 9–10, 39–52, 54, 101, 115, 391; aesthetic judgments about actions, 40; aesthetic response to tragedy, 47; Aristotelian vs. Augustinian interpretation, 39–40; death, 42; faith in God, 41; God in nature, 22; intellect as coping power, 44; limits of moral and religious judgments, 47; nature, equilibrium with, 112; self-reliance, 260; temperament as source of tragic sense, 40; tragedy as relational, 42, 43; tragedy, four interpretations, 40–43. *See also* tragedy, Transcendentalism
emotions, 101, 173; emotional response, to ideas, 286; to discovery, 313; to reality in itself, 349
empathy, 248–49
epistemology, 95
equilibrium, 127; Dewey's goal of adaptation, 111–12
The Essentials of Formal Axiology (Edwards), 140
ethics, dependence on aesthetics (Peirce), 299, 384
Evans, Bill, 201
events, material basis, 370
everyday aesthetics, 22, 23, 339–56; basic questions, 343; capacity to shatter ordinary experience, 351; contribution to human welfare, 350; ordinary vs. extraordinary, 339, 342. *See also* dilemma of everyday aesthetics
everyday tragedies: aesthetic judgments required, 40, 47
everydayness, 46, 129, 238, 339–42; Boetticher Westerns as pointing beyond, 331; meaninglessness of, 322–23. *See also* everyday aesthetics
evil, 39, 50
evolution, 144–45; of aesthetic sensitivity, 99; of mind, 70; of social landscape, 146
existential depth, 221
existentialism, 39–40. *See also* Sartre
existentialist interpretation of Boettticher Westerns, 326–30
experience, always mediated by signs, 222
Experience and Nature (Dewey), 50, 111, 116

fabric of Thirdness, 298, 306–7
feeling, 4, 7, 11, 17–20, 32, 80, 130, 166, 168, 191, 283, 289, 343–46; aesthetic types of, 19; context for expression, 192; four connotations, 18, 236
Felski, Rita, 34
feminist philosophy, 53
Firstness, 160–61; quality and possibility, 163
fitness landscapes, 142–47
fittingness, 132
Fleisher, Leon, 308
Ford, John, 325–26, 329
form, 213; as field of significance, 125
formal simplicity, purity, 285
Foster, Hal, 29
Freud, Sigmund, 47, 382
Fry, Roger, 30
fun and enjoyment comparable to aesthetic experience, 226, 233

Gablik, Suzi, 34
Game of Thrones, 154
ganzfield, 274, 277
Garcia-Rivera, Alejandro, 34
Gaskill, Nicholas, 157–75

Gerhard Richter Painting, 85
Gibson, Eleanor and James J., 206
Gilbertson, Leanne, 257-71
Giotto, 262
Glass, Ira, 83
God, arguments for existence, 59-60, 66; beauty of idea, 64; concepts, 150; Edwards on, 211; intuition of through light, 279; Neville's view, 331; Poe's view, 180; Sartre's interpretation, 328. *See also* Neglected Argument
Goetze, Mary, 313, 319
Goodman, Nelson, 25
Goodson, Jacob, 39-57
goodness, 140, 213, 232; relational, 215, 219; social construction, 153
Gracyk, Theodore, 34
Greenberg, Clement, 25, 26, 28, 261-64, 268, 270; formalistic criticism, 261; modernism's booster, 261
Greenhouse, Bernard, 359, 369, 372
Grene, Marjorie, 207
The Great Gatsby (Fitzgerald), 342
Gulick, Walter, 3-35, 236, 237, 246, 257-71, 283-96, 343-46, 360, 357; aesthetics, theory of, 211

habits, 9, 67, 164; habits of feeling, 166
Hafiz, 287
Hamlet (Shakespeare), 268
Hancock, Herbie, 200, 204
Handel, George Frederick, 239
harmony, 211-21, 276; characteristic of everything determinate, 211; existential field constituted by roles, 215; fittingness, relational, 212; four traits, 213; object of longing, 112; threefold analysis of its goodness, 216-19
Hart, Steven, 308, 311-19

Hartley, Dorothy, 372
Hartshorne, Charles, 149
Hauerwas, Stanley, 54
Hegel, G. W. F., 94, 103, 197, 347
Heidegger, Martin, 206, 362, 373, 389; being toward death, 181, 190-91, 193
Henderson, Eddie, 200
Heraclitus, 363
hip-hop music, 27
historical judgment vs. aesthetic judgment, 237
history, 152, 237
Hölderlin, 181
Hopper, Edward, 283
horror, 45
Housman, A. E., 163
Howard, Delton Thomas, 207
Hoyle, Fred, 145
Hudson, W. H., 113-15
Hume, David, 59, 64

icons, 77-79; pure icons, 77-79
ideologies, 265
imagination, 6, 163, 173, 245, 285, 335
imitation, 94
impressionism, 262
Indecent Theology (Althaus-Reid), 239-40
individualism, 269, 290; self-interest and bad faith, 328-29
induction, 71
ingression, 207
Innis, Robert E., 111-34
inquiry, 155
insecurity, 41
installation art, 27, 273
intentionality, 224; contribution to aesthetic experience, 224, 229
The Interface Between the Written and the Oral (Goody), 241

internet: aid to international perspective, 29
interpretants, 79–81, 380; emotional, 80
interpretation, 222; three streams of, 80–81
intuition, 173; feeling of coherence, 19

James, William, 9, 48–49, 65, 69, 93–109, 157, 161, 333, 383; aesthetic experience evoked by struggle, 17; aesthetic influences on thought, 95–96; aesthetic judgment, rich varieties of, 12; attention, 74, 95; bodily basis of aesthetics, 97; clothing as a value, 108; critique of abstract thought, 94; democratic taste, 98, 108; Emerson, dependence upon, 109; empathy stimulated by literature, 169; emotion, theory of, 96; feelings of relation, 106, 131; feelings as source of cognition, 17; ineffability of aesthetic judgment, 93; Kant, critique of, 94; limits of language, 93; perchings, 105–6; play, 99; reality of relations, 162, 172; stream of consciousness, 105
Japanese tea ceremony, 352–54
Jaspers, Karl, 386
jazz: improvisation, 200
Jefferson, Thomas, 288
Johnson, Mark, 23, 33
Judd, Donald, 284
Jung, Carl, archetypes, 324, 381; collective unconscious, 381; individuation, 379; unconscious complex, 382

Kaag, John, 23
kalos, 299–300, 306
Kandel, Eric, 134
Kandinsky, Wassily, 292

Kant, Immanuel, 11–15, 32, 33, 49, 61, 94, 101, 242, 345; aesthetic judgment, 11–13; aesthetical ideas, 13; beauty, analysis of, 11–12, 385; disinterested judgment, 7, 12, 31, 257–58; genius, 13, noumena, 350; transcendental argument, 380. *See also* sublime
Keating, Ann Louise, 55
Kellner, Douglas, 28
Kelly, Ellsworth, 284, 285
Kennedy, Burt, 324
Kent, Sister Mary Corita, 222
Kitses, Jim, 322, 326, 329
Kivy, Peter, 25
knowledge, 102
Kohut, Heinz, self-objects, 382
Koppman, Debra, 33
Kramer, Hilton, 271
Kristeva, Julia, 55

landscape, felt matrix of existence, 121
Langer, Susanne, 9, 124, 125, 134, 188, 207–8; autonomy of art, 16; critique of Dewey, 16; feelings as actions, 18; presentational symbolism, 192–93, 203, 284; semblance, 204; symbols, 31, 183
language, 174; autonomy of critiqued, 162, 172
Leddy, Thomas, 339–58
Lee, Sung Hyun, 74
Leitch, Vincent, 24
Leonardo da Vinci, 260
Lewis, C. I., 340
Li Zehou, 347
light as aesthetic object, 275
Lichtenstein, Roy, 283
Liszt, Franz, 304
literary criticism, autonomy of text rejected, 24–25; ideal impact,

167; and pragmatism, 157; virtual connection to life, 158
literary language: immediacy plus interpretation, 161
literature, creates new modes of relating, 165; politicians as fiction writers, 267; writing as self discovery, 260
Livingston, Paisley, 339–40
Lopez, Michael, 47, 53
love expressed in painting, 295–96
Lyotard, Jean-François, 29

Mallarmé, Stéphane, 351
Malle, Louis, 199
Marcuse, Herbert, 351
Martin, Agnes, 285, 289
Marx, Karl, 259, 347, 351–52
Massumi, Brian, 171, 173
Mateen, Omar, 153
Matisse, Henri, 125
Matthay, Tobias, 303–4
May, Rollo, 115
McKibben, Bill, 373–75
McKinney, Kurl, 208
McLachlan, James, 321–35
McTernan, Vaughn Durkee, 273–81
Mead, George Herbert, 158, 165
meaning, 164, 168, 204, 270; conversation between components of network, 290; literary: Firstness combined with Thirdness, 161–64; musical, 298; relation to possibility, 185
Melchionne, Kevin, 351–53
meliorism, 100, 267; broadening of taste, 100; literature's cultivation of good habits, 170
memory, aesthetic role, 201
Mendelssohn, Felix, 243
metaphor, 165, 287
metaphysics, 388

The Mill on the Floss (Eliot), 115
mimicry, 99
mindfulness, 73, 353, 392
minimalism, 264, 284
Mona Lisa, 119–23
Mondrian, Piet, 284, 285
moral pluralism, 154
Morris, William, 10
Mozart, Wolfgang Amadeus, 299
musement, 61–64, 70; aesthetic contemplation, resembles, 61; Buddhist mindfulness, 62; Schiller, originator of term, 61
music and dancing: mediators between experience and actuality, 196
music, 80, 182, 235, 318; semiotic analysis, 78–80; solitary and social aspects, 178–80; unintentional absorption, 182, 198
musical experience, 184
musical notes to *not* play, 200, 302
musical performance, 311; emotional meaning, not dynamic markings, 316; excellence, contributors to 300–1; live performance, importance of, 375; peak aesthetical experience, 311; from technique to mystery, 298
mysticism, 286
myth, of the entirely new, 266; of settling the West, 329

narrowness, 217, 219, 224, 227
natura naturans, natura naturata, 389; source of art, 393
natural beauty, 229, 230
natural order, 288
natural selection, 143
natural theology, semiotic approach, 72
nature, 111, 213, 242, 372, 389; celebrated in Ford, Boetticher films, 326, 330; source of aesthetic joy, 114–15; unconscious of, 391

Nature's Sublime (Corrington), 242
Neglected Argument (Peirce), 59–72; not about God's existence, 65; pragmaticism, 61; self-control, 63; vagueness of God idea, 65
Neville, Robert Cummings, 149, 211–33, 322, 330–34, 372; need for symbols that engage one, 332. *See also* broken symbols
New Age, 290
New Criticism, 23–25; exclusive focus on literary object, 24; reaction against reductionism, 24
New Deal WPA, 259
New Yorker, 259
Newman, Barnett, 26, 284
Niebuhr, Reinhold, 48
Nietzsche, Friedrich, 47–49, 155, 187, 345; aesthetic judgment of tragedy, 48
nihilism, 53
Noë, Alva, 23
nominalism, 226, 304–7
nominalist fallacy, 307
Normative Cultures (Neville), 140
novelty, 3, 275; aesthetic experience, 158–60, 166
nudes, 127–28

Odin, Steve, 222
Oedipus Rex, 265
O'Keeffe, Georgia, 285, 289
Oliver, Mary, 287
On Suicide Bombers (Asad), 46
ontological depth, 221
Ozu, Yosujiro, 322–23

paintings, artist's biography crucial for understanding, 261; primacy of emotional response, 91; recognizing vs. perceiving aesthetically, 125; semiotic interpretation, 79–82; spatial and temporal components, 117, 214
passion, 335
participation, art's invitation, 117
Pater, Walter, 10
Peirce, Charles Sanders, 9, 17, 18, 22, 23, 59–73, 121, 149, 150, 238, 246–48, 297–302, 305–8, 380–82, 390; abduction as feeling impending coherence, 18; aesthetic theory, 60; aesthetics as basic normative science, 17; autonomy of texts rejected, 160; beauty, 62; community of inquiry, 379; critique of his philosophy, 390–91; Firstness, 131, 161, 305–7; habits of feeling, 166; inquiry, its reach, 249; meaning subsequent to thought, 168; musement, 61–67; normative sciences, 172, 237, 247, 298; panpsychism, blocking psychic otherness, 382; pragmaticism as long-run view of reality, 62–63, 298, 307; reality distinguished from existence, 161; scientific intelligence, 302; scientific method, expansive view of, 71, 91; Secondness, 305–7; semiotics, 75–82; synechism, 250–51; *summum bonum*, 67; theory of signs, 158–61; Thirdness, 305–8. *See also* fabric of Thirdness, *kalos*, musement, Neglected Argument, semiotics, signs
Pepper, Stephen, 51
perception, 108, 114; influence of context on, 96
perceptual feelings, 89–90
performance: questions to be answered, 314; emotional expression to be sought, 318
performance art, 27
person, 177, 204–5, 268

phenomenology of human experience, 341
philosophy, 109; art as stimulant, 169; concern with humans' place in the world, 350
pianos, 301
Pickpocket, 322, 323
Pink Floyd, 209
Pirsig, Robert, 360, 376
place, soulless sprawl, 366
"place" of meaning, 184, 189, 193–95, 206; in choral music, 315. *See also* "space" of action
Plato, 370
Platonic form, 268
play, 73
Plotinus, 150
Poe, Edgar Allan, 178–80, 188, 193–99, 207, 208; dying, images of, 186; "The Island of the Fay," 178; "The Masque of the Red Death," 193. *See also* death, possibility
Poetics (Aristotle), 41–43
The Poetics of Space (Bachelard), 240
poetry, 163, 168, 318; in choral music, 315
Poirier, Richard, 174
Polanyi, Michael, 206; indwelling, 113
Poole, Adrian, 48
possibility, 95, 147, 159, 161, 177–205, 207; egress of, 185, 191, 204; ingression, 179, 204. *See also* affordance
postmodernism, 28–29, 35
practice for performance, 302–5
pragmatism, 15, 51, 71, 157, 167, 383, 392; affirms subjective experience and effective action, 171; fallibilism, 141; meaning understood as effects, 157–58, 167; process emphasized, 159

pragmatist aesthetics, 22, 94, 162; authors supportive of, 175; experience, not object, emphasized, 81–82; pluralistic democratic view affirmed, 98. *See also* Dewey, aesthetic experience
pragmatist literary theory, 158, 169–70
Prall, D. W., 31
presentational symbols, 113; as context for linguistic expression, 192. *See* Langer
Principles of Psychology (James), 94, 101
The Problem of Christianity (Royce), 49
process aesthetics, 269, 273, 275
Process and Reality (Whitehead), 149
public space diminished, 369

Quéré, France, 122
Quine, W. V. O., 207

Rank, Otto, 380; art as seeking wholeness, 383; birth trauma, 382
Ranown cycle (Boetticher Westerns), 322–34; attractive landscape, 325–26; broken symbols, 331; low budget "B" films, 324; morality tales, 333; mythic meaning, 332; villains appealing, 327; villains desire complete control, 328–29
Ransom, John Crowe, 23
Raposa, Michael, 59–74, 251
Rautio, Pauline, 340
Read, Herbert, 286
reality, 392; aesthetic and practical contributions, 102; Peirce's notion, 307; pragmatist understanding, 226
reason; aesthetic and practical basis of, 102
Redcoatism, 265

relationship, 124
religion, 392; practice vs. explanation, 241; source of aesthetic values, 21, 287
religious aesthetics, 21–22; American, 22. *See also* transcendence in aesthetic experience
religious extremism, 153
religious studies, experiential base vs. historical analysis, 239; historical-aesthetic complementarity, 249; use of aesthetic analysis, 238
Renoir, Auguste, 127–29
representation, inadequate in world of process, 160; expressed even in abstraction, 125
rhythm, 199
Richards, I. A., 23
Riefenstahl, Leni, 333
Richter, Gerhard, how completion of work known, 85–86
Rilke, Rene, 287
ritualization, 352–53
Rohr, David, 75–91
Rorty, Richard, 15
Rosenberg, Harold, 26, 258–71; anti-universalism, 263; history, two views, 268; independence of American art, 262; individual creativity, emphasis on, 260; inspiration, quest for certainly of, 267; life experience, 259; political commitment vs. aesthetic idealism, 266; social and political concern, 263
Rosenthal, Sandra B., 247–48
Rothko, Mark, 284, 289
Royce, Josiah, 9, 49–50, 63, 204, 206; community of interpreters, 379
Rubens, Peter Paul, 88
Ruscha, Edward, 340, 354
Ruskin, John, 10

Saito, Yuriko, 339–40
Santayana, George, 9, 112, 379
Sargent, John Singer, 124
Sarris, Alexander, 322, 329
Sartre, Jean-Paul, 197, 260, 269, 327–29, 335
satisfaction, 15, 296, 373; gratefulness as indicator of completion, 287–88
Saussure, Ferdinand, 171
Schapiro, Meyer, 83
Schelling, F. W. J., 35, 380, 391
Schiller, Friedrich, 3, 59, 61–63
Schnabel, Artur, 298–300, 302–4, 308
Schopenhauer, Arthur, 155, 242, 348, 385
Schrader, Paul, 321–24, 332
science: reinvigoration needed, 181
Scott, Randolph, 322, 326–30; characters alienated, independent, stoic, 327; iconic symbol of transcendence, 330
Selving process (Corrington), 379–84, 386–88, 393; aesthetic drive as inner telos, 383; beauty as spiritual food, 386; evolving self as work of art, 388; finite/infinite contrast in great art, 387; positive gains, 381; power and structure of unconscious, 384
semeiosis (Peirce's term), 76. *See* semiotics
semeiotic (Peirce's original spelling), 75. *See* semiotics
Semiotics of Religion (Yelle), 241
semiotics, 60, 68–69, 148, 158–62, 168, 247, 381
sensation, 95; its contextual and aesthetic sensitivity, 96
shallowness, 218
Shakespeare, William, 50, 268
Shapiro, Meyer, 26
Shane, 326

Shaw, Robert, 317, 319
Sheriff, John, 172–73
Short, T. L., 78, 79, 91
The Shortest Route to Pianistic Perfection (Leimer & Gieseking), 303
Shusterman, Richard, 22, 33, 93–109, 173
Siedell, Daniel, 267
signs, 379; definition, 76; dynamic nature, 160; information, 77; interpretation, 70
Silence: A Christian History (MacCulloch), 241
singers as aesthetic decision makers, 313
Slater, Gary, 235–51
Sommer, Frederick, 285
"space" of action, 180, 184, 191, 193, 204
space-time matrix, 129–32
Spinoza, Benedict, 349, 350
spiritual aspect of world, 348
spirituality, 284, 291–93
spontaneous creativity, 221
square, 288; symbol of sacredness, 284
St. Augustine, 121
Stewart, Arthur, 297–309
story, world forming, 373
Strong, David, 359–77
style, musical, 299
sublime, 12, 147, 193, 345, 385, 388
Suburban Nation (Duany, Plater-Zyberk & Speck), 365
Sunsets, beauty of, 223–26
symbols, 77, 192, 332–34. *See also* presentational symbols

Taj Mahal, 228
taste, classic, 108
Tate, Allen, 23

Taylor, Joshua, 22
technology, 360; aesthetically attuned philosophy of, 376; maximum, 369, 375; its promise, 361, 369
Technology and the Character of Contemporary Life (Borgmann), 361
teleology, primal, 188
television, 368
Ten Commandments, 321, 323, 333; Cold War mythology, 333
terror, 43–46
theater, 265
Theogony (Hesiod), 145
theory, not essentially distinct from criticism, 175; theory selection, aesthetic influence, 103
theosemiotic, 74
Thích Nhất Hạnh, 73, 353
things. *See* centering things
Thirdness, 305–8, 381; Firstness of Thirdness, 65; interpretation of Firstness, 161, 248
Thompson, Paul, 364
Thoreau, Henry David, 374
Tillich, Paul, 332, 383
time (temporality), 147, 178–87, 199; development of aesthetic appreciation, 314. *See also* death, evolution, space-time matrix
Titian, 131
Trachtenberg, Alan, 175
tragedy, 39–52, 265; aesthetic judgments as best response, 47, 52
transcendence, in aesthetic experience, 312, 317, 321–22; Dewey's reflections, 345; infinite ground resistant to explanation, 331
Transcendentalism, 47–50, 350, 388
Transcendental Style in Film: Ozu, Bresson, Dreyer (Schrader), 321–24; disparity, 323; everydayness, 322; stasis transcending disparity, 324

transformation, crucial for art, 323, 393
Tree of Life, 144–45
triviality, 218, 223, 227
truth, 292, 334; framework-relative approach, 155; influence of interest, 102
Truth of Broken Symbols (Neville), 331
Turrell, James, 208, 274–80; beauty in changing light, 274, 277; light framed by structures, 274–75; participation in installation, 278; Quaker influence, 279; sacred spaces, 278

unity of consciousness, 104–7

vagueness, 65–66, 218, 227
valuation, co-primal with physicality, 149; objectively afforded, subjectively assessed, 142; simultaeously individual and social, 142
valuational pluralism, 148
value, resident in things, 232
value histories, structure and process summarized, 142–43
van Eyck, Jan, 120
van Gogh, Vincent, 83–85, 88–89, 146, 375
Verlaine, Paul, 121

visual culture, 30

Ward, Graham, 55
Washington, George: portrait, analysis of, 218
Weil, Simone, attention, its importance, 69
West, Cornel, 48–52; prophetic pragmatism, 52
What is Value? (Frondizi), 140
Whicher, Stephen, 53–53
Whitehead, Alfred North, 9, 33, 149–50, 185, 197, 199, 203, 225, 390; aesthetic appreciation, 269; beauty, 273; beauty and discord, 266; beauty's components, 275; effective art, 280; eternal objects (better called possibilities), 178, 207; feeling, 17; harmony of contrasts, 295; intensity of contrast, 217, 276; massiveness, 275; prehension of possibilities, 179; simple location, 215; tragic beauty of perishing, 222
Whitman, Walt, 9, 169
wholeness, art as manifestation, 117
width, 217, 225, 227
Wilberg, Mac, 316
Wildman, Wesley, 139–56, 212, 229
Williams, Raymond, 52
wisdom, 387
workaholic society, 368–69
Wright, Sewall, 143